The Handbook for Working with Difficult Groups

The Handbook for Working with Difficult Groups

HOW THEY ARE DIFFICULT, WHY THEY ARE DIFFICULT AND WHAT YOU CAN DO ABOUT IT

Sandy Schuman
Editor

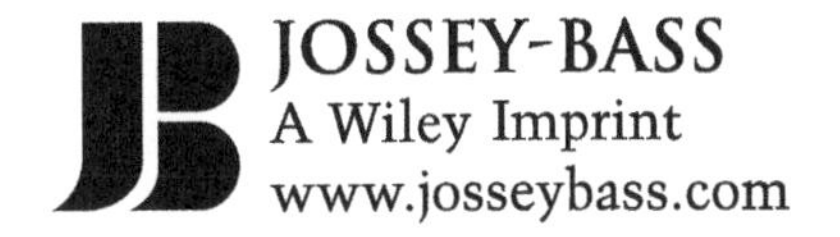

Published by Jossey-Bass
A Wiley Imprint
989 Market Street, San Francisco, CA 94103-1741—www.josseybass.com

Library of Congress Cataloging-in-Publication Data
The handbook for working with difficult groups : how they are difficult, why they are difficult and what you can do about it / Sandy Schuman, editor. — 1st ed.
p. cm. — (The Jossey-Bass business & management series)
Includes bibliographical references and index.
ISBN 978-0-470-19038-8 (cloth)
1. Conflict management. 2. Interpersonal relations. 3. Interpersonal conflict.
4. Teams in the workplace. I. Schuman, Sandy, 1951-
HD42.H357 2010
658.3'145—dc22

2009051940

Printed in the United States of America

FIRST EDITION
HB Printing 10 9 8 7 6 5 4 3 2 1

The Jossey-Bass
Business & Management Series

CONTENTS

PREFACE

"Isn't this the most difficult group you've ever worked with?" a group member asked earnestly. As a group facilitator, I have heard this question—in one form or another—many times. For years I responded by downplaying or outright denying the group's difficulty. "Oh, this group isn't so difficult; it's not that unusual." "Really?" the group member responded. "I thought this was a really bad group!" and the eagerness and energy that came with the initial question would fade.

After many such exchanges, I finally realized two things. First, from my perspective the group did not seem unusual or difficult, but from the perspective of its members, it was. Second, instead of hearing me deny their reality, these group members wanted me to acknowledge that their group was indeed difficult, provide some insight into why it was difficult, and suggest what they could do about it.

When I finally caught on to the meaning of this question, I started responding differently. Instead of negating people's sense of the group's difficulty, I replied, "That's an interesting question! What makes this group difficult from your perspective?" The responses I heard were often illuminating, and they helped me appreciate the many ways in which groups can be experienced as difficult. And indeed, even for the most experienced and wise group members, leaders, and facilitators, there are "difficult groups."

This leads to an important element in how we think about our work with groups: rather than think in terms of *how to work with difficult groups,* the approach we take in this book is to think in terms of *what makes working with groups difficult.* That is to say, a particular group is not innately difficult; rather, there are various things that make working with the group difficult. Wouldn't it be useful if we had a way of thinking systematically about all the ways in which working with a group might be difficult? That would provide a basis for understanding *why* working with the group is difficult and then *what* you could do about it.

In the Introduction, John Rohrbaugh and I present a conceptual framework for thinking about groups and how they might be effective or ineffective. In brief, the framework presents three high-level factors that affect group performance: *context, structure,* and *process.* In addition, it adopts four perspectives on group performance: *relational, political, rational,* and *empirical.* These factors and perspectives are integrated to result in twelve conditions. The framework was presented to prospective authors in the "call for chapters" that initiated this book. I asked the authors to locate their chapters within this framework, and I appreciate their willingness to work with it. However, the authors were not limited to addressing one factor, perspective, or condition. Rather, most of the chapters address multiple parts of the framework, as should be expected when dealing with real groups. The framework is intended as an intellectual tool for helping you think about the difficulties that groups encounter, not as a way to categorize groups.

The value of this structure to you is—I hope—twofold. First, *any structure* is valuable if it helps you make sense of the content of the book. Second, the structure itself is *informative.* It provides a framework for thinking about the full range of issues, not just those presented in the book, but in the full domain of concern—group effectiveness.

But why *this* structure? As we say in the Introduction, "Rather than provide a long list or an all-too-simplistic categorization of the ways in which working with groups can be difficult, we would like to present a framework for thinking about groups and what makes them effective or ineffective." Because it is based on several decades of research and thinking about organizational and group effectiveness, the framework is time tested and able to accommodate virtually any group-related topic and place it in the context of others. If you are already familiar with the three factors and four perspectives, their juxtaposition will not present a great challenge. If you are encountering them for the first time, I hope you can make sense of our presentation and see how the framework applies in each of the chapters and in your everyday work.

In addition, I asked the authors to address each of the following questions.

How the group is difficult: a brief story that presents a group and the observable phenomena that reflect the group's difficulty

Why the group is difficult: an exploration of the underlying causes of the difficulty

What you can do: what you as a group facilitator, leader, or member can do to help the group

Initially, I thought I would use the framework to order the chapters in the table of contents but, as I noted earlier, most of the chapters address multiple aspects of the framework, so this didn't work. However, I noticed that most of the chapters were in predominantly intragroup settings (Chapters One through Nine), a few addressed both intra- and intergroup settings (Chapters Ten through Twelve), and a few addressed intergroup settings (Chapters Thirteen through Fifteen). In addition, a number of chapters dealt directly with the roles of leadership and facilitation (Chapters Sixteen through Twenty). I arranged the chapters in this order, but I did not want to reinforce these categories by labeling these as formal parts of the book.

As the third in a series of edited collections sponsored by the International Association of Facilitators (IAF), the idea and planning for this book emerged from the efforts of Tammy Adams, then IAF's strategic initiative coordinator for communications and publications; Betty Kjellberg, then IAF's executive director; and Kathe Sweeney, senior editor at Jossey-Bass/Wiley. Without them, this book would never have been conceived, much less implemented. Fifty-three individuals thoughtfully reviewed and evaluated the chapter proposals that were submitted in response to the call for chapters. The Center for Policy Research at the University at Albany provided support throughout, with Paul Dickson playing a key role in managing the chapter review process. John Rohrbaugh's contributions to the Introduction, and his advice throughout my editorial work, were invaluable. More than I can say, I am indebted to the thirty-seven authors who contributed to this volume, responded thoughtfully and graciously to my comments, made multiple revisions, and saw through the details of bringing this book to publication. Although I hope that everyone has gained something through this process, no one has gained more from these interactions than I.

August 2009

Sandy Schuman
University at Albany
Albany, New York
sschuman@albany.edu

ABOUT THE CONTRIBUTORS

Deborah Ancona is the Seley Distinguished Professor of Management at MIT Sloan School of Management. Her work is focused on distributed leadership and team process and performance and has appeared in a wide range of journals, including *Administrative Science Quarterly* and *Academy of Management Journal.*

Anna C. Boulton is program manager of community development for the Utah Arts Council. Her program focuses on enabling arts and cultural organizations to grow and stabilize through professional development. She created and facilitates the Utah Change Leader Institute, a National Endowment of the Arts–funded program to train community arts administrators and volunteers to become the initiators of change in their local communities using the arts as a vehicle for economic development. She authored two arts administration handbooks, *The Art of Board Development* (State of Utah, 2000), and *The Art of Volunteer Development* (State of Utah, 2004). Anna is also an adjunct instructor of communication at Weber State University.

Füsun Bulutlar is assistant professor of organizational behavior at Yeditepe University, Istanbul. She has been teaching research methods and management courses at the undergraduate level and human resources and organizational behavior courses at both the undergraduate and graduate levels. As the vice chair of the International Trade and Business Department, she is well accustomed to working with diverse and difficult groups. Her interest areas are positive organizational behavior, positive scholarship, emotions in the workplace, and business ethics. Her primary aims are to stress the importance of the human side of the organization and to reveal that the efficiency and effectiveness of groups and organizations can flourish when the quality of work life and the well-being of employees are improved.

David F. Caldwell is the Schott Professor of Business at the Leavey School of Business, Santa Clara University. His research on individual and team processes has appeared in *Administrative Science Quarterly, Academy of Management Journal,* and *Organization Science.*

Michael Cassidy is a professor of information technology and management science at Marymount University's School of Business in Arlington, Virginia, with teaching responsibilities in research methodology, statistics, decision analysis, simulation modeling, and task groups. He is past coeditor of *Performance Improvement Quarterly,* a peer-reviewed journal whose focus is human performance at the individual, group, and organizational levels. He is also senior principal analyst at Innovative Decisions, Inc., in Vienna, Virginia. Professor Cassidy has an active and diverse research agenda, including the areas of decision making, human deception, and epistemology, and he has published in fields including management, education, sociology, and law enforcement. He has worked with multiple agencies in the U.S. federal government, the World Bank, and other organizations.

Ingrid C. Chadwick is completing her Ph.D. in organizational behavior at Queen's School of Business, Queen's University, in Kingston, Ontario. She has an international background in human resources, and she has worked with employee and organization development initiatives at Volvo, Ford, and PepsiCo. Her research focuses on teams, interpersonal relations, diversity, learning, and leadership. She completed a master's degree in education at Queen's University prior to pursuing her Ph.D.

Mark A. Clark is an associate professor at the Kogod School of Business, American University, Washington DC, and Visiting Scholar at the Instituto de Empresa (SEK) in Madrid. His research on team performance contexts, culture, diversity, and strategic human capital has appeared in *Group Dynamics, Academy of Management Journal,* and *Journal of Applied Psychology,* among other outlets, and has been presented internationally to both academic audiences and business executives. Dr. Clark's background includes experience as a treatment specialist, trainer, program administrator, and consultant. He earned his Ph.D. from Arizona State University.

Taya R. Cohen (Ph.D. in psychology, University of North Carolina at Chapel Hill, 2008) is a visiting assistant professor and postdoctoral fellow at the Kellogg School of Management at Northwestern University. Dr. Cohen's research focuses on understanding differences between group and individual behavior in a variety of contexts, including ethical dilemmas, social dilemmas, and negotiation. She investigates these issues by comparing interactions between groups to interactions between individuals in mixed-motive situations, such as the prisoner's dilemma game and the deception game. She studies how moral emotions (for example, guilt, empathy) affect interactions in these contexts.

Philip Gamaghelyan is the co-founder and co-director of the Imagine Center for Conflict Transformation that works primarily with Turkish-Armenian and Armenian-Azerbaijani conflicts. Philip's research focus in on the role of historical memory and education in identity-based conflicts. He developed a facilitation methodology that uses historical timelines as a tool for analysis of the underlying reasons for the "historical hatred" of groups in conflict and also for outlining solutions to the conflict through a structured mediated discussion of events alive in the historical memories of the involved groups. Prior to starting the Imagine Center, he lectured at Tufts University Experimental College, served as a fellow at the International Center for Conciliation and worked with Arab and Israeli educators at Seeds of Peace. Philip has a master's degree in conflict resolution from Brandeis University and a B.A. in Political Science from Yerevan State Linguistic University. He is the author of a number of articles on Nagorno-Karabakh and Turkish-Armenian conflicts, including publications in the *International Negotiation Journal* and *Peace and Conflict Monitor.*

Dennis S. Gouran (Ph.D., University of Iowa, 1968) is a professor of communication arts and sciences and labor studies and employment relations at the Pennsylvania State University. Professor Gouran has been president of both the Central States Communication Association and National Communication

Association. He has served as editor of *Communication Studies* and *Communication Monographs.* Professor Gouran's scholarship focuses on communication in decision-making and problem-solving groups. He is author or coauthor of more than one hundred books, book chapters, and journal articles dealing with the subject. For his contributions to scholarship, in 1993 Professor Gouran was named one of the first ten National Communication Association Distinguished Scholars.

Verlin B. Hinsz received his undergraduate degree in psychology and sociology from North Dakota State University and his Ph.D. in social-organizational psychology from the University of Illinois at Urbana-Champaign. Since earning his doctorate, he has been on the faculty of North Dakota State University, where he is now a professor of psychology. Professor Hinsz has published primarily in the areas of group and individual judgment and decision making. In addition, his research has ventured into social psychology topics of mate attraction, mood, and nonverbal expressions. Professor Hinsz's research in organizational psychology has focused on team performance and goal setting by groups and individuals. Professor Hinsz is currently associate editor of the Interpersonal Relations and Group Processes section of the *Journal of Personality and Social Psychology.*

Astrid C. Homan (Ph.D., University of Amsterdam, 2006) is an assistant professor of social and organizational psychology at VU University, Amsterdam, The Netherlands. Her research interests include team diversity, team processes, team performance, subgroup salience, and diversity beliefs. She is particularly interested in determining how to harvest the potential value in diversity. She has published her work in such journals as the *Journal of Applied Psychology* and *Academy of Management Journal.* Her most recent area of interest is team member change and leadership of diverse teams.

Chester A. Insko received his A.B. in philosophy from the University of California, Berkeley in 1957, his M.A. in psychology from Boston University in 1958, and his Ph.D. in psychology from the University of California, Berkeley in 1963. Since 1965, he has been on the faculty of the University of North Carolina at Chapel Hill, where he is now a professor of psychology. He is a past associate editor of the *Journal of Experimental Social Psychology* and past editor of the Interpersonal Relations and Group Processes section of the *Journal of Personality and Social Psychology.* His current research focuses on interindividual-intergroup discontinuity—the tendency in some social contexts for relations between groups to be more competitive than relations between individuals.

Sandra Janoff, Ph.D., a psychologist and consultant, works with corporations, government agencies, and communities worldwide on issues of globalization, sustainability, and humane practices. She was staff member for Tavistock conferences sponsored by the Tavistock Institute of Human Relations in Oxford, England. She is coauthor with Yvonne Agazarian of "Systems Thinking and Small Groups" for the *Comprehensive Textbook of Group Psychotherapy,* and was a member of the European Institute for Transnational Studies. Sandra Janoff and Marvin Weisbord codirect the international nonprofit Future Search Network, and they are coauthors of *Future Search: An Action Guide, 2nd Edition* (Berrett-Koehler, 2000), and *Don't Just Do Something, Stand There! Ten Principles for Leading Meetings That Matter* (Berrett-Koehler, 2007). They have managed planning meetings in Africa, Asia, Australia, New Zealand, Europe, India, and North and South America and have trained more than thirty-five hundred people worldwide in using their principles.

Karen A. Jehn (Ph.D., Northwestern University, 1992) is a professor at Melbourne Business School at the University of Melbourne, Australia. Her research examines intragroup conflict, group composition, and lying in organizations. Professor Jehn has authored numerous publications in these areas, including articles in the *Academy of Management Journal, Administrative Science Quarterly, Journal of Personality and Social Psychology,* and the *Journal of Business Ethics.* She has served as a director of the Solomon Asch Center for the Study of Ethnopolitical Conflict and the Sloan Foundation's Diversity Research Network. Her most recent area of interest is in asymmetric perceptions within workgroups.

Simone Kauffeld (Ph.D., University of Kassel, Germany, 1999) is a professor of work, organizational, and social psychology at the Technische Universität Braunschweig, Germany. Her research focuses on teams, competencies, training and transfer, consultant-client interaction, leadership, and innovation in organizations. Professor Kauffeld has edited three volumes on competence management and development, developed several instruments in organizational psychology, and written more than one hundred contributions to textbooks and peer-reviewed journals, such as the *Journal of Occupational and Organizational Psychology*, the *European Journal of Work and Organizational Psychology*, and *Personnel Review*. After managing numerous team and organization development projects, she founded the spinoff 4A-SIDE (www.4a-side.com) to carry her scientific instruments and approaches into the field.

Celia Kirwan is a consultant with Robert H. Schaffer & Associates (RHS&A), a management consulting firm based in the United States and London. RHS&A helps organizations conduct rapid-cycle, results-driven experiments that stimulate large-scale systems change and develop the capabilities needed to sustain those changes. Celia has used this approach to help organizations in the financial services, consumer goods, health care, insurance, and nonprofit sectors improve their internal processes and ensure that those processes yield the desired results. Prior to joining RHS&A, Celia worked for Kinsley Lord–Towers Perrin in London and Mercer Management Consulting (now Oliver Wyman) in London and Boston. In 2008, Celia coauthored "Healthcare Rx: Start with Results Today" in *OD Seasonings* (the online publication of the OD Network). Celia has also coauthored a chapter on RHS&A's Rapid Results approach in the second edition of *The Change Handbook* (Berrett-Koehler, 2007). Celia has an undergraduate degree in geography, German, and European studies from the University of Sussex, United Kingdom, and an M.A. in geography from Boston University.

Theresa J. B. Kline is a professor in the Department of Psychology at the University of Calgary. She has an active research program in the area of team performance, and her other research interests include psychometrics, organizational effectiveness, and work attitudes. Theresa has published two books on teams, *Teams That Lead* (Erlbaum, 2003) and Remaking Teams (Jossey-Bass, 1999), and one on psychometrics, Psychological Testing (Sage, 2005), and over fifty peer-reviewed articles. Theresa teaches statistics and methods and organizational psychology at both the undergraduate and graduate levels. She has an active organizational consulting practice with projects ranging from individual and organizational assessment to strategic alignment.

Dagmar Kusa is a senior fellow and program coordinator at the International Center for Conciliation (ICfC) and a Ph.D. candidate at Boston University and at the Ethnology Institute of the Slovak Academy of Sciences. She is currently in the final stages of writing her thesis on the role of historical memory in the politics of Central Europe. She has written a number of publications and chapters—most recently a chapter on Slovak citizenship (in R. Bauböck, B. Perchinig, & W. Sievers, *Citizenship Policies in the New Europe,* Amsterdam: Amsterdam University Press, 2007) and Alternative Conflict Resolution I and II for the Foundation Against Discrimination in Slovakia (EU Project EQUAL). Dagmar has a background in political science and human rights, and has worked in the field of conflict resolution since 1999, leading workshops in Slovakia, India, Cambodia, The Netherlands, and the United States. She has been developing an "historical conciliation" approach, focusing on working with the collective memory of the groups involved in identity-based conflict.

Mary Laeger-Hagemeister has spent her career living and working with diverse populations in the United States, from the plains of the Midwest to an inner city on the East Coast and the mountains of Appalachia. Her adult students have included incarcerated individuals, people in poverty, people in a mental health facility, immigrants, and members of the general population. In addition to developing curricula and teaching topics ranging from parenting to leadership and facilitation, Mary has served as a community coach. For the past twenty years she has been employed in the extension system at the Pennsylvania State University and, most recently, the University of Minnesota. Presently, Mary is finishing her Ph.D. at the University of Minnesota. Her dissertation is on social capital networking and immigration populations in rural Minnesota.

John Landesman is the founder and current coordinator of the Montgomery County Public Schools Study Circles Program. The program has organized over two thousand parents, teachers, administrators, and students in dialogue and action to address racial and ethnic barriers to student achievement and parent involvement. Landesman also consults with government agencies and community organizations to develop public engagement programs on race, education, neighborhood issues, and immigration. Landesman is a senior associate and former director of community assistance for the national organization

Everyday Democracy, and has written curriculum guides for facilitating dialogues on a variety of challenging public issues.

Nale Lehmann-Willenbrock received her undergraduate and graduate degrees in psychology after studying at the University of Göttingen (Germany) and the University of California, Irvine. She has worked in human resource development as a team trainer and has been a faculty member at the Technische Universität Braunschweig (Germany) since 2007. She is currently working on her Ph.D. thesis concerning trust in the workplace, based on a study of fifty groups from two companies. Her research interests further include intragroup processes, teamwork, communication, and heterogeneous teams. She has written several book chapters and articles in such peer-reviewed journals as the *European Journal of Psychological Assessment* and the *Journal of European Industrial Training.*

Ann Lukens promotes collaborative and reflective working practices in local government, corporations, and partnership groups through strategic activities such as mergers, reorganizations, public consultations, and change programs. As a mediator and facilitator, Ann designs and delivers training and facilitated sessions to develop cross-sector and partnership working, collaborative leadership, and conflict management and resolution, and she supports teams and groups working through conflict and difficult times. Her M.Sc. research centered on the availability of training that effectively combines group work and conflict work. Ann is a practitioner at heart—she enjoys training and being trained, but loves "the doing" even more.

Brian P. Meier received his undergraduate degree in psychology and his Ph.D. degree in social psychology from North Dakota State University. He has been a faculty member at Gettysburg College in Pennsylvania since 2005. Professor Meier's primary research interests lie in emotion and social cognition. His recent publications cover a wide range of topics in these areas, including embodied cognition and emotion, personality and aggression, and implicit processes in emotion and social cognition.

Steven Ober, Ed.D., is founder and president of Chrysalis Executive Coaching & Consulting. He is a leading executive coach and has created a breakthrough approach to executive coaching: Creating Your Leadership Story. Steve has worked successfully with senior executives in business, high-tech, government, health care, and education—helping them produce outstanding results in complex systems. He was a vice president at Arthur D. Little, a principal in Innovation Associates, a thought leader in ADL's strategy and organization practice, and leader of Innovation Associates' team learning practice. Steve is the author of numerous articles and professional guidebooks, including "Encouraging Enrollment: Personal Stories as a Vehicle for Change" (*Prism*, 2000), *Cracking the Culture Nut: Human Systems Consulting* (Innovation Associates/Arthur D. Little, 2000), and "Lies About the Learning Organization" (in *Lies About Learning*, ASTD, 2006). Steve has conducted sessions on organizational learning and executive storytelling in numerous workshops and national conferences. He is known for his frankness, openness, honesty, and ability to unravel very difficult team and organizational problems.

Thomas A. O'Neill is a Ph.D. candidate at the University of Western Ontario, Canada, where he is studying industrial/organizational (I/O) psychology. He completed his B.A. Honours in psychology at the University of Calgary and his M.Sc. in I/O psychology at the University of Western Ontario. His varied research interests include the effects of personality in explaining teamwork, the antecedents of effective teleworking arrangements, methodologies of group research, alternatives to selection test validation, the usefulness of broad versus narrow traits in predicting organizational behavior, and virtual teamwork and leadership.

Jana L. Raver, Ph.D., is an assistant professor at Queen's School of Business, Queen's University, in Kingston, Ontario. Her expertise covers topics including interpersonal relations in work teams and workplace diversity. Her award-winning research has been published in top-tier management journals, such as *Academy of Management Review, Academy of Management Journal,* and *Journal of Applied Psychology,* and has been disseminated widely through media outlets. She teaches undergraduate, M.B.A., and Ph.D. courses on team processes, human resource management, and multilevel topics in organizational behavior. She has also consulted and conducted applied research with a number of public and private organizations. She completed her Ph.D. in industrial and organizational psychology at the University of Maryland.

John Rohrbaugh earned his Ph.D. in social psychology at the University of Colorado and currently serves as full professor in the Rockefeller College of Public Affairs and Policy at the University of Albany (SUNY). Professor Rohrbaugh's research has focused on the problem-solving processes of management groups, executive teams, and expert task forces in an effort to identify methods that would improve both the efficiency and effectiveness of organizational decision making. His work has been published as articles in more than thirty different journals and as chapters in nearly as many books. As a consultant and facilitator, Professor Rohrbaugh has worked with over thirty-five agencies of the federal and state governments in the United States, and participated on project teams engaged with governments in Chile, Egypt, Somalia, Lebanon, and Hungary.

Adam Saltsman is a fellow and program officer at the International Center for Conciliation (ICfC). With the ICfC, Adam spent nearly two years in Phnom Penh, Cambodia, between 2005 and 2007, establishing an office and projects related to historical conciliation. Collaborating with local Cambodian non-governmental organizations, Adam started the Social Justice and History Outreach project in three villages throughout Cambodia with the goal of sparking public discussion about history in conflicted communities. As part of this project, Adam worked to bring together former Khmer Rouge cadre and survivors from the Cambodian genocide to develop conciliatory dialogue strategies to address village access to Cambodia's transitional justice process. Adam is also a doctoral student in the Department of Sociology at Boston College, where he focuses on the political economy of forced migration and participatory action development and research.

Donna Rae Scheffert writes for to the Washington Times Communities. Her column is called Making Change: Getting Involved in Helping Others. She is also a senior consultant with Action Wheel Leadership, Inc., and an associate with deepSEE Consulting. A former extension professor at the University of Minnesota she still teaches a graduate course on facilitation. Along with colleagues, she codeveloped the Facilitation Resources capacity-building program for adults to increase their facilitation skills and then volunteer to help create solutions for public problems. Scheffert has helped bring facilitation training, leadership development, and community visioning and action to hundreds of high-poverty communities in eight northern states to reduce poverty and grow prosperity (Horizons program). She received the Distinguished Extension Campus Faculty Award, University of Minnesota Extension, and the FUTURES award, Minnesota Rural Futures.

Sandor Schuman helps organizations work more effectively to solve complex problems and make critical decisions. He is a group facilitator, collaborative process advocate, and storyteller. He helps groups create shared meaning, make critical choices, and build collaborative relationships. Sandy is the editor of the International Association of Facilitators handbooks, including *Creating a Culture of Collaboration* (Jossey-Bass, 2006) and *The IAF Handbook of Group Facilitation* (Jossey-Bass, 2005). He was the long-term editor of *Group Facilitation: A Research and Applications Journal* and moderator of *The Electronic Group Discussion on Group Facilitation.* Sandy is a director of the Program on Strategic Decision Making at the Center for Policy Research, University at Albany, SUNY, and president of Executive Decision Services LLC.

Carol Sherriff is a Certified Professional Facilitator with more than eight years' experience in facilitating events and projects in the United Kingdom. Before setting up her own facilitation business, she was CEO of two not-for-profit organizations. She has an M.Sc. in psychology and an M.B.A., and is an associate lecturer with Open University Business School. Carol Sherriff and Simon Wilson have presented at IAF conferences in Europe, Asia and North America. They contributed a chapter, "Metaphors at Work," for the IAF handbook *Creating a Culture of Collaboration* (Jossey-Bass, 2006) and wrote the IAF Europe professional development pamphlet "Does He Who Pays the Piper Call the Tune?"

Wes Siegal is an organizational psychologist and a senior consultant at Robert H. Schaffer & Associates (RHS&A), a management consulting firm based in the United States and London. RHS&A helps organizations conduct rapid-cycle, results-driven experiments that stimulate large-scale systems change and develop the capabilities needed to sustain those changes. In his role as the firm's team leader for practice development, Wes has worked with dozens of top-tier organizations to transcend the organizational dynamics that so often frustrate critical strategic goals. He has helped clients achieve breakthrough results in areas as diverse as sales growth, manufacturing efficiency, certification of renewable energy sources, and HIV mitigation in developing countries. Wes has spoken about consulting and change dynamics at the national SIOP and ASTD conferences, and he has written about these topics in two recent articles in the journal *Consulting to Management.* Wes has an undergraduate degree in cultural anthropology from Brown University, and a Ph.D. in organizational psychology from Columbia University.

Stanford Siver, Ph.D., Dipl.PW, is a certified process work diplomate, conflict facilitator, organizational consultant, and coach. He is a cofounder of the Deep Democracy Institute, an NGO dedicated to training individuals, groups, and organizations in process oriented leadership development, community building, organizational change, and conflict facilitation. He is formerly a sales and marketing manager; an organizational change, people empowerment, and quality improvement process facilitator; a military intelligence analyst; a numerical systems development analyst; a shipwright and sailor; and director of the Institute for Multi-Track Diplomacy. Stanford's work focuses on the psychology of conflict and the relationship between our inner experience and community, organizational, and global conflict.

Richard W. Sline (Ph.D., University of Utah, 1999) is associate professor of communication at Weber State University in Ogden, Utah, where he teaches organizational communication, interpersonal and small group communication, group facilitation and leadership, intercultural communication, and communication theory. He has been designing and facilitating organization needs assessments, interventions, and training programs for private corporations and nonprofit organizations for over twenty years. His major areas of specialization include organizational assessment, team building, organization change, and conflict management. His research interests include work team effectiveness, teaching teamwork, and relational dialectics in retirement. He has written book chapters and conference papers on group facilitation techniques, the effects of emotionality on work team collaboration, and member commitment to their work team and organization.

Glyn Thomas, Ed.D., is the director (learning, teaching, and international) in the Centre for Excellence in Outdoor and Environmental Education at La Trobe

University in Australia. His research and teaching primarily focus on the education of facilitators to work in experiential education settings. Over the last twenty-two years, he has taught in a range of educational contexts and is committed to the values, principles, and practice of ecological sustainability.

Marvin Weisbord consulted with business firms, medical schools and hospitals from 1969 to 1992. He was a partner in Block Petrella Weisbord, Inc., a member of the NTL Institute and the European Institute for Transnational Studies, and is a fellow of the World Academy of Productivity Science. He received a Lifetime Achievement Award from the Organization Development Network, which in 2004 voted his book *Productive Workplaces* (1987) among the five most influential books of the past forty years. He also is author of *Organizational Diagnosis* (1978), *Discovering Common Ground* (1992), and *Productive Workplaces Revisited* (2004). Marvin Weisbord and Sandra Janoff codirect the international nonprofit Future Search Network and are coauthors of *Future Search: An Action Guide, 2nd Edition* (2000), and *Don't Just Do Something, Stand There!* (2007). They have managed planning meetings in Africa, Asia, Europe, India, and North and South America and trained more than thirty-five hundred people worldwide in using their principles.

Simon Wilson is a Certified Professional Facilitator with extensive experience in facilitating events and projects in the government, public, and private sectors. He is chair of a not-for-profit national organization and holds an M.B.A. Simon Wilson and Carol Sherriff have presented at IAF conferences in Europe, Asia, and North America. They contributed a chapter on metaphors at work for the IAF Handbook *Creating a Culture of Collaboration* (Jossey-Bass, 2006) and wrote the IAF Europe professional development pamphlet "Does He Who Pays the Piper Call the Tune?"

Working with Difficult Groups: A Conceptual Framework

Sandor Schuman and John Rohrbaugh

Working with groups can be difficult in innumerable ways, but working without groups is nearly impossible. The aim of this book is to help your working with difficult groups become easier. Indeed, instead of thinking in terms of difficult groups, we would rather think in terms of what makes working with groups difficult and, for that matter, what makes working with groups effective. Rather than provide a long list or an all-too-simplistic categorization of the ways in which working with groups can be difficult, we would like to present a framework for thinking about groups and what makes them effective or ineffective. This framework is not offered as definitive, but it is nonetheless useful for organizing the book. Other recent frameworks are highly instructive as well (see, for example, Rousseau, Aube, & Savoic, 2006).

Three factors (context, structure, and process) and four perspectives (relational, empirical, political, and rational) provide the organizing framework for *Working with Difficult Groups.*

Each chapter of the book focuses on aspects of one or more of the factors or perspectives. In this way, while each chapter addresses particular aspects that make working with groups difficult, the book as a whole presents an integrated view of group effectiveness and ineffectiveness. The following sections describe this framework more fully.

THREE FACTORS CONTRIBUTING TO GROUP PERFORMANCE

For nearly fifty years, effectiveness or ineffectiveness of group performance has been linked in both theory and research to at least three high-order factors: context, structure, and process (McGrath, 1964; Gladstein, 1984; Schwarz, 2002), as illustrated in Table I.1. A group's *context* takes into account environmental variables and can be characterized by the multifaceted external circumstances that both support and constrain collaboration. A group's *structure* reflects the variables of design and is evidenced by its many formal and informal aspects. A group's *process* derives from the confluence of interaction variables and subsumes a wide variety of behaviors pertaining to exchanges before, during, and after meetings. A group may be difficult due to some particular attribute (or combination of attributes) of its context, structure, or process.

Table I.1
Three Higher-Order Factors of Group Performance

	Context	Structure	Process
McGrath (1964)	Environment-level factors	Group-level factors	Group interaction process
Gladstein (1984)	Organizational resources and structure	Group composition and structure	Group process
Schwarz (2002)	Group context	Group structure	Group process

Context

All external variables that may directly or indirectly affect a group's performance can be considered its *context.* These environmental factors may be described as (but not limited to) physical, social, economic, political, or organizational. In some ways, the context of a group can be beneficent and enhance its performance; in other ways, its environment can be hostile or even catastrophic in character, making any group achievement unlikely, perhaps impossible. Many groups function with considerable ignorance of the full context in which they are working, except for only the most apparent variables. As a result, they may fail to take advantage of substantial resources readily available to them, or to prepare adequately for emergent obstacles that eventually thwart them.

Resource dependence theory instructs groups to devote considerable attention to understanding the key aspects of their context and to making a concerted effort to communicate with external individuals and groups. Such strategic alliances initially may seem beyond the agenda of the group, but building successful networks of partners can serve to accumulate additional resources that may prove essential to positive outcomes. Furthermore, strong coalitions reduce the vulnerability of any one group standing alone.

Structure

Even groups that have come together organically and developed unintentionally with no oversight of membership and no succession of leadership do have *structure*—that is, a distinctive design. To describe a group's design does not imply that there was a designer but merely that a pattern of characteristics is apparent. A simple head count at each meeting can be an indicator of group size, which is a key structural variable; group size, as is true of any aspect of group design, need not be fixed but can vary over time. A group with too many participants (or too few) or a group lacking members' relevant knowledge or skills may be challenged in accomplishing its goals. In addition to its size and composition, a group's structure includes many other aspects, such as its communication patterns, norms, and roles.

A group's goals and objectives are often considered part of its structure as well, because the extent to which they are understood, accepted (shared), and valued will affect group outcomes. However, tasks officially assigned to a group may differ from the tasks that engage the efforts of its members. This is an important distinction. *Formal* structure refers to any aspect of design that has been planned for (and, perhaps, imposed on) a group; *emergent* structure refers to the distinctive pattern of group characteristics that actually are observed over time. We should not be surprised if the formal leadership structure and the emergent leadership structure of a group are not the same. In fact, the divergence of formal structure and emergent structure can be a potential impediment (or, alternatively, the essential key) to a group's success.

Process

Group interaction exhibits a large variety of facets of patterned verbal and nonverbal behavior. Exchanges between group members have been roughly categorized as focused on the task or focused on the group, a long-standing and useful but simplistic bifurcation. To be effective, of course, members need to work constructively toward accomplishing their objectives, but they also need to ensure that their group remains a cohesive collectivity. If an excessive task orientation begins to fragment the group or if meeting the socioemotional needs of individuals largely competes with goal achievement, failure can be imminent. How a group balances its task orientation and its social orientation is an important aspect of its process.

Group conflict, of course, is not limited to the tension between task and socioemotional interests. Conflicts of opinion, conflicts of value, and conflicts of interest (to name only a few) emerge in any group process. As has been well established in the formal study of groups, diversity (or heterogeneity) of membership can contribute positively to task performance. Groups composed of highly similar members may "get along" well, but typically do not have a large enough pool of abilities, experiences, skills, and perspectives to respond effectively to complex problems. Whereas a group's composition is an aspect of its structure, the use of tools and techniques to enable conflict to emerge and be used constructively is a key element of its process.

FOUR PERSPECTIVES ON GROUP EFFECTIVENESS: THE COMPETING VALUES APPROACH

Contemporary standards for both organization and group performance were well anticipated by the theory-building work of the sociologist Talcott Parsons (1959; Hare, 1976). Parsons proposed that there are four key functions of any collectivity (or system of action): pattern maintenance, integration, adaptation, and goal attainment. The essential nature of these four functions—and their appropriate balance—has been the emphasis of the Competing Values Approach (CVA) to organizational analysis (Quinn & Rohrbaugh, 1983; Rohrbaugh, 1983; Belasen, 2008). (An introduction to the CVA is given in the appendix to this chapter.) At the group level in particular, the CVA has been used to identify four domains of collective performance that parallel Parsons' functions: relational, empirical, political, and rational (Rohrbaugh, 2005).

Relational Perspective

> *We are all dependent on one another, every soul of us on earth.*
>
> —George Bernard Shaw (1913/2008, p. 119)

The relational perspective places emphasis on achieving the pattern maintenance function and focuses on full participation in meetings, with open expression of individual feelings and sentiments. Extended discussion and debate about conflicting concerns should lead to collective agreement on a mutually satisfactory solution. Such team building would increase the likelihood of support for any solution during implementation. This very interpersonally oriented perspective is dominant in the field of organization development.

For example, when group members are divided in their values and have conflicting interests, it is important that the conditions under which they are collaborating fully support their joint efforts. In addition to such incentives that would motivate collective work, group composition should be characterized by such attributes as sincerity and openness to others' views so that trust can be encouraged. Groups that are skillful in expressing and using their conflicts constructively will benefit substantially over time.

Empirical Perspective

> *A patient pursuit of facts, and cautious combination and comparison of them, is the drudgery to which man is subjected by his Maker, if he wishes to attain sure knowledge.*
>
> —Thomas Jefferson (Lipscomb & Bergh, 1903–04, vol. 2, p. 97)

Group observers who take an empirical perspective place emphasis on achieving the integration function and stress the importance of documentation. They pay particular attention to the ways in which groups secure and share relevant information and develop or rely on comprehensive databases to support problem solving. Proponents of this perspective, typically trained in the physical and social sciences (especially management information systems) believe that, to be effective, group deliberation should allow thorough use of evidence and full accountability.

In addition to the availability of external information, group composition should be characterized by an appropriate pool of necessary skills, abilities, and expertise to address the focal issues. Furthermore, communication channels must remain open, so that group members can better inform and learn from each other. From the empirical perspective, widening communication beyond single channels and specific occasions (for example, beyond only spoken communication during face-to-face meetings) will enhance group achievement.

Political Perspective

It is not necessary to change. Survival is not mandatory.

—W. Edwards Deming

The political perspective emphasizes the adaptation function and takes the view that group flexibility and creativity are the paramount process attributes. One indication of adaptability is the extent to which the group is attuned to shifts in the nature of the problem, accordingly altering its focus and approach to finding solutions. The search for legitimacy—the acceptability of solutions to outside stakeholders who are not immediate participants but whose interests potentially are affected by the group deliberations—would be notable through a fully responsive, dynamic process.

From the political perspective, a group is credited rather than shamed by explicitly taking into consideration how its standing in the eyes of outside interests is maintained or enhanced. An effective group is one that works to increase its own authority and influence. Over time, such a group improves its readiness to adjust both structure and process to better position itself in the ongoing competition for resources, especially external financial support.

Rational Perspective

> *Our plans miscarry because they have no aim. When a man does not know what harbor he is aiming for, no wind is the right wind.*
>
> —Marcus Annaeus Seneca (Cook, 1999, p. 352)

The priority of clear thinking as the primary ingredient for successful group performance is the hallmark of the rational perspective, which emphasizes the goal attainment function. From this very task-oriented approach (particularly common in management science and operations research), groups should be directed by explicit statement and understanding of their primary goals and objectives. Methods that assist group members to be more efficient planners are valued for improving the coherency and consistency of decision making.

For example, rational planning includes thorough consideration of the physical aspects of face-to-face meetings. Collaboration is enhanced when group members are comfortably seated in well-lighted, temperature-controlled, appropriately furnished and equipped rooms, well protected from the distractions of hour-to-hour organizational life. Prerequisites for virtual meetings are adequate hardware and software that are readily available to—and easily used by—participants. Ensuring optimal conditions for the most efficient use of resources, including the investment of everyone's time and attention, is paramount.

TWELVE CONDITIONS THAT CAN SUPPORT OR UNDERMINE GROUP EFFECTIVENESS

Any aspect of a group's context, structure, or process might have profound consequences for its performance. These aspects can be categorized as relational, empirical, political, or rational in nature. As shown in Figure I.1, these factors and perspectives can be juxtaposed. Such a juxtaposition produces not

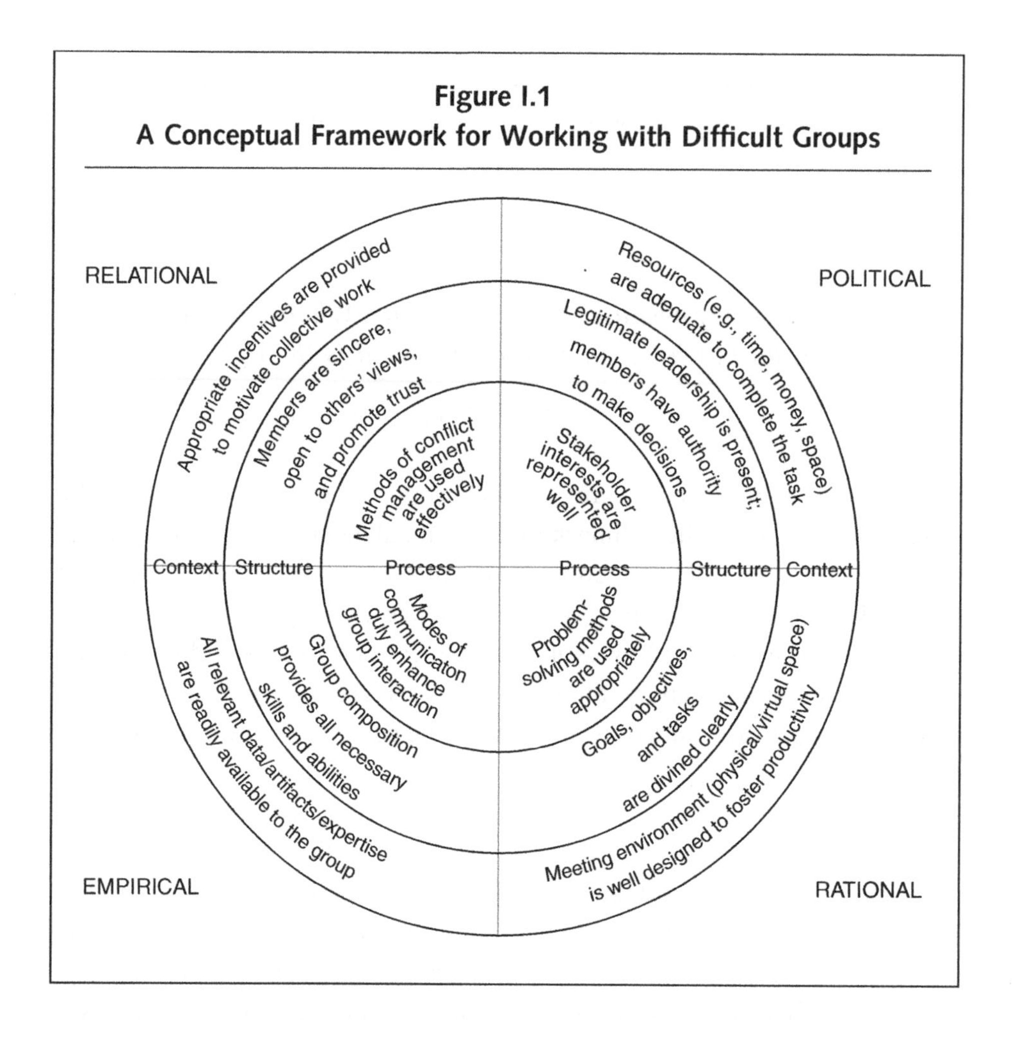
RELATIONAL
POLITICAL
EMPIRICAL
RATIONAL
Context
Structure
Process
Process
Structure
Context
Appropriate incentives are provided to motivate collective work
Members are sincere, open to others' views, and promote trust
Methods of conflict management are used effectively
Resources (e.g., time, money, space) are adequate to complete the task
Legitimate leadership is present; members have authority to make decisions
Stakeholder interests are represented well
Modes of communicaton duly enhance group interaction
Group composition provides all necessary skills and abilities
All relevant data/artifacts/expertise are readily available to the group
Problem-solving methods are used appropriately
Goals, objectives, and tasks are divined clearly
Meeting environment (physical/virtual space) is well designed to foster productivity

Figure I.1
A Conceptual Framework for Working with Difficult Groups

an exhaustive laundry list of conditions but rather a relatively concise framework of twelve conditions that can either support or undermine group effectiveness. The framework is further elaborated in Table I.2, with specific examples of each of the twelve key conditions having particular influence on a group's level of accomplishment. Exhibit I.1 provides an additional example showing how the Competing Values Framework can be used to assess the need for an outside facilitator—that is, one who is not a member of the group or organization.

Table I.2

Conditions That Can Support or Undermine Group Effectiveness

	Context		Structure		Process	
	Support Effectiveness	Undermine Effectiveness	Support Effectiveness	Undermine Effectiveness	Support Effectiveness	Undermine Effectiveness
Relational	Appropriate incentives are provided to motivate collective work.	When participants are not extrinsically and/or intrinsically engaged in the group effort, weak cohesion can undermine cooperative achievements.	Members are sincere, open to others' views, and promote trust.	Destructive conflicts result from personal animosities that emerge in groups composed of disrespectful, defensive, and/or deceitful participants.	Methods of conflict management are used effectively.	Groups without tools for constructive use of conflict cannot take advantage of (and may avoid) significant disagreements that can lead to synergistic solutions.
Empirical	All relevant data/artifacts/expertise are readily available to the group.	A group will fail if members are ignorant about critical aspects of their work due to restrictions on their access to external records, reports, and other forms of useful information.	Group composition provides all necessary skills and abilities.	When participants are not adequately prepared to deal with the difficult cognitive and/or physical challenges that their group is facing, task performance will suffer.	Modes of communication duly enhance group interaction.	Faulty communication, including inappropriate, confusing, and often unavailable channels, will limit necessary exchanges of ideas and information and hinder a shared understanding of problems and solutions.

(*Continued*)

Table I.2

(Continued)

	Context		Structure		Process	
	Support Effectiveness	Undermine Effectiveness	Support Effectiveness	Undermine Effectiveness	Support Effectiveness	Undermine Effectiveness
Political	Resources (e.g., time, money, space) are adequate to complete the task.	When groups are "short-changed" on requisite resources essential to eventual success, it is unreasonable to expect any outcome other than failure.	Legitimate leadership is present, and members have authority to make decisions.	Powerless groups have difficulty organizing themselves and even greater trouble in accomplishing tasks in a timely and consensual manner.	Stakeholder interests are represented well.	Although excluding the concerns of unrepresented parties will reduce the complexity of most problems that groups confront, beyond near-term advantages are long-run disasters.
Rational	The Meeting environment (physical and virtual space) is well designed to foster productivity.	A room that is too hot or too cold, noise, hard chairs, no writing surface, faulty equipment, bad coffee, distractions, too confined a space, unreadable projection, interruptions, difficult-to-learn technology, and so on will all impede effectiveness	Goals, objectives, and tasks are defined clearly.	Group members who do not understand their roles and responsibilities cannot be expected to meet performance expectations that have not been made explicit.	Problem-solving methods are used appropriately.	In the absence of even the most basic tools and techniques employed by well-skilled facilitators, groups will founder when faced with interpersonal challenges and demanding tasks.

Exhibit I.1
When to Use an Outside Facilitator

A group member can effectively perform the role of facilitator in many situations. This is especially true when group members have attended facilitator training and gained some experience. Nonetheless, periodically the question arises, "When should we bring in a facilitator who is not a member of the group or perhaps even not a member of the organization, or who has some particular type of process expertise?" Another way of thinking about this question is, "How difficult will it be for this group to work effectively, what type of difficulty will they encounter, and will bringing in an outside facilitator be justified?"

Building on the conceptual framework described in this chapter, we could systematically assess the group's situation on each of the twelve conditions. The guide that follows is less ambitious, providing some guidelines using only the four perspectives of the Competing Values Framework—the relational, political, empirical, and rational perspectives—without differentiating between context, process, and structure.

Considerations from the Relational Perspective

From the relational perspective, thinking about distrust, bias, and intimidation can provide useful insight into the challenges faced by the group and the potential value of an outside facilitator.

Distrust or Bias

In situations where distrust or bias is apparent or suspected, collaborating groups should make use of an impartial process expert to facilitate (and perhaps convene) the group.

Those whose job it is to manage the process, such as project leaders, bear an enormous influence on the process, and potentially the outcome. Their decisions—such as the choice of participants, analytical methods, social interaction methods, and agenda topics and tasks—have fundamental influence on the group's collaborative efforts. To give this power

(*Continued*)

Exhibit I.1

(Continued)

to anyone who has a stake in the outcome gives that person potentially more power than the others. Consequently, the other group members might view such leaders as biased, steering the process in some way to favor their own ends. This might be true, but even if not, it might be perceived as such. A facilitator who does not have a stake in the outcome is less likely to be perceived as being biased.

Intimidation

The presence of a facilitator can foster the participation of individuals who might otherwise feel intimidated.

In situations where participants are of disparate educational, social, or economic status; are at different levels in organization hierarchies; or are in other types of control relationships (such as clients and service providers or small businesses and government regulators), some participants might feel intimidated and be disinclined to participate. Often the presence of a facilitator provides participants with a neutral-status person to whom they can direct their comments more comfortably. The facilitator is skilled in eliciting information in a nonthreatening way, thus fostering productive conversations. However, in some situations, the presence of intimidation, distrust, or bias might suggest that private or anonymous information collection is appropriate.

Considerations from the Political Perspective

From the political perspective, rivalry between individuals and organizations, and the degree to which the problem is well defined and widely shared, can be useful indicators of the difficulties to be encountered by the group and the contributions an outside facilitator might make.

Rivalry

Rivalries between individuals and organizations can be mitigated by the presence of an outside facilitator.

Participants are often reluctant to exhibit personal rivalries or attacks in the presence of an outsider. They might realize that their claims might not seem valid when viewed externally, and so do not even raise them. Participants are often surprised at how polite they are to each other. When rivalries surface, a facilitator can work with the group to determine if they are relevant to the task at hand, and if not, whether the group can refocus on its stated purpose. When rivalries are germane—either to the task at hand or to the long-term development of the group—the facilitator can assist the participants in understanding them as part of the issues to be addressed collaboratively by the group.

Problem Definition

If the problem situation is poorly defined, or defined differently by different parties, an impartial listener and analyst can help the group construct a complete, shared understanding of the problem.

When people come together with disparate views, they are often more concerned with having their own point of view understood by others than they are in gaining an understanding of others' views. A facilitator can guide the group through listening, analyzing, and summarizing each point of view; help members understand and learn from each other; and work with the group to create a shared understanding of the problem.

Considerations from the Empirical Perspective

From the empirical perspective, the information demands that the group must face, and the degree to which the group is practiced at integrating that information for the particular type of problem at hand, are important concerns.

Human Limits

The depth and breadth of substantive issues may be so great that to think about them and the group's process issues is too much for any person to think about all at once.

(*Continued*)

Exhibit I.1

(Continued)

The demands of attending to the content—the volume and complexity of the substantive information—in addition to the group process issues that come into play at each moment in a collaborative meeting may be too much to expect a single human being to meet. Our cognitive capabilities, though great, have limitations. Running a meeting and participating in a meeting are each sufficiently demanding tasks that in complex situations, we ought to focus on one or the other. Having a facilitator whose attention is focused largely on process issues can be a relief to group members, who can then attend more fully to the content issues.

Complexity or Novelty

In complex or novel situations, the group should bring in facilitators who are familiar with and have process expertise for those types of situations.

Meta-decision making—that is, making decisions about the problem-solving and decision-making process—is a legitimate specialty in which experts can accumulate a wealth of knowledge, expertise, judgmental capability, and practical skill. Although groups often have developed their own expertise for addressing recurring decisions, when approaching novel situations or tasks that they encounter infrequently, such as strategic planning, it might be valuable to call in process experts who work with that type of problem frequently.

Considerations from the Rational Perspective

From the rational perspective, the efficient use of the group's key resources—time and money—are important considerations.

Timeliness

If a timely decision is required, as in a crisis situation, the use of a facilitator can speed the work of the group.

For example, if all the metadecisions were made by the group—considering alternative process scenarios and carefully planning each meeting—it would take valuable time away from treating the substantive issues they want to address. Unlike parliamentary procedure, for which there are prescribed rules that address nearly every procedural issue that a decision-making group can encounter, there is no widely accepted rule book for collaboration. Groups are faced with either making up the rules as they go along or using the rules of the process expert as a "collaborative parliamentarian" who will choose which procedures to apply, make up new ones as appropriate, steer the group through their application, and explain them as needed.

Cost

A facilitator can help the group reduce the cost of meeting as a barrier to collaboration. When the participants find it difficult to get together, either because of the cost of travel or other obligations, use of a facilitator can reduce the cost of collaboration. By vesting responsibility for process in the facilitator, the group reduces or eliminates the time it has to spend on metadecisions, makes use of more effective methods known to the process expert, and takes advantage of the facilitator's attention to helping the group accomplish its goals.

Although these considerations are not exhaustive, they do provide some assurance that you are thinking about each of the four perspectives when considering whether to bring in an outside facilitator. The following summary is intended to help you assess each of these considerations. Higher ratings suggest that the person in the role of group facilitator should be clearly differentiated from that of participant or that an outside facilitator (someone who is not a member of the group or organization) should be engaged.

Note: Earlier versions of this assessment guide appeared in "The Role of Facilitation in Collaborative Groups" by S. Schuman, 1996, in C. Huxham (Ed.), *The Search for Collaborative Advantage,* London: Sage; and in "What to Look for in a Group Facilitator," by S. Schuman, 1996, Quality Progress, 29(6), 72.

(*Continued*)

Exhibit I.1

(Continued)

When to Use an Outside Facilitator

1	2	3	4	5	6	7	8	9	10

interpersonal trust — **DISTRUST OR BIAS** — suspicion

1	2	3	4	5	6	7	8	9	10

low status differential — **INTIMIDATION** — high status differential

1	2	3	4	5	6	7	8	9	10

low competition — **RIVALRY** — high competition

1	2	3	4	5	6	7	8	9	10

well defined, held in common — **PROBLEM DEFINITION** — poorly differently defined

1	2	3	4	5	6	7	8	9	10

low demands — **HUMAN LIMITS** — high demands

1	2	3	4	5	6	7	8	9	10

simple or familiar situation — **COMPLEXITY OR NOVELTY** — complex or unfamiliar situation

1	2	3	4	5	6	7	8	9	10

no rush — **TIMELINESS** — pressure to solve quickly

1	2	3	4	5	6	7	8	9	10

easy to get together — **COST** — difficult to get together

APPENDIX: A PRIMER ON THE COMPETING VALUES FRAMEWORK

"What problems or difficulties have you encountered when working with groups?"

I often begin with this question when I lead a workshop on group facilitation, teamwork, or leadership. I ask the participants to think about this question privately for several minutes. When it comes time to solicit and record their responses, instead of listing them, I organize them "on the fly" using the four perspectives on group effectiveness described in this chapter. That is, after I hear each item, I decide where it belongs in the framework illustrated in Figure I.1 and then write it on the wall in the corresponding position.

I don't introduce the framework first, so my choice of where to record each person's contribution naturally stimulates some curiosity. Invariably, someone asks why I recorded the items where I did. When I respond to this question, I explain that the question of what makes groups and organizations ineffective or effective has been a central question in organizational theory and leadership theory for decades. For example, many people would agree that the purpose of group facilitation or of leadership is to help an organization become more effective, but unless you know what "organizational effectiveness" means, it would be difficult to know if your leadership was fulfilling its purpose.

In the 1970s, John Campbell, professor of psychology and industrial relations at the University of Minnesota, addressed this question systematically. He reviewed the literature on organizations and identified what each author found to constitute organizational effectiveness. He found thirty criteria of organizational effectiveness (Campbell, 1977). In a subsequent study, another pair of researchers (one of whom, John Rohrbaugh, is coauthor of this chapter) engaged a panel of organizational effectiveness researchers to reduce the criteria, resulting in the list that follows. (An explanation of the rules they used to reduce the list can be found in Quinn & Rohrbaugh, 1983.)

Organizational Effectiveness Criteria

Conflict/cohesion

Control

Efficiency

Evaluations by external entities

Flexibility/adaptation

Growth

Information management and communication

Morale

Planning and goal setting

Productivity

Profit

Quality

Readiness

Stability

Training and development emphasis

Utilization of environment

Value of human resources

In my workshops, I propose that although it would be useful to memorize and apply this list of seventeen criteria, it would be better still if they could be organized in some way that made more sense and was easier to remember, something more useful than a seventeen-item laundry list. I ask people to work in small groups to organize these seventeen criteria into some scheme or framework. Conveniently, I just happen to have a deck of cards for each small group. Each deck has seventeen cards, and on each card is printed one of the criteria. I invite them to deal the cards out on their tables and move them around into whatever organization makes sense to them. Affectionately, I refer to this exercise as "Organizational Effectiveness: The Card Game."

After ten minutes or so, each group has come to terms with each of the criteria and developed some sort of organizing scheme. I ask two or three groups to report out. Invariably, there are both similarities and differences among the groups. So I ask, "Who's right? Is there a *correct* way to organize these criteria?"

Now I take a small digression and turn the workshop participants' attention to a mathematical-spatial problem. I ask them to work again in small groups and draw a map showing the relative locations of cities A, B, and C, given that their distances are as follows. Give it a try and see if you can create a map yourself.

The distance between City A and City B is 138 miles.

The distance between City A and City C is 122 miles.

The distance between City B and City C is 175 miles.

I have not yet found a group that could not create a reasonable map given this information. To strengthen the idea that they can map the relative locations of cities given just their distances, I ask them to add a fourth, City D, which has the following distances.

The distance between City D and City A is 76 miles.

The distance between City D and City B is 113 miles.

The distance between City D and City C is 67 miles.

Having added the fourth city, I now ask them to orient their maps so that City A is to the north and City B is to the south. Figure A.1 shows the real map, with the following locations in New York State: A, Albany; B, Brooklyn; C, Cortland; D, Downsville (not an especially well-known location, but the only one in the vicinity that starts with a *D*).

Next, I ask if they think they could do the same with stars in the sky rather than cities on Earth. That is, if given the same kind of distance information, could they locate the stars in a three-dimensional space rather than cities in a two-dimensional space? After some thought, the workshop participants tell me that this seems a feasible if more difficult task.

Could we do this same kind of mapping with ideas? Say, for example, if two ideas were almost alike, we would give them a 1, and if another two ideas were very dissimilar, we would give them a 7. Yes, we could do that! So, for a set of ideas, such as the seventeen organizational effectiveness criteria, we could compare the ideas, two at a time, and numerically assess how similar or dissimilar they were. This would give us the "distance" data for each pair of ideas, and we could use those data to construct a map. In fact, we could ask a number of people each to make independent assessments of the similarity-dissimilarity distance for each pair, and then statistically integrate the data for all individuals. This would give us a map of the ideas, not just based on each individual's judgment, but—if the individuals' judgments were sufficiently similar—representing a collective judgment.

This is just what Quinn and Rohrbaugh did. They asked the same panel of organizational effectiveness researchers, and then a larger number of organizational theorists and researchers, to numerically assess the similarity or dissimilarity of the seventeen criteria. (Of course, they had to do this for each possible pairing, so they had to do this for $17 \times 16 \div 2 = 136$ pairs.) Using a

Figure A.1
A Map of Four Cities

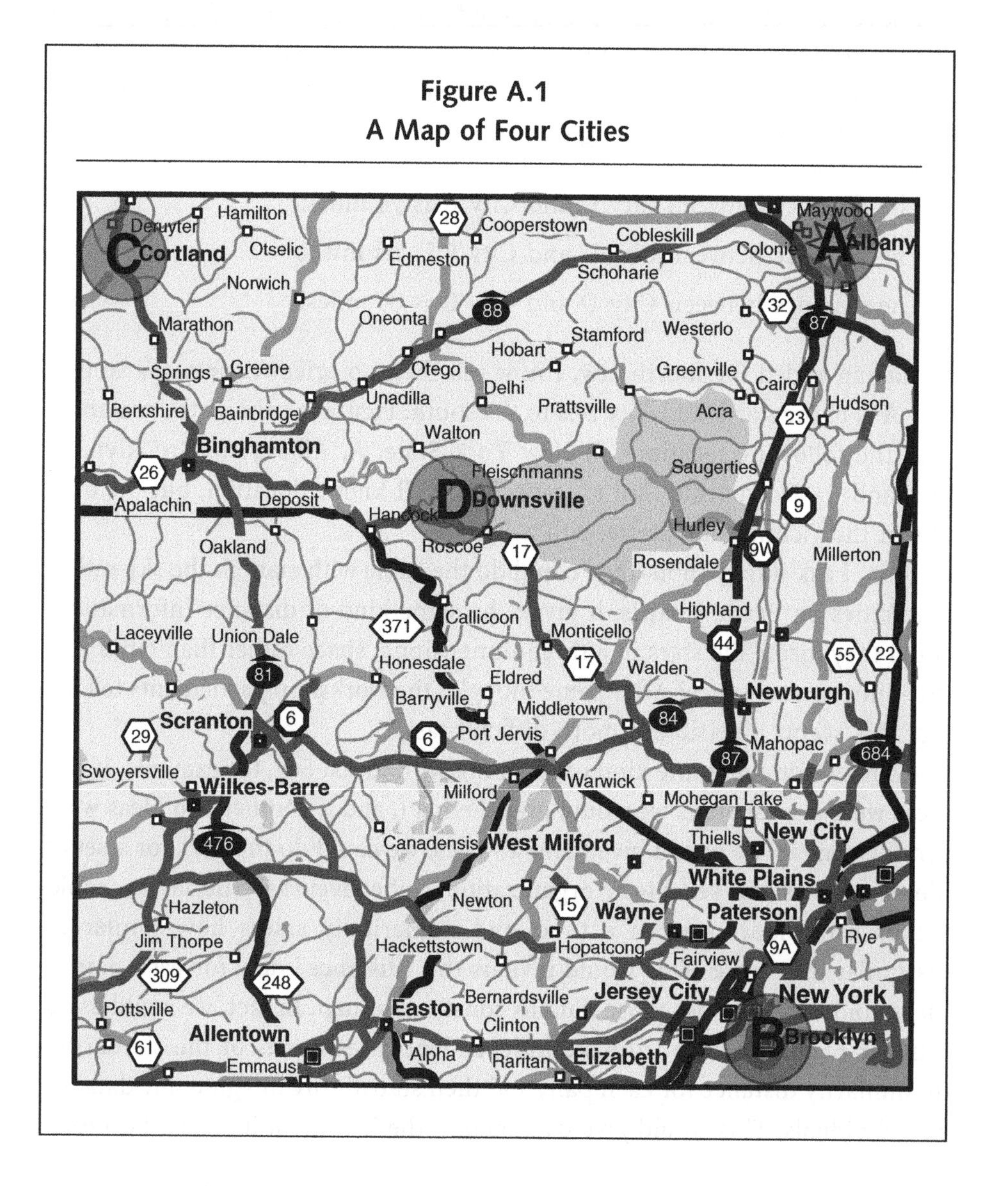

specially designed computer program, they mathematically analyzed the data and found that the researchers shared an implicit cognitive framework for these criteria, which they represented in a three-dimensional map. Figure A.2 shows the map as it was reported in *Management Science* (Quinn & Rohrbaugh, 1983).

Just as we can name the dimensions in a map of the cities—the east-west dimension and the north-south dimension—Quinn and Rohrbaugh named the dimensions in the spatial map of organizational effectiveness criteria. Notice

Figure A.2
The Spatial Map of Organizational Effectiveness Criteria

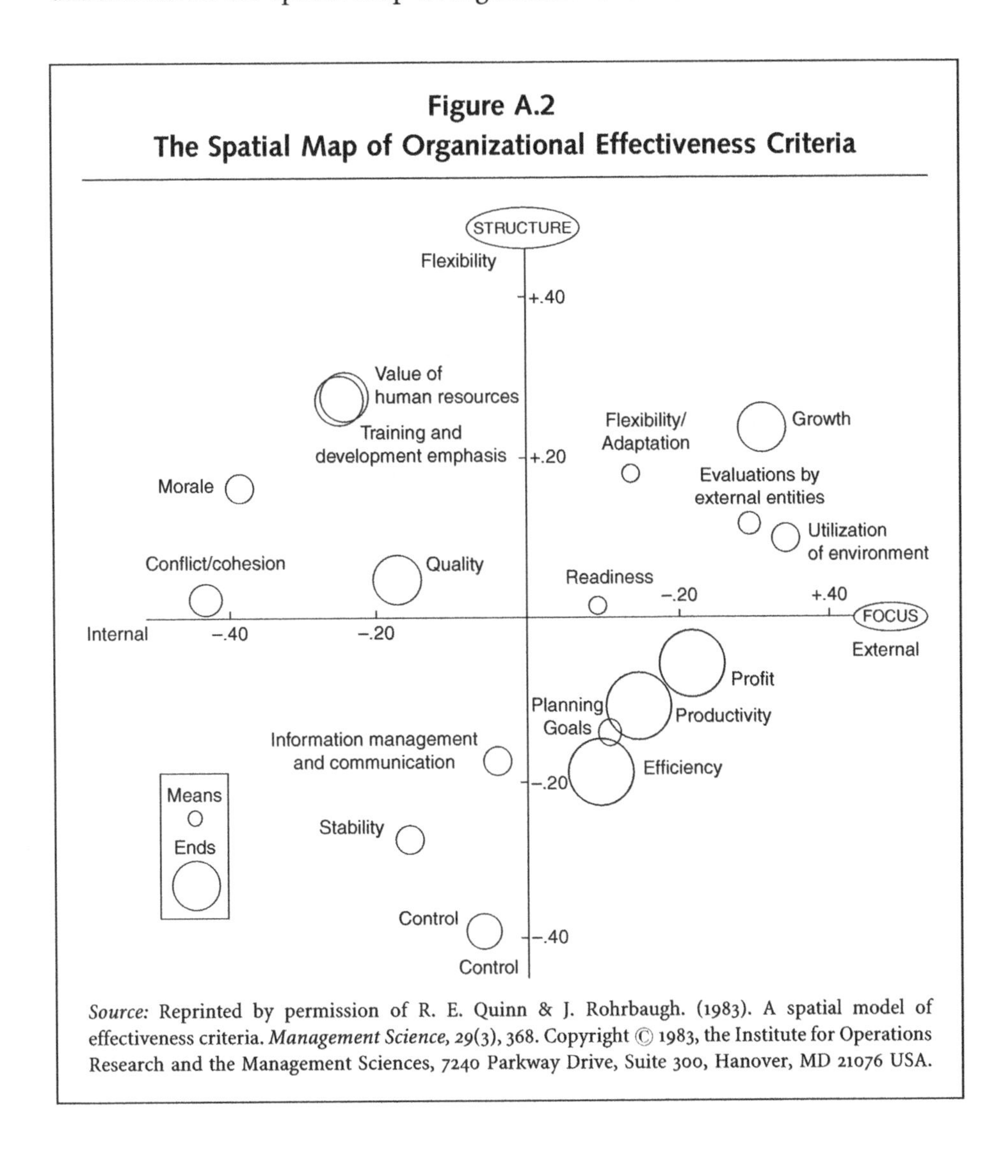

Source: Reprinted by permission of R. E. Quinn & J. Rohrbaugh. (1983). A spatial model of effectiveness criteria. *Management Science, 29*(3), 368. Copyright © 1983, the Institute for Operations Research and the Management Sciences, 7240 Parkway Drive, Suite 300, Hanover, MD 21076 USA.

that in addition to the seventeen criteria, the map shows a horizontal line or dimension labeled Focus that ranges from Internal to External. In organizations, concerns for the internal workings of the organization and its human and information systems compete with concerns for external resources and relationships with customers and other organizations. Also, the map shows a vertical dimension labeled Structure that ranges from Flexibility to Control. The need for organizational flexibility and adaptability compete with the need for organizational stability and control. A third dimension, Means-Ends, is indicated in the diagram by the size of the circles associated with each criterion. The concern for ends is nearer and larger; the concern for means is farther away and smaller. Organizations often experience competing concerns with regard to means and ends. Quinn and Rohrbaugh named their spatial map of effectiveness the *Competing Values Approach* (also referred to as the Competing Values Framework) because it captures so well these fundamental organizational tensions. I find these dimensions—Internal-External, Flexibility-Control, and Means-Ends—to be the most useful in understanding and applying the Competing Values Framework. I will return to them shortly.

A virtue of the Competing Values Approach is that it allows for multiple levels of group and organizational concerns to be viewed in the same framework. The original article on the Competing Values Approach (Quinn and Rohrbaugh, 1983) placed four models of organizational effectiveness in the Competing Values Framework, as shown in Figure A.3:

The open systems model, where flexibility and an external focus are valued, and the primary system function is adaptation

The rational goals model, where control and an external focus are valued, and the primary system function is goal attainment

The internal processes model, where control and an internal focus are valued, and the primary system function is integration

The human relations model, where flexibility and an internal focus are valued, and the primary system function is social maintenance

Rohrbaugh (1989) extended the Competing Values Framework to group decision-making processes, as shown in Figure A.4. This is the source of the four perspectives on group effectiveness we described earlier in the Introduction: *relational, political, rational,* and *empirical.*

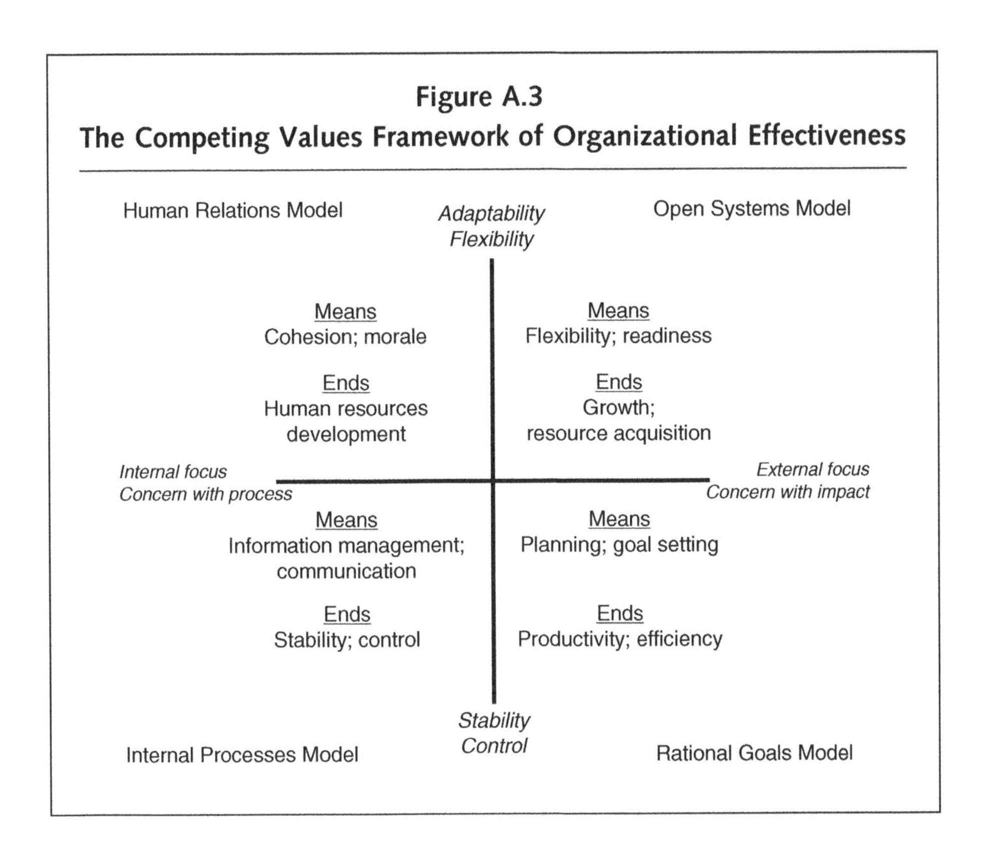

Figure A.3
The Competing Values Framework of Organizational Effectiveness

In my workshops, I integrate the dimensions of the Competing Values Framework, in particular the Internal-External and Flexibility-Control dimensions, with the four perspectives. I would like to "walk you through" the model, integrating these dimensions and perspectives. To make the connections in my workshops, I move around so I can point to various parts of the framework while I explain them, but here you will have to do the footwork and pointing on your own.

The Internal-External dimension. The relational and empirical perspectives, on the left, are internally focused and concerned with process, whereas the political and rational perspectives, on the right, are externally focused and concerned with impact.

On the left, the relational perspective is concerned with interpersonal relationships *within* the group, whereas the empirical perspective is concerned with the internal systems for collecting and integrating pertinent information and expertise.

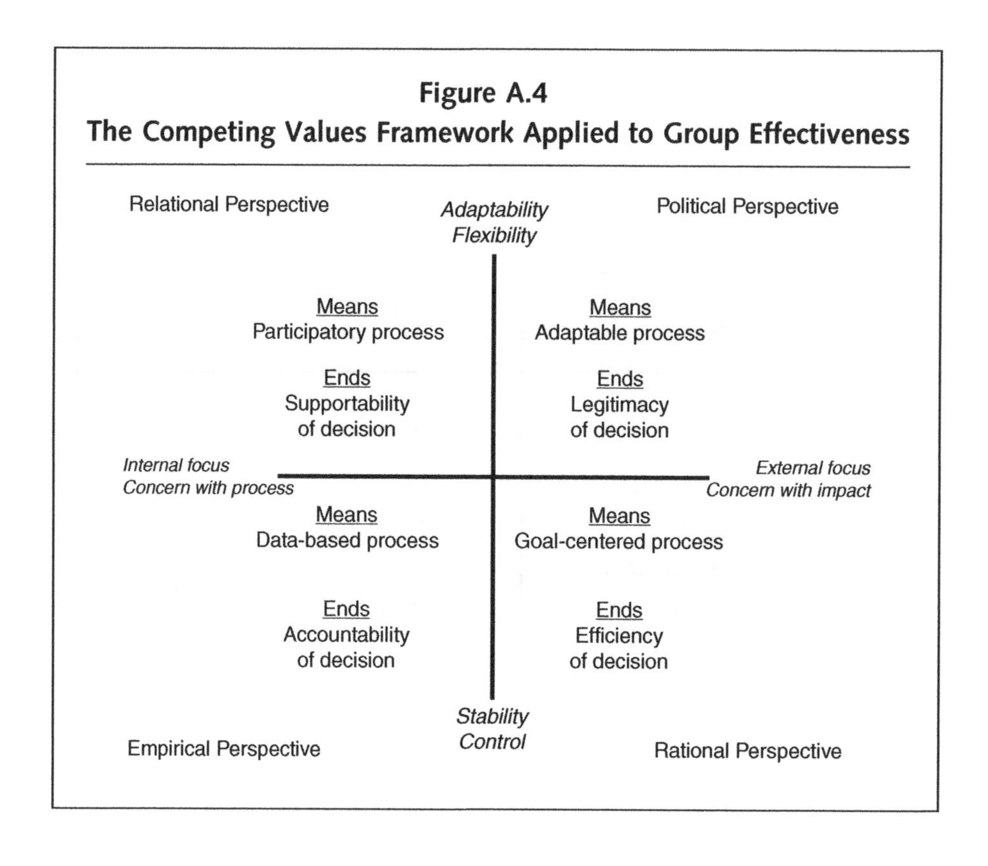

On the right, the political perspective is concerned with relationships between the group and others (other individuals, groups, and organizations) that are outside the group, whereas the rational perspective focuses on establishing goals that will be recognized and valued by those outside the group (such as customers, funders, and oversight bodies), and using resources efficiently to attain them.

The Flexibility-Control dimension. The relational and political perspectives, in the upper half, are concerned with flexibility and adaptability, whereas the empirical and rational perspectives, in the lower half, are concerned with stability and control.

In the upper half, the relational perspective focuses on cultivating the group's human capital, acquiring new knowledge and skills, and continuously learning and developing. By making appropriate use of members' contributions, the group's actions receive their support. The political perspective is concerned with the group's ability to take advantage of its external sources of information and ideas, and to respond innovatively and adaptively. Consequently the group can be viewed as having involved others and taken their concerns into account, thereby achieving legitimacy.

In the lower half, the empirical perspective values information used to monitor the group's status, identify any emerging problems, and take corrective action to maintain the group's internal processes. The record of this activity enables the group to be accountable for its actions. From the rational perspective, the concern is that the group is stable, predictable, and productive in achieving its goals. The task and goal orientation of this perspective ensures that the group's actions result in efficient use of resources.

Although the Competing Values Framework is now decades old, it continues to be used and developed, a tribute to its robustness. Further applications of the Competing Values Framework continue to be made, as illustrated by its application to communications (Belasen, 2008).

The Handbook for Working
with Difficult Groups

chapter
ONE

Keeping Difficult Situations from Becoming Difficult Groups

Marvin Weisbord and Sandra Janoff

We were managing a welfare-to-work meeting in a midwestern county to involve citizens in carrying out a new federal law. The meeting included bankers, business owners, social workers, county officials, and welfare recipients. People started with considerable goodwill as the sponsors spoke about the importance of finding solutions that would benefit families and employers, solutions that would take into account needs for training, transportation, and child care if full-time parents on welfare were to be employed. Early on, the welfare group told how hard it was for them to find work. Soon after, the employers' group announced that together they had one thousand unfilled jobs. "If you were really motivated," said one business owner to the welfare group, going on the attack, "you could easily get one those jobs!" A welfare mother rose to the occasion. "You have no idea what my life is like!" she shot

---

This material is adapted from "Principle 6: Master the Art of Subgrouping," in Marvin Weisbord and Sandra Janoff, *Don't Just Do Something, Stand There! Ten Principles for Leading Meetings That Matter* (San Francisco: Berrett-Koehler, 2007).

back, anger building with every word. "I've applied for some of those jobs, and all your interviewer sees is my black face!"

In fifteen seconds, people were ready to fight. Our task was to help the stereotypical subgroups become functional. This we did by means that we will describe in this chapter. For purposes of this example, we can say that the turning point came after a long dialogue when another employer faced the angry woman and said, "You're right. I have no idea what your life is like, and I would like to know more."

For twenty years we have been leading planning meetings and teaching our methods in many of the world's cultures. Typically we work with groups of twenty to eighty people for two or three days. We work only on tasks with a goal requiring collaborative action. It could be creating a welfare-to-work program like the one cited here, demobilizing child soldiers in southern Sudan, devising a joint strategy among global agencies working on disaster risk reduction, or creating a sustainability plan for a worldwide retailer. Nearly always our groups include people from many walks of life who usually don't work together.

We have known difficult times in groups—when we've been anxious, annoyed, confused, and uncertain about what to do. We have greatly reduced our difficulties, however, by acting primarily on structural issues that we can control. We came to this decision during years of working with people in diverse cultures whose worldviews differed from ours and from each other's. We have come to believe that calling a group "difficult" is a perceptual act leading to a self-fulfilling prophecy. We now act on the assumption that we don't know how to fulfill the needs of people who have little cultural affinity except the task they share. The difficulty in such groups is in us, not them. To the extent that we treat differences as a problem to be solved rather than a reality to be managed, we set ourselves up for endless diagnosis and intervention at the expense of doing the work.

As a result, some years ago we stopped labeling individual and group behavior. We dropped categories like "defensiveness" and "resistance to change." Instead we chose to see people doing their best with what they had. We began paying attention to the way structure influences a group's dynamics. Instead of behavior, about which we could do little, we began attending to what we could control. In particular, we interested ourselves in those aspects of meetings that predict whether a group will succeed or fail in its task. When we ran into difficult people, nearly always they were enmeshed in difficult structural situations that were mostly avoidable. So we taught ourselves by trial and error to control those few factors that help people find the best that is in them. We have found this to be the shortest route to helping people—regardless of age, culture, education, ethnicity, race, class, and language—create action plans they are committed to implementing.

We have identified four key conditions under which diverse groups are most likely to accomplish their tasks: (1) matching people to the task, (2) making sure we have enough time, (3) making sure everybody knows the goal, and (4) heading off potential conflict that might result in flight from the task. Whereas the first three points are widely understood, it is the fourth one that for us holds the key to productive meetings.

For this chapter, then, we will limit ourselves to describing how we head off fight or flight in a group otherwise structured for success. We will describe a theory and practice that we use to keep a group on task with minimal intervention. Our experience is that when differences cause frustration, fear, or anger, people will keep working on the task to the extent that they view the situation as normal. When people learn to contain their anxiety, they are unlikely to become a "difficult group." Our job is to help people accept their differences with the least intervention. In particular, we seek to minimize "authority projections"—that is, having people turn to us as saviors, or turn on us as enemies. Rather, we invite people to be responsible for themselves. Our interventions are few and brief. However, the underlying theory requires some explication lest you dismiss what we shall describe as oversimplified.

DEALING WITH DIFFERENCES

We trace the evolution of our practice back more than half a century. Not long after World War II, a German refugee psychologist named Solomon Asch (1952) conducted a series of legendary group experiments. Asch was interested in the conditions under which people will maintain their independence from group pressure. He hypothesized that individuals faced with an obvious choice will choose correctly no matter what other group members do. He presented student volunteers with a line drawn on a card. They were asked to select an identical line from another card containing three lines, two of them of different lengths. All group members but the subject were briefed in advance to give wrong answers. The subject disagreed repeatedly, becoming more agitated and uncertain. Within a dozen trials, most subjects went along with the group, feeling a little crazy to deny their own reality. Although the correct line was obvious, only one person in four held out against group pressure.

Untangling from Group Pressure

Seeking to free people from group pressure, Asch tried variations. He gave dissenters a (secret) ally briefed in advance to give an answer contrary to the majority. Now the subjects stood firm. The correctness of the ally's answers didn't matter. So long as one other person dissented from the majority, subjects stayed true to what they believed to be right. Asch then had the ally leave the room on a pretext. Many subjects reverted and after a few trials went along with the wrong choice. To maintain their reality, people needed support from another dissenter (Asch, 1952; Faucheux, 1984). We now call what Asch did in his experiments *subgrouping.* He created two-person subgroups united by their dissent. Without support, few people could stay independent. (See also the discussion of "pluralistic ignorance" in Chapter Eight.)

Validating the Power of Subgroups

Now fast-forward several decades. Yvonne Agazarian (1997), developer of Systems-Centered Group Theory, was experimenting with a theory that groups develop new capacity as they discover and integrate differences. She found that a person who makes an anxiety-producing statement risks being ignored, coerced, or attacked. Should that happen, the group abandons its task, moving instead to feelings, overt or unstated, about right and wrong. In effect, people create informal subgroups in the moment, pro, con, or neutral about every statement. Given enough emotionality, such subgroups can easily divert a meeting down unintended paths.

Agazarian hypothesized that all it takes to keep groups whole and working on their task is to make sure that nobody risks ridicule or rejection for saying something out of synch with other group members. Such statements could be as simple as, "My time is being wasted in this meeting, and I don't like it!" or more complicated—for example, "We have talked a long time about X and Y, and what none of you will accept is that Z—as I have said repeatedly—is the key to the problem." The key to managing these challenges is to make visible an informal subgroup of those who share the feelings being expressed. When people at risk have allies, as Asch showed long ago, they are more likely to stay engaged in an authentic way. More, as Agazarian has shown, when people realize that more than one person has a particular concern, all are more likely to stay on task.

Agazarian learned that she easily could make people aware of informal subgroups whenever differences threatened to subvert a task. By surfacing a subgroup for emotionally charged differences, she reduced the possibility of fight or flight. Often, nothing more was required to keep a group working than to say, "Anyone else feel we are wasting time?" or "Are there others who believe Z also is relevant?" Simply having allies identify themselves was all that was needed to keep people engaged and working. Exploring these dynamics, Agazarian made a further significant discovery. Between subgroups that appeared to differ, there were always similarities. Within subgroups of people sharing similarities, there were always differences. When a group was at risk of splitting apart, now and then surfacing allies was not enough to keep the task alive. In those cases, Agazarian found that helping people express the whole spectrum of thoughts and feelings held the key to integrated solutions for complex problems.

Heading Off Group Splits

Over time, we adapted Agazarian's insights to task-focused meetings, using techniques that she developed. If you choose to use the practice outlined here, you will discover a simple way of keeping groups on task regardless of their differences. You can let go of diagnosing a group's behavior, its stages of development, or its members' personalities. You won't have to confront anybody's behavior. You may free yourself from the burden of needing to fix every problem that comes up. You become active only when disagreements might end productive work. Instead of dreading conflict, you may come to experience differences as a creative opportunity to keep people working without their having to agree on everything.

A THEORY OF DIFFERENCE: WHY WE CAN'T ALL GET ALONG

What makes leading meetings a challenge is that nobody is indifferent to differences. We may hate them, love them, avoid them, or rub everybody's noses in them, but the one thing we are not likely to do is remain neutral about them. When a group starts poking at contrary views, dialogue may turn into dismissal or attack. The task goes out the window. Some may feel the need to convince others they are wrong; some may worry about hurting other people's feelings; some may start labeling others as "change resisters" or "touchy-feelies" or whatever comes into their heads.

Whether any of this is said or not, once these (largely unconscious) processes get under way, you can say good-bye to task focus, creative solutions, and committed implementation. When a topic is hot, what ought to be ordinary matters of fact—"You believe this; I believe that"—quickly become "my good views" versus "your bad ones." Those who feel superior start throwing their weight around; those who feel inferior give up or rebel.

Frustration rises. How will you keep the lid on? When views collide, you may be tempted to smooth over the differences. We want to fortify you to respond to tension by moving toward it. Getting people to differentiate themselves—to heighten their awareness of their differences—holds the key to integrated problem solving and decision making.

We Upset Ourselves over Differences

There is one near-universal experience that makes the practice we advocate a personal challenge. Heading off potential splits requires new behavior if you are not used to staying with tension when differences arise. From the days when our ancestors lived in caves, people have stereotyped without a moment's reflection other families, tribes, or villages. It is our lot to categorize people before we know them.

We walk into a meeting with strangers and gravitate toward people similar to us and away from those who are not. We judge people on the basis of very little contact. This process is as natural as breathing. Much of the time our judgments do no harm. If we need to work with others, however, we may escalate first impressions into divisive stereotypes. Think how easily we dichotomize men and women, rich and poor, old and young, fat and thin, light skin and dark, able and disabled, short and tall, sick and healthy, housed and homeless, working and unemployed.

The list never ends. And our negative predictions about "them" can turn deadly, as anyone can tell you who has lived in Northern Ireland, the Middle East, and parts of Africa. There, stereotyping begins with "Catholics are . . . ," "Protestants are . . . ," "Israelis are . . . ," "Palestinians are . . . ," "Blacks are . . . ," "Whites are . . . ," "Latinos are . . . ," "Asians are . . . ," "The rich are . . . ," "The poor are . . . ," and ends with vile attributions, hostility, and aggression persisting over centuries. To experience the tip of this iceberg, you need not go to places of hair-trigger conflict. You may encounter incipient aggression in any meeting. Indeed, if you look hard enough, you may find some inside yourself.

Subgrouping Goes on All the Time in Meetings

Every meeting provides a forum for mutual stereotyping, drawing on the best and worst parts of our psyches. No matter what formal structures you use, group members from the first moment will be drawn into informal subgroups. Because people keep most projections secret, even those meetings that seem smooth and orderly have as subtext a jumble of unspoken wishes, energies, and frustrated impulses. Somebody forms a judgment and becomes part of a subgroup that includes every other person with similar thoughts. Of course, none know this unless somebody polls the group. There is at work in every meeting an informal system functioning apart from the people in it. This system only becomes a problem when some people silently stereotype a speaker's comments to the point where they abandon the task. On the surface, you have people doing what they do in meetings, speaking, listening, doodling, daydreaming. Underneath, people are aligning with, distancing from, or ignoring every statement made. Each audible remark becomes a focal point for new subgroups forming and reforming from moment to moment. If a meeting were a cartoon panel, you would see little cloudlike balloons over each person's head. Inside would be unspoken comments like "That's the dumbest thing I ever heard" or "I'd never say anything like that!" or "This is a huge distraction" or "I'm glad someone had the guts to speak up." If the comment stirs enough emotionality, informal subgroups, unknown to participants, can derail a meeting.

Rarely do people voice their judgments of one another. Most of us discover early in life the psychic risks of antagonizing a group. When somebody heeds the impulse to do that, tension rises. Some manage their discomfort by hoping, even expecting, that the leader will take care of it. Others ask challenging questions. Others patiently explain how the deviant missed the point. Some practice a firm, friendly coercion toward their own view. No wonder so many people sit on ideas or feelings that might violate a group's unspoken norms.

YOU CAN TURN STEREOTYPICAL SUBGROUPS INTO FUNCTIONAL ONES

Fortunately, just knowing about this phenomenon gives you leadership options you never had. With a few well-chosen words, you can change a stereotypical subgroup, one based on emotional judgments, into its functional equivalent. We use the adjective *functional* here to mean "contributing to growth," not to describe people's jobs. Functional subgroups transcend the stereotypical subgroups that people form and reform in their heads. Asch showed that so long as each person has an ally, people maintain their independence. Agazarian demonstrated that so long as there is a subgroup for every viewpoint and all voices can be heard, the whole group is more likely to keep working on its task. This point is so easy to miss that it bears repeating. So long as every person has a functional ally—somebody who carries similar ideas or feelings—a group is more likely to keep working. It will not distract itself with side trips into rejecting, rescuing, or scapegoating the member with a difference. Our minimal job becomes helping people experience their functional differences when stereotypes might cause them to abandon the task. If we do this job right, group members will take care of the rest. Our practice, derived from Agazarian's work, is simple, fast, and effective.

Minimal Intervention: When to "Just Stand There"

When we lead meetings, we just stand there so long as people are

- Putting out their own ideas
- Asking questions
- Answering questions
- Asking for or giving information
- Building on each other's ideas

All these behaviors contribute to the task. We even stand there when people flounder, stumble, express confusion, wander off the subject, or dream out loud. Usually a group recovers quickly from occasional side trips. We also believe deep in our beings that every contribution has value, even though that value may not be obvious. Groups usually ignore one person's stumbling, and so do we. If the flow of conversation veers away for several comments in a row, we consider it our job to point that out. Typical comment: "Let's pause and see where we are. I think I'm losing the thread."

Now and then one of us will ask someone who seems to have wandered far alone and is at risk of not coming back, "I know there is a connection between what you are saying and the topic we're discussing. How does it connect up for you?"

Even when we seem quiet on the outside, just standing there for us involves actively listening with awareness of the way informal subgroups can influence the work.

FOUR WAYS TO ENABLE FUNCTIONAL SUBGROUPS

When people say or do something that visibly heightens tension, when we hear the crackle of fragmentation and splitting, fight or flight, we go on high alert. Those are the moments when we must be ready to act. Here we describe four key techniques that make up the core of our meeting management.

Technique 1: Ask an "Anyone Else" Question

This practice is stunningly simple. Take action when you hear people make statements so emotionally charged that they put themselves at risk of being isolated or labeled. For example:

Participant: "We have been at this for two hours, and I'm frustrated that the rest of you just want to talk instead of acting!"

We judge the impact of such statements by the extent to which tension rises in the group. Sometimes people jump in to challenge the statement, putting the speaker on the defensive. The temptation is to let the antagonists have it out while others watch. This can make for entertaining reality television, but it rarely expedites the task.

You can do better. What is needed now is neither confrontation nor a search for "truth." Rather, you need to head off the split so that people keep working. The best way to do that is to invite a *functional* subgroup for the risk taker. For many people, this will be counterintuitive. Rather than look for somebody who is *not* frustrated to counterbalance the first person, your best move is to get the frustrated person joined.

Leader: "Anyone else feeling frustrated?"

We expect one or more people to raise their hands. When they do, we ask for their experience. Usually we discover they have a spectrum of frustrations. The speaker is not alone. Frustration is OK. Confrontation is avoided. Everyone has new information on where others stand. The group moves on. We call such subgroups functional because they advance the task. Note that in highly charged situations, we do not ask people to join the speaker's contention, only the feeling. If some share any source of frustration, let them say so. Often, people have other reasons. Rather than debate talk versus action, we seek to legitimize frustration by finding a subgroup for that feeling. Only then can we attend to what the meeting should be doing.

Sometimes, however, people ignore the frustrated person, moving on to other topics, leaving emotionality hanging like fog in the air. Is frustration legitimate?

Leader (recognizing unfinished feelings): "I want to go back to what ______ said a minute ago. Is anyone else feeling frustrated?" We stop. We look around. We repeat the question if necessary. We watch for heads to nod.

Leader (to those nodding): "What frustration do you experience?"

One person gives his or her version. Perhaps another chimes in. At this point the group is working again. What might have been a fight becomes a dialogue on a key issue—the degree to which the work frustrates people. This is not a denial of the reality of the person who brought up the issue.

In the welfare-to-work meeting cited at the outset, we allowed the confrontation between the employer and welfare mother to continue for a bit as tensions rose in the room. Before things turned really ugly, we invited the contentious parties into the same functional subgroup by asking, "Anyone else feeling deeply about this issue?" Hands went up around the room from all stakeholder groups. Now several people chimed in with their concerns, enlarging the subgroup. This paved the way for the employer who then asked to know more about the lives of welfare mothers.

By finding an ally, in effect creating a subgroup, we kept both the employer and the welfare mother from becoming isolated and perhaps unwitting scapegoats. We acted to help the group accept frustration rather than turn it into further aggression. See Exhibit 1.1 for specifics.

Informal Subgroups Emerge During Meetings Note that we expect functional subgroups but cannot know who will be in them, or when they will become important. We discover all this as the meeting progresses. It takes only one ally to form a subgroup, validate a person's right to an opinion, and keep the meeting on track. As people learn that there is a subgroup for every issue that matters, they

Exhibit 1.1
Rules for Asking "Anyone Else?"

1. Listen for the intensity of feeling, and note what happens in the group. If anxiety rises, if you sense more tension in yourself, that could be a moment to ask an "Anyone else" question. (Many statements require no response. The person making them is satisfied to get it out, and people accept the comment as part of the dialogue.)
2. Cite the content of a statement only when the content does not threaten a personal attack or a divisive argument.

   Participant: "I'm confused about what's going on right now."

   Leader: "Anyone else confused?" (Rather than "Let me explain it to you.")
3. Cite only the feeling behind the statement if the issue is potentially divisive. In other words, find a subgroup for the *emotion,* so that all emotions remain legitimate.

   Participant: "I'm getting impatient with the idea that ___________."

   Leader: "Is anybody else impatient right now—for any reason?"

are more likely to join the conversation and create a more realistic portrait of the whole. The "Anyone else" question also preempts a habit that we often run into, namely somebody saying, "I'm sure I'm the only one who feels this way, but . . . " or "I know I speak for many others when I say . . . " Whenever we hear this, we ask the person to ask if anyone else feels the same way.

In managing meetings, we need to emphasize, we are not standing there saying "Anyone else?" every few minutes. Even in meetings lasting two or three days, we rarely ask this question more than once or twice. We attribute this to the fact that we seek from the start to validate every person's experience. When the context includes everyone, most groups then handle what comes up without fleeing or fighting. When groups come to recognize the power of joining, individuals will ask as a matter of course if anyone else feels the way they do. Indeed, if you are participating in a group, not leading, and wonder whether you are alone with a particular view, you can easily ask, "Anyone else?"

rather than wonder. That is the best form of reality check. You keep yourself engaged by surfacing your own subgroup.

Suppose Nobody Joins? In our learning workshops, somebody inevitably asks, "Suppose nobody joins?" Well, we have been there too. Once in a great while—maybe every year or two—one of us will ask an "Anyone else" question and be greeted by silence.

Participant: "This has been a big waste of time for me."

Leader: "Anyone else feel they are wasting their time?"

Nobody says a word.

In that case, we see whether we can authentically join the person who has gone out on a limb. We may wait as long as twenty seconds after asking, "Anyone else?" which seems like an eon longer than eternity. When nobody speaks, tension builds while we consult our experience for an honest response.

Leader: "I've had moments here when I thought I was wasting my time, too."

Suppose we can't authentically join. The meeting has been great from our point of view.

Leader: "It seems you're the only one at this moment. Are you able to move on?"

Technique 2: Use Subgroup Dialogue to Interrupt Polarization

Asking "Anyone else?" is not always the end of the story. Now and then people become deeply polarized over conflicting beliefs, problem definitions, solutions, or decisions. In such cases, people may strongly disagree without stereotyping each other, but their conflict threatens to derail the task. There is a second technique we use for instances that paralyze a group. Our objective is to have people explore both sides of the conflict, but not in the way you might imagine. So if people overtly split on an issue, we stop the action. We ask people to identify which subgroup they belong to. However, we do not encourage a confrontation between subgroups, as you might do in a debate. Rather, we encourage the A's to talk *with each other* while the B's listen. After all the A's have had their say, we ask subgroup B to do the same while subgroup A listens.

The reason for this may not seem obvious. When people engage in dialogue with those who are ostensibly similar, comparing notes on what they believe and why, they nearly always discover differences that were not apparent at first. There is a spectrum of views within subgroup A and within subgroup B (just as members of a political party vote the same way for different reasons). Often this comes as a surprise to both subgroups. Moreover, as people listen in on conversations among those they consider different, they nearly always discover positions similar to theirs that they could not discern until now.

In short, we affirm Yvonne Agazarian's principle that similarities always exist within apparent differences, and that within apparent similarities there always are differences. As people make these finer distinctions, they develop a more grounded sense of what they consider relevant. They experience a continuum of opinions rather than two opposite poles. They suspend for the time being their stereotypes and projections and get on with the business at hand. Differentiation leads to integration. Both-and replaces either-or as the unspoken group assumption.

Example: Mending a Split over Decision Making In a business meeting, people split over what they believed were the principles underlying effective company decisions. Fact-based decision making ranked high for one vociferous person. A vice president hesitantly noted that feelings and intuition often entered into his decisions. The first speaker, surprised by this, heatedly asserted the centrality of facts. We asked her to find out if anyone else shared her view. Several raised their hands. Next, we asked who believed intuition and feelings entered in. Many other hands went up. Two functional subgroups became visible. We asked each subgroup to explore thoughts and feelings among themselves while the other subgroup listened. Members of both soon found differences in their apparent similarities. One woman, for example, admitted that to stay fact based, she had to struggle to keep feelings and intuition out. On the other side, one man said, "Of course I pay attention to data, and I also use information that is not based on hard numbers."

The subgroups integrated their views by validating each other's stand under certain conditions. People later said they were astonished that no confrontation was necessary. Indeed, they had created a larger third subgroup, those who could accept that this might be a both-and proposition. The whole exchange took less than ten minutes.

Technique 3: Listen for the Integrating Statement

How do you know when a group is ready to take a next step? One clue is when people start recycling earlier statements. This usually indicates that a spectrum of views is now on the table. No one has more to add. An even more reliable sign that a group has all it needs to move on is what we call an *integrating statement.* Polarized groups often get stuck in tense either-or conversations. An integrating statement takes the form of a both-and comment, recognizing that each side of a polarity has validity. When we wait long enough for a dialogue to run its course, a group member will nearly always volunteer such a statement.

In a housing conference, people split over what kinds of housing they wanted to see built. The group was on the verge of a stalemate. At that point, a group member, who had been listening intently, said, "Well, some people want to build high-rise apartments, and others are in favor of townhouses, and others fear public housing in their neighborhoods. We all agree more affordable housing is needed. We don't have to agree on what form it should take in order to move forward at this stage. We have to take everybody's concerns into account."

Technique 4: Get Everybody to Differentiate His or Her Position

Throughout, no matter what else goes on in a meeting, we stay mindful that people can integrate only to the extent that they make functional differences public. People need to know who they're dealing with and what they bring to the table. If they don't, their apparent agreements could be perfunctory, superficial, and unlikely to stand up. We never run an interactive meeting without giving all participants a chance to comment on what they do, why they came, what they want, and what they know. In groups of up to fifty or sixty, we nearly always start with a go-around. We might ask people for their name, role, and interest; for their expectations; or for their understanding of the goal. In larger groups, we might have several small groups do this simultaneously. This technique also becomes a dependable security blanket when there is uncertainty about what to do next. We use the go-around any time we feel stuck and need to break an apparent logjam.

We were managing a workshop in Germany on 9/11. When the news came, several group members said they felt they could no longer stay with the agenda. They wanted to change to a conversation about terrorism, peaceful change, and other concerns. Feelings ran high. Everyone was upset. We stopped the action and said, "We'd like to hear one sentence from each person who wants to speak. How do you feel about this situation? What would you like to do now?" About a third of the fifty participants spoke. Soon there was a spectrum of views to consider. In the end, the group decided to proceed with the original agenda.

Nearly always, this act of differentiation produces information that gives everyone choices not obvious a few minutes earlier.

SUMMARY

For twenty years we have been leading planning meetings in many of the world's cultures. We learned to reduce our difficulties in multicultural groups by acting on structural issues that we can control. We stopped labeling individual and group behavior and dropped categories like "defensiveness" and "resistance to change." Instead we chose to see people doing their best with what they had. In this chapter, we described how we head off fight or flight in groups otherwise structured for success—that is, groups that include the right people for the task, have sufficient time, and accept their goals. We described a theory and practice of subgrouping that we use to keep a group on task with minimal intervention.

We cited the work of German refugee psychologist Solomon Asch (1952) and of Yvonne Agazarian (1997), developer of Systems-Centered Group Theory. Both did experiments showing how to help people stay reality focused and engaged despite their differences. Our practice relies on recognizing the existence of informal subgroups that form and reform around every statement people make. We noted the differences between stereotypical subgroups, based on people's judging others on little information, and functional subgroups, based on people sharing feelings and views relevant to their work. Such subgroups become significant when somebody makes a statement so emotionally charged that others may project negative stereotypical characteristics on that person, causing people to abandon the task. Our intervention is to surface a functional subgroup for the person at risk by asking "Who else feels the same way?" This legitimizes that a spectrum of responses is possible. Most times, this simple intervention is enough to keep groups whole and working. We use it sparingly, as groups tend to catch on quickly that we consider all statements valid.

Sometimes groups polarize around a sticky issue. In such cases, we identify subgroups for each position and ask each subgroup's members to engage in dialogue among themselves while others listen. Usually this leads to a realization that a full spectrum of views exists in each group. The issue appears more nuanced than it seemed at first. This procedure usually produces enough new information for people to find a creative resolution. We described two other techniques ancillary to our method: listening for a both-and integrating statement and asking group members when they are stuck to differentiate themselves by hearing each person who wishes to state his or her views.

chapter TWO

Building an External Focus: Avoiding the Difficulties on an In-grown Team

Deborah Ancona and David F. Caldwell

As part of a new strategy, a government agency providing consulting services to other agencies reorganized into teams that focused on specific geographic regions. The broad goal of the strategy was to be more responsive to client agencies, in part by identifying issues that might exist within a particular region. One of these new consulting teams was headed by an experienced manager named Chris. (This description is a composite of different groups rather than one team.)

A DIFFICULT GROUP?

The move to the use of regionally focused teams was greeted with a mix of skepticism and concern by most of the consultants. Although consultants had sometimes worked together on projects in the past, this new structure was seen as a radical departure from the way the work had been done. Before, teams had been made up of similar specialists; now different types of specialists were combined on teams to serve the needs of a particular region. Because of this, one of Chris's primary goals was that members see the team as something of an island of stability in a sea of change. In putting her team together, Chris tried to select people who had experience in working with some of the agencies in the region and who knew each other from past projects. Her initial focus was on ensuring that team members would get to know one another, figure out what they hoped to accomplish, and develop effective processes for getting the work done.

Because the team members had experience with various agencies, they spent a great deal of time exchanging information with one another about their experiences and how they saw the challenges the team would face in implementing the new strategy. During this time, Chris saw her role as that of a facilitator, working to ensure that the team effectively exchanged information and moved toward developing a set of goals for expanding services to agencies. If the team needed resources or information from others in the organization, Chris would handle it, although this was relatively rare. Once the team members had identified an initial model of the kind of services they could provide to the agencies in the region and an ability to work together, Chris planned to spend less time working with the team and a substantial amount of time out meeting with agencies in the region.

Overall, Chris's plan seemed to work well. Compared to the members of other teams, members of Chris's team reported higher levels of satisfaction, more cohesiveness, and much less conflict. Further, when the team was asked to assess its own performance, the members described the success the team had in laying out goals for itself, identifying a timeline, meeting objectives, and efficiently making decisions about the services they could provide. Chris herself echoed these comments. In fact, when asked to assess the performance of her team, Chris reported that the team had been very effective in creating a trusting environment for team work. She went on to compare her team with some of the other newly formed teams that seemed to have more conflict, a tougher time arriving at a strategy, and less cohesiveness. When asked about the difference between her team and others, she attributed a large part of her team's success to its ability to maintain its focus and avoid distractions. She said that some other teams never seemed to jell because they kept getting distracted by "extraneous" information. The other consulting team managers and the vice president of the organization didn't have much to add to Chris's evaluation of her team. The vice president said that she had not spent a lot of time with Chris other than during regular meetings. The other managers reported that they had not spoken extensively with Chris, and their people had not been talking much with the members of Chris's team.

About six months after the reorganization, the consulting teams were scheduled to begin marketing new products and services to the agencies in their regions. Most of the teams had already begun informally meeting with agencies in their areas, so formally rolling out the new services was an easy process. A couple of the teams found that one or two of the agencies in their regions were interested in services that a consulting team in another region had developed, and they were able to partner with consultants from the other region to deliver the new service. None of this was the case for Chris's team. Although Chris had tried to meet with agencies and outline what her team was developing, when the consultants began to work with the agencies, they had little success. When they did get an opportunity to make a formal proposal, a comment they frequently heard was that their offering did not really fit some of the new constraints the agencies were facing. About a year after the reorganization, Chris's team was far behind the other regions in both contracts and billings. As the bad news came in, the tenor of the team's meetings changed. The group became much more critical of the strategic change that had led to the new organization and voiced complaints about the lack of support from management for the new effort. Within the group, much of the blame for the team's failure was attributed to problems with the region the group had been assigned. Some members of the team began to speak with consultants on other regional teams to try to understand how they had succeeded; they generally got some broad advice, but little specific help. Over the next few months, performance continued to be substandard, the team began to fracture, and Chris was replaced.

WHY DID THE CONSULTING TEAM FAIL?

Explaining why a team might fail is not easy. Every team that fails has a different story—yet when asked to describe those stories, leaders and members of those failing groups often identify the same set of problems. In our experience, the issues that are most frequently raised include the difficulty in arriving at a common goal, conflicts between members, lack of clarity about roles and responsibilities, and a lack of cohesiveness. In short, most of the failures of groups are attributed to the inability of the members to work together effectively to get the job done. When explaining the performance of a group, most people—including authors of books about effective teams—focus on what is going on *inside* the group rather than how the team interacts with those outsiders who provide resources to it, will use its product, and will ultimately evaluate its success. Yet despite this bias, our research suggests that teams often fail because of an inability to do the right kind of *external* outreach.

Although the causes of a group's failure are often not straightforward, nor do they always have an immediate effect, in retrospect the cause of this failure seems clear. Chris's team never established relationships with the outside groups—both the agencies that would be their clients and the other entities within the organization—that could provide the resources and information that might help the team be successful. Instead, by relying only on its own resources, the team began a vicious downward spiral. As the team became more internally focused, the members became more disengaged from the organization and therefore lost the potential for support from others who could help deal with the inevitable setbacks a team experiences. The lack of external focus prevented the team from being able to move beyond the information that team members possessed and to develop products that its clients valued. In addition, it also limited the team's ability to build a positive reputation within the organization. As the group learned that it was not succeeding, the team began to blame outsiders for its difficulties, further limiting its ability either to develop effective relationships with clients or to gain support from others within the organization, thereby cementing a downward spiral of failure, as shown in Figure 2.1.

The focus of this chapter is on how successful teams must develop productive interactions with important outsiders, both inside and outside the parent organization. A team may do a very good job of developing cohesiveness, reducing conflict, and meeting the objectives it sets for itself, yet still fail if it is unable to obtain information and resources from outside the group and build support for the group's work. This implies that teams must effectively manage their cultural and strategic contexts in order to obtain the important information and resources that are necessary for success. Successful teams must also manage the political process to ensure that data and concerns from important external stakeholders are considered in decisions. (See the Introduction for an explanation of the political perspective.)

Figure 2.1
The Downward Spiral of Failure

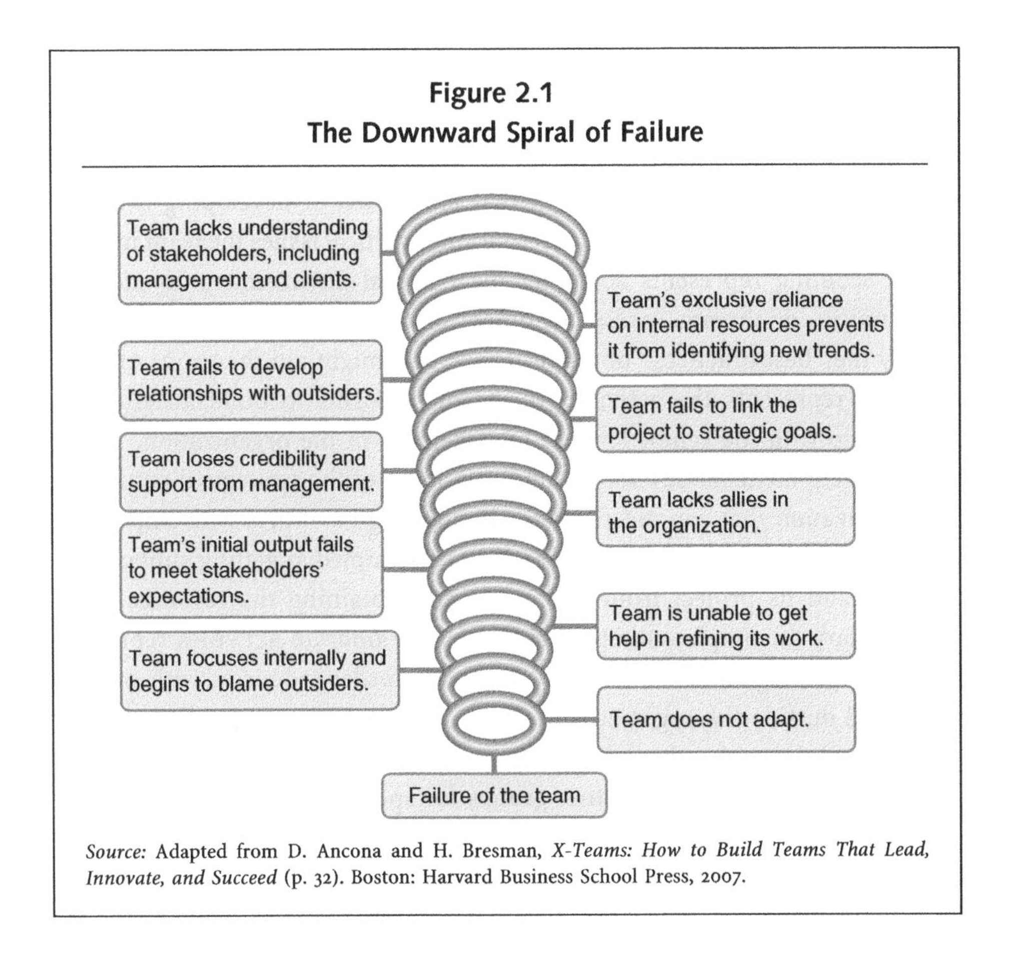
Team lacks understanding of stakeholders, including management and clients.
Team's exclusive reliance on internal resources prevents it from identifying new trends.
Team fails to develop relationships with outsiders.
Team fails to link the project to strategic goals.
Team loses credibility and support from management.
Team lacks allies in the organization.
Team's initial output fails to meet stakeholders' expectations.
Team is unable to get help in refining its work.
Team focuses internally and begins to blame outsiders.
Team does not adapt.
Failure of the team

Source: Adapted from D. Ancona and H. Bresman, *X-Teams: How to Build Teams That Lead, Innovate, and Succeed* (p. 32). Boston: Harvard Business School Press, 2007.

WHAT IS AN EXTERNAL PERSPECTIVE?

As the failure of Chris's team illustrates, the inability to build links with other groups, both inside and outside the organization, can begin a downward spiral that is difficult to correct. Systematic research on teams has confirmed this. In an early study, Gladstein (1984) demonstrated that group process has an external dimension as well as the well-established internal dimensions related to task and maintenance activities. She found that this external dimension was related to the performance of the teams, but that the internal dimensions alone were not. Ancona and Caldwell (1992) took this idea further and identified the specific activities defining this external dimension. They identified three independent sets of activities—what they referred to as Scouting, Ambassadorship, and Task Coordination—that were related to the performance of teams. In the framework described in the Introduction to this book, Scouting and Ambassadorship primarily reflect the political perspective, and Task Coordination most closely aligns with the rational perspective.

Scouting includes those activities that are aimed at developing a broad understanding of the technical, marketing, and political issues the team may be facing. Scouting represents scanning the external environment to identify opportunities or threats, assess customers or competitors, spot trends, and identify the "best practices" of other groups that might aid the team. *Ambassadorship* represents the activities the team performs to build an effective relationship with the senior level of management in the organization. These activities help the team develop an understanding of the strategic direction of the organization that can aid the team in aligning its efforts with important organizational priorities. Ambassadorship is also aimed at getting support for the team and its project from executives and obtaining the resources that are necessary to complete the project. *Task Coordination* activities represent the ongoing things that are done to manage interdependencies with others, inside and outside the organization. These activities can range from coordinating schedules with other groups, to meeting with customers to fine-tune products, to negotiating with other groups for specific resources. Like Scouting, Task Coordination involves communication with other groups throughout the organization or even outside the organization. However, unlike Scouting, Task Coordination is much more focused; the goal is not general understanding, but rather the resolution of specific issues. Scouting and Task Coordination activities generally involve other groups in the organization that are at a similar level to the team; in contrast, Ambassadorship activities are most frequently directed up the hierarchy of the organization.

Ancona and Caldwell (1992) found that these specific boundary activities were related to the performance of product development teams. In particular, teams that engaged in large amounts of Ambassadorship and Task Coordination were both more innovative and efficient than teams that engaged in smaller amounts of these activities. Somewhat paradoxically, although Scouting is a key activity for teams, too much Scouting or Scouting that is not combined with Ambassadorship or Task Coordination can actually be detrimental to a team's performance. This happens because the team may constantly change its decisions in response to general information from outside. Also, it is worth noting that assessments of team performance by independent evaluators stand in contradiction to those of team members. Specifically, independent evaluators saw team performance as related to external activities, whereas team members did not. Instead, team members' self-ratings of performance were related to cohesiveness and effective internal processes. In many cases, team members come to associate good internal processes with effective performance and ignore the other factors that are necessary for a team to be successful.

Overall, this research and other similar studies (see, for example, Bunderson & Sutcliffe, 2002; Cummings, 2004) provide the basis of the external perspective and lead to a number of conclusions. First, external activities are related to a team's performance. Second, it is not simply the amount of communication that a team has with outsiders but the nature of that communication that leads to high performance. Third, and consistent with the perspective of this volume, the optimal pattern of activities for a team can change over time.

Ancona and Bresman (2007) describe specifically how the necessary boundary activities change over the life of the team. Early in its life, the critical task for a team is discovery—that is, developing a clear understanding of what customers will require and acquiring broad knowledge of best practices, technology, and market considerations. During this time, the team must also begin to develop the support within the organization. Effectively meeting these challenges requires substantial Scouting and some Ambassadorship. But a team cannot "play in the sandbox" for too long. To keep the team moving forward, the critical task of the team needs to shift from discovery to design. The team needs to narrow its search for broad information and work to fully develop its product, process, or idea. During this time, the team must make sure that it can acquire the resources necessary to meet its objective and to ensure that its efforts are aligned with the strategic direction of the organization. This focus on building support within the organization requires a high level of Ambassadorship. In addition, the team should begin working the other groups that ultimately adopt or receive the product of the team. This requires some Task Coordination. Once a design is completed, the challenge for the team becomes that of successfully transferring it either to customers or to those in the organization who move the project forward. During this time, finalizing specifications, schedules, and new responsibilities is critical. This speaks to the need for a high level of Task Coordination. Because the diffusion of the team's output will be easier if it is supported by higher-level management in the organization, some Ambassadorship is called for.

WHAT ARE THE CHALLENGES TO AN EXTERNAL PERSPECTIVE?

Although substantial research suggests that an external perspective will aid team performance, these activities must be effectively managed. Recall that this external perspective involves working with other entities both inside and outside the organization. Some teams may concentrate so much on external activities, particularly Ambassadorship, that they are seen primarily as "political" entities, rather than real performers. More problematic, if a team continues to engage in a large amount of Scouting activity late into the design phase of the project, the group may have difficulty in deciding on what its final outcome will be. This is likely either to delay the project completion or even to prevent the group from agreeing on the specifications of the project. If Scouting is taken to an extreme, group members may spend so much time with outsiders—either those inside or outside the organization—that the group runs the risk of becoming "underbounded," in that the group never really creates a boundary between itself and other entities. When this happens, members of the group see their primary connections outside the group and therefore may never identify with the group or its effort.

Even if external activities are effectively managed, they may affect the internal operations of the group. As group members bring in outside information from divergent sources, conflict and uncertainty may increase. When group members spend time with outsiders, the links they develop with each other may not be as tight as they would be if they worked solely with each other. This can create a situation where the external activities necessary to perform effectively may *undermine* the internal processes that team members often see as the road map to high outcomes. In evaluating the progress the team is making, leaders and members need to understand the importance of appropriate external activity and how it affects the internal dynamics of a team.

HOW CAN ONE FACILITATE AN EXTERNAL PERSPECTIVE?

Building an external perspective in a team is based on three things. First, one needs to understand what the team will require from outsiders. Whether it is information, resources, or support, identifying what will be needed is vital. Second, one needs to put together a team that has the potential to acquire what is necessary. Finally, the external interfaces need to be managed successfully. This third step involves both developing a structure for ensuring that external activity takes place, and creating processes in the group for successfully dealing with new information.

Understanding What the Team Needs from Others

The first task for a leader or facilitator is to begin to develop a sense of what information and resources the team will need from outsiders. Although the list of what is needed will change as the project evolves, beginning with an understanding of the outside requirements is important. One important aspect of this is identifying the specific people who can provide resources or information to the team. A second aspect is determining the areas where Scouting needs to take place. Assessing potential markets, competitors, technologies, and the strategic and political issues within the organization is an important early step. Anticipating how the team's efforts will unfold is important in establishing areas where in-depth Task Coordination will be necessary. The team leader also plays a critical role in structuring the team to ascertain what resources the team may need, any opposition from others in the organization, and who in the hierarchy can provide support for the team. This analysis helps build a plan for Ambassadorship activities.

As the team does its work, new needs for external activity will emerge. Resources that can provide background information will be identified, areas where extensive coordination is needed will emerge, and politics within the organization may require interactions that were not forecasted. However, establishing an initial road map for managing external interactions will get the team off to a good start.

If we look back at Chris's team, it is clear that little was done to plan for external interactions. Chris seemed to focus almost exclusively on creating a safe haven for the team. Despite the team's developing new services, there was no plan for collecting current information from potential clients, nor was there a plan for learning from groups doing similar work. Because the strategic change was new and potentially still evolving, understanding how the group could match its efforts to the new strategy became critical. Chris neglected important Ambassadorship activities by not checking her plan with the vice president or adapting her plan to shifts in strategy. Despite the need for coordinating the team's efforts with other teams, no plan was made for working with them. Chris seemed to believe that little external action was necessary, especially at the start of the team's effort, and that what was needed, she could do.

Composition of the Team

A key way to develop an external perspective is to put together a team that includes members who can easily build links with other important outsiders. Two common ways of doing this are by selecting people who come from different functions in the organization and by including people who already have well-developed relationships with relevant outsiders.

Building a team of members who come from different functions, regions, or divisions can provide the range of data that is necessary to understand the external challenges the team will face. In addition, people from different areas can provide multiple perspectives for assessing the information. Reviews of research on teams suggest that this type of diversity is related to overall performance primarily because of the diversity of knowledge and the potential for easier connections with the range of functional groups within the organization (Williams & O'Reilly, 1998). In some cases, it may not be easy to bring people from different functions, regions, or divisions into a team. The task may not require people from all areas, or people may not be available. Even if it is not possible to include in the team people from all the different relevant backgrounds, there is evidence that the same advantages can be obtained if the team contains individuals who have previous experience in such contexts (Bunderson & Sutcliffe, 2002).

A second approach for managing external interactions is to include individuals on the team who have connections or relationships with others outside the group. These connections could come from working together in the past, common experiences in the organization, or simply personal relationships. When individuals have connections with outsiders, the transfer of knowledge becomes easier.

The types of connections individuals develop with one another vary. Some relationships are strong in that they are characterized by closeness, reciprocation, and substantial time spent together. Other relationships are weaker and are based on more superficial connections in which individuals know one another but do not have a particularly close relationship. In understanding how relationships can help a team develop an external perspective, it is useful to keep three things in mind. First, in strong relationships, people are likely to be willing to extend considerable effort to help each other. In weak relationships, people are likely to share information or provide advice, but may not be willing to provide extensive help. Second, because weak relationships require less effort to develop and maintain than strong ones, most individuals will have more weak relationships than strong ones. Third, individuals will develop different patterns of relationships. Some people may develop relatively few ties to others. Others may concentrate on developing and maintaining a small number of close relationships. Still others may concentrate on building up a large set of more superficial relationships at work.

Both strong and weak relationships can help a group build an external perspective. When members of a team have extensive relationships with outsiders, the team should be able to locate useful information and resources throughout the organization. Even if the relationships are weak, outsiders can provide advice, identify information sources, and keep the team informed of events. Although these weak relationships can provide extensive information, a strong relationship with a team member will enhance the motivation of an outsider to actively help the team. An external perspective is enhanced when team members have extensive contacts inside and outside the organization—even if the relationships are weak—and strong relationships with individuals whose active help may be critical to the group.

Looking back to Chris's team, it seems that little thought went into selecting team members who had either a variety of experiences in the organization or who had established connections with important outsiders. In fact, Chris seemed especially concerned about selecting people who either already had ties with one another or who would be able to develop strong relationships with each other. To Chris, the advantage of this strategy was that the members would quickly form a cohesive team and be able to work together. However, such a strategy makes it difficult to build an external perspective. There is evidence that when team members develop strong ties within the group, they may have a hard time developing relationships with outsiders (Reagans & Zuckerman, 2001). By starting with a team whose members had similar experiences and relatively few external connections and then focusing on building relationships within the group, Chris developed a team that would have difficulty accessing the critical outside information. The lack of relationships with outsiders made it hard for Chris's team to easily complete the Scouting necessary to identify resources and needs. In addition, if members of Chris's team had had strong relations with members of other teams, they might have been able to enlist their help in understanding clients' needs and in gaining an in-depth understanding of the types of programs other teams had developed and successfully sold.

Managing External Relationships

After developing an initial road map for external interactions and selecting team members, the leader or facilitator faces the challenge of managing those interactions across the life of the project. At the very beginning of the project, the major issues for the team leader are in laying the groundwork for developing an effective external perspective. Once the team begins its work, maintaining the external perspective through effective Scouting, Task Coordination, and Ambassadorship becomes critical. Doing this requires actively managing team members' efforts and ensuring that information the team obtains is included in ongoing decisions. As discussed earlier, and elaborated below, the pattern of external activities will change as the group does its work. During the early stage, the key challenge is developing a clear understanding of the specifications for the project. During the middle stage, the major task of the team is developing a prototype or initial design. The final stage is oriented toward refining the initial design, finalizing it, and transferring it to the end users. The following are some of the critical tasks the team leader or facilitator should address in each stage so as to maintain an effective external perspective across the life of the team.

Starting Up Even before formal work on the project begins, the following activities are important for positioning the team for success.

- Complete an external map by identifying the groups or individuals that can provide information or resources and that the team will need to deal with in the future.
- Have team members describe their external networks and help the team allocate responsibilities for dealing with outsiders.
- Begin to develop internal processes for sharing and processing information. Bringing in outside information is likely to create conflict within the group; therefore, the challenge for the leader is to create an environment for productive conflict.
- Expose all team members to the end users or final consumers of the team's output. Having all members meet end users will help the team develop a collective sense of customer needs.

- Build a log for recording and maintaining the information the team members receive from outsiders. This helps keep external information salient for all members of the team.

Early Stage Developing a clear sense of the specifications for the project requires a great deal of external activity.

- Substantial Scouting efforts are needed to develop a model of the environment as it is seen by the ultimate users of the team's output. Scouting is also important in understanding what competitors may be doing and identifying resources within the organization, including other groups that may have experience with the type of work the team is doing. Developing this model will require the efforts of most members of the team.
- Task Coordination at this stage of the project will focus on identifying the other groups that will need to work with the team in the future or that will be affected by what the team produces. An important focus will be on beginning to work with the groups that will ultimately take over the team's output. The team may also begin to identify other people who might be brought in to provide specific information or resources as the project progresses.
- Ambassadorship in the early stage is necessary to understand the strategy of the organization and communicate how the team's efforts contribute to that. This may require substantial dialogue with others to determine how the team's output can fit the overall strategy. At this stage, most of the Ambassadorship activity can be done by the team leader or other team members with the communication skills to interact with top management.

Middle Stage Even though the primary focus of the team is on the project, external activities are still important.

- The primary purpose of Scouting shifts from general scanning to filling in specific blanks in the group's knowledge, testing possible solutions with clients, learning from others who have engaged in similar tasks, and tracking any environmental changes that have implications for the team's proposed direction.
- During this stage, Task Coordination becomes more important than it was earlier. The team may need to develop shared timelines and formally negotiate specifications with other groups. Individuals who have relationships with

important outside groups may need to tap those to manage the shared work that the team will do with these other groups. For the leader, the key task is ensuring that these external links are developed, making sure that needed connections are made and shared milestones reached.

- During this stage, strengthening the relationship between the team and top management is important. Top management support may be necessary to facilitate cross-boundary work that challenges traditional stovepipe communications. The team leader and selected others should look for opportunities to present the team's perspective to others.

Final Stage Transferring the work of the team to other units changes the focus of the team's external activities.

- Scouting shifts its emphasis to collecting best practices about how the team can transfer its output to others. Overall, Scouting becomes less important during this stage.
- Task Coordination will focus on negotiating the transfer of the output of the team. Team members will need to involve other groups in this to ensure their support. The team will also need to build excitement for the project.
- During this stage, Ambassadorship will be directed primarily toward keeping top management's support in order to deal with any unexpected problems that might arise and on conveying enthusiasm for the team's work.

CONCLUSIONS

The Introduction of this volume describes three broad factors that influence group effectiveness (context, structure, and process) and four different perspectives that reflect the performance of a group (relational, empirical, political, and rational). In our view, one of the critical aspects of the context is the external environment of the team. This external context includes both what is going on inside the organization in which the team operates and the larger external environment. Understanding both is critical for team success. When the team is unable to manage its relations with outsiders effectively, performance will suffer. In particular, when evaluated in terms of the political perspective, failure to manage external relations will prevent the team from fully understanding the context in which it must operate. Similarly, failure to influence outsiders may prevent the team from creating allies and countering adversaries, thus undermining effectiveness from the political perspective. Effective external relations are also central to aspects of the process factor. If the concerns of all stakeholders are not considered and if multiple teams cannot work together, then political pitfalls will hamper the organization's ability to create synergies and higher performance within and across teams.

We began this chapter with the observation that there are many reasons a team can fail. In our view, one frequently overlooked cause is the inability of the team to effectively manage its relations with outside groups. Looking back at Chris's team, it is clear that much of the failure can be traced to lack of management of external activities. Rather than seeking out information from outside the team about the agencies' needs, the team members relied exclusively on their own experiences. Chris did not work with management to understand how the group's efforts could be aligned with the new strategy. Team members did not tap into what other groups were doing until it was too late. Overall, Chris failed to stimulate the group to bring new information into its decision making, had minimal contact with top management, and did not push members to develop creative solutions in concert with other teams. Although our focus has been on why a team might fail, there is a positive side to the story. In both our research and consulting, we have seen teams achieve exceptional results by combining an external perspective with good internal processes (Ancona & Bresman, 2007). This is not always easy, but with effective facilitation and leadership, teams can do it.

chapter THREE

The Downside of Communication: Complaining Cycles in Group Discussions

Nale Lehmann-Willenbrock
and Simone Kauffeld

It is my belief we developed language because of our deep inner need to complain.

—Lily Tomlin

The six-member team has worked together for some years in a company that established teamwork as the norm. The teams are asked to meet regularly to discuss their work, talk about problems, and exchange and develop their ideas for improvement. However, this particular team has come up with very few ideas recently, and has not implemented any ideas for a while. Their meetings tend to focus on problems in their work, but do not yield any solutions and thus do not lead to change. This situation is due somewhat to their working environment: their supervisor "grew up" in the company before team work was adopted and does not see the benefits. Previous ideas and proposals made by the team have found little or no support by their supervisor. However, another issue concerns the communication within the team.

In one of their meetings, team member A complains, "No one cares about our ideas." Team member B has been in a positive or neutral affective state until now, but upon hearing this statement starts thinking about all the events in the past where that statement may have been true. An adaptation of mood follows whereby team member B adopts a similarly negative mood; B starts complaining as well. This adaptation supports team member A and gives the impression to other team members that this is an acceptable, socially desired behavior. Team member A now feels free to go on complaining rather than contributing to the discussion in a constructive manner. Other team members become involved. The rest of the meeting is spent talking about their heavy workload, their unsupportive supervisor, and past attempts at change that have failed. A "complaining cycle" is born. The team members leave the meeting feeling frustrated, but they have grown accustomed to this over time.

Recent research has shown that group mood affects group members' behavior and has an impact on social interaction (for an overview, see Kelly & Spoor, 2006). We analyze group interaction on the basis of group discussions (verbal behavior) by means of Advanced Interaction Analysis (Kauffeld, 2006a, 2006b; Kauffeld, Lorenzo, Montasem, & Lehmann-Willenbrock, 2009). We have gained some insights concerning positive verbal behavior (for example, solution-oriented statements) as well as negative verbal behavior (for example, complaining).

In addition, we have found evidence that group mood develops through interaction. More specifically, we identified patterns of complaining behavior. Results by Kauffeld (2006b) demonstrate that negative interaction such as complaining has a negative impact on both team-level outcomes (for example, satisfaction with the discussion) and organization-level outcomes (for example, productivity). Furthermore, our results hint at intervention opportunities for negative communicative behavior such as complaining.

We focus on the detrimental effects of complaining cycles as an indicator of negative group mood. A summary of theories and scientific evidence of group mood sets the course for a discussion of our research results concerning negative group mood, which we conceptualize as dysfunctional interaction. We finish with implications of our findings and intervention opportunities, in the context of both group interaction and human resource development.

HOW THE GROUP IS DIFFICULT: INEFFICIENT GROUP DISCUSSIONS

What was described in the opening story of this chapter is familiar ground for many teams. You may recognize this from your own field of work: in any group meeting, a new solution (implying change) rarely leads to spontaneous support by the others. In contrast, when somebody starts complaining about his heavy workload, the others are much more likely to support this or follow with more complaining.

In the last few decades, organizations have increasingly implemented teams or work groups as a structuring principle with the intention of taking advantage of the performance potential inherent in teams (for example, Jordan, Lawrence, & Troth, 2006; Nielsen, Sundstrom, & Halfhill, 2005). Teams can enable an efficient exchange and an optimal combination of a wide spectrum of individual resources (Brodbeck, Anderson, & West, 2000). Although the general notion is that teams improve organizational performance (for example, Wheelan, 1999), not all teams achieve the performance expected of them (for example, Sims, Salas, & Burke, 2005). Why do some teams develop and implement innovative ideas, while others fail to utilize the autonomy that is given to them by the organization?

There is a consensus among several models of team performance (for example, Tannenbaum, Beard, & Salas, 1992; Gersick, 1991) that interaction between team members is crucial for high team performance. In practice, regular team meetings and group discussions have been implemented as a standard procedure in many contemporary organizations—for instance, as part of the Continuous Improvement Process (CIP; for example, Liker, 2006). Meetings and group discussions carry the potential for exchanging and building new knowledge in the team, enabling members to discuss current problems and develop solutions and innovative ideas. Therefore, intrateam communication plays an important role. One of the reasons some teams do better than others in this respect concerns the mood that is built within a team through interaction.

Although there is some research on interaction in teams, the effect of team members' moods on interaction and subsequent performance has been rather neglected (cf. Jordan et al., 2006). Only recently have researchers begun to look into group mood as an influential factor in team performance. For example, Jordan et al. investigated student groups and found that negative mood compromised team processes and team performance. But do these findings hold true for real teams in the workplace?

After a brief introduction to group mood, we will present research findings from real teams in the workplace, linking employee interaction in group discussions to team and organizational performance outcomes.

Group Mood

Moods have been described as low-intensity, diffuse feeling states that usually do not have a precise antecedent (for example, Forgas, 1992). They are longer in duration, less focused, and less intense than emotions (Watson & Tellegen, 1985). Group mood may be understood as synchronized moods of individuals (for example, Hackman, 1992). Moods can be classified in various ways. The model we refer to was developed by Larsen and Diener (1992).

In this model, moods are arranged circularly, illustrated in Figure 3.1, their position depending on their similarity or polarity. This means that two aspects that are close to one another, such as "warmhearted" and "calm," are highly correlated. The various group moods are classified on two orthogonal or independent dimensions: (1) behavior willingness or activation (high to low activation) and (2) hedonistic value (pleasant to unpleasant).

Because mood can be observed in terms of behavior (for example, Barsade, 2002; Bartel & Saavedra, 2000), we look at a specific communicative behavior:

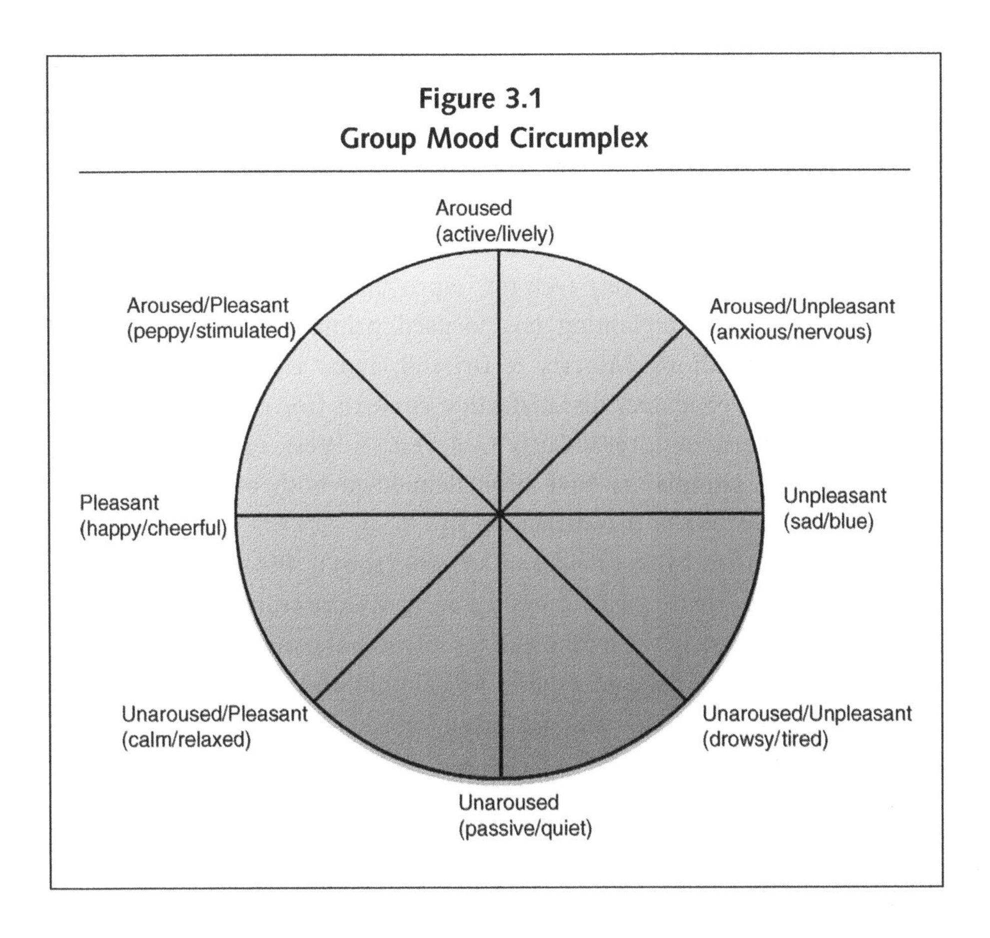

Figure 3.1
Group Mood Circumplex

complaining. Within the model, complaining behavior can be described as an expression of an unpleasant mood (cf. Kauffeld, 2007; Kauffeld & Meyers, 2009).

Complaining Behavior in Group Discussions

Complaining is a rather common activity. It is socially accepted and even expected that people complain about the weather and about politicians, government, and taxes. Complaining serves several functions (cf. Kauffeld & Meyers, 2009):

- Provides a common ground in conversation and may serve as a subject for small talk
- Offers a vent for frustration and experienced inconvenience
- Presumably, allows us to make the best of a less than ideal situation and to share this with others

It should be noted at this point that complaining in the working context is a natural reaction to dissatisfying circumstances and working conditions. Examples include monotonous work, low team cohesion, a nonsupportive supervisor, or a lack of opportunities to participate in organizational change. However, some conditions can be changed if team members are willing to use their (partial) autonomy and actively seek for improvement.

Past research on complaining has focused primarily on interpersonal communication situations (Alberts & Driscoll, 1992; Hall, 1991; Newell & Stutman, 1988) and consumer dissatisfaction contexts (for example, Brashers, 1991; Fornell & Wernerfelt, 1988; Garrett, Meyers, & West, 1996, 1997; Sellers, 1988). In general, complaints have been defined in both of these research domains as expressions of dissatisfaction.

As has been shown by Kauffeld and Meyers (2009), dissatisfaction, along with complaining behavior, also occurs regularly in work teams. Moreover, not only do team members in the workplace complain, but complaining also leads to more complaining. This can result in self-maintaining complaining cycles, which we describe as an expression of group mood. An essential underlying process is emotional contagion.

Emotional Contagion

Emotional contagion has been defined as "The tendency to automatically mimic and synchronize facial expressions, vocalizations, postures, and movements with those of another person and, consequently, to converge emotionally" (Hatfield, Cacioppo, & Rapson, 1994, p. 5). This definition emphasizes the unconscious process of emotional contagion. In conversations, people automatically mimic the facial expressions, voices, postures, and behaviors of others (Bavelas, Black, Lemery, & Mullett, 1987; Bernieri, Reznick, & Rosenthal, 1988), and people's conscious experience may be shaped by such facial feedback (for example, Laird, 1984).

There is, however, a second way in which people may "catch" another's emotions. Contagion may also occur via a conscious cognitive process of "tuning in" to the emotions of others. This will be the case when individuals try to imagine how they would feel in the position of another and, as a consequence, experience the same feelings. Thus the realization that another person is happy or sad may trigger memories of the times we have felt that way, and these reveries may spark similar emotions (Hsee, Hatfield, & Chemtomb, 1992).

Figure 3.2
Emotional Contagion Through Interaction

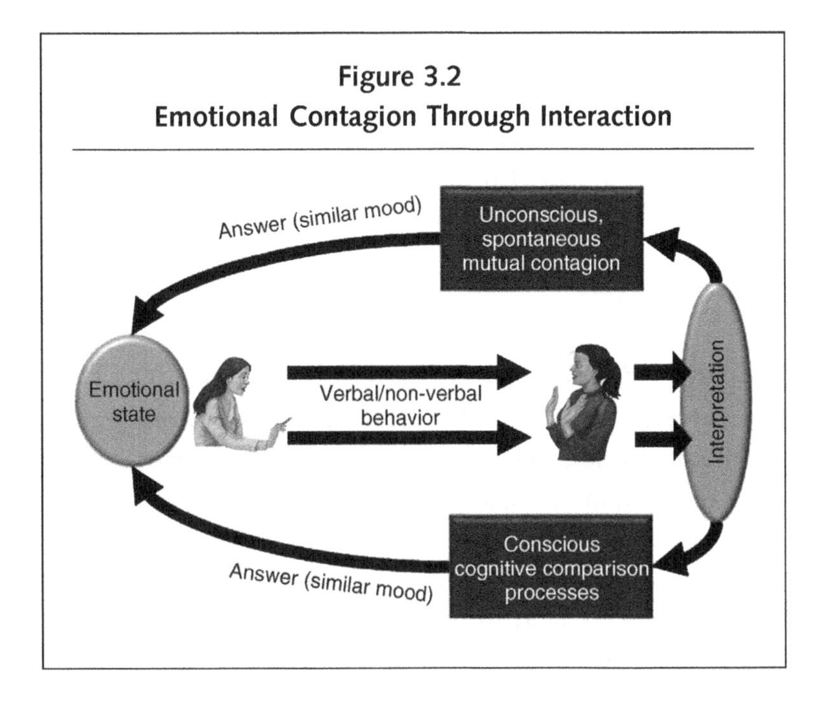

Figure 3.2 shows the two ways in which emotional contagion may occur. The route illustrated on top is the unconscious, spontaneous mutual contagion that automatically occurs in interaction. The route on the bottom is conscious and driven by cognitive comparison processes, whereby we actively adjust to the mood exhibited by our interaction partner(s).

Regardless of why such contagion might occur, researchers from a wide range of disciplines have described phenomena that suggest that emotional contagion does exist (for overviews, see Hatfield et al., 1994; McIntosh, Druckman, & Zajonc, 1994).

How does emotional contagion apply to complaining in group discussions? Figure 3.2 shows an interaction between two group members. Recall the example from the beginning of this chapter: Group member A (on the left in Figure 3.2) starts with a complaining statement, group member B follows with a similar statement, and so forth.

The unconscious contagion in this example would concern the fact that group member B does not make a conscious choice as to changing her mood. The conscious cognitive process in this example concerns the reasoning that sets in upon hearing the statement: Why does group member A feel that way?

What happened in the past that led to this emotion? Why is it reasonable to feel the same way?

This example demonstrates that although complaining may fulfill a normal human need, it can also cause group members to bring each other down. In the following section, we will report some empirical evidence for this phenomenon.

WHY THE GROUP IS DIFFICULT: COMPLAINING CYCLES

Kauffeld and Meyers (2009) showed that complaining in work groups occurs in communicative cycles; that is, complaining leads to more complaining (as opposed to solution-oriented verbal behavior) and eventually causes a negative group mood. As mentioned earlier, complaining would be characterized as an active-unpleasant affective state within the circumplex model. Complaining statements tend to focus on the perceived negative and unchangeable actual state as well as the perceived role of victim. Complaining is often expressed by using "killer" phrases such as "Nothing could be done," or "Nothing works." Such statements are not facilitative to the group's decision-making process and in fact will inhibit progress toward the solution or group goal.

To examine whether complaining really leads to more complaining in groups, we examined real groups in the workplace. These are autonomous groups who have usually worked together for years. Group discussions are a regular part of their work routine. When we videotaped their discussions, there was no supervisor present. Anonymity was guaranteed to ensure realistic data. Occurrences such as backbiting the absent supervisor, answering cell phone calls, and so on indicate that this seems to be the case (cf. Kauffeld, 2006b). To evaluate these discussions, we used a process-analytical instrument named Advanced Interaction Analysis (act4teams®; Kauffeld, Lorenzo, Montasem, & Lehmann-Willenbrock, 2009). We use this instrument to measure groups' work-related interaction when completing a real, relevant optimization task (for example, how to improve material sourcing in production teams). The instrument comprises four areas of competence that can be observed through interaction: problem-focused statements, procedural statements, socioemotional statements, and action-oriented statements, measured by a total of forty-four categories of observable behavior. In Table 3.1, the four areas of interaction are shown in

Table 3.1
Interaction-Based Competencies (in Column Headings) and Their Aspects (in Gray Highlight) and Categories (in Italics)

Problem-Focused Statements	Procedural Statements	Socioemotional Statements	Action-Oriented Statements
differentiating a problem	positive structuring statements	positive socioemotional statements	positive statements promoting action
problem	*goal orientation*	*encouraging participation*	*interest in change*
identifying a (partial) problem	pointing out the topic or leading back to it	e.g., addressing the quiet participants	signaling interest
describing a problem	*clarifying*	*providing support*	*personal responsibility*
illustrating problems	ensuring contributions are to the point, clarifying	agreeing to suggestions, ideas, etc.	taking on responsibility
cross-linking a problem	*procedural suggestions*	*active listening*	*action planning*
connections with a problem	suggestions for further procedure	signaling interest ("mmh," "yes")	agreeing on tasks to be carried out
e.g., naming causes and effects	*procedural questions*	*disagreeing*	negative statements inhibiting action
differentiating a solution	questions about further procedure	contradiction based on facts	*no interest in change*
defining the objective	*prioritizing*	*giving feedback*	e.g., denial of optimization opportunities
vision, description of requirements	stressing main topics	e.g., signaling whether something is new or already known →	*complaining*
solution	*time management*	*lightening the atmosphere*	emphasis on the negative status quo, pessimism, killer phrases

(Continued)

Table 3.1

(Continued)

identifying (partial) solutions	**reference to time**	**e.g., jokes**	*empty talk*
describing a solution	*task distribution*	*separating opinions from facts*	**empty talk**
illustrating a solution	delegating tasks during the discussion	marking one's own opinion as an opinion, not as a fact	*seeking someone to blame*
cross-linking a solution	*visualizing*	*expressing feelings*	personalizing problems
problem with a solution	**using flip chart and similar tools**	**mentioning feelings like anger or joy**	*denying responsibility*
objection to a solution	*weighing costs/ benefits*	*offering praise*	pointing out hierarchies and competencies
connections with a solution	**economical thinking**	**e.g., positive remarks about other people**	*terminating the discussion*
e.g., naming advantages of a solution	*summarizing*	negative socioemotional statements	ending or trying to end the discussion early
statements about the organization	**summarizing results**	*criticizing/running someone down*	
organizational knowledge	negative structuring statements	**making disparaging comments about others**	
knowledge about organization and process	*losing the train of thought in details and examples*	*interrupting*	
statements about knowledge management	examples irrelevant to the goal, monologues	cutting someone off while speaking	
knowing who		*side conversations*	
reference to specialists		simultaneous talk on the side	

question	*self-promotion*
question about opinions, content, experience	pointing out work experience, duration of employment at this company, etc.

Source: As used in the Advanced Interaction Analysis Instrument

the four columns. Each of these areas comprises two or more aspects, highlighted in gray, which in turn contain the forty-four categories (in italics) that describe the individual statements.

Problem-focused statements, shown in the left-hand column in Table 3.1, concern problems and solutions discussed in the team. Examples are categories such as *problem* or *describing a solution.* These types of remarks can be distinguished as problem-focused statements because they relate to content rather than to the structuring of the discussion (procedural), the relationship between group members (socioemotional), or participation (action-oriented statements).

Procedural statements, depicted in the second column in the table, refer to remarks that are aimed at structuring a discussion, such as *goal orientation* or *procedural questions.* However, there are also negative structuring statements (*losing the train of thought*).

Socioemotional statements, in the third column, are coded with categories such as *active listening* or *feedback.* As in the procedural area, there are also negative statements in the socioemotional area, represented by the categories in the aspect "negative socioemotional statements" (for example, *criticizing/running someone down*).

Action-oriented statements, listed in the right-hand column, concern a group's willingness to actively create conditions for improving its work. Such participation-oriented behavior can be described as proactive behavior. Positive statements that promote action can be coded with the categories *interest in change, personal responsibility,* and *action planning.* The following categories describe negative statements inhibiting action: *no interest in change, complaining, empty talk* (which only wastes time and does not lead to progress in the discussion), *seeking someone to blame* (instead of tackling the underlying causes of a problem), *denying responsibility* (for example, by emphasizing the others' responsibility and authority), and *terminating the discussion* (not using the time available).

To evaluate a videotaped group discussion, thoroughly trained raters analyze the group interaction with Advanced Interaction Analysis. In the coding procedure, the videotaped discussion is cut into small segments, where each segment is equal to one remark or verbal statement.

Every verbal statement or sense unit uttered by any individual group member is then ascribed an observation category. A sense unit is defined as a communication that, in context, may be understood by another group member as equivalent to one single simple sentence of the discussion (Bales, 1950). To facilitate the coding, we use a customized version of the Interact software by Mangold (2005) as well as a specially designed keyboard. Figure 3.3 depicts a screenshot of the software with the individual sense units. The duration of each sense unit is depicted on the left, followed by the individual

Figure 3.3
Coding Group Discussions with act4teams®:
Interact Software and Keyboard

Individual codes are added to calculate a team score.
00:00:28:11

participant (for example, person A) and finally the observation category (for example, P for *problem*). The keyboard in the bottom right corner is programmed to contain the forty-four coding categories, the letters A through G for the participants, and some keys for cutting and editing the video in order to further facilitate the coding procedure.

Through extensive research, Advanced Interaction Analysis has been psychometrically validated (Kauffeld, 2006b; Kauffeld et al., 2009) and shows excellent inter-rater reliability.

Complaining is an example of negative statements inhibiting action (see Table 3.1). As this is only one category out of the forty-four, one might suspect that complaining does not have much of an impact on the discussion outcome. Although this is intuitively plausible, our findings consistently show a very different picture.

In a large study of fifty-nine groups from nineteen companies in Germany, Kauffeld (2006b) demonstrated that complaining has a statistically significant, strong negative impact not only on the discussion outcome (group member satisfaction and applicability of the solutions that were developed in the discussion) but also on organizational outcomes, such as corporate success and corporate innovation. Table 3.2 shows the correlations between complaining and these outcomes (cf. Kauffeld, 2006b).

As mentioned earlier, complaining can be quite legitimate when working conditions are bad. Arguably, the negative relationships we found could also

Table 3.2
Pearson's Correlations Between Complaining Behavior and Success Measures

	Group member ratings		Observer ratings	Management ratings	
	Satisfaction with the discussion	Applicability of solutions	Implication of solutions in the workplace	Corporate success	Corporate innovation
Complaining	−.32**	−.37**	−.69**	−.41*	−.46*

Note: *significant at a level of $p < .05$; **significant at a level of $p < .01$

have been due to bad working conditions. For example, if teams cannot manage to implement their solutions in the workplace, or if corporate innovation is low, this might actually cause complaining. However, all the criteria were assessed *after* the group discussions. Whereas the group member ratings were performed immediately after each discussion, the observer ratings were made with a delay of three months (so that the teams had sufficient time to implement their solutions), and the management ratings were made 2.5 years after the discussions. Thus, at least in the context of this study, complaining can be viewed as an antecedent.

Although complaining is a very human, everyday habit, the results presented in Table 3.2 show that it can be rather harmful not only for the group but even for the company as a whole. Why is it that complaining has such a strong impact? Suppose that complaining is not something that is uttered by individual team members every once in a while, but rather a collective phenomenon in terms of the expression of a negative group mood. As we explained, emotional contagion describes the process by which complaining may lead to more complaining. This makes sense intuitively, but we also found empirical support for this process.

Complaining cycles can be defined as sequences of complaining statements (complaining – complaining – complaining) or sequences of complaining, support, and subsequent further complaining (complaining – support – complaining). Here are some examples of these communication patterns:

Example 1

Group member A: We've tried to do that like five times now and nothing ever changed. (*Complaining*)

Group member B: Whatever you try in this company, nothing ever happens. (*Complaining*)

Group member C: It's like, we've had all these ideas and they've never gone anywhere. (*Complaining*)

Example 2

Group member B: No one cares about our problems. (*Complaining*)

Group member A: Yeah, exactly. (*Support*)

Group member C: It's like you don't count at all. (*Complaining*)

The second example points out the potentially deleterious effect of support. In our opinion, supporting a complaining statement should be seen as complaining itself because it can lead to a complaining cycle and thereby build a negative group mood.

Kauffeld and Meyers (2009) examined thirty-three group discussions with video recordings and Advanced Interaction Analysis coding. To determine whether complaining cycles actually exist, they used lag sequential analysis. This statistical method determines the likelihood of specific statements following one another. They found that indeed, complaining cycles as communication patterns occur significantly more frequently than chance would indicate. Moreover, sequence analysis showed that complaining statements inhibited subsequent solution-oriented statements, which are crucial for discussion and team success. We have replicated these findings with other samples. Complaining cycles seem to be pervasive in all kinds of groups and business branches. Considering the results of Kauffeld (2006b) as shown in Table 3.2, it becomes evident that complaining cycles are dysfunctional not only in terms of group mood and team member satisfaction but also in terms of team-level and organizational outcomes. So what can be done to counteract this dysfunctional communication pattern?

WHAT YOU CAN DO: COUNTERACTING COMPLAINING CYCLES

Complaining is not an inherent quality or personality trait, but a behavioral expression of a passive-unpleasant. Complaining cycles may be tackled in several ways. First of all, the employing organization can take measures to design work in a way that puts more emphasis on employees' ideas and innovation potential (cf. Kauffeld, 2006b). Second, methodological or structuring statements can be used to consciously break up complaining patterns and get back to the topic. Our research has demonstrated that methodological statements inhibit complaining behavior. Sensitizing a team to these matters may include facilitator training for one or all group members. Third, an external consultant or group facilitator can be useful for reflecting on the team situation and developing a more constructive group mood. Teams can be educated about the negative effects of complaining behavior on not only the discussion but also team and organizational outcomes. We will elaborate on these three possibilities a little further.

Organizational Design Against Complaining

When employees complain, this does not necessarily mean that they have a bad attitude; as we mentioned, complaining may actually be due to an unfavorable work environment. Within the conceptualization of Advanced Interaction Analysis, complaining statements are characterized by an emphasis on the negative status quo, pessimism, and killer phrases. Representative of a negative and unpleasant mood, complaining is an expression of a pessimistic perspective. Although team members differ in their amount of complaining in a discussion, they often share experiences where they indeed have not been able to make a change or optimize their work according to their ideas. For example, a team can have many insights and improvement suggestions concerning their work processes, but if they have a supervisor who does not support these ideas, they tend not to go very far. Our facilitation experience has shown over and over again that whereas the management may be well aware of the benefits of teamwork, the immediate supervisors of work teams often are not, and will not support their teams appropriately.

One important job design factor that can help increase positive self-competence (that is, interest in change, personal responsibility, and action planning in a discussion) and help diminish the negative aspect of self-competence (for example, complaining) is job autonomy. There is a substantial amount of research demonstrating the beneficial effects of giving more autonomy to work teams (for an overview, see Sundstrom, McIntyre, Halfhill, & Richards, 2000). Kauffeld (2006a) found that work characteristics such as participation, formal team communication, continuous improvement processes, training, and team-oriented tasks were beneficial in self-directed work teams. It can be deduced that giving employees the opportunity to actively participate in and autonomously improve their work processes is a promising approach for triggering the potential inherent in teams.

Methodological Statements Against Complaining

Before turning to team consulting or coaching, there is a simple way for team members to break up complaining cycles.

In sequence analysis, we have not only examined complaining cycles but also taken a closer look at other statements preceding or following complaining statements. Research results demonstrate that one way to break up complaining cycles is to make a positive structuring statement (see Table 3.1). The following positive structuring statements have been shown to consistently inhibit complaining, and thus carry the potential of breaking up complaining cycles (Kauffeld, 2006b, 2007; Kauffeld & Meyers, 2009): *Goal orientation* (for example, "Let's get back to our topic, which is . . . ")

- *Clarification/concretization* (finishing the sentence for someone who is missing a word)
- *Procedural suggestion* ("Let's hear what everyone thinks about this one.")
- *Procedural question* ("Should we move on to the next point on our agenda?")
- *Task distribution* ("Please write that down.")
- *Visualization* (using a flip chart)

Reflection Workshops Against Complaining: Toward More Positive Participation

When the organizational environment is designed in a way that gives autonomy and responsibility to the teams, but they do not use this freedom in terms of improving their work where possible, a team trainer or consultant may help. In a recent longitudinal study, we conducted a workshop designed to foster the positive aspect of self-competence with each of the fifty-four teams. The self-competence categories *interest in change* and *action planning* (see right-hand column in Table 3.1) have been demonstrated to have a strong positive impact on team-level and organizational outcomes (cf. Kauffeld, 2006b). The workshops started out with an exercise that shows the benefits of teamwork over individual work units. Next was an assessment of the team's current situation: (1) What is going well in our work? (2) What isn't working/Where do we have problems? (3) Where and how do we want to improve?

This assessment was followed by in-depth discussions that were aimed at pointing out ways in which the teams themselves can make a difference in their work (rather than waiting for supervisors or other departments to make a change, for example). We also included some simple team-building exercises to enhance the team climate.

Over time, we found a significant positive impact of these workshops on the self-competence of the teams involved (Neininger & Kauffeld, 2009). That is, in group discussions some months after the workshops, teams who participated in the workshops were voicing more interest in change, taking more personal responsibility for the solutions they discussed, and planning more actions than those teams who did not participate in a workshop. Likewise, teams who participated in a workshop were making significantly fewer negative remarks concerning participation after the workshop. We used an experimental group versus waiting group design. Teams who functioned as a waiting group during the first phase of the study received a workshop in the second phase (see Neininger & Kauffeld, 2009).

These preliminary findings demonstrate that it is indeed possible to employ team consultation to address dysfunctional communication in teams. Future research will show whether the effects we found can hold in a follow-up design.

Team Coaching with act4teams® as a Continuous Process

How can team members be sensitized to complaining cycles and the chance to break these with structuring statements? Although team members are probably not too excited about looking into methods such as sequence analysis, we have had good experiences with examples taken from group discussions such as the two we described earlier. Team members usually benefit from such examples if they are asked to think about their own discussion, how they interact with each other, and what results they are able to generate. The video analysis and evaluation present the team with a good starting point for reflecting on their own interaction processes. Seeing the assessment of the team's competencies (for example, in charts that depict the frequency of behaviors in each of the four interaction-based competency areas) in comparison to a reference sample may have a stronger effect than listening to implications provided by an external trainer. Moreover, podcasts of the group discussion video can help underline specific strengths (such as solutions) or weaknesses (such as complaining) observable in the group discussion. Video analysis is a useful feedback instrument for teams who want to improve and tap the potential inherent in their team.

Also, it can be useful to present the findings by Kauffeld (2006b) as depicted in Table 3.2. These results underline the fact that it *does* matter a great deal what goes on in a group discussion and what the team members make of their ideas and solutions afterwards. The sensitization to the importance of these processes could be implemented as part of the standard group facilitator training in companies, or it could be included in team-building workshops. In any case, it should be considered that teams as a whole need to be sensitized to these processes. If, for example, only the team leader receives this knowledge, there will probably be very little acceptance in the team of insights about complaining cycles as dysfunctional interaction. Moreover, when educating a team about these negative communication patterns, it should be made very clear that these occur in all kinds of groups and at all levels of an organization, rather than leaving them with a feeling of being picked out for bad communication. Finally, successful team coaching requires a continuous process. In the context of interaction, this should involve an initial interaction assessment as a basis for evaluating where a team stands, subsequent reflection and optimization periods during which the team is actively involved in making changes, and process and result evaluations to point out where these changes have been successful and where there may still be some work to do.

As depicted in Figure 3.4, both measurement and evaluation are embedded in a continuous team coaching process comprising six modules. This continuous coaching process has been implemented in act4team-coaching® (cf. Kauffeld et al., 2009). Trainers who work with this system start out with an Activation module that focuses on the current state of affairs in the team and some initial team development. The second module, called Action, involves supervisor coaching (consistent with the notion that the supervisor may play a crucial role in any team's potential for change and improvement), as well as the first evaluation (the video coding and analysis is provided by a research team). The results are a basis for reflection and subsequent team development measures in Module 3, Reflection, which is comparable to the "reflection workshops against complaining" described earlier. In some interventions, this module is followed by an individual evaluation, in which the coach meets with the individual members to discuss their respective results and implications. In the fourth module, Progress, the team (as well as the supervisor) reflect on recent changes and developments, and proceed to plan further measures for improvement. Advanced Action, the fifth module, includes a second measurement of the four competencies. This second discussion is evaluated again as a basis for objectively measuring the progress that the team has made in the various competence areas over time. This evaluation takes place in the sixth module (Evaluation), in which the team decides, together with their supervisor, whether they will continue or conclude the team coaching.

Figure 3.4
The Team Coaching Process as Implemented in act4team-coaching®

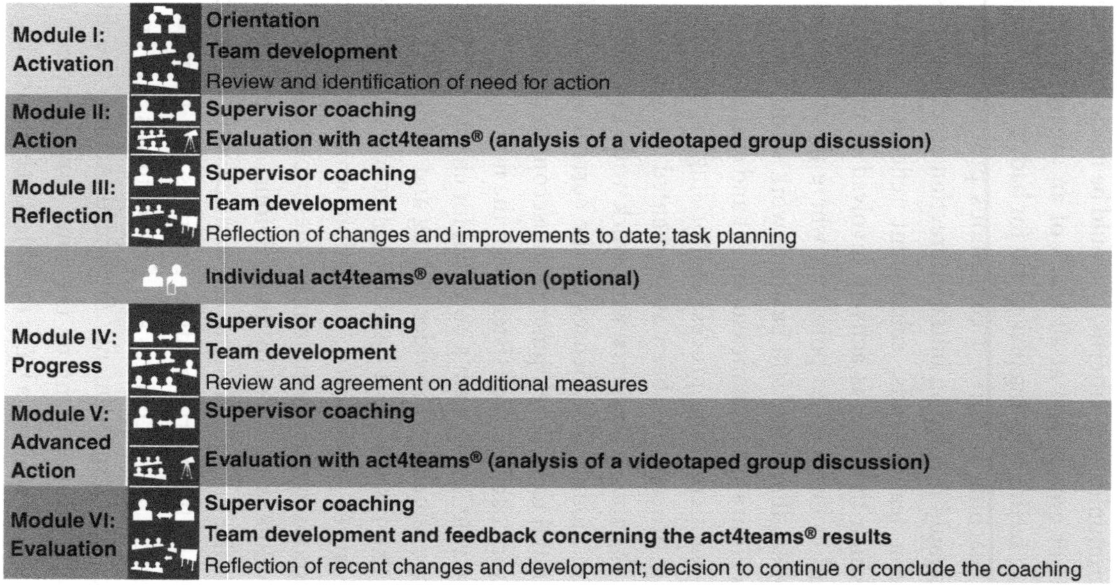

Module I: Activation	**Orientation** **Team development** Review and identification of need for action
Module II: Action	**Supervisor coaching** **Evaluation with act4teams® (analysis of a videotaped group discussion)**
Module III: Reflection	**Supervisor coaching** **Team development** Reflection of changes and improvements to date; task planning
	Individual act4teams® evaluation (optional)
Module IV: Progress	**Supervisor coaching** **Team development** Review and agreement on additional measures
Module V: Advanced Action	**Supervisor coaching** **Evaluation with act4teams® (analysis of a videotaped group discussion)**
Module VI: Evaluation	**Supervisor coaching** **Team development and feedback concerning the act4teams® results** Reflection of recent changes and development; decision to continue or conclude the coaching

Source: © 4 A-SIDE (www.4a-side.com)

All of these measures described measures are aimed at helping a team get out of the complaining loop and turn to solution-oriented interaction instead. This does not mean that complaining should be prohibited per se. Complaining may be useful at the beginning of team interventions or change processes—for example, as a way to give everyone a chance to "vent." However, team members should then commit themselves to the convention that complaining is out of place in optimization discussions. When team members succeed in making this shift to solution orientation, they can rise to their full potential: tackling their problems, optimizing their work processes, and being more productive and innovative than any individual alone.

chapter FOUR

Facilitating Multicultural Groups

Donna Rae Scheffert and
Mary Laeger-Hagemeister

Anytown Health Care Systems and its partners provide the gamut of health care services to a Minnesota city of twenty-four thousand and the surrounding area. A majority of the population served by the hospital and clinic are descendents of settlers from northern Europe. Over the past decades, new immigrant communities have settled and stayed in Anytown. Mexican men came first, as longtime migrant workers for the food processing industry. Then demands for a more permanent workforce grew, and Mexican families settled in. They were followed by Somali families, whose leaders proactively recruited to fill workforce shortages for local industry.

Anytown's health care practitioners are used to getting good results. Hard working, professional, and thorough, they deliver tertiary care and effectively engage the community in prevention. However, in 2005 it was recognized that health outcomes for Somali and Mexican community members were not as

Special thanks to Joyce Hoelting, assistant director of the University of Minnesota Center for Community Vitality, for assistance with composition and editing of this chapter.

good as those achieved in the rest of the area. Training provided to staff about multicultural health care was helpful, but was not concrete enough to be practical. The health care community needed to know: What do Somali and Mexican families do when they get sick? What do they do with mental health difficulties? Who makes the decisions about health care in families? Why is there sometimes a difference between what health care providers prescribe and what action is taken?

Ann, an R.N. and hospital nurse manager, decided to be proactive. She had heard about a forum in a nearby community between community leaders and Mexican immigrants. "We hadn't talked to anyone here about how we can best serve our clientele," Ann said. "I wanted to have this conversation." She contacted Mary from the University of Minnesota Extension, who facilitated the nearby Mexican forums, and asked her to create a similar forum about health care for the Mexican and Somali cultures in Anytown. Setting the goal for this community-wide effort and bringing in a facilitator were important first steps toward building multicultural teams.

> We not only need these voices to understand their world view, but we also must ask them what solutions would work for them. . . . Listening to those voices forces us . . . to confront the inadequate ways in which we organizationally, intellectually, and professionally deal with social class differences and face up to the shortcomings of our systems in serving all people honorably and equitably (Beegle, 2006, p. 97).

WHY THE GROUP IS DIFFICULT

Forums for conversations among Somali, Mexican, and United States health care communities would be difficult to facilitate because there were no existing relationships among the groups, and many behaviors and norms differ within the three cultures. The most obvious were language and health-care practices. Less obvious were differences in power distance, individualism, and masculinity (Hofstede, 2003). These differences impact convening a leadership team, developing relationships, engaging participation, fostering dialogue, minimizing direct conflict, leveraging social capital, navigating power and influence, and creating fruitful communication channels.

Moreover, *culture* is a broad term that includes many variables:

1. Demographic: age, gender, place of residence
2. Status related: social, educational, economic
3. Affiliative: formal and informal connections
4. Ethnographic: nationality, ethnicity, language, religion

In this case, the construct of *multicultural* refers to the three national cultures (United States, Somalia, and Mexico) but also to differences within those cultures. No cultural group is homogenous (Pedersen, 2000). It is difficult for a facilitator to focus on hundreds of differences within a group while making progress toward the goals. So how does a facilitator decide what to focus on?

WHAT YOU CAN DO

The University of Minnesota Extension was contracted by the Anytown health care system to do the facilitation. The goal of this facilitation was to create stronger relationships between the Mexican and Somali communities and the health care system. An immediate goal, that of giving and receiving information, needed to be achieved. Beyond that, the process needed to allow three different communities (Mexican, Somali, and health care professionals) to be seen, understood, and responded to, so that an ongoing pattern of fuller participation and better health could be achieved.

One way to see differences is to focus on observable markers. Cultural markers delineate basic areas of difference between cultures (Taylor, 2007). Cultural markers are *the differences that make a difference* when individuals and groups enter relationships to accomplish a task. Cultural differences make multicultural facilitation complex, so cultural markers can guide the facilitator in anticipating differences and making wise facilitation choices. Table 4.1 identifies nine cultural markers that Mary (as the facilitator) and Ann (as the client) could consider.

Facilitation of groups with national or ethnic differences requires extra self-examination by the facilitator. "Be aware that all facilitation strategies contain a cultural imprint, whether implicit or explicit. Facilitation is not value free" (Hogan, 2005, p. 279). Distefano and Maznevski (2000, cited in Hogan, p. 262)

Table 4.1
Cultural Markers in Multicultural Settings

Context: Environmental or External Influences	Structure: Formal and Informal Design	Process: Interactions Before, During, and After Meetings
The **intercultural sensitivity** of the facilitator and its monitored effect on the task	Different views of **leadership present** among and within the cultures	Different types of **relationships present** among and within the cultures
Different beliefs about **participation** in society **present** among and within the cultures	Different techniques of **dialogue present** among and within the cultures	Different expressions of **conflict present** among and within the cultures
Differing levels of **social capital present** among and within the cultures	Differing levels of **power present** among and within the cultures	Different styles of **communication present** among and within the cultures

researched multicultural teams and found that they perform either better or worse than homogeneous teams. The key to being successful was the quality of the interaction processes rather than the team membership. Multiculturally sensitive facilitation is facilitation that intentionally considers differences in the knowledge and meaning systems of group members and the implications of those differences for facilitation. Relational aspects of facilitation are essential to the interaction processes.

The remainder of this chapter describes relational aspects of facilitation. Strategies and solutions are documented for the nine cultural markers. The dynamics of intercultural facilitation are framed by challenges from the Anytown case in chronological order. Six challenges were important to designing, implementing, and sustaining the multicultural discussion:

1. Acknowledge and adapt to cultural differences
2. Engage leaders and build trusting relationships
3. Gain participation and manage power dynamics
4. Build systems for productive dialogue

5. Accommodate communication needs and styles
6. Make optimum use of social capital

ACKNOWLEDGE AND ADAPT TO CULTURAL DIFFERENCES

We don't see things as they are. We see them as we are.

—Anaïs Nin

The first challenge any experienced facilitator may encounter when taking on multicultural facilitation may be with herself. Each facilitator brings to the job a set of reactions to difference that are the result of experience (or lack thereof) in intercultural settings. The facilitator's world view may range from ethnocentric (my own culture is central to reality) to ethnorelative (culture is experienced in the context of other cultures). The Developmental Model of Intercultural Sensitivity (Bennett, Hammer & Wiseman, 2003) can guide self-examination. Its six stages of intercultural competence are as follows:

- *Denial* of cultural difference, or disinterest in cultures
- *Defense* against cultural difference, where one's own culture is experienced as the only good one
- *Minimization* of cultural difference, where one's own cultural views are experienced as universal
- *Acceptance* of cultural difference as an interesting phenomenon
- *Adaptation* to other cultures and a shift to seeing the world through others' eyes rather than one's own
- *Integration* with other cultures in ways that do not undermine one's own, but allow one to move in and out of others'

A facilitator who has greater intercultural sensitivity (operating at the acceptance, adaptation, or integration levels of competence) will be most effective in multicultural facilitation settings because these levels are characterized by a greater ability to adapt group interaction to other cultures. In Anytown, Mary's previous experience in multicultural community settings and graduate coursework in cultural communication gave her sufficient understanding of cultural differences to adapt facilitation processes to the situation.

To see the world through the eyes of people raised in Mexico and Somalia, Mary explored the knowledge base about the dimensions of culture. Geert Hofstede's research from over three decades can inform a facilitator about cultural relativity of organizational practices and theories (1983). His theory was that the cultural context in a country of origin influences a culture's values and behaviors. He identified five dimensions that differ across societies (2003).

1. The **Power Distance Index** focuses on the degree of inequality or equality that people consider to be normal among people in a country.

A *high power distance* score indicates that inequalities of power and wealth are perceived as normal within the society. These societies are more likely to have a caste system that reinforces status differences. People in high power distance societies are comfortable with status differences. Relationships are formal, titles are used, and people wait for direction from authority figures. There are standard and fixed approaches to how the world operates.

A *low power distance* score indicates that equality is more socially desirable, and there is less of a focus on the differences among citizens' power and wealth. People in low power distance societies easily interact across positional lines. In these societies, opportunity is stressed. Relationships are casual, with few titles used. People are expected to be self-starting and to take initiative at work and in the community. In a low power distance society, being spontaneous and trying various approaches are expected.

2. The **Individualism Versus Collectivism Index** focuses on the degree to which the society reinforces individual interest and values versus collective values and goals of the group (extended family, ethnic group, or company).

A *high individualism* score indicates that self-expression and individual rights are highly valued. Individuals are expected to speak about their own views and ideas. The public decision-making model is based on individuals voting depending on what they believe is best for them.

A *low individualism* score typifies societies with a collectivist nature where conformity to the group is the mode of operation. Elders or others often speak on behalf of the group. Harmony within group relationships is emphasized over individual wants and opinions. Although consensus building takes more time in making a decision, it is highly valued in a collectivist-oriented society.

3. The **Masculinity Versus Femininity Index** focuses on the degree to which a society is conducive to assertiveness and achievement versus conducive to

modesty and caring for people. Males differ more on this index, whereas females score higher toward femininity.

A *high masculinity* score describes a culture that emphasizes assertiveness and a competitive drive for money and material objects. It is socially desirable, especially for males, to be viewed as decisive and to seek career advancement. Assertive, career-oriented women may also be more accepted in these cultures.

A *low masculinity* score (femininity) indicates that a culture values developing and nurturing personal relationships, with obligations to family and friends coming before a career. Because both males and females tend toward low scores in low masculinity cultures, there is less differentiation between genders. Both genders, especially women, tend to be negatively judged if they are perceived as too assertive.

4. The **Uncertainty Avoidance Index** focuses on tolerance for ambiguity and uncertainty within the society. It influences whether people are uncomfortable or comfortable in situations that are different from usual structures.

A *high uncertainty avoidance* score is found in societies where situations are well structured and predictable. People are comfortable when the future is relatively certain. Therefore, they prefer to operate with strict laws and rules. Surprising and unknown situations produce stress and may be avoided.

Low uncertainty avoidance scores are prevalent in societies that value situations involving novelty and surprises. Most people are comfortable with and accept the unknown and tolerate risk and unpredictability. They tend to prefer to have as few rules as possible.

5. The **Long-Term Versus Short-Term Orientation Index** refers to societal values about what is important to focus on while living life—the past, present, or future.

A *high long-term orientation* score is found in countries that place great value on future generations. Therefore, they are thrifty and persistent in achieving goals. People with a long-term orientation are less likely to expect immediate results on investments of any type.

A *low long-term orientation* score (short-term orientation) describes societies that respect tradition and fulfilling social obligations. They place great value on immediate needs and see the future as a blank slate. Societal members with short-term orientation may see immediate gratification as a priority along with living for the present.

Table 4.2
Cultural Dimensions for Three Societies

	Power Distance	Individualism	Masculinity	Uncertainty Avoidance	Long-Term Orientation
Eastern African	64	27	41	52	25
Mexican	81	30	69	82	No data
United States (facilitator and health care workers)	40	91	62	46	29

Note: Long-term orientation is a dimension recently added, with incomplete data to date.
Source: Excerpted from *Culture and Organizations* (2nd ed.), by G. Hofstede, 2005, New York: McGraw-Hill.

Table 4.2 shows the scores of the U.S., Somali, and Mexican cultures based on Hofstede's research conducted in those countries. The scores lie between 1 and 100, with higher numbers indicating stronger tendencies to exhibit the orientation (Hofstede, 2005).

Mary identified the implications of each dimension and the facilitation adaptations required to address them. Differences among the cultures can be seen across all five dimensions, but the three indexes that made this facilitation complex were power distance, individualism versus collectivism, and masculinity versus femininity. Uncertainty avoidance was managed by a simple solution: direct involvement of leaders in the planning of a highly structured forum. There are no data available about the long-term versus short-term orientation of the Mexicans, so that dimension was not considered.

1. The power distance scores indicate that, compared to the U.S. culture (40), the Mexican and Somali cultures (81 and 64, respectively) have a more unequal view of power. Power and decision making are concentrated in certain strata of the communities. This would indicate that some members of the community would not be likely to speak, on their own, directly to institutions about a concern to try to effect change.

The facilitation response was to reach out first to leaders. The community would expect leaders to speak on their behalf to an institution. Community members would then be asked to assist their own leaders during the forum.

2. Individualism scores showed that Somali and Mexican cultures (27 and 30, respectively) have a much more collectivist view than the U.S. culture (91), meaning that Somali and Mexican cultures were less likely to engage in a discussion about their personal needs than to work on behalf of the whole community.

The facilitation response was to use the power of these closely bonded networks to help the whole community find its voice and express it collectively.

3. Masculinity scores showed that Somali culture (41) values caring relationships and modesty; individual assertiveness is less desirable. They are more likely to value women in nurturing roles and less likely to value women in higher-profile public leadership roles than the U.S. (62) or Mexican (69) cultures.

The facilitation response was to seek buy-in from male leaders in the Somali community before Mary assumed the assertive role as the facilitator. She asked whether she should ask a male facilitator to join her or replace her. They responded that they would support Mary in the facilitator role because she was from the United States, where women are in careers. They requested that Somali elders be seated in positions of influence during the forum to show respect to the process. Table 4.3 shows differences among the cultures relating to masculinity and femininity.

Mary and Ann put much time and attention into planning and prefacilitation work to address differences in power distance, individualism, and masculinity as well as accommodate language differences. Prefacilitation work included paying attention to their own intercultural sensitivity, engaging both Somali and Mexican leaders, and establishing trusting relationships with them.

ENGAGE LEADERS AND BUILD TRUSTING RELATIONSHIPS

Leadership may be assigned or emergent (Northouse, 2001). Assigned leadership results from a person's position or status in a community (for example, elder or spiritual guide). The group confers power and influence to these leaders. This is a common basis for leadership in collectivist cultures like

Table 4.3
Perspectives on Gender Roles Related to Masculinity

Masculinity	Femininity
Societies such as Mexico and the United States that score higher on masculinity tend to:	*Societies such as Somalia that score lower tend to:*
Appreciate assertiveness	**Exhibit more modest and caring values—both men and women**
Be achievement oriented	**Display less assertiveness and workplace achievement orientation—both men and women**
Reinforce for both men and women traditional workplace values of power and control (that were once more the male model and now are more common for women also)	**Have a more traditional male model of public decision making, as the women are honored in family and nurturing roles**

Source: Adapted from *Culture and Organizations* (2nd ed.), by G. Hofstede, 2005, New York: McGraw-Hill.

Somalia and Mexico. Mary and Ann started making inroads into the Somali and Mexican communities by reaching out to assigned leaders who could guide them about how to involve and engage the Mexican and Somali communities.

Both Mary and Ann had already worked with two organizations in town: Centro Campesino and the Somali American Organization. Two men who led the Somali organization were very well educated in their own country and were considered leaders for the entire community. The director of Centro Campesino and her staff were overseeing a health program that tapped special funding to make certain that migrant health care was sufficient. These leaders were selected to plan the exchanges.

All the leaders were bilingual, which created a communication bridge between the cultures and the health care system. Their assistance was critical to the process. As noted by Schauber, "Cultural informants are bridge builders. They can walk in two worlds with a conscious understanding of the differences. Thus, they can help cultures understand each other" (2002, p. 311).

Mary facilitated a series of planning meetings with leaders from all three cultures. At their first meeting, Ann described the help the health care sector needed—help and answers that only people from their communities could provide. This first conversation created mutual understanding of issues that undermined the effectiveness of health care for these communities. Mary and Ann asked the Somali and Mexican leaders for help with four things: (1) articulating the questions from the health care sector to their communities; (2) designing meetings that would engage community members in productive conversation; (3) seeking questions and concerns from their communities—questions that could be answered by health care staff; and (4) recruiting a wide group of people from their communities into the conversation. The leaders agreed to help Mary and Ann with the four tasks. The planning group operated as one entity for the entire process.

Once the leadership was in place, preparatory meetings were held to build trusting relationships and make decisions about the forums. In more collectivist cultures like Somalia and Mexico, trust is based on credible roles in a reputable organization, dependable family and kinship networks, and consistency between words and actions maintained over the long term. In more individualist societies like the United States, trust is based on charismatic personality traits, personal credibility, reliability, persuasive words, and decisive actions (Ting-Toomey, 1999). Thus earning trust in all communities would require deeper relationships, and time to establish credibility.

During a series of meetings, the level of trust between the sponsor, facilitator, and leaders improved. For example, during one meeting, Ann asked the Somali leaders whether it was all right for doctors and nurses to discuss birth control and family planning with Somali women. The men confided that it wasn't all right yet, but that as a community they were realizing how difficult it is to have families of thirteen children in America. They thought that soon birth control would be more acceptable. Ann then shared that it was only in the past several decades that American Catholics and others made that same decision. This helped the Somali leaders see their evolution as more normal in relation to that of others in America.

Self-disclosure helps others see more fully what you believe, value, and do, and allows for finding common ground. Facilitators can pay attention to the level of communication that is happening among cultures in the group, seeking to move to stages of sharing that promote identification—levels two and three in the following model (Beegle, 2006).

Level one: sharing information regarding specific subject matter

Level two: sharing personal information about you and your family or community

Level three: sharing values and beliefs

Much of the exchange of information in the health care forums stayed at level one; however, when the conversation stimulated moments of self-disclosure, such self-disclosure was useful. In both the Mexican and Somali groups, mothers and fathers described home remedies they used to care for sick children. Many of these home remedies were familiar to some of the older medical professionals. The discussion led medical professionals to admit that there was value to those home remedies, and that members of the U.S. culture might be too quick to show up at Urgent Care. The exchange overcame some of the community's sense of separateness from the U.S. medical system.

GAIN PARTICIPATION AND MANAGE POWER DYNAMICS

The goal of the Anytown project was to involve Mexican and Somali community members in an open discussion that improved health care outcomes in the entire community. To think about how to engage community members, Mary needed to revisit the influence of power distance. Table 4.4 describes views of equality and inequality in cultures.

One of the challenges identified by the planning team was that Somali and Mexican community members needed to believe that their involvement mattered to the health care institution. Background and experience influence whether people are apt to participate in organizations and institutions, and if they do, experience *marginality* or *mattering*.

> Marginality is a feeling that we do not belong or matter. People may be marginalized by race, ethnicity, nationality, socioeconomic background or language. People ask themselves: "Are we part of things; do we belong; are we central or marginal? Do we make a difference; do others care about us and make us feel we matter?" (Schlossberg, 1989, p. 2)

To manage intracommunity power dynamics, Mary facilitated two separate dialogues—one with the health care providers and Somali residents, one with

Table 4.4
Perspectives on Participation Related to Power Distance

Equality	Inequality
In low-distance societies like the United States:	*In high-distance societies like Somalia and Mexico:*
People believe that all are "created equal" and have an equal opportunity to succeed in life.	Unequal status is the norm and is accepted. Those with more authority tend not to interact with those with lower class or status unless in an authoritarian manner.
People assume that all individuals have a right and responsibility to fully participate in the public domain and to share their ideas.	Rank, status, and authority give people a sense of security and certainty. It is reassuring to know, from birth, who they are and where they fit in society.
People interact across class and authority lines as a matter of fact.	Low-status individuals may not willingly approach those with higher status. Thus, participation with leaders, institutions, and power structures is uncomfortable.

Source: Adapted from *Culture and Organizations* (2nd ed.), by G. Hofstede, 2005, New York: McGraw-Hill.

the health care providers and Mexican residents. This reinforced the power of participation by the people. Because the representatives of the health care providers were perceived to be of high status, representatives of the Somali and Mexican communities saw themselves as being very distant from the health care providers. The rank and status of the Somali and Mexican leaders involved in planning and cohosting the forums gave community members a greater sense of security. These leaders created a bridge spanning the power distance and made it more likely that community members would participate.

The leaders decided to generate questions for the forum by seeking them from their group—the Somali, Mexican, and health care communities. Then the leaders brought the potential questions that they had collected to the planning group. Mary worked with them to cluster the questions into themes and issues that warranted discussion. Half were questions for Somali and Mexican community members from health care providers; the other half were questions for health care providers from Somali and Mexican community members. The topics included Cesarean birth, circumcision, interpreter availability, insurance, use of the emergency room, ideas to improve service, and more. The final set of twenty questions was approved by the leaders. Agreement was reached about the order in which they would be asked. Some of the questions follow.

From health care providers to community members:

- What are the obstacles or challenges you face in gaining access to care and providers (that is, in obtaining services from clinics, hospitals, public health, school nurses, and first responders)? What suggestions do you have for addressing them?
- What are some educational topics that you would like to have offered so that you can better understand health care in the United States?
- If each provider group did one thing to improve services, what would it be?
- What are the best ways for health providers to communicate with patients from your culture?

From community members to health care providers:

- Can there be more information on various diagnoses translated into informational flyers for patients to take with them when they leave?
- Has there been any thought into considering having specific Somali and Spanish days for public health and the Women, Infant and Children program?
- We need help understanding insurance coverage and paperwork and how to get insurance issues resolved. What is the best way to work with the health providers to address these concerns?
- Somali specific: there needs to be a dialogue concerning women's health concerns—for example, birth control, female circumcision, birth, male doctors, and so on.

BUILD SYSTEMS FOR PRODUCTIVE DIALOGUE

The next step included identifying the format and supports needed for the facilitated dialogues so that all attendees could fully participate. Child care was

Table 4.5
Perspectives on Dialogue Related to Individualism

Individualism	Collectivism
In highly individualist societies like the United States:	*In low individualistic (collectivist) societies like Somalia and Mexico:*
Individuals feel free to voice their personal opinions, believing what is good for them is what they should strive toward. Voting is used to determine which individuals "win."	There is a strong sense of shared accountability and responsibility because of the emphasis on the group. Consensus and group decision making is preferred.
Individual contributions and accomplishments are highly prized.	Being "singled out" may be embarrassing, and individual accomplishment and initiative are downplayed and even discouraged.

Source: Adapted from *Culture and Organizations* (2nd ed.), by G. Hofstede, 2005, New York: McGraw-Hill.

discussed. The Somali group said that the women would take care of their children at home, but the Mexican group did want child care so that everyone could participate and their children would be next door to them. Refreshments were available after the sessions to add a social component to the exchange.

To stimulate dialogue about the questions, Mary and Ann considered the preferences of the cultures in the group, as shown in Table 4.5.

About fifty people were involved in each of the two discussions, including Somali and Mexican community members, physicians, public health and school nurses, hospital administrators, and social services case workers. For the Somali forum, a special request was to have a gynecologist attend to address several questions focused on childbirth and women's health concerns.

Circles were used for both groups to ensure that participants and the facilitator were able to see and hear each other and to create a sense of equity between the health providers and the community participants. The facilitator stated the questions to the group and moderated the dialogue. Questions raised by health care providers were responded to by community members; questions raised by community members were responded to by health care providers. Many voices were heard; this dialogue created greater recognition and

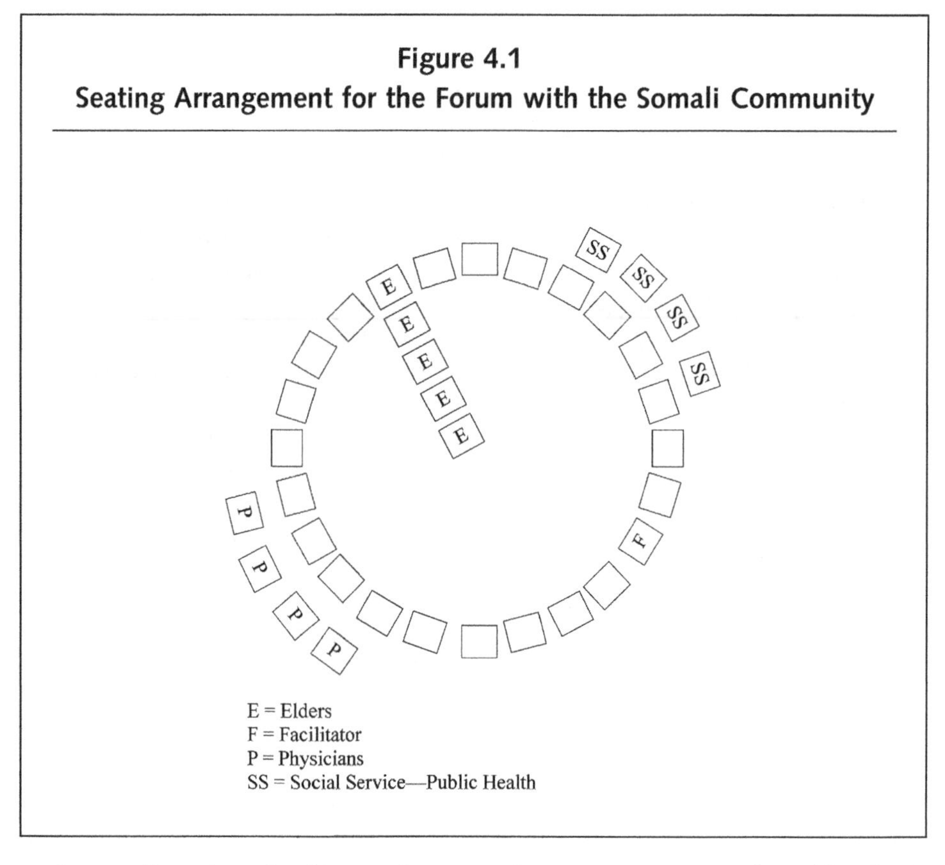

Figure 4.1
Seating Arrangement for the Forum with the Somali Community

understanding about health care issues and more appreciation for each other's health practices.

As shown in Figure 4.1, the Somali discussion circle was arranged so that the male elders were seated in a line inside the circle. The shape allowed the leaders to be recognized for their hierarchical role within their collectivist society. The facilitator sat in the circle, across from the elders. Priority was given first to seating Somali community members in the circle. Health care providers sat outside the larger circle.

As shown in Figure 4.2, the Mexican forum used a more traditional circle format. Health care providers were interspersed with community members so that no one was singled out within the circle. Mary and the Spanish-speaking physician's assistant sat beside each other. The interpreter clarified information about health issues by speaking in both Spanish and English. The seating arrangement was the Mexican culture's way of honoring two people whom they saw as having authority.

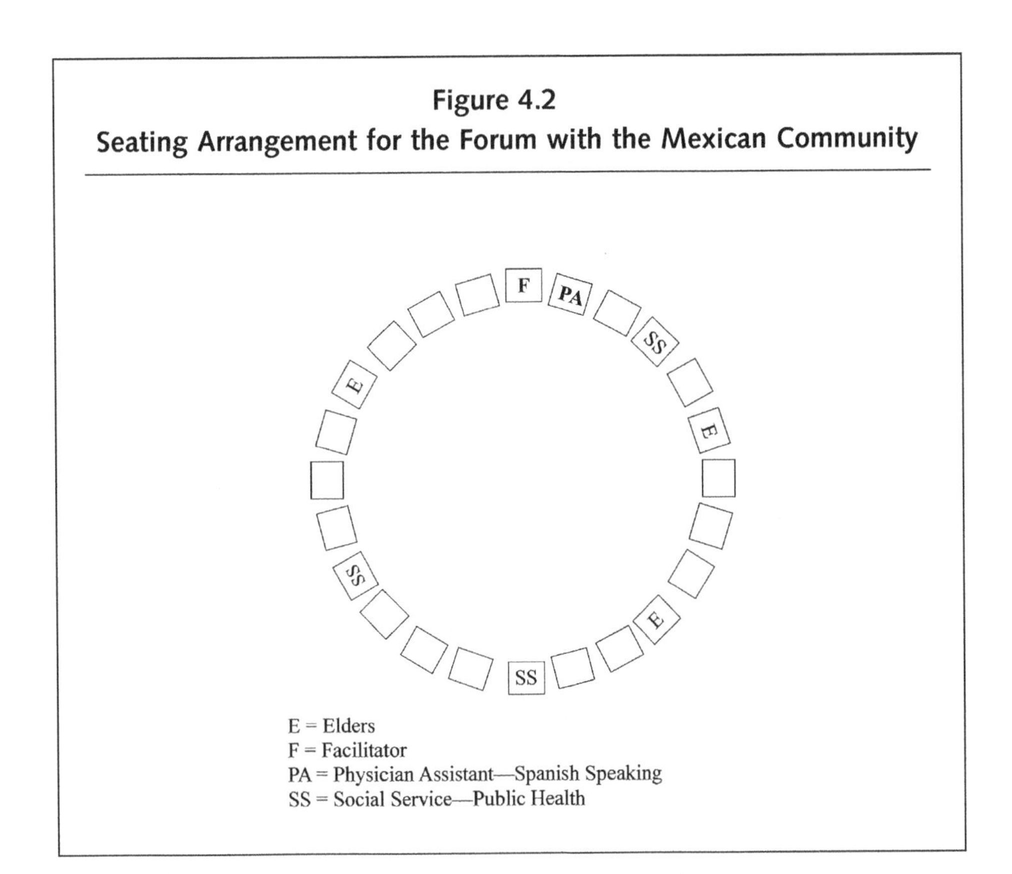

Figure 4.2
Seating Arrangement for the Forum with the Mexican Community

ACCOMMODATE COMMUNICATION NEEDS AND STYLES

Of course, interpreters are necessary for conversation in multicultural forums. In Anytown, the leaders in both communities selected trusted interpreters for the forums. The Mexican group selected a bilingual physician's assistant who was able both to interpret and to respond directly with accurate medical information and system practices to the community in response to questions. Extra time was built into the agenda for language interpretation.

There are two key cultural elements that shape conflict styles. The first is a culture's shared beliefs about *harmony and conflict.* The second is how a *culture communicates,* both verbally and with gestures (Hammer, 2002).

Mexican and Somali immigrants are oral in their communication style because English is not their first language, and also because many are not literate in their own language. In oral cultures, communications emphasize connections between people. Information is sought from people with whom one can identify—within the community and among family and friends

(Beegle, 2006). The collection of questions and the discussion format accommodated the oral culture that is predominant in both cultures.

Given their collectivist orientation, the Mexican and Somali cultures value harmony highly. Relationships may be prized more highly than any task; thus harmony is seen as a way to maintain relationships. The facilitator was mindful of normal cross-cultural expressions, including the use of indirect speech, stories, third-party intermediaries, and expressing emotions. For example, expressing emotions and talking "with their hands" are also indications of how much some people care about the issue and not a distraction from the task (Hammer, 2002). By being aware of these modes of communication, the facilitator was able to recognize that emotive expressions did not indicate anger or frustration, but were typical means of conversing.

MAKE OPTIMUM USE OF SOCIAL CAPITAL

One challenge for multicultural groups and facilitators of multicultural groups is to make use of existing networks to achieve the goal of the group, and to broaden those networks for the good of the whole. Social capital is the collective value of networks and the inclination to help one another that arises from these networks (Putnam, 2000). The basic idea of social capital is that a person's relationships are an important asset, one that can be called on for its own benefits and enjoyment, and leveraged for material gain.

Three types of networks are valuable. Networks can be weak or strong; strong is preferable (Scheffert, Horntvedt & Chazdon, 2007):

- *Bonding networks* are the close ties (usually with family, friends and neighbors) that give people a sense of belonging and a sense that someone is available to help them get by in times of trouble.
- *Bridging networks* are weaker ties (like a friend of a friend) that create networks with people who are from different social backgrounds, interests or occupations, organizations, or neighborhoods. These ties can provide access to opportunities that close networks cannot.
- *Linking networks* are with private and public leaders and systems that have resources, such as banks, foundations, and institutions. They can be accessed to bring about changes or attract resources such as loans or grants.

The social capital networks of Anytown were informally assessed by Mary the facilitator, as summarized in Table 4.6.

The assessment revealed that opportunities existed for bridging and linking. It was also clear that the bonds of the Somali and Mexican cultures were an asset that could be tapped to introduce and propagate new health care behaviors. An example of how the culture-specific group discussions stimulated more informed discussion came when questions about Cesarean births arose. Young Somali women asked the medical professionals to tell them why "every Somali woman is being told to get a Cesarean." This question revealed that a rumor had caught fire among Somali women, creating suspicion. A medical professional, through the Somali interpreter, described the actual circumstances under which Cesareans were recommended.

Even then, the women were doubtful. "But we had many babies in Somalia, and we never used Cesareans."

A frank medical professional replied, "And how many of your babies and mothers died in Somalia?" The women grew quiet, and eyes grew wider. The consequences of childbirth in Somalia took hold. It was a discussion that reverberated throughout the community after the forum ended, and the Anytown doctors recognized that they needed to more thoroughly describe to Somali women the reasons they had when recommending Cesareans.

Bridging networks were developed within the leadership team that supported the design of the forums. In those planning conversations, the leaders recognized common needs and concerns. One example of this was the need for consistent availability of interpreters. By voicing those concerns and hearing the limitations of the health care sector, the leaders began to work together to solve problems.

The groups also began to recognize better the contributions of those persons in the culture who were bridges between the health care sector and their culture. In the Mexican forum, for instance, the bilingual health care provider was able to provide key information. The health care administrators in the room quickly saw the value of bilingual providers, and considered that value in future hiring efforts.

Links between immigrant communities and health care professionals resulted in tangible first steps. The dialogue helped the health care institution prioritize investments that would best strengthen the links between the community and the health care system.

Table 4.6
Assessment of Social Capital in the Communities

	Type of Network		
	Bonding	**Bridging**	**Linking**
	Trust and engagement with others like them within their community	Trust and engagement between Somalis, Mexicans, and U.S. health care workers	Connections of trust and engagement to the local health care system
Somalis	**Strong (within group)** Two Somali groups that settled in the area had been at war with one another in Somalia. Each sect was bonded within themselves but not to the other. They lived in two different parts of Anytown.	**Weak** Very few connections	**Weak** Very few connections
Mexicans	**Strong** Many families came from the same area within Mexico or Texas to settle in this U.S. town	**Weak** Very few connections	**Weak** Very few connections
U.S. health care workers	**Strong** Those in the health care industry in the community were well connected to each other and knew the health care services available in the community.	**Weak** Although some effort had been made in the past for health care workers to learn about their new clients' culture, they had not been deliberate in talking directly with the population.	Not applicable

The answers to the questions posed by health care providers became a wish list that health care organizations used to better connect immigrant communities to their institutions. An example of one tangible outcome was to produce picture and word cards in English and either Spanish or Somali for first responders to use in emergency situations.

The facilitated process created a win-win situation for institutions that needed to make strategic investments to reach immigrants, and for immigrants who would otherwise have a steep climb to improve health care. The forums improved understanding and trust across all three populations and clarified best practices for getting and giving culturally sensitive health care. The Somali and Mexican participants thanked the health care members for caring, for spending their off-duty time to participate, and for demonstrating how much they really cared about them.

chapter FIVE

Interpersonally Hostile Work Groups: Precipitating Factors and Solutions

Jana L. Raver and Ingrid C. Chadwick

Pierre Lebrun worked at the OC Transpo bus company in Ottawa, Ontario, for over ten years. He was a quiet man who kept to himself, yet he also had an embarrassing disability: he stuttered. He was bilingual, but speaking English was more difficult for him and caused his stuttering to get worse. Lebrun's coworkers frequently teased and humiliated him as a result. He complained to supervisors, but they did nothing, so the harassment went on for some time. One day, Lebrun was facing a reflective window and noticed that a coworker was mimicking him behind his back. He got angry and slapped his coworker. The other employee reported the incident, and Lebrun was fired. Lebrun filed a grievance with the union; he won his grievance

We thank the Social Sciences and Humanities Research Council of Canada for research funding that helped facilitate the completion of this chapter.

and returned to work on a strict "last chance" contract, which required him to take anger management and speech therapy courses. His coworkers who harassed him were not punished. This sent the disturbing message that teasing and psychological harassment were acceptable so long as employees did not actually touch the victim. Upon Pierre's return to work, he was transferred into a new group with friendlier coworkers, and he worked very effectively there. However, he was later promoted to a nonunionized job (with no protection from harassment) in a different group, where he was again harassed by colleagues. About six months after this promotion, he suddenly quit.

Four months later, on April 6, 1999, Lebrun arrived at OC Transpo carrying a Remington high-power hunting rifle and forty-five rounds of ammunition. He set fires in a chemical storage room and then shot and killed four workers, injured two others, and committed suicide. While hunting his former coworkers, he shouted, "Do you think it's funny now?" The coroner's inquest into the tragedy revealed a workplace at OC Transpo that workers described as "toxic" or "poisoned" and where everything was done with threats. Pierre Lebrun had long been harassed by numerous coworkers, and management had done nothing. Lebrun's suicide note blamed his problems on the hostilities and humiliation inflicted on him by coworkers. The lawyer representing the chief coroner went so far as to conclude that the shootings were the result of harassment of Lebrun by his coworkers. Of the seventy-seven recommendations made by the inquest's jury, twenty-five were specifically aimed at OC Transpo's work environment, sixteen addressed workplace harassment, and twelve addressed health and safety. Overall, although Lebrun's actions were inexcusable, much of the blame was placed on OC Transpo for doing little to prevent the creation of an interpersonally hostile environment that resulted in violence (McLaughlin, 2000).

This tragic case illustrates the extreme dark side of interpersonal relations in groups, where hostile acts were inflicted over time by colleagues and caused the victimized employee to finally reach the breaking point and enact revenge. Of course, only a small minority of cases escalate to this point; however, there is substantial evidence that even relatively minor hostile acts can cause severe harm to victims and the organizations where they work. Unfortunately, despite extensive efforts to educate organizational leaders and practitioners regarding how to build collaborative and respectful groups, the reality is that many groups are still characterized by high levels of interpersonally hostile actions among the members. These hostile acts have been variously called *harassment, bullying, mobbing, aggression,* and *emotional abuse,* among other terms. Although these negative acts fit within the domain of relationship-based conflicts, they need to be addressed differently because of their unique characteristics. In particular, people often become victimized to the extent that they can no longer defend themselves (that is, it is not a conflict between equals), group members often "gang up" on victim(s), and these acts become embedded within group norms. In addition, antiharassment legislation exists to protect members of underrepresented groups (for example, women, racial minorities, disabled), and broader legislation that protects targets from harassment and bullying regardless of their characteristics is beginning to appear in nations around the world (for example, Australia, Canada, France, Germany, Sweden, and the United Kingdom).

The goal of this chapter is to offer a systems approach to understanding and preventing interpersonal hostility in organizational work groups. Our approach contrasts with many managers' and practitioners' conclusions that hostility is due to "bad apples," a conclusion that encourages individualistic interventions that address only a small part of the problem. We focus on how *group processes* (for example, communication patterns, conflict climate, identity, and emotions), *group structure* (for example, leadership, power distribution, and work stressors), and *group context* (for example, harassment policies, appraisal and reward systems, expectations, and training on respect) independently and collectively influence the levels of interpersonal hostility. We also provide advice to help prevent the formation of interpersonally hostile groups and to facilitate these situations should they arise. However, before analyzing the causes of hostility in groups, we first explain the nature of the problem.

HOW INTERPERSONALLY HOSTILE GROUPS ARE DIFFICULT: PATTERNS AND IMPACT

This section addresses the nature of hostility in groups, including different types of outcomes associated with this problem.

The Nature and Outcomes of Hostility

The variety of ways in which employees may be harassed, bullied, mobbed, victimized, or abused by fellow employees is virtually endless (Einarsen & Hoel, 2001; Keashly & Jagatic, 2003; Neuman & Baron, 1996, 1998), yet the patterns of escalating hostility and their effects on targets are remarkably similar across cases. Some employees are harassed for characteristics that are legally protected (for example, gender, race, disability). Other employees are harassed because their personality or values do not fit with those of others in the group, or because other members find it entertaining to ridicule their characteristics (for example, jokes about stuttering, obesity). Still other employees are subjected to hostility for violating performance norms (over- or underperforming). One common theme in these situations is that the hostile acts are enacted in a manner that inflicts harm on a target while protecting the perpetrator(s) from culpability (Björkqvist, Østerman, & Lagerspetz, 1994). For example, a perpetrator may hurl insults at targets to denigrate their self-worth, but is most likely to do so when the situation allows this (for example, in private, when observers do nothing, with implicit support from management). Perpetrators also frequently aim their attacks at a target's social relationships (for example, spreading rumors), reputation, or work (for example, attacking quality of tasks) in subtle ways that are difficult to police. Ostracism or social isolation is another very common way to inflict harm without detection.

With regard to targets' outcomes, employees who experience any type of interpersonal hostility—even if it is at a relatively low level—are at increased risk for negative psychological and physical outcomes. The set of personal outcomes includes anxiety, depression, burnout, frustration, negative emotions at work, lowered self-esteem, poor life satisfaction, poor job satisfaction, low organizational commitment, and physical symptoms (for example, headaches, sleep disorders), among others. (For reviews, see Bowling & Beehr, 2006; Hershcovis & Barling, 2008; Raver & Barling, 2008.) Targets of hostile acts also tend to have high absenteeism, impaired job performance, and high turnover (Bowling & Beehr, 2006). Research on group-level outcomes has illustrated that groups with high levels of sexual harassment (Raver & Gelfand, 2005), interpersonal deviance (Dunlop & Lee, 2004), and bullying (Mathisen, Einarsen & Mykletun, 2008) perform worse on various group performance outcomes—including financial performance—than those groups with low levels of harassment. In many cases, employees believe that the organization is to blame for their harassment because leaders did little or nothing to prevent the situation (or made it worse), so targets may also attempt to get even with the organization and their coworkers (for example, sabotage, theft, undermining colleagues, harming the organization's reputation) (Bies & Tripp, 2001). Thus the evidence is clear that interpersonally hostile acts between employees are detrimental *both* for targets and for the organizations where they work.

Patterns in the Chaos: When Minor Hostilities Escalate

Incidents such as the one at OC Transpo that escalate and result in workplace homicides are fortunately rare, largely because most targets eventually leave their organizations without engaging in such extreme acts of retributive justice. However, this case illustrates several events that occur when interpersonally hostile acts in work groups begin to escalate into more severe bullying and persistent abuse. Exhibit 5.1 details the escalation steps identified in Leymann's early research on victims of mobbing (1996), and this sequence of events has been corroborated in other research (for example, Andersson & Pearson, 1999; Zapf & Gross, 2001). This sequence of minor hostilities leading to extreme victimization is also seen again and again in case reports of workplace bullying (for example, Davenport, Schwartz, & Elliott, 2002; Field, 2008; Namie & Namie, 2000; Randall, 1997). In short, this is the pattern of events that tends to occur if the group context is permissive toward hostility (as we discuss below) and no intervention is enacted to prevent escalation.

Exhibit 5.1
The Course of Escalating Hostility

1. There is a conflict trigger that begins the sequence of events. This may be a dispute between two parties, but it may also be unilateral, such that only one party perceives a threat (for example, the target's characteristics are seen as undesirable). The hostile acts begin.
2. One of the parties gets the upper hand through more formal or informal power, political tactics (for example, turning the rest of the group against the target), more aggressive techniques, or simply inflicting more harm. In cases where the perpetrator is a supervisor, this power differential is already embedded in the relationship. The target is put in a low power position such that it is difficult to defend himself or herself. Bullying begins in earnest, often with the involvement of coworkers who become convinced that the target "deserves it."
3. The target seeks help by appealing to management or human resources. In many cases, support is immediately denied, and targets are told that they are overreacting and should cope and handle the conflict themselves. In cases where allegations are investigated, there is insufficient evidence to support the target's position because of the subtle nature of the acts and the group's implicit corroboration. The target returns to work.
4. The target is stigmatized; he or she is branded as a "difficult" or "troubled" employee who is disrupting the group. The bullying escalates. Over time, the target begins experiencing mental strain and physical ailments, which impair work and life quality.
5. The target is eventually pushed out of the work context. Voluntary resignations are most common, although involuntary resignations and stress leaves also occur frequently. In rare cases, victims may attempt suicide or try to "get even" by enacting violence.

Now that we have identified the problem, illustrated its nature, and detailed its outcomes, we turn to a detailed examination of the reasons interpersonal hostility is sustained in work groups.

WHY INTERPERSONALLY HOSTILE GROUPS ARE DIFFICULT: PRECIPITATING AND SUSTAINING FORCES

To date, scholars and practitioners have generally adopted one of two alternative approaches to understanding and addressing hostile and abusive behaviors at work. The first, the *individualistic perspective,* illustrates that certain individual attributes (for example, negative affectivity, trait anger) have been associated with reports of enacting aggression (Fox & Spector, 1999; Hershcovis et al., 2007). Recommendations for change have consequently focused on removing those "bad apples" (Felps, Mitchell, & Byington, 2006; Sutton, 2007b), including instituting integrity tests, background checks, or both to filter out the potential troublemakers (Neuman & Baron, 1996). The second, the *policy perspective,* has emphasized that abusive behaviors at work persist in large part due to the absence (or lack of enforcement) of regulations, laws, or policies that prohibit these behaviors, and thus formal regulations and better enforcement procedures are needed to begin to address this pervasive problem (for example, Namie & Namie, 2008). We agree that both individualistic and policy interventions may be beneficial; however, they only tell part of the story. Hostility at work occurs in an interpersonal context where more than one perpetrator is typically involved (Raver, 2008), the behaviors are condoned by other group members and by management, the group's task structure is the source of stress and frustration that creates conflicts, and the larger organizational culture and practices may be implicitly communicating acceptance of hostility. We argue that to fully understand and prevent interpersonal hostility, it is essential for scholars and practitioners to adopt a *group perspective,* which advocates attention to the facilitating and sustaining forces within work groups.

The framework for our approach, summarized in Figure 5.1, is grounded within the relational perspective and incorporates insights with regard to process, structure, and context. At the core of this figure, we depict a work group where eleven members of the group, including the group leader (D), have exhibited hostility toward member A. Member A also engaged in some counterhostility toward B, E, and I; however, nearly all members of the group have turned against A, and she is unable to defend herself. Her lone alliance is F, who has remained supportive of her despite the fact that member A has been stigmatized. Due to this, F has also started to become "stigmatized by association" and is now enduring harassment from the leader and from E

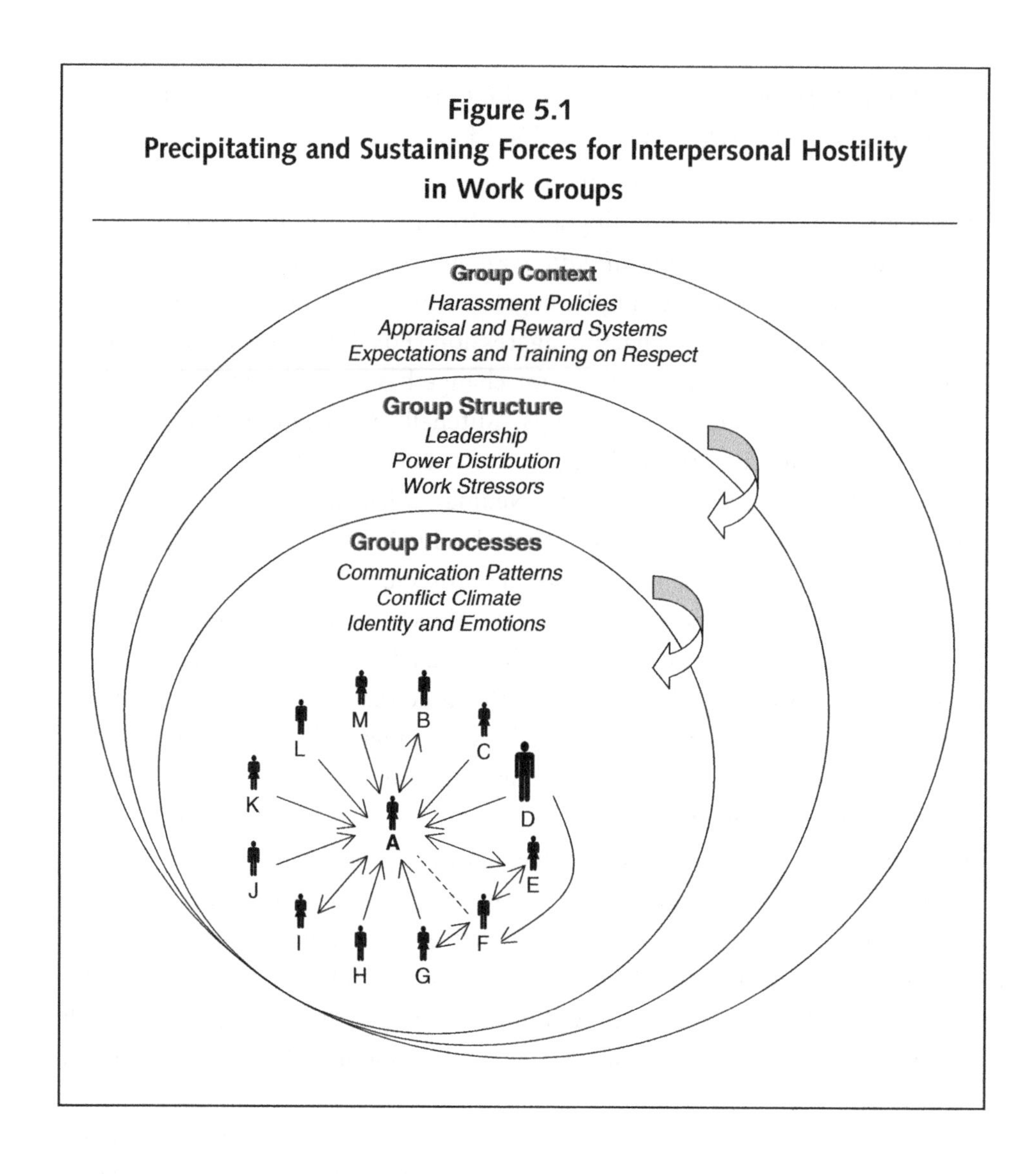

Figure 5.1
Precipitating and Sustaining Forces for Interpersonal Hostility in Work Groups

and G. These interpersonal dynamics of hostility and alliance building are necessarily part of the group's processes and are thus depicted within the first circle along with communication patterns, conflict climate, and group identity and emotions. In the sections that follow, we elaborate on each of the process, structure, and context factors in the model to illustrate their role in precipitating and sustaining levels of interpersonal hostility in groups.

Group Processes

Group processes, such as communication patterns, conflict climates, group identity, and emotions, greatly affect interpersonal relations in groups. Following we elaborate on the particular influence of each of these types of group processes in precipitating and sustaining levels of interpersonal hostility in groups.

Communication Patterns

> They don't want to attack a problem so it never goes away. When they should speak up to resolve this, they don't. They don't want to be bothered by it (Jehn, 1997, p. 543).

Communication is clearly a mechanism through which perpetrators inflict harm on their targets (for example, with insults, slurs, jokes, "silent treatment"); however, the nature of communication in a group may also help determine whether hostility will arise in the first place, how it might spread throughout the group, and the extent to which it is sustained. First, hostility can arise in groups due to deficient communication channels, such as poor flow of information or lack of mutual conversations about tasks (Vartia, 1996). Similarly, defensive communication between group members can be a conflict trigger that starts the hostility process (Gibbs, 1961). Second, the nature of communication patterns (that is, who talks to whom) also influences the spread of hostility in groups. Research indicates that individuals with lower communication capabilities have a higher chance of becoming "attacked" (Zapf, Knorz, & Kulla, 1996). Not surprisingly, targets often have sparse communication networks with little political influence, whereas perpetrators benefit from greater influence through communication. Finally, as illustrated in the quote, the patterns of communication in a group can create conflicts, and the absence of communication can help sustain those conflicts. Even though hostility often begins with direct talk or talk behind the target's back, eventually the goal is to treat the stigmatized target as if he or she were invisible. Ostracism threatens individuals' fundamental needs of belonging (Williams, 2007), which can lead to severe feelings of sadness and anger (Smith & Williams, 2004). Accordingly, such exclusion can move hostility toward step 5 in Exhibit 5.1, where the target feels forced to leave the group.

Conflict Climate

> I was at the college for eight years where stabbing in one's back was pretty much the accepted way of life. It was not something that was provoked by a change in the CEO. It was built into the culture ("Steven," quoted in Davenport et al., 2002, p. 64).

Sometimes, groups simply do not know how to respectfully disagree. A member might strongly criticize the group's plan without realizing that other members' egos were closely intertwined with that idea. In many groups, critiques are ego threats that are interpreted to mean that you did something wrong or failed to "win" everyone's esteem. In short, some groups have climates that fail to encourage constructive controversy, and thus any number of task- or process-related disagreements hold the possibility of escalating into interpersonal hostilities (Jehn & Bendersky, 2003). In addition, targets of bullying are often principled and moral individuals who stand up for what they believe is right (Davenport et al., 2002). However, upholding these principles may be unpopular when it means that others' egos or territories may be harmed in the process. Once hostilities begin, the target's conflict resolution strategies may exacerbate the problem; in fact, research suggests that collaborating strategies that work with other types of conflict are ineffective in situations of escalated hostility (Aquino, 2000; Zapf & Gross, 2001). Therefore, it is important to address the group's conflict climate from a systems perspective, rather than simply teaching individuals new resolution strategies.

Group Identity and Emotions

> A group of workers make jokes about black people in front of Sarita. At first she pretends she does not hear, but as the jokes continue, she tells them they are offensive. They retaliate by saying, "That's the trouble with you Pakis—no sense of humour," and increase the frequency of jokes and comments. Eventually, one member of the group pushes Sarita roughly when she comments about their racism. She tells the supervisor, who says, "They're only having a joke. Don't be so sensitive" (Randall, 1997, p. 120).

The creation and maintenance of a group identity is one of the most fundamental tasks for group formation because shared group identities help members make sense of their reality, clarify expectations for desirable members and behaviors, help motivate collective effort, and provide reassurance when setbacks occur (Tajfel & Turner, 1985). Although the identity creation process is beneficial when it is inclusive, the downside is that the group boundaries may be drawn too narrowly, such that members who do not "fit" the ideal prototype are rejected and ridiculed. Members may actually bond emotionally through their shared experiences of bullying the rejected target (Leymann, 1993). The victimization process becomes a way in which the group reinforces its identity—that is, by identifying and ridiculing an *undesirable* member—which then produces positive emotions and cohesion among the rest of the group. When a few members begin to enact deviant behaviors, other group members follow (Robinson & O'Leary-Kelly, 1998). Even when some members of the group are uncomfortable with the hostility or silently support the target, very few publicly stand up for the target out of fear of becoming targets themselves (for example, member F in Figure 5.1). Unfortunately, being singled out as the sole target is the most damaging type of interpersonal hostility (Duffy, Ganster, Shaw, Johnson, & Pagon, 2006).

Group Structure

Another set of group factors influencing interpersonal hostility in groups is based on the group's structure. In this section we address structural elements including leadership, power distribution, and work stressors, and we discuss how they influence the levels of hostility in groups.

Leadership

> After three months of being bullied he . . . reported the young men. The response was brief and cruel: the young men were right in that he was too fat so he should expect to be made fun of (Randall, 1997, p. 15).

Leaders are the lens through which employees interpret the organization and its practices, and they are also important role models whose actions define the range of acceptable behavior (Judge, Woolf, Hurst, & Livingston, 2009). Charismatic leaders who act as ethical and supportive role models can reduce the levels of aggression in groups (Brown & Trevino, 2006; Hepworth & Towler, 2004). (For further discussion in the context of authentic leadership, see Chapter Seventeen.) In the same way, however, leaders can also create more hostility in a group by either allowing it or modeling such behaviors themselves (through social learning; Bandura, 1977). For example, leaders who form unsupportive relations with certain employees (Townsend, Phillips, & Elkins, 2000) or who use a laissez-faire leadership style and do nothing to intervene (O'Reilly & Raver, 2008) can generate higher levels of hostile behaviors in a group. Indeed, a recent large-scale study of aggression rates in hospitals throughout England revealed that inaction after hostile incidents was one of the best predictors of organization-wide rates of aggression from supervisors, coworkers, and patients (Raver, Dawson, Grojean, & Smith, 2008). Consequently, it is essential to ensure that leaders have the right awareness and skill set to be able to create more collaborative and respectful work groups.

Power Distribution

> It began with the little comments. . . . Most of these comments came from one middle-aged woman who worked there two days a week. Unfortunately for me, she was also good friends with the directors of the company, and was so far up their behinds; well you get the picture (Field, 2008, case history 5).

Hostilities can be exchanged between any two parties regardless of their formal or informal power; however, the unequal distribution of power becomes increasingly important as conflicts escalate to become bullying (Einarsen, 1999; Leymann, 1996; Keashly & Nowell, 2003). Clearly, formal power differentials between supervisors and subordinates facilitate the development of bullying; however, evidence indicates that coworker-perpetrated aggression is common and that most instances of supervisor aggression are accompanied by coworker aggression as well (Raver, 2008). Zapf et al. (1996) and Einarsen (1999) described how bullying may result between "equals" when one party becomes disadvantaged during the conflict process such that he or she no longer has the resources to defend himself or herself. Thus one important precursor to the development of bullying between group members is that the environment must permit one party to use his or her personal power bases (French & Raven, 1959) to gain an advantage over the target (Salin, 2003). In the case briefly quoted above, the primary perpetrator was friends with the directors (that is, she held referent power), and she was able to get insider information because of it (information power), which helped her gain power over her coworker. Power in organizations is also influenced by roles in society, where members of groups who hold less sociological power (for example, women and minorities) are more likely to become victims of hostilities (Berdahl, 2007; Cortina, 2007).

Work Stressors

> Ambiguous situations, or situations where the real source of frustration is unclear, also represent fertile ground for scapegoating processes (Hoel & Cooper, 2001, p. 10).

The presence of structural stressors within work groups, such as role ambiguity, role conflicts, and work overload, can greatly influence the way employees treat each other. These stressors have been argued to be the result of the "leaner and meaner" direction of the contemporary workplace (Neuman & Baron, 1996). As organizations compete globally, employees are forced to repeatedly adapt to new organizational realities. Accordingly, many employees suffer from the uneasiness of role ambiguity as they struggle to understand what their responsibilities are in organizational structures that emphasize flexibility (for example, matrix structures, self-managed teams). Similarly, role conflicts appear as a result of the communication of different and competing expectations for work and responsibilities, leading to confusion among group members regarding their respective roles. Another common stressor today is work overload, which can lead employees to feel overwhelmed by the additional work responsibilities and demanding time pressures to deliver more with less (Zapf, 1999). Together these job stressors create high levels of stress and frustration that have been shown to result in counterproductive behavioral responses (Bowling & Beehr, 2006; Fox & Spector, 1999).

Group Context

The context of a group is also highly relevant for assessing interpersonal hostility in groups. In this section we explicate how contextual factors, such as harassment and respectful behavior policies, appraisal and reward systems, and finally, expectations and training on respect, can influence levels of interpersonal hostility in groups.

Harassment and Respectful Behavior Policies

> The impression I've had from the reaction of senior managers is that to act on this now would be an admission of their failure to deal with this situation when others first reported it, and rather than risk it becoming known that they have failed miserably in upholding their own policy on bullying, they are going to try and sweep it all under the carpet (Field, 2008, case history 32).

Most companies have sexual harassment and discrimination policies in place for legal compliance, yet some are beginning to adopt broader anti-harassment policies or codes of conduct regarding respectful behavior, which protect employees against all forms of hostility, bullying, harassment, and abuse (Namie & Namie, 2008). By clearly articulating what workplace harassment is and why such behaviors are unacceptable, organizations can establish guidelines for respectful employee relations. Resources are available to help draft broader harassment prevention policies (for example, Hancocks, 2006a, 2006b), yet many North American organizations still focus their efforts only on antidiscrimination legal compliance. In addition, as the quote above shows, it is not enough simply to introduce a policy or code of conduct; managers and employees must be aware of it, know how to use it, and actually be willing to use the procedures specified. Having an antiharassment policy on the books without enforcing it may actually lead to backlash where the company is seen as hypocritical (Sutton, 2007a). Organizations' policies will be more effective if they establish procedures for how employees report cases of harassment and what the sanctions will be if the policy is violated. Moreover, managers must be trained in how to respond to potential policy violations and how they can help employees through this process (Saint-Cyr, 2004).

Appraisal and Reward Systems

> When Joan was [bullied] by a former colleague who became her boss, she said to him: "You told me the first time I met you that you wanted my job. I believe that you have gone out of your way to look for any and every opportunity to embarrass me professionally and to discredit me" (Davenport et al., 2002, p. 62).

Hostile behaviors in groups are often described as having little instrumental purpose, other than to reinforce the group's identity or to have some fun at someone else's expense. However, Salin (2003, p. 1223) argued that "there are several instances where it might be individually 'rational' or rewarding to bully a colleague or a subordinate." In organizations that have ranking-based appraisal and reward systems, group members must compete against each other for the few prized "outstanding performer" slots (typically the top 20 percent), and managers also feel a strong pressure to be ranked highly, so they will pass this pressure on to their subordinates (Ryan, 2007). To our knowledge, only one study has investigated the link between competitive reward systems and harassment (Raver, 2007), and the results demonstrated that when group members perceive that they have to compete with each other to gain desirable rewards, harassment levels increase significantly. If employees find themselves in the bottom 10 percent in a ranking system, they are generally encouraged to leave. We know that the ultimate result of escalated harassment and bullying is expelling "undesirable" employees from the work context, so this strategy is preferred by some leaders as a means of "letting go" of employees without having to fire them or pay severance (Salin, 2003).

Expectations and Training on Respect

> Putting the right practices and policies in place is useless if they don't set the stage for civilized conversations and interactions. People must treat the person in front of them, right now, in the right way, and they must feel safe to point out when their peers and superiors blow it (Sutton, 2007a, p. 54).

Ensuring that the organizational policies forbid harassment and also that the appraisal and reward systems encourage collaboration are both necessary steps toward creating a respectful environment where hostility will not occur; however, they are not sufficient. The organization must also clearly and repeatedly communicate expectations regarding employees' respectful behaviors. For example, Bell, Quick, and Cycyota (2002) discuss the importance of "harassment-free notifications," including signage posted throughout the workplace. Also, we encourage communication regarding the importance of respect through policy documents at hiring, orientation, leadership training, newsletters, intranet sites, and so forth. The absence of this communication leads to lack of awareness where many employees simply fail to understand what is going on until incivilities escalate to aggression. Moreover, group contexts exacerbate bystanders' tendency to do nothing, due to the Abilene paradox and groupthink tendencies (Namie & Namie, 2000). (For related discussions, see Chapter Eight on pluralistic ignorance and Chapter One on subgrouping.) It is therefore important to instruct all employees that it is their responsibility to report harassment that they observe, not just harassment that happens to them; to ensure that this becomes a normative and nonstigmatized behavior; and to provide anonymous channels for reporting. Perhaps most important, when leaders receive interpersonal skills or conflict resolution training that provides them with exercises that expand their behavioral repertoires (for example, role playing, perspective taking, simulations), they are more likely to transfer the training back to the context where it is most needed (see Sutton, 2007a).

WHAT YOU CAN DO: INTERVENTIONS FOR REDUCING HOSTILITY IN WORK GROUPS

Now that we know about some important factors that precipitate and sustain hostility in work groups, the important question still remains: What can we do about it? The answer depends on whether facilitators are dealing with a situation where (1) escalated hostility has already occurred and the group needs immediate intervention, or (2) the goal is to improve the functioning of the group and organization to ensure that hostilities do not occur in the first place. Of course, even if the situation requires immediate intervention to address a case of bullying, the ultimate goal should be to design a long-term solution for the prevention of hostility. We begin by describing the scenario where a facilitator is brought in to avert an immediate crisis situation, and then turn to the longer-term solution.

Immediate Intervention

Facilitators are commonly called in to "fix" a difficult group once the conflict has moved beyond step 3 in the sequence of escalation described in Exhibit 5.1. In this scenario, a facilitator's first priority is to stop the harassment. Despite the urge to point fingers, facilitators must protect the stigmatized employee from getting further attacked, blamed, or pushed out of the work context (steps 4–5, Exhibit 5.1). Facilitators should listen nonjudgmentally to all sides of the story. They must recognize that the target may have been victimized long-term and that both supervisors and coworkers may have passively (or actively) been involved in sustaining the hostility. Facilitators need to further ensure that the target is aware of counseling resources available to help victims of bullying. Mediation between the bullies (or bully) and the target(s) is often successful; for example, 97 percent of bullying complaints filed in Québec (which has antibullying legislation) are settled at either the early investigation or mediation stage (Hébert & Ravary, 2008). Moreover, facilitators should educate leaders and group members about the nature of workplace bullying and its negative effects on targets and groups. Finally, in severe cases, it may be helpful to encourage a job transfer because it is exceedingly difficult to destigmatize a formerly stigmatized member; most targets have solid job performance records before and after their bullying episode, and only experience complaints in the toxic group. Once the immediate harassment situation has been averted, the facilitator can begin to address contextual and structural factors for the prevention of future conflict and harassment.

Long-Term Prevention Strategy

> One cannot coach a poorly designed team to greatness (Wageman & Donnenfeld, 2007, p. 273).

To effectively prevent the development of hostile groups, each of the precipitating and sustaining forces that we discussed (see Figure 5.1) needs to be addressed. Although harassment is witnessed and experienced in relationships, it is not at the level of group interpersonal processes where interventions may be most effective. In fact, research suggests that interventions against interpersonal conflicts should take the opposite direction of the order in which we have discussed the group factors (Wageman & Donnenfeld, 2007). More specifically, an effective prevention strategy should ensure that the organizational context and supporting group structures are addressed before attempting to change any interpersonal processes. By addressing the organizational context and structural factors, it is possible to build group contexts where interpersonal hostility will not occur in the first place. That is, the goal is to design healthy groups rather than to focus solely on providing resources and recourse for victims to cope with the stressful experience once it has occurred (see Bell et al., 2002).

The first step of an effective long-term prevention strategy is to ensure that the organizational and group contexts are supportive of the change initiative (Hoel & Giga, 2006). To avoid the intervention being seen as "just another HR initiative," the management team needs to be an advocate for it and to introduce it as an important part of the organizational vision or culture (Schein, 1985). The intervention can be framed more broadly as a "respect" or "healthy workplace" initiative. Organizational policies, practices, and informal norms must be implemented in alignment to ensure that no mixed messages are sent. Consistent with the discussion in this chapter, it is important to ensure that policies are clear regarding the unacceptability of disrespectful and demeaning treatment, that the performance management process rewards collaboration, and that there is genuine adherence and ongoing communication regarding respect.

Next, it is important to address the structure of the group (Wageman & Donnenfeld, 2007) to ensure that members have clear boundaries, roles, and direction toward which they should interdependently work. The group needs to be supported with sufficient resources and an appropriate group composition to prevent the exacerbation of conflict due to work overload or harmful competition. Coaching regarding the group's task processes can be beneficial for improving strategy and skills in the group. Many conflicts emerge and escalate due to power struggles, unclear roles, or poor leadership, so hostilities can be indirectly reduced by addressing these structural elements.

Finally, once these first two steps have been successfully carried out, the group can be coached on its interpersonal processes. Conflict process coaching, which involves techniques to reduce relational conflicts while maintaining constructive debate (Wageman & Donnenfeld, 2007), can be beneficial for directly addressing conflict and mistreatment. Trust-building exercises, role playing, and training on conflict management and effective communication can be beneficial. Keep in mind, however, that interpersonal interventions are often ineffective if structural or contextual problems are not addressed first, so conflict process coaching is best treated as a final point of intervention.

This prevention strategy requires high investments of time and energy, yet if the intervention is successfully carried out, the benefits are countless in terms of improved employee well-being, satisfaction, and productivity.

chapter
SIX

Diversity by Design: Creating Cognitive Conflict to Enhance Group Performance

Michael Cassidy

This chapter begins with a description of two groups, whose many differences illustrate the main points of this chapter.

THE SYSTEM SELECTION GROUP

Several years ago, my colleagues and I were asked to facilitate a group whose task was to select a telecommunications system that would be used to offer a new business service. The decision that the session could not exceed one day had been made. As well, all but two system options had been eliminated from consideration: system A and system B. Both systems were capable of satisfying technical requirements, but each had unique strengths and weaknesses. The stakes were high. The unit responsible for the system selected would likely gain in budget, personnel, and prestige. We selected a multiattribute utility analysis approach (MAU) to structure the evaluation of the two systems. MAU decomposes overall utility into a hierarchically structured tree, comprising criteria and attributes. The relative utility of each level of the hierarchy is expressed numerically as weights.

Working in consultation with the client, attendees were selected on the basis of their knowledge in key domains (for example, engineering, operations and maintenance, marketing); decision-making authority; and organizational affiliation. In essence, attendees came from two matched groups, one representing system A and the other system B. Attributes such as implementation and operating costs, service speed, flexibility to grow with emerging needs, and so forth were defined, reviewed, and vetted by the client and participants prior to the face-to-face meeting.

At the start of the session, we reviewed the criteria to ensure that everyone held consistent, operational definitions. The group agreed on working utility weights, retaining the option of conducting sensitivity analysis later using modified weights. System A and system B were then assessed against each attribute. Approximately seven hours after the meeting began, the session ended with unanimous support for the selection of system A. One attendee representing system B remarked that although he was disappointed that the system he was representing was not selected, he thought the process to be fair, adding that he believed he would be able to justify it to his senior management, supported by documentation developed at the session.

THE MICROCOSM GROUP

Within a large corporation, two organizations, Alpha and Beta, were identified by executive management as performing essentially identical functions; as a result, the two were merged, with the expectation of enhanced efficiency. A new director was named; this individual had a strong technical background, management experience limited to oversight of a laboratory with a half-dozen scientists, and no prior association with Alpha or Beta. The newly integrated management team of the new organization was directed, as part of its charge by executive management, to select and promulgate best practices from each of the two organizations.

A small external consulting organization was secured by the director to help facilitate the transition. The merger had resulted in widespread vocal dissatisfaction within the new organization. Resistance to change and suspiciousness of those from the "other side" were evident from those who had come from both Alpha and Beta. The consulting organization designed and facilitated a two-day retreat for all managers, largely devoted to team-building exercises with no direct relevance to the issues the group was facing. On the day following the retreat, members returned to their regular responsibilities with only one apparent demonstrable difference: cynicism had increased. Perceiving a rapidly deteriorating situation, the director accepted the consulting organization's recommendation to form an ongoing working group, representative of the entire organization. The group was named the Microcosm.

Over the course of the next twelve months or so, the Microcosm met weekly for several hours to discuss issues. The fifteen people invited to join the group had been selected to represent diversity within the organization, as defined by race, ethnicity, tenure, age, organizational unit, and hierarchical level. The consultant who had recommended forming the group facilitated it. Her approach to facilitation was desultory. After suggesting a topic or two, she let the group talk with virtually no intervention except when personal affronts reached some unspecified threshold. For example, when asked by a frustrated attendee, "What are we doing?" she responded, "What do *you* think we are doing?" Although the consultant observed at the initial meeting that the sessions were not private, she recommended that members not convey to others in the organization anything beyond the names of the topics being discussed. The recommendation was, for some time, a de facto rule to which group members abided.

The group had no specific mission beyond helping the organization "heal." Several initial attempts by members to secure from management a more specific charter were unsuccessful. The consultant responsible for designing and facilitating the group met regularly and privately with the director, advising him what to do. She publicly derided the need to develop a more specific group charter, and the group worked without criteria against which to evaluate progress. Absenteeism was frequent, and it increased over the year the group existed. Some attendees periodically used the group as a forum for vitriolic tirades against particular organizational units and persons. Passive-aggressive behavior was not uncommon. Some members attended largely to appease management while actively avoiding participation.

THE MEANINGS OF DIVERSITY

It would be easy but incorrect to offer a simple explanation for why the system selection group was, by all apparent accounts, a success, whereas the

Microcosm was largely a failure, and I harbor no illusions about the scientific accuracy of my conclusions. Nonetheless, the groups provide interesting case studies with which to examine factors that might strongly influence a group's functioning. In the sections following, I consider some of these factors, with particular attention to the diversity of group membership.

The *American Heritage Dictionary* (Morris, 1982) defines diversity as "1a. The fact or quality of being diverse; difference. b. A point or respect in which things differ. 2. Variety; multiformity." Logically, for diversity to exist in a set, the elements of the set must to some demonstrable extent differ or vary from one another. That they must be unlike in one regard or another begs the question, in *which* regard(s) should they be assessed for homogeneity or heterogeneity? In the popular media, diversity implies differences in race, age, gender, and other, largely perceptible differences among people. In recent years, however, diversity has assumed more nuanced connotations (for example, Chapter Eighteen of this volume; van Knippenberg & Schippers, 2007). This emerging vantage, while retaining as relevant perceptible differences, is broader in scope, embracing a wide range of imperceptible psychological and cognitive attributes including, for example, attitudes, values, and knowledge. One goal of this chapter is to argue that when narrowly defined, diversity will not necessarily enhance group performance; indeed, it might unintentionally foster interpersonal conflict that detracts from a group's performance.

Over the past decade or so, I have been asked to conduct what are sometimes referred to as diversity audits for several organizations. A diversity audit is concerned, in large part, with calculating the proportions of persons representing different groups (ethnic, racial, gender, and so on) who are entering, leaving, and being promoted at organizational and unit levels. Initially, the task seemed relatively unambiguous, and amenable to objective quantitative analysis. It was, for example, relatively easy to calculate the rate at which Hispanic women were being promoted from one level to the next over a specified time period. Increasingly, however, what at first appeared straightforward became increasingly complex and methodologically murky. For example, I began to question the logic underlying the definition of the units of analysis such as race and ethnicity, and to question potential limitations of these definitions as they pertained to organizational performance. When I began work in this arena, I was unaware of an ongoing and sometimes contentious debate within parts of the academic community as to whether race is a biological or social construct.

Table 6.1
A Comparison of Traditional and Nontraditional Perspectives on Diversity

	Focus	Goals	Sample Metrics
Traditional	Legal	Redress past injustices related to race, ethnicity, gender, and so on; ensure nondiscriminatory practices	Legal compliance
	Ethical	Ensure fairness, inclusion, developmental opportunities for all; recognize the value of a diverse workforce	Assessment of trends within the organization over time benchmarking against comparable employers
Nontraditional	Functional task capability	Optimize staffing to facilitate task execution in support of organizational mission and goals	Organization-specific task requirements; "getting the job done"

As I searched for answers in the literature, debates such as these became increasingly salient.

Table 6.1 summarizes and compares traditional and nontraditional perspectives on diversity. Although the unit of analysis that stimulated it was organizational, it is equally if not more pertinent at the group level, as I will argue shortly.

The traditional approach to diversity comprises two foci: legal and ethical. In a number of countries, including the United States, laws have been enacted to counter discrimination in the workforce. Such laws have arisen largely in response to discriminatory practice. For example, in the United States, Title VII of the 1964 Civil Rights Act was enacted in response to forms of discrimination based largely on perceptible, or surface-level, differences among people. Section 703 states that it is unlawful for an employer to "limit, segregate, or classify his employees or applicants for employment in any way which would deprive or tend to deprive any individual of employment opportunities or otherwise adversely affect his status as an employee, because of such individual's race, color, religion, sex, or national origin." The classification scheme on which discrimination is predicated has thus become, de jure, the classification basis for its response. Evaluating organizational diversity from this perspective is essentially equivalent to assessing the degree to which the organization is in legal compliance.

Numerous organizations have made public commitment to exceed legislatively mandated requirements and to adhere to policies and practices guided by an egalitarian ethos, namely, to provide all organization members the opportunity to develop professionally and realize their individual potential. Ample evidence of this exists on many corporate Web sites. Inherent in these espoused commitments is a recognition of the value of a diverse workforce, albeit a recognition still largely predicated on perceptible, surface-level diversity, sometimes broadened to include, for example, sexual preference. Offices of diversity have emerged as distinct units within Equal Employment Opportunity (EEO) offices, or as independent diversity offices. Diversity audits, including the calculation of statistics to assess patterns in hiring, promotion, turnover, and so forth, are segmented by biodiversity categories. The organization might enact policies and procedures aimed at encouraging managers to develop diverse work groups or establish policies aimed at increasing the representation of minorities at organizational levels in which they are proportionally underrepresented.

Although I accept, a priori, the value of initiatives arising from legal and ethical foci as necessary, the question of whether these foci are sufficient to improve organizational performance is unresolved. As summarized in this chapter, empirical evidence indicates that they are likely not to be adequate. What is labeled in Table 6.1 as functional task capability refers to diversity defined in light of mission-specific goals. From this nontraditional perspective, the definition of diversity is grounded in group and organizational goals; the meaning of heterogeneity is a function of those differences salient to facilitating the organization's mission. When assessing diversity from a traditional perspective, the organization is likely to be the appropriate unit of analysis. Given the task-specific nature of organizational and ad hoc groups, however, the relevance of functional task capability assumes prominence. The contributions arising from differences is an acute issue.

The bulk of the research conducted in approximately the past quarter century has operationalized diversity similar to that of the popular media; that is, it has examined diversity as it is perceptibly manifested (gender, race, and so on). These largely observable attributes are sometimes referred to in the literature as examples of surface-level diversity, demographic diversity, or biodemographic diversity (for example, Phillips & Loyd, 2006). By contrast, more recent research has begun to investigate deep-level diversity, referring to attitudes, values, opinions, information, and the like (for example, Harrison, Price, & Bell, 1998; Cunningham & Sagas, 2004; Jehn, 1995). The shift in empirical emphasis was spurred in part by the inherent methodological problems associated with using demographic variables as predictors of outcome at the organizational or group level (Lawrence, 1997); although these demographic variables are simple in definition, they are not particularly precise in their operational boundaries, nor are they particularly effective surrogates for differences in internal states (for example, Priem, Lyon, & Dess, 1999).

Surface-Level Diversity and Group Performance

Another reason for the aforementioned shift in defining diversity arises from the findings that have emerged from surface-level diversity research. When the impact of surface-level diversity is examined at the team level, the results are consistent: with few exceptions, there is virtually no evidence to support a positive relationship between surface-level diversity and group performance. Cunningham and Sagas (2004), for example, studied the impact of both surface-level and deep-level diversity variables on employment satisfaction and stated intent to remain with the organization, and reported that ethnic dissimilarity was unrelated to the criterion variables.

In my opening examples, membership in the Microcosm was carefully considered by the consulting team that designed it. The racial, ethnic, and gender composition of the group was intended to reflect the proportions that existed in the entire organization. So also, attention was paid to ensuring representation from all units and employment levels. To what extent was this selection strategy appropriate? The Microcosm group was formed in response to a merger of two organizations with different policies and practices, and with an executive directive that implied winners (best practices) and losers. There was no evidence that race, ethnicity, or gender were related to dissent within the organization. By contrast, each member of the system selection group was selected largely on the basis of the person's knowledge about and ability to represent a key functional aspect of each system. The surface-level diversity criteria used in selecting Microcosm members was not salient; the criteria used to select members of the system selection group were directly pertinent to the group's task.

As part of a methodologically rigorous meta-analysis of research on the relationship between team diversity and team outcomes, Horwitz and Horwitz (2007) examined seventy-eight correlations, representing more than a thousand subjects from thirty-five peer-reviewed articles published between 1985 and 2006. The studies examined in the meta-analysis related to the relationship between biodemographic diversity (that is, observable and categorized) and the quality and quantity of team performance. The authors examined as well the relationship between task-related diversity (acquired attributes such as functional expertise, education, and tenure in the organization), and the same outcome variables of quality and quantity. Their principal finding related to surface-level diversity was that "bio-demographic diversity exhibited virtually no relationship with the quality of team performance" (p. 1001). With a single exception largely unrelated to the topic at hand, the results and conclusions were virtually identical when the authors controlled for theoretically based moderators (task complexity, team type, task interdependence, and so on) and three methodological moderators (setting, type of criterion report, and criterion measure type).

The research has consistently found that surface-level diversity does not have a positive impact on group performance. Might it have a negative impact? Phillips and Loyd (2006) investigated the impact of surface-level and deep-level diversity on team performance, and reported that surface-level similarity among members engendered an expectation of homogeneity in deep-level diversity as well. That is, similarity in appearance might engender an expectation of similarity in perspective. When this expectation was violated, dissenting persons from the social majority exhibited surprise and irritation with those with whom they shared surface-level similarities rather than with those different from them on a surface level. The authors remark that "[c]onventional wisdom assumes that diversity is beneficial to groups because people who are 'different' bring different perspectives to the table. Although this is sometimes true, this assumption implies that the person who is different always brings a different perspective to the table" (p. 158). van Knippenberg, De Dreu, and Homan (2004) argue similarly that bias toward one's subgroup may adversely influence group functioning. The diversity criteria used to select members of the Microcosm were likely to have had no positive impact on group functioning, but they might have inadvertently introduced a negative factor, fostering a stronger identification of persons within each subgroup with one another than with the Microcosm and, in turn, with the organization from which it was formed. Before considering the topic of how diversity might be beneficially defined, I turn briefly to the topic of deep-level diversity.

Deep-Level Diversity and Group Performance

Whereas the meta-analysis of Horwitz and Horwitz (2007) largely revealed that surface-level diversity and group performance were not related, their investigation into the relationship between task-related diversity and the quality and quantity of group results was substantially different. Task-related diversity (for example, variation in members' task-salient knowledge, functional expertise, and organizational tenure) was found to be positively correlated with both the quality of what the group produced and the quantity of its outcomes. These findings, the authors wrote, "suggest that diversity in teams can potentially provide organizations with competitive advantages if they consider these results in determining the composition of teams while discarding a simple, myopic understanding that team diversity has a uniform effect on team outcomes" (page 1009). This conclusion is echoed in a review of peer-reviewed psychological research on the topic of diversity published between 1997 and 2005 (van Knippenberg & Schippers, 2007). The authors suggest that potential benefits might emerge from a more thorough consideration of four issues: better linking of diversity effects by diversity type; moving beyond demographic and functional diversity; conceptualizing diversity as more than simple dispersion; and explaining diversity outcomes as interactions rather than additive effects.

Although deep-level diversity has the potential to contribute to group performance, there is evidence that performance is higher in groups whose members have shared rather than diverse values. Reflecting on finding a positive relationship between task conflict and performance but a negative relationship between interpersonal conflict and performance, Jehn (1997) wrote, "For a team to be effective members should have high information diversity and low value diversity. For a team to be efficient, members should have low value diversity. For a team to have high morale (higher satisfaction, intent to remain, and commitment) or to perceive itself as effective, it should be composed of participants with low value diversity."

Although the literature reflects a shift in the fundamental meaning of diversity, it has not resulted to date in a universally accepted conceptual structure. As an illustration, Harrison and Klein (2007) proposed a diversity typology with three levels (minimum, moderate, and maximum) and three types (separation, variety, and disparity), in an effort to distinguish forms of diversity. Separation, drawing from McGrath, Berdahl, and Arrow (1995), refers to differences among people related to values, beliefs, and attitudes. Variety relates to qualitative differences in knowledge, skills, and abilities among people. Disparity relates to variation in such dimensions as power and prestige. In their investigation of the relationship between diversity and group performance in a software environment, Liang, Liu, Lin, and Lin (2007) reported that diversity in knowledge among group members was positively related to performance, whereas diversity in the values held by group members adversely affected interpersonal relationship, which, in turn, adversely affected group performance.

Until this point, I have considered deep-level diversity largely as a matter of selecting group members. Although who participates in a group is important to group performance, also important is how group members interact with one another. To take advantage of relevant differences among group members argues for facilitating conflict of a particular type: cognitive conflict.

CONFLICT: COGNITIVE AND AFFECTIVE

Groups are inherently multidimensional, interactive, and nonlinear. At the core of these dynamics is conflict. Stemming from the work of Amason (1996) and Jehn (1995), a distinction is commonly made between cognitive and affective conflict. Cognitive conflict refers to the expression of differing interpretations, perspectives, and attitudes about task elements. Affective conflict (sometimes referred to as relational conflict, as in Chapter Seventeen) pertains to differences attributable to values, emotions, and personal attributes. Although the two forms of conflict may interact in positive and negative ways (for example, Mooney, Holahan & Amason, 2007), in what might be an oversimplified reduction, cognitive conflict appears to stimulate positive outcomes, whereas affective conflict does not. What aspects of cognitive conflict relate to improved group performance?

There is evidence that groups benefit from participating in the elaboration of diverse, task-related information (for example, van Knippenberg et al., 2004; Chenhall, 2004). Although such participation implies the presence of diverse knowledge in the group, it is not the diverse information per se that is beneficial, but rather the exchange among group members operating on that information that has a positive effect. Creating an environment in which such elaboration occurs requires mutual trust in members' abilities, knowledge, and perspective. Although cognitive trust can positively impact the outcomes of cognitive conflict, it may also lower affective trust and adversely affect performance (Parayitam & Dooley, 2007). Other research, however, has generated different results. Mooney et al. (2007), for example, found a positive relationship between cognitive conflict and functional diversity, turnover, and team culture; these variables, however, were not found to be related to affective conflict. Some research suggests as well that affective conflict may be exacerbated by the subgroups emerging from surface-level attributes. For example, as noted by Ilgen, Hollenbeck, Johnson, and Jundt (2005), a group of four persons—composed of two women and two men, two of whom are Caucasian and two African American, and two from marketing and two from operations—will have stronger subgroups if both women are African American and come from marketing. In their review of the literature on teams, Ilgen et al. (2005, p. 526), noted that "Teams learned best when there were a moderate number of weak subgroups." Attempts to reduce subgroup strength through recategorization (integrating multiple groups into a single group), however, may not be successful in reducing intragroup bias (Cunningham, 2006). The use of structured techniques has been proposed as one approach to engendering productive cognitive exchange (for example, Parayitam & Dooley, 2007). Kerr and Tindale (2004) suggest, on the basis of their review of a number of investigations, that interventions intentionally designed to counter members' "hidden profiles" (unexpressed preferences resulting in excluding select information from discussion) should be considered. Examples of such interventions include training members to explore additional information; ensuring that all pertinent information is brought forward by assigning group members responsibility; and separating the task into information sharing, integration, and decision.

THE SYSTEM SELECTION AND MICROCOSM GROUPS: A RECAP

The membership of the system selection group was essential to its success, and membership criteria were predicated on task-salient diversity. It was necessary to have persons with sufficient knowledge and expertise to engage in evaluative dialogue about the two systems. It was also necessary for all pertinent functions to be represented in the group. For example, had operations and maintenance not been represented, those domains might have escaped scrutiny. Even if they had been considered by members who lacked expertise in those domains, the results of the group's deliberations might have lacked validity.

A second factor contributing to the apparent success of the system selection group was the use of an evaluative structure that encouraged cognitive conflict. Each attribute agreed to by the group as pertinent was systematically considered on the basis of fact, where possible, and on the basis of judgments openly stated and actively debated. The presence of a specific purpose of the session provided a fertile environment for highlighting differences and systematically assessing the positive and negative aspects of those differences. As a third factor, the highly structured nature of the session offered little opportunity for personal vitriol. Had it emerged, the facilitators were prepared to question the relevance of the statement and turn the group's attention back to the analytic task at hand.

As previously suggested, the criteria used to select membership for the Microcosm was largely irrelevant to the group's ambiguous goal of healing. Arguably, functional representation was germane, as was hierarchical representation. The merits of trying to ensure that the membership of the Microcosm physically resembled the population it was intended to represent, however, are without foundation. To what extent did the Microcosm's structure encourage conflict, and of what type?

The Microcosm's structure was, in essence, a lack of structure. Lacking a clear purpose, there was no impetus to drive development of a task-salient structure. Cognitive conflict was serendipitous and infrequent. The format did permit, perhaps even encouraged, interpersonal conflict. By allowing the group to move among topics and levels of detail, the facilitator seemed to be embracing the view that this apparently aimless wandering would ultimately result in a relevant and previously unrealized insight among group members. Acting in a somewhat secretive manner engendered suspicion across the organization. In the end, the Microcosm seemingly only exacerbated the organization's problems.

A FRAMEWORK FOR DEFINING DIVERSITY

In this section, I present a framework to assist in defining salient diversity within the context of the specific and general missions of groups and organizations, respectively. In particular, it facilitates how one might define the nontraditional diversity dimension reflected in Table 6.1.

Groups vary widely in their tasks and their relationship to organizational missions. In Table 6.2, entries under the heading Group's Mission, Function, and Tasks are illustrative. Using an example that is elaborated later in the chapter, I have listed some purposes for which a group might be formed, ranging from those more common, such as strategic planning and resource allocation, to more specialized activities, such as market research in a geographic region with which an organization might have no experience. The descriptors that populate this column should emerge from the particular purpose of a specific group and context. In Table 6.2, I have included some illustrative details based on the later example.

In Table 6.2, the three columns under Group Members' Salient Attributes, Skills, and Knowledge represent an attempt at a set of categories by which diversity of group membership might be assessed: innate, developmentally and incidentally acquired, and intentionally acquired characteristics. Although the attributes, skills, and knowledge represented in the three columns will be sufficient for most organizational settings, further breakdown might be needed for unusual circumstances. For example, a governmental covert intelligence organization might profit from distinguishing between attributes acquired developmentally and incidentally, those of the latter category being potentially more suspect to detection. Each of these three categories is described more fully in the next sections.

Innate

Innate attributes are determined largely by biology and comprise surface-level attributes, such as gender, height, and skin color. Although this dimension will have limited applicability for most organizationally sponsored task groups, its importance, when salient, may be substantial. A law enforcement agent working

Table 6.2
A Framework for Defining Task-Salient Diversity Needs

Group's Mission, Functions, and Tasks	Group Members' Salient Attributes, Skills, and Knowledge		
	Innate	Developmentally and Incidentally Acquired	Intentionally Acquired
Strategic planning		Knowledge of past successes and failures; awareness of organizational politics acquired through tenure; ability to discriminate among potential external alliances; and so on	Skills in selecting and applying appropriate strategic planning models to assess potential market mix and so on
Market feasibility in Saudi Arabia	Arabic lineage; gender; and so on	Nuanced understanding of Arabic culture resulting from extensive experience living in a Arabic communities	Arabic language proficiency; marketing and sales knowledge and skills
Budget planning and allocation		Tacit understanding of where reallocation of resources is genuinely feasible, based on tenure with the organization	Knowledge of project-specific budgets, schedules, and the relationship of these factors to overall mission

covertly to infiltrate a group whose identity was based on an ethnic characteristic, for example, would obviously need to share ethnic characteristics with the group. This dimension, although somewhat similar to the Equal Employment Opportunity Commission classification scheme in use in the United States, is also quite different. That scheme, arising from legislation, classifies persons as "white" whether they are Swedish, Italian, Saudi Arabian, or Iraqi.

Developmentally and Incidentally Acquired

This category encompasses those characteristics acquired as part of the normal maturation process, or acquired through exposure to and experience in a given milieu. It is evidenced by such elements as language proficiency, dialectic variation in speech, and tacit knowledge of cultural norms and taboos stemming from being raised in a specific environment or developing as a function of being a member of a particular organization or practicing a given profession.

Intentionally Acquired

This group represents skills and knowledge developed as a function of deliberate intent, and is illustrated by such things as academic degrees, certifications, and licenses.

AN ILLUSTRATION OF THE FRAMEWORK

Whereas the descriptions of the system selection and Microcosm groups were based in real events, the example used here is fictional and unrealistic in its simplicity. I trust that you will permit some unlikely departures from reality. For example, in the following scenario, the three groups are assumed to be operating concurrently. In reality, they might well operate to some extent consecutively, and have formal linkages not here assumed.

A large, for-profit U.S. organization is starting three concurrent initiatives. A group approach has been selected for each initiative. The initiatives pertain to strategic planning, investigating the potential market in Saudi Arabia for a product in development, and budget planning and allocation. What attributes might be salient for selecting members for each group?

Strategic Planning

Were this a community planning group, potential members' innate attributes would likely be pertinent. In this example, however, such attributes are unlikely to be relevant. By contrast, those characteristics acquired through tenure—for example, an understanding of the organizational politics, shareholder preferences, and past organizational successes and failures—would be important. Representative persons with such incidentally acquired knowledge would bring to the group both applicable content knowledge and, particularly for senior members, the meaningful involvement necessary for buy-in and support. In addition, persons with knowledge and skills from all relevant areas within the organization would be required to have a role, including finance, marketing, and HR.

Market Feasibility in Saudi Arabia

Here the task is to investigate potential market feasibility in Saudi Arabia for a new product. Persons with acquired skills and knowledge in marketing, sales, and the language and culture of Saudi Arabia would need to be involved in this initiative. The organizational knowledge that accompanies with experience might contribute to the group's success as well. However, the knowledge that some employees might have acquired in Arabic language and culture, though useful, pales in comparison to what someone inculcated in the Arabic culture would bring to the effort. Persons with such characteristics would likely have an advantage over those with different personal histories in interacting with Saudi nationals; they would be better prepared to correctly interpret subtle nuances of interaction.

Budget Planning and Allocation

In many ways, this initiative would benefit from having group members with the same characteristics as those working on the strategic planning initiative. However, of primary relevance in this instance are attributes in the intentionally acquired category. In particular, persons from each unit whose budget is at stake—with the knowledge and skills needed to present accurate and detailed information about costs, schedules, and projects' relationships to the overall mission of the organization—would need to be directly or indirectly involved.

CONCLUSION

When diversity is defined traditionally, its potential positive impact on group performance is serendipitous at best; at worst, it might adversely affect group performance. As it relates to team functioning, diversity is best defined in light of group responsibilities. Group sponsors and facilitators should be aware of the potential and the pitfalls of failing to consider diversity from this perspective. In some instances, surface-level diversity might be relevant; in others, irrelevant. Worse, reliance on surface-level diversity might obscure the need to incorporate task-related diversity that could contribute to group performance. Facilitators, in particular, should collaborate with organizational sponsors, where possible, to ensure the selection of group members whose diversity best reflects those attributes most pertinent to the tasks the group faces. In addition, facilitators should be conscious of the potential causes and consequences of subgroup polarization.

Group facilitators should aim to stimulate and facilitate salient cognitive conflict arising from the task-related diversity present in group members, while working to manage affective conflict. In designing and conducting groups, facilitators should use tactics that will assist group members in understanding differences among themselves and appreciating the potential value of divergent perspectives.

Finally, group facilitators should be realistic in their expectations. Nothing, not even diversity, is a sinecure.

chapter SEVEN

Facilitating Inclusion: Study Circles on Diversity and Student Achievement

Mark A. Clark and John Landesman

The red-headed woman looked across the room, bewilderment creasing her brow. "But I don't see anyone's color. I thought that's what this is all about."

Some eyes were drawn to the mosaic patterns of the cafeteria floor, while others exchanged meaning among cliques. Hips shifted, frowns danced. Finally, a small eruption: "You don't see . . . ppsshww . . . forget it."

The facilitator, Gloria, grimaced as well. This was clearly an important juncture—a teachable moment, in education parlance. But how could she steer the conversation in the right direction? And what direction would that be?

Group facilitation is a dynamic balancing act, never more so than when the topic involves deeply held beliefs, assumptions, emotions, and uncertainty about both process and outcomes. The facilitator charged with bringing together the members of such a group must be sensitive to both the participants' feelings and the goals of the facilitation (Everyday Democracy, 1998). A push too far, and some participants might opt out of the experience. No push at all, however, could lose the rest or fail to move the group toward the program goal. In the moment described here, the facilitator, Gloria, must assess the group—members' emotions, factions, readiness—and her own state of mind, consider a range of possible responses, then choose a course of action that balances the group dynamic with the need to move them toward their ultimate purpose. In short, Gloria faces a difficult context in which her choice of facilitative structure and process will determine group effectiveness.

This chapter examines the structure and process of facilitating dialogue in diverse groups charged with sensitive, uncertain topics, illustrated through a study circles Program charged with addressing the link between race and student achievement in the Montgomery County Public Schools (MCPS) system. First, we will describe the facilitation context in terms of the general environment, including the area demographics and resources, and in relational terms, issues unique to diverse groups, such as communication difficulties, fault lines, and trust. Next, we will discuss the intended structure of the Study Circles Program, including adaptations for specific geographic areas, age groups, and community needs, as well as the emergent patterns spurred by group interests, power differentials, and community issues. This structure will include considerations of group composition and school-based goals.

Following our look at structural considerations, we will discuss the facilitative process of the study circles. We will offer a set of practices consistent with the group effectiveness framework presented in the Introduction, applied to the Study Circles Program. We describe a menu of techniques, procedures, and facilitative tools; they enable response to emergent issues within a structured program. The section will conclude with an estimate of program impact on participants, students, and the school system, as evidenced through designated metrics and stakeholder feedback.

Finally, we will contemplate how this facilitative structure and process might be applied to different contexts and issues. Many aspects have significant potential for generalized use; for instance, the structure of dialogue-driven small groups could be utilized for policy development, cross-functional product development teams, corporate diversity training programs, or any topic with inherent differences in perspective or experience. Other processes may be more specialized for use in a school context, such as the focus of action planning on programs related to removing barriers to student achievement.

CONTEXT

In the back of her mind, Gloria considered what she knew about moving diverse groups toward a goal. It was apparent that Joyce's resolution to be color-blind—well intentioned and perhaps somewhat innocent—had loosely, but effectively, divided the circle participants into groups based on skin color. Most of the African Americans were surprised, some suspicious, that a fellow parent could state that she didn't notice race. The Latino and white participants' reactions ranged from hesitant agreement to blatant confusion.

The Study Circle Program in Montgomery County, Maryland, brings together school personnel, parents, and students in a structured dialogue on issues relating to race and student achievement. To attain its desired ends of community involvement and improved student scores on educational assessments, the program must overcome difficulties present in its particular environment. Although the particular characteristics of Gloria's scenario above aren't necessarily typical—most of the study circles address the "color-blind" issue, but few of them fracture along a skin color gradient—all study circles in the program encounter challenges related to understanding the experience of diverse others. In this case, there is a difference of opinion as to whether racial differences, especially skin color, can be ignored. Although to be "color-blind" may be an aspiration of members of a dominant racial group, it is a questionable goal for people of color, who may instead choose to vest positive identity in human differences. In addition to these issues inherent in facilitating diverse groups, the overall context here includes the school system and its immediate community, glimpsed further in the next section.

Community

Montgomery County borders Washington DC and includes urban, suburban, and semirural areas. With approximately two hundred schools and 140,000 students, the school district is the largest in Maryland and the sixteenth largest in the United States. Although as recently as 1970 the schools were 95 percent white and 4 percent African American, today there is no racial or ethnic majority in the schools, with 22.9 percent African American, 0.3 percent American Indian, 15.2 percent Asian American, 21.5 percent Hispanic, and 40.1 percent white students. Students come from 163 countries, and nearly fifteen thousand students are enrolled in courses teaching English as a second language. However, as the student diversity has changed significantly, the teaching staff remains predominantly white. Added to the mix is the broad range of economic strata covered by the school district. It is typical for students who live in subsidized housing to attend school with others who live in million-dollar homes.

Although the school district is well funded and regularly places on the nation's lists of top schools, it also has a racial achievement gap. Individual students from all backgrounds compete at the highest levels; however, the average achievement of racial groups varies significantly. As stated in the school system's 2003–2008 strategic plan (Montgomery County Public Schools, 2003), "White and Asian American students significantly outperform Hispanic and African American students in nearly all assessments of student performance. This trend . . . also exists in schools where poverty and language development are minimal."

The MCPS Study Circles Program was implemented to complement other, more "teacher-focused" initiatives to close the achievement gap. The program provides a process for engaging diverse stakeholders in dialogue and problem solving by connecting active community outreach with honest, facilitated dialogue, and in shared action. The Study Circles Program helps schools, first, by providing a process for parents, teachers, and students to develop trust, learn about each other's cultures, and talk honestly about their different experiences and viewpoints. The efficacy of this approach is supported by research, which reports, for instance, that students who make friends across ethnic lines perform better academically (Guzmán, Santiago-Rivera, & Hasse, 2005). Second, the program acknowledges the importance of family involvement in minority student achievement (see Slaughter-Defoe, Nakagawa, Takanishi, & Johnson, 1990), guiding participants through the process of finding common ground on related racial-ethnic barriers, then creating action steps to overcome the prioritized barriers. (A more complete overview of the Study Circles Program's vision, goal, and objectives follows here.)

MCPS Study Circles Program Vision, Goal, and Objectives

Vision: A school system where all students succeed regardless of racial and ethnic background

Goal: To remove racial and ethnic barriers to student achievement in Montgomery County Public Schools

Objectives for individual study circles are to

- Build a unified group of diverse parents, teachers, and students that understands the challenges and benefits of a diverse school
- Create personal and group action steps that address racial and ethnic barriers to student achievement
- Encourage an environment in which racial and ethnic issues are discussed openly and productively

From 2003 to 2008, the MCPS program organized 111 study circles, engaging seventeen hundred participants in over fifteen thousand hours of dialogue, and the program continues its expansion each school year. As impressive as the numbers have been, the success of the Study Circles Program is measured in more than the quantity of participants. At its core, study circles are about the meaningful interaction between diverse stakeholders. Participant data and feedback from evaluations show that the program has been successful in having parents, staff, and students who represent the school's diversity participate together. Said one participant (Landesman, 2008, p. 1), "The parents who were involved in the study circle aren't the usual parents that are involved in everything. This is a different group of parents. And we really became a close group."

Another added (Landesman, 2008, p. 1), "The experience has made a significant difference in the understanding of how a variety of stakeholders view the school and staff. I have established relationships with individuals that will help me provide a more inclusive school environment."

In addition to the specific action plans that are developed in every study circle, there is evidence that participants are personally changed by the experience in ways that positively influence the communication and learning environment at the school. An evaluation reported noted (Wade, 2007, p. 24), "Many principals remarked that the study circle provides a forum for difficult but important conversations, and . . . that those conversations and relationships have led to greater focus and understanding of the impact of race and ethnicity."

Student and Group Diversity

Facilitators in the MCPS Study Circles Program must grapple with the topic of diversity at two levels: (1) helping the participants focus on the experience of the student, including the differential achievement of racial groups and the day-to-day experiences in school, and (2) working with the differences among the study circle participants themselves, which influence interaction, understanding, and the group's ability to achieve coordinated action. For the first level of diversity, evidence for racial disparity exists locally in each school's report of student achievement test scores and discipline records. For example, countywide averages on the mandatory state test for eighth-grade math show that scores of "proficient" or better were achieved by 86.9 percent of Asian American students and 84.6 percent of white students, yet by only 43.7 percent of African American students and 46.1 percent of Hispanic students. At one school where race is not viewed as a particularly egregious problem, discipline records show that African Americans were approximately seventeen times as likely as whites to be suspended in the 2006–2007 school year (17 percent of eighty-one African American, 3 percent of Hispanic, and approximately 1 percent of White and Asian students were suspended). Research in education and psychology generally reinforces these correlations, explaining the differences as products of academic preparation and engagement (for example, Ogbu, 1992), identity (Guzmán et al., 2005; Spencer & Markstrom-Adams, 1990), belongingness (for example, Faircloth & Hamm, 2005), motivational environment (Wigfield & Wentzel, 2007), language use (Collier, 1992), family involvement or value placed on education (Slaughter-Defoe et al., 1990), and teacher preparation (Darling-Hammond, 2000), among other factors. Facilitators can expect the group to have some difficulty in sorting out these many factors, describing what they might mean to their own school, and how best to plan actions to address them.

At the second level of diversity, facilitators can expect to encounter challenges related to the differences among members of the study circles, especially as their sensitivities may be activated due to the uncertain and potentially contentious topics under discussion. Essentially, the same diversity that enriches the dialogue often creates difficulties in arriving at shared meanings. Members from varying backgrounds—racial, cultural, socioeconomic, educational, and further areas of difference—can be expected to have distinctive ways of communicating, such as word choice, nonverbals, tone, and eye contact (see Asante & Davis, 1985; Larkey, 1996). In addition, dissimilar backgrounds may engender differences in viewpoints, assumptions, information exchange, and the ways solutions are constructed (Clark, Anand,

& Roberson, 2000). This effect may be exacerbated when multiple areas of difference—for example, a group containing Hispanic females of a similar age and an older set of white males—solidify divisions between subgroups, causing further communication problems (Lau & Murnighan, 1998). If difficulties within a diverse group are left unchecked, it may suffer increased conflict and lose members over time (see Milliken & Martins, 1996), impeding its ability to make good decisions and to act on them.

Full participation of group members may therefore become more dependent on interventions and task directives by the facilitator. Such intervention is necessary to achieve functional levels of communication (Gouran & Hirokawa, 1996, 2005), in which groups exchange the information necessary to reveal their expertise and make optimal decisions. In the next two sections, we detail the structure and facilitation processes used in the MCPS Study Circles Program, including the role, function, and techniques employed by facilitators to move their diverse groups through information sharing, mutual understanding, and action planning.

STRUCTURE

This was the third weekly session of a six-week sequence, thought Gloria. Is it OK that participants are upset at this point? Is this just the thing to shake them from the comfortable, feel-good conversations on valuing racial diversity that we've had in the first two weeks? Or will the divisiveness prevent them from engaging in further dialogue? Should I intervene, or let the process play out? What can I do to nudge this in the direction of its relationship to student achievement, without preaching or patronizing?

The design of the Study Circles Program maps the general direction of the group experience, giving structure to the interactions of perspectives described in the framework presented in the Introduction. Care is taken to form groups whose members represent the diversity of perspectives in the school, legitimizing the participants in the eyes of the constituent groups that they formally or informally represent. This structure also provides a rational basis for the group experience, setting a specific goal of planning steps toward overcoming racial barriers to student achievement while giving the participants room to define their own specific actions.

Understanding how the sessions fit together helps the facilitators accomplish their goals, guiding the group through a successful growth cycle. Typically, a study circle has between twelve and twenty-three participants who represent the racial and ethnic diversity of the school, meets for six weekly two-hour sessions, and is led by two impartial facilitators from different racial-ethnic backgrounds. Sessions one and two are designed to develop trusting relationships. Sessions three and four are designed to have honest and challenging conversations about race and the impact of race on student achievement and parent involvement. Sessions five and six are meant to develop action steps that will address the racial and ethnic barriers. The role of the facilitator changes slightly, in accordance with the goal of each session. The program is usually spaced with one week between sessions, to allow participants to reflect on their progress, but variations occur according to the needs of each school.

When conflict arises through the dialogue, the facilitator must remember to rely on the planned structure in conjunction with the use of a variety of specific process techniques. For instance, it's no accident that the conflict described in Gloria's vignette occurred in session three. This third session was designed to provoke participants to challenge each other about their views on race, stereotypes, and racism in a way most people would not usually do with people from different backgrounds. It is unlikely that such a challenging issue would come up in the first two sessions, when the structure and process focus more on building relationships and sharing positive differences.

As can be seen, the MCPS Study Circles Program goes beyond superficial dialogue, spurring action through community organization. To accomplish this, the program staff focus their efforts on recruiting community members who do not traditionally participate, winning over school-based decision makers, and readying a cadre of facilitators.

Most of the recruitment is focused on getting parents and students to an information meeting organized for each participating school. (Figure 7.1 illustrates an overview of this procedure.) The county's Study Circles Program staff provides flyers to the schools, which are sent to the local community. Announcements are also made in principal newsletters, Parent-Teacher-Staff Association (PTSA) e-mail lists, informational flyers, and at Back-to-School Night and other local meetings.

Figure 7.1
Overview of MCPS Study Circles Program Structure

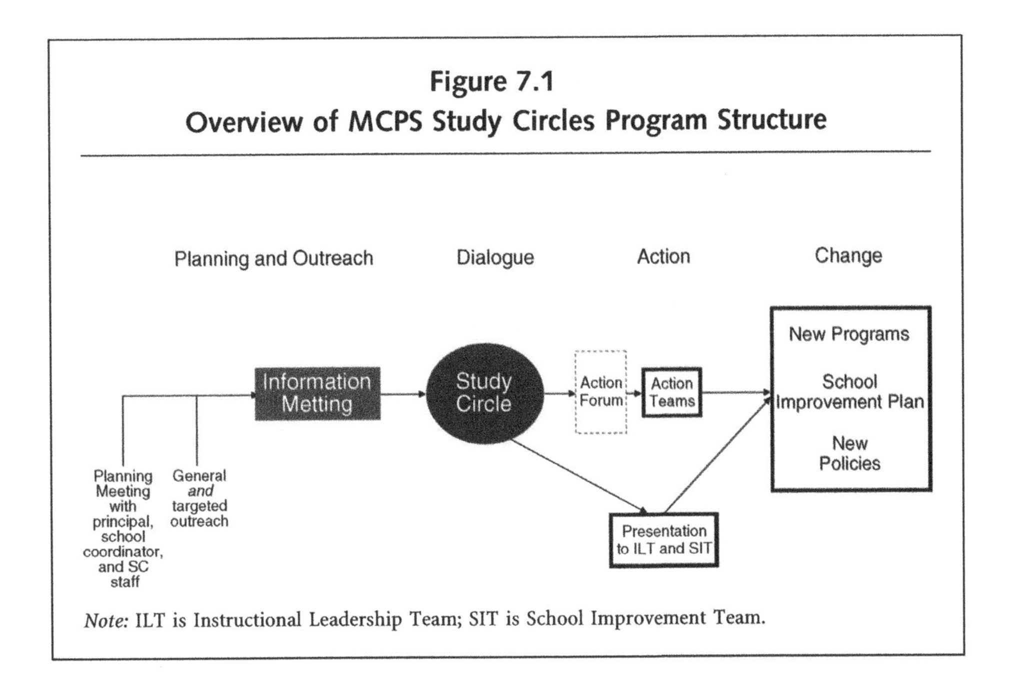

Note: ILT is Instructional Leadership Team; SIT is School Improvement Team.

More targeted outreach is used, however, to reach parents who would not be likely to attend solely on the basis of a flyer. Principals are asked to work with teachers, guidance counselors, and parent groups to create of list of sixty to eighty families who have been infrequent participants in school activities, then to send a personal letter inviting these parents to attend a local Study Circles information meeting. This is followed up with personal phone calls by the county Study Circles staff. Calls are made in the evening, on weekends, or at any time that a parent will most likely be reached. To increase the ease and likelihood of participation from all segments of the community, Study Circles staff members work with each school to provide child care, a light dinner, and multilingual interpreters. At the end of the experiential information meeting, attendees are asked to sign up for the six-week Study Circles Program. Further recruitment efforts are undertaken if the registered participants do not represent the diversity of the school.

The MCPS Study Circles Program developed its own curriculum based on the model created by Everyday Democracy in Connecticut (www.everyday-democracy.org). The curriculum is designed to lead participants to action, each session building on the one before (as outlined in Figure 7.2), under the premise that sharing past experiences will help participants understand one

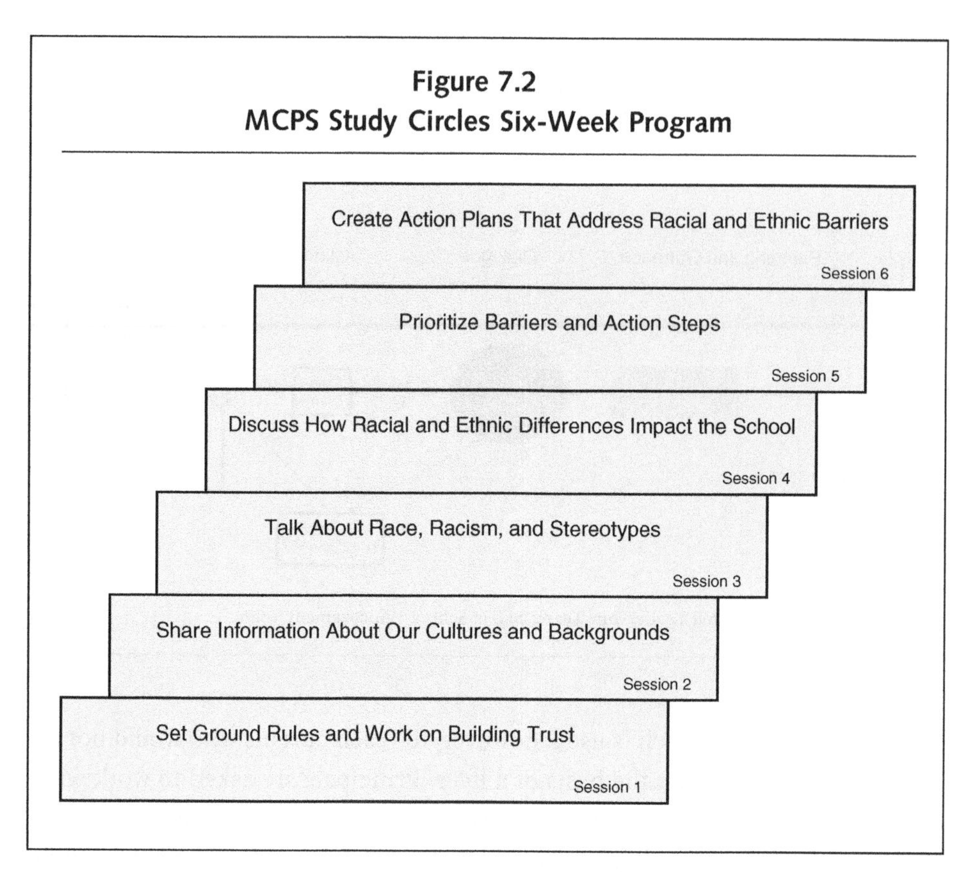

Figure 7.2
MCPS Study Circles Six-Week Program

another's perspective. Further, it is difficult to develop meaningful action plans if participants have not first talked about the racial issues influencing the school. The curriculum calls for impartial facilitators to guide participants, posing questions and using exercises to get them thinking and talking in different ways.

The two trained facilitators leading each study circle are drawn from a pool of over two hundred who have participated in the program's twenty-two-hour facilitator training. All potential facilitators are evaluated at the conclusion of the training to determine if they are ready to cofacilitate in a local school. Facilitators are a mix of MCPS staff, parents, and professional trainers from businesses, organizations, and government agencies in the metropolitan area. Approximately twenty students have also been trained as peer facilitators as of fall 2008.

In 2006, a team of lead facilitators was established to meet the growing demand for study circles and to function in an advisory capacity to professional program staff. This team comprises experienced facilitators who can work with and mentor less experienced facilitators. Lead facilitators also assist in the training of other facilitators and in reviewing and suggesting changes to the curriculum and process.

The study circle facilitator is not meant to be an expert on the issue of race relations and student achievement. Rather, the role of the facilitator is to function as a process expert who manages the discussion while maintaining an impartial stance—not teaching or giving personal opinions, but rather helping the participants express their divergent perspectives and moving them from dialogue to action. This role includes helping the group set up and follow ground rules to govern acceptable behavior within the circle while encouraging participants to examine issues from multiple points of view, not joining the discussion but challenging participants with probing questions when appropriate (Study Circles Resource Center, 2006). The next section of this chapter gives more specific information about lessons, exercises, and facilitator techniques to support the structure and goal of the program.

PROCESS

The standoff over the "color-blind" issue continued. Gloria sensed a bit of anger, a lot of confusion, and some pure exasperation. OK, she thought, they need a nudge—maybe in two parts: first, an opportunity to express themselves, then an orientation toward our overall purpose of student achievement. This will remind participants that this is both personal and at the same time bigger than just their own feelings. After all, this was just one of many resolvable conflicts, and the group should learn how to effectively bring valuable perspectives to the table. She turned to a face that was more sad than angry. "Carole, how are you feeling right now? What would you like to say to your group?"

Within the structure of the Study Circles Program, a planned curriculum sequence including lessons and exercises is used in conjunction with visual aids and facilitation techniques to encourage participation and move the group from dialogue to action. These lessons, exercises, and techniques work to achieve relational coordination, as defined in the group effectiveness framework, by encouraging participation of all members with honest and "open expression of individual feelings and sentiments" (p. xxxiii in the Introduction to this volume). They also facilitate performance from the political perspective, in that they are designed to shepherd the group through a process bringing together various stakeholders to find a solution that works for their specific situation. Finally, these techniques are conducted in the spirit of community building, what Schwarz (2002) referred to as "developmental" facilitation, which goes beyond a basic practice of helping a group solve a problem. Instead, facilitators in developmental mode help the group and its members increase their own skill and efficacy in problem solving—teaching them to fish, rather than simply giving them a meal for the day.

The six sessions have a number of common elements designed to encourage honest participation, provide continuity, and improve the flow and direction of shared information. First, participants are encouraged to arrive early by holding a regular presession period, with snacks provided, during which participants can congregate, refresh themselves, and fill out program paperwork (including attitudinal surveys that are administered again, after the sessions). Chairs are placed in a circle so that, once seated, participants can maintain eye contact in a setting without obvious status differences. The two facilitators generally seat themselves across from one another, in order to keep the focus distributed around the circle.

The room is set up with graphic aids—posters, illustrations, and flip charts to record comments, such that participants "literally see what they mean" (Sibbet, 2005, p. 155). One permanent poster depicts an overview of the six-week structure (see Figure 7.2), referred to at the beginning of each session and whenever necessary to remind the group of where they've been and where they are heading. Other posters revised from session to session include the Parking Lot, for ideas that are worth considering but aren't immediately relevant to the discussion, and Things We Are Already Doing, on which to record positive efforts while avoiding duplication. Illustrations include the Cultural Timeline (explained later in this chapter) and various charts describing school characteristics.

Each session generally begins with some variation of an icebreaker exercise. Most typically, participants complete a Hello Circle in which everyone stands and welcomes each other with a hug, handshake, or other greeting. Smaller breakout groups—three- to four-person subgroups working on similar topics—are used to encourage full participation in various exercises such as those described here. Other aids and techniques, such as videos, brainstorming, group discussion, and posting notes on a board are used when appropriate. Finally, sessions are closed ceremoniously, with exercises such as a One-Word Close where the circle stands as a group, shoulder to shoulder, and sums up their feelings or observations about the session with one word (or as close to it as they can manage!).

The six sessions, structured as noted in the preceding section, follow the general curriculum outlined in the following sections, with variations tailored to each school and group and to the skills of the facilitator.

Session 1

The first session is designed to ready participants for future sessions, without talking much about racial issues or their own school. It begins with the facilitator explaining the program goal and sequence, then guiding participants through the development of ground rules and small group activities that help them feel comfortable, get to know each other, and begin building trust. Creating an adequate level of trust is vital to the future challenges of the group: honest discussion in sessions three and four, and action planning in sessions five and six.

Adding complexity to the relational and political coordination are the multiple areas of difference among members of the study circle. In addition to the racial diversity, most study circles have participants with different levels of education, economic status, proficiency with English, and experience in meetings. There are also potential power dynamics to overcome in groups that often include the school principal, teachers, parents, and sometimes students. The activities in the first two sessions help put participants on the same level, asking them to speak about their past experiences in small groups or in pairs, focusing on commonalities and differences ("Find three things you have in common and three things that make you unique") and descriptions of the community in which each was raised. ("What was the racial and ethnic makeup of your neighbors? What role were parents expected to play in the school you attended as a child?")

Session 2

Session two continues to build relationships through having participants talk about their culture and their experiences—their unique story. This allows individuals to share aspects of themselves that are more complex than what can be immediately seen, which also provides empirical information needed to overcome the difficulty encountered in forming action plans (see the Introduction). The facilitator's role is to create a comfortable atmosphere where everyone can participate, share, and listen. By the end of this session, most believe they have gotten to know their fellow participants on a deeper, more personal level. For example, the Cultural Timeline activity—in which participants are asked to think about and share global, national, personal, and racial events that have had an impact on their lives—helps participants understand past experiences that have shaped the way they view issues today. Examples from recent study circles include

- A parent who walked 372 miles to get to this country.
- A student who was detained at Union Station in Washington DC because the security guards did not believe she attended a private school that had the day off. Her white friends were able to walk right through.
- A teacher who as a student walked miles to a segregated school as the white children rode past her on the bus.
- A teacher who had not been around people different from her until her first year of teaching.
- A principal who was no longer allowed to visit his father's store after riots destroyed the neighborhood following the assassination of Dr. Martin Luther King Jr.
- A parent who kept her child home during the 2002 Washington DC, area sniper crisis because of her memories of living through a civil war in her country.
- A parent who struggles to teach her children about their mixed-race heritage while their social environment treats them as "purely" African American.
- A student who witnessed his uncle being killed in gang violence soon after immigrating to the United States.

Session 3

We all carry records about other groups that prevent us from building effective alliances.

—Brown & Mazza, 2005, p. 34

In session three, the focus and tone of the study circle changes to lead participants to challenge one another about racial issues. Because the participants usually have very different levels of experience discussing race and racism, the session uses three activities to spark conversation, beginning with light conversation in small groups, then becoming increasingly provocative before participants can contemplate politically correct responses.

The first activity has participants reflect on the racial and ethnic backgrounds of the people in different parts of their lives (for example, people at their grocery store, friends whom they have over to their house, the characters in their favorite television programs). The second activity focuses on stereotypes. Participants are encouraged to give three words that they think describe their racial or ethnic group and three words they think others would use to stereotype their group. This activity leads into a dialogue about stereotypes and their impact on the school and community.

The session closes with Does Skin Color Make a Difference? an exercise on relative privilege of race in U.S. society. Participants stand side by side to form a line at one end of a clear room, listening to a facilitator's statements and moving forward if they believe each to be true for them. After hearing and responding to about ten statements, such as "Schools that have large numbers of students who look like me are considered good schools," participants are asked to look around at their peers. In most cases, white participants will have advanced the most; Asian, Latino, and lighter-skin African American participants are in the middle; and darker-skin African American participants are in the back of the room. The activity gives the participants a visual understanding of how skin color can result in different experiences. Maintaining the visual effect and tweaking participants' comfort by having the participants continue to stand in place, the facilitator leads a discussion about white privilege. Gloria's scenario in this chapter describes a conversation that resulted from this activity.

Session 4

Whereas session three promotes discussions of difficult racial issues that most participants do not want to address among people from different backgrounds, session four brings the focus back to the school with activities that push discussion of the racial issues that affect the school. By the end of the session, the group should have identified and prioritized specific racial and ethnic barriers to student achievement and parent involvement. The session begins with a brief look at school performance and disciplinary data that illustrate the racial achievement gap that the study circles were organized to address. Facilitators guide discussion from the empirical perspective by asking participants to comment on *what* they notice about the data.

The next activity, Where Do You Stand? is designed to encourage relational participation across power dynamics and comfort zones. It proceeds by asking participants to interpret data and discuss *why* they look like they do. The activity proceeds as follows:

- Participants straddle a "neutral" line drawn down the middle of the floor. A sign on the right wall reads "Strongly Agree"; one on the left reads "Strongly Disagree."
- A facilitator reads a series of statements, such as "Some students get pressure not to succeed" and "Racism keeps some students from getting access to good programs, while making it easier for other students to get access." After hearing each statement, participants move to the side of the line that represents agreement or disagreement with the statement.
- The use of physical movement has two benefits: it allows participants (1) to "voice" their opinions without worrying about having the right language to explain their position and (2) to make a decision before they can think about whether or not they are offending someone.
- After each statement, the facilitator calls on two or three people to explain why they chose that side. Participants are encouraged to question each other and engage in dialogue.
- Frequently, participants will move closer to the "neutral" line as a result of the dialogue.

The session concludes with a brainstorm, based on the first four weeks of discussion, of what participants see as the most important racial and ethnic barriers to student achievement. After brainstorming, participants vote on the top three barriers to consider in future sessions.

Session 5

In session five, the facilitator's role changes from facilitating relational dialogue to guiding action planning, a difficulty that pertains more to the rational perspective. This requires a more directive approach to facilitation. The session begins with the facilitator asking participants to create a vision of a school without racial and ethnic barriers. They then work in small groups to brainstorm action ideas that would address the barriers. The participation of school staff becomes very important here, especially in regard to how to leverage existing resources and programs. Near the end of the session, the participants bring together the ideas from the various subgroups, voting or otherwise reaching consensus on the top three ideas.

Session 6

In session six, participants begin to plan action for each of the top three ideas, using a template provided by the facilitators. In addition, participants discuss how they will connect the action plan to other committees and initiatives in the school, and how to communicate their experience to the rest of the school community. By the end of session six, the study circle has led to new relationships across groups, increased awareness of the influence of race on student achievement and parent involvement, and devised two or three action plans that address barriers to these aims. Frequently, participants plan to continue their dialogue, informally or formally.

CONFLICT AND FACILITATOR CHALLENGES

Throughout the six-session sequence, a variety of challenges present themselves with regard to the participants' comfort with the dialogue and its associated conflict. Study circle facilitators are trained not to fear conflict among group participants, as healthy debate often requires oppositional stances. Conflict relating to differences of opinion about the topic at hand, referred to as task or cognitive conflict, is therefore necessary to fully address complex issues, whereas conflict of a more interpersonal nature can be detrimental to discussion progress (see Jehn, 1994; see also Chapter Eighteen of this volume). The challenge is thus to achieve an appropriate level of task conflict, minimize interpersonal conflict, and guide the group into understanding the difference. In our role as MCPS Study Circles facilitators, we have noted that racial, economic, and educational differences influence the groups' levels of conflict and willingness to work through it. For instance, participants often seem more comfortable sharing their perspectives in economically homogeneous groups or subgroups. Likewise, it is often easier to get participants talking when they have similar levels of education. When helping the group bridge these zones of misunderstanding, it is useful for the facilitator to be familiar with a variety of process techniques, while being careful not to step into the role of content expert. Some specific suggestions follow.

Spend time doing activities that develop trust and relationships: When pushed for time, facilitators might be tempted to skip the activities that help participants get to know each other at deeper levels, a move that could be fatal to meaningful dialogue. As noted, the first two sessions are devoted to activities that help participants develop their relationships, such as the Hello Circle and structured closings—from One-Word Close to group hugs, depending on the group. For the participants, these activities may make it harder to completely discount someone's opinion, considering they have spent several hours hearing about very personal stories and experiences (see Lasley, 2006). In an interview after the study circle, one principal said, "When you hear some of those experiences, all other differences kind of melt away. . . . [T]he study circle helped make people strong to deal with these issues" (Wade, 2007, p. 10).

Address feelings, not just facts: When there is conflict in a group, participants often hunker down into their own views of the facts, no longer able or willing to hear another person's perspective. In this situation, the facilitator can probe participants to address their feelings about the issue. For example, after the Does Skin Color Make a Difference? exercise and its discussion of white privilege, the facilitators read through a list of feelings, such as *frustrated, hopeless, embarrassed, guilty, empowered, victimized, validated,* and *angry,* asking participants to raise their hands for each that they are feeling at that moment. Through this focus on feelings, the facilitator changes the dynamic of the dialogue.

Bring other participants into the conversation: It is not the facilitator's role to resolve conflicts that arise in a study circle. Rather, the facilitator should engage other participants to address the conflict through such questions as "Does anyone else feel as these two participants feel?" "What are some other perspectives?" or "What is blocking the conversation?" In one study circle, two adult participants were locked in a heated argument. The facilitator turned to the rest of the group and asked why these two did not seem to be able to hear each other. A student participant responded that the adults brought too much history and baggage into the conversation and seemed unwilling to listen to each other's perspective. The response was much more effective coming from a participant than the facilitator.

Use activities that provide a visual expression of the issue: Activities such as Does Skin Color Make a Difference? help participants see the differences in perspective before having any conversation. This is useful because without the activity, some participants would shut down before the dialogue began. Even if no agreement is reached on the issues of racial privilege, the activity illustrates differences in participant perceptions that often fall along racial lines.

Be transparent about the process: Facilitators should not think that all conflicts need to be resolved within the session; it is acceptable, sometimes desirable, for some participants to leave a session feeling frustrated or angry. This is one example of the program structure and process working together, with specific outcomes for each session. To keep the focus on the participant, and mitigate beliefs that the program shouldn't make them feel uncomfortable, the facilitator should inform participants that conflicts may arise, reminding them that the six-week structure will give them opportunity to resolve their discomfort.

Remind participants of experiences discussed earlier: The activities in the early sessions help the facilitators as much as the participants, assisting facilitators in understanding participants' backgrounds and providing experiences that can be brought up later in the dialogue. For example, an activity in session one has participants talking about the communities in which they were raised. During a conflict, the facilitator could remind the participants about that early discussion and ask how participants' different experiences influence the current conflict.

Know the group: Each group will react differently to the same questions and activities. As the sessions progress, the facilitator should gain understanding of how the group interacts, and adjust accordingly. Facilitators can ask themselves the following questions:

- What are the communication styles and patterns in the group? For example, are there participants who dominate the discussions and others who sit back?
- Are there educational differences that influence participation?
- What power dynamics are at play? In many study circles, a teacher is participating with his or her supervisor, or a student with a teacher.
- Is everyone starting from the same historical perspective on race in America? Many newcomers to the United States are unfamiliar with this country's history of race issues.

- Is language an issue? Many MCPS study circles have interpreters for those who do not speak English. It is important not to isolate speakers of other languages in small groups, and to periodically invite them into the dialogue if they are not participating. The facilitator must stay connected with the interpreter, as some concepts are not easily translated.

This list of process techniques is by no means exhaustive. A good facilitator will use a variety of resources, including the group members themselves, to discover tools that work best for their particular group. It isn't always immediately apparent whether the process has been effective, but as the next section shows, the participants' process efficacy and reaction may provide some indication of facilitation effectiveness.

OUTCOMES

In December 2007, MCPS published an evaluation based on data from forty-three study circles conducted in 2005–2006 and 2006–2007, stating that "Findings from surveys and interviews provide evidence that the Study Circles Program is having a positive impact on both the participants and the school communities. . . . Evaluation of the broader impact of the program using measures of school climate, student engagement, parent involvement, and progress on study circle action plans shows positive gains" (Wade, 2007, p. iii.).

The following are some major findings from the evaluation.

Positive experience: Perceptions of the study circle experience were highly positive, both immediately following the six sessions (post-SC survey), as well as two or more months after the sessions ended (follow-up survey). During each of the two years, 90 percent or more of the parents, staff, and students responding to the post-SC survey, and 80 percent of those responding to the follow-up survey rated the Study Circles Program as "Very good" or "Good," and reported that they would tell a friend to participate in a study circle ("Strongly agree" or "Agree").

Increase in understanding others' attitude and beliefs: After participating in a study circle, 92 percent (2005–2006) and 86 percent (2006–2007) of parents and 87 percent and 85 percent of staff reported an increase in understanding others' attitudes and beliefs. A teacher said,

> I didn't understand why one of the parents was always upset or always pushing or always being a certain way towards the teachers.

> Then I heard her talking about her childhood and what her experiences were. That was a huge ah-ha for me. Where she was coming from made so much more sense . . . (Landesman, 2008, p. 1).

Impact on the school community: All twenty-one principals interviewed during the year following their school's study circle reported that progress in the priority action areas had taken place. Schools are implementing their actions in different ways:

- In several schools, action areas were included in the school improvement planning process.
- Some study circles have joined with the PTSA in efforts to reach out and recruit underrepresented parents, as well as to plan school and family activities.
- Some study circles have led to changes in school policy.

A participant said, "I think it made teachers and parents who participated more aware of . . . racial issues that we didn't know we had. And it set us on the path to deal with those issues" (Wade, 2007, p. 13).

Engaging diverse stakeholders: The Study Circles Program has been successful in helping schools engage parents who do not traditionally participate in school programs. In the two years covered in the evaluation, 29 percent of participants were African American, 8.2 percent were Asian American, 25.5 percent were Hispanic, and 32.9 percent were white. Further, participants in 2006–2007 represented fifty-seven different countries of origin and named twenty-four different languages spoken at home. Of the total number of participants in the two years evaluated, 50 percent were parents, 34 percent were school staff, and 16 percent were students.

Understanding and involvement: Sixty-nine percent of parents reported increased understanding of the school system, 70 percent indicated that their participation with the school increased, and 88 percent indicated that their connections with staff or other parents increased. Explained one principal, "The study circle participants are now active in the PTSA. . . . These parents had not been involved in school activities prior to the study circle" (Wade, 2007, p. 24).

Said another, "I feel that more minority parents are becoming involved in school activities and programs. I think it has brought us together and better enabled us to work as a team" (Wade, 2007, p. 25).

IMPLICATIONS

After a cautious start, session four was a watershed success, thought Gloria. There had been a lot of tension built last week, and she'd only allowed a bit to steam out before dismissing the group to simmer for a week. This time, at least, the technique appeared to have paid off. No one had wanted to bypass the feelings of last week, but insisted on discussing it in the cool of a week's contemplation. And what a conversation! Now the group was ready to focus on identifying barriers within the school and plan workable actions to enhance student achievement.

Bringing together persons with disparate perspectives to discuss differences and plan actions poses challenges to the best of facilitators and groups. Such difficulties are not unique to the Study Circles Program, however. When viewed through the group effectiveness model, the set of study circle structures and processes are seen to be special instances of generalized perspectives, which can be tailored to a number of topics and contexts. As such, from both the political and empirical perspectives, study circles bring together the stakeholders needed to adequately define an issue—members of varying racial backgrounds and degrees of involvement in the school system—and legitimize the resultant action plans. These are couched within a well-defined, rational goal system—that of augmenting student achievement—but without easily identifiable means to accomplish the end.

Thus small, issue-driven groups that explore multiple perspectives over a set number of weeks can be effectively employed for a number of topics. For example, a community in Virginia is at the early stages of organizing study circles on immigration. The county recently passed legislation requiring the police to arrest undocumented residents. The legislation has had a wide impact not only on the immigrants but also on the economy, the county budget, and housing. Public debate on the issue has been polarizing and rancorous, with little opportunity to listen to or understand others' perspectives. Organizers believe that a large segment of the population feels caught in the middle. The study circles would be an opportunity to have a productive dialogue on the issue and find common-ground solutions.

Further, the processes used are readily transferable to multiple contexts, from civic organizing to corporate settings. For example, study circle structures and processes can be applied to the task of product innovation in the automobile industry, given a goal of producing a marketable vehicle with a reduced reliance on fossil fuels. With this goal, it would be necessary to build the empirical base of useful resources, such as persons with essential backgrounds or perspectives. The study circle application for this task would be to meet the potential participants on their own turf, speak to them in their own language, provide inducements to ensure their comfort, and assure them that their input is important and valued. This implies that the automotive product development team should seek out perspectives from outside the traditional automotive industry partners—perhaps consulting bioengineers for alternate fuel sources, flight specialists to explore streamlined shapes, or artists to envision what might be aesthetically pleasing to the masses—and go to lengths to understand what the new participants need to get their work done.

Further, the study circles model would suggest that the product development team should plan and implement relational processes that deliberately seek out contrary information, using nonstandard (and perhaps nonverbal) exercises designed to upend the status quo. It would be necessary to stir up conflict, as when challenging participants on conceptions of racial privilege, while keeping any contention focused on the task rather than allowing it to become interpersonal. It may therefore be useful to include modifications of study circle process status checks, such as One-Word Close, to ensure that all participants are still feeling involved and to prepare the manager for any upcoming issues. Finally, participants coming from outside the traditional hierarchy may need assurances that their voices will be heard throughout the discussion. Study circle processes address this in many ways, including recording even those ideas that are not immediately useful and empowering individual members to deliver their concerns to key decision makers of the organization.

In this way, the study circles approach offers broad lessons that may be useful for other groups, topics, and contexts. The key is to get a clear sense of the goals associated with the issue at hand, structure a path to sufficiently address relevant perspectives, and involve the necessary constituents and give them the opportunity to voice their concerns and ideas. Inclusion of members' differences, whether in backgrounds, perspectives, or resources, is thus important to maximizing the potential of facilitated groups.

chapter
EIGHT

Overcoming Sources of Irrationality That Complicate Working in Decision-Making Groups

Dennis S. Gouran

Senator Browne, although eager to meet with the Agenda Committee to answer questions concerning the report of his Faculty Senate Committee recommending changes in the size of the membership to make it a more efficient body, was also a bit apprehensive. He had never before appeared before the committee and was not quite sure what to expect. The members, he had been informed, were to assess the readiness of the report for consideration by the full Senate in its next regular meeting. Instead of receiving questions along these lines, however, Senator Browne found himself on the receiving end of criticisms of the recommendation his committee had reached and the rationale for it. Upon being told by the Agenda Committee that the recommendation was unacceptable and that his committee needed to do more work and come up with something better, he left the meeting completely demoralized and without a clear sense of what the members expected his colleagues to produce. Equally frustrated were members of the Agenda Committee who tried, without success, to convince the majority during the grilling and prior to the vote that it was not the body's responsibility to assess the merits of the recommendation Senator Browne's committee had hoped to take to the Senate floor. One was so outraged that she decided not to stand for re-election.

As this fictional incident illustrates, working in decision-making groups is an experience that many find difficult, if not distasteful to the point of developing what some refer to as "grouphate" (see Keyton & Frey, 2002; Socha, 1997, p. 19), especially when stakes are high and the consequences of choosing inappropriately can be costly. Under these circumstances, one's impulse is to attribute the problems encountered to such causes as incompetence, sinister motivations, and personality characteristics of one or more of the members. To be sure, such sources of influence are often operative and contribute to the frustrations and disaffection of those who see themselves as doing their best to ensure desired outcomes, but without much cooperation from others. In other instances, however, such perceptions are misplaced and serve only to exacerbate tensions among members to the extent that poor outcomes become even more likely, if not inevitable.

There is a more charitable explanation of why decision-making groups often go awry. Its premise is that members, despite their best intentions and desires to reach good decisions, frequently become immersed in communicative processes that are suboptimal, in the sense that they reflect insufficient attention to one or more critical task requirements, insensitivity to sources of interference in their fulfillment, or both, and hence predispose group members to behave inadvertently in a less than rational manner. In the analysis that follows, I develop this thesis more fully in respect to an ongoing group of which I am a member; note ways in which it frequently proves to make life difficult for at least some of its members, not to mention external constituencies affected by it; and examine what forms of facilitative action might serve to bring the members' performance into greater alignment with interests of rational choice.

THE GROUP AND HOW IT IS DIFFICULT

The University Faculty Senate Council meets six times each academic year two weeks in advance of the six meetings of the Senate. Its principal function is to determine the readiness of reports that various other committees seek to place on the Senate agenda for whatever type of action the sponsors wish the Senate to take—for instance, discussion (as in the case of forensic reports), acceptance (as in the case of informational reports), or action (as in the case of advisory-consultative and legislative reports). In this capacity, the Council serves as an agenda committee.

The membership of the Council is fluid. Some voting units repeatedly return the same representatives to it, whereas others exhibit a good deal of change in whom they elect from year to year. The group then is never exactly the same body for any two years in succession, even though in a given term it may more nearly resemble a former manifestation and in another year less nearly resemble any of its predecessors. With variation in the tenure of members and the concomitant mix in any particular term also come a range of knowledge relating to the work of the group and its external constituencies, different proportions of well-formed and barely formed relationships, and considerable diversity in the members' potential for the exercise of influence. The chemistry of the Council is thus continually in flux, which can be a strength, but also a source of difficulty. There are years in which the members function in a highly amicable, effective fashion and others in which they experience both internal strife and difficulties with those whose proposed agenda items they have to consider.

In regard to its role in setting the agenda for Senate meetings, the Council's responsibilities are explicit. On the surface they would seem to leave little doubt as to what is expected of the members and would make behaving in a manner consistent with rational-choice theory (see Beach & Connolly, 2005) a relatively simple matter. The pertinent item in the bylaws of the organization reads as follows: "It [the Council] shall provide a mechanism for Council members' review of all legislative, consultative, and informational reports submitted for the Senate Agenda. Decision on whether or not an item is to be placed on the Agenda for full Senate discussion is to be based on whether a report is adequately prepared and documented" (*Constitution, bylaws, and standing rules of the university faculty senate,* 2009, p. 10). Despite the clarity of the agenda function, the performance of the members is not always congruent with this specification. Following is an overview of how the group can be difficult.

Failing to Satisfy Task Requirements

Depending on its profile and the confluence of the preceding characteristics of the membership at play, life in the Council can prove to be difficult when it comes to fulfilling the function of interest. What frequently occurs in the consideration of proposed items for the Senate agenda is that rather than offer assessments of the readiness of particular items for senators' consideration in subsequent meetings of the Senate, members of the Council begin advancing their personal views concerning what they find objectionable about particular provisions of the legislative and advisory-consultative reports. Surprisingly, they even do this in the case of informational reports, which are not ones for which senators are asked to vote. They merely receive them. It is as if some of those who take issue with the substance of reports, rather than remaining focused on the readiness of those reports, see themselves as self-appointed guardians or as having the responsibility to prevent fellow senators from being exposed to certain matters. This is not their charge and represents a failure on their part to satisfy the requirements of the task.

Making Inappropriate Decisions

When members of the Council who fail to address task requirements prevail, their decisions are more apt to be inappropriate. That is, items for the Senate agenda warranting approval are rejected, and ones that do not satisfy the criterion of readiness may appear on it and unnecessarily consume valuable time in Senate meetings. If the reports that are actually ready make it to the agenda and those that are not fail to, it is more a matter of accident than of the pertinence of Council deliberation.

Creating Intragroup Tensions

If those who are insensitive to task requirements display the tendency repeatedly and in the process contribute to the number of inappropriate decisions concerning the readiness of agenda items, the climate of group interaction often takes a turn for the worse. Other members, resenting diversions, begin to develop a sense of ill will toward the offending parties, a case of task and process conflict producing relational conflict (Jehn &

Mannix, 2001). Future exchanges can also suffer, as those who are upset by the lack of consideration for what the participants are supposed to be doing become more curt, if not belligerent, in how they respond to such individuals. At the other extreme, they may adopt a more passive-aggressive posture that they convey with a thinly disguised air of resignation.

Complicating the Lives of Others External to the Group

In addition to what sometimes occurs in respect to the interpersonal relationships among members of the Senate Council, sponsors of reports may find themselves subject to a good deal of unnecessary additional work, or they may even give up in frustration and decide not to go forward with a report they originally felt worthy of full Senate consideration. Such obstructionism does little to encourage sponsors of reports to invest energy in, and to be as committed to, the work of the Senate as they might otherwise be.

Adversely Affecting the Members' Credibility

In addition to complicating the lives of others, the Council, in being less than rational in the way it makes decisions concerning the readiness of reports for the Senate agenda, can and does make its own life more difficult. It has frequently been the target of charges of elitism, obstructionism, abuse of power, and what Senge (1990) refers to as "political decision making" (p. 60), or the tendency to choose on the basis of who among those external to a group may be approving or disapproving rather than on the basis of evidence and sound arguments. Such attributions do serious damage to the Council's credibility, albeit only temporarily. In my view, members of the Council do not see themselves as acting in a political way even if others do. Insofar as damage is concerned, however, they might as well be, because the end results are the same.

Given the published charge of the Council with respect to approving items for inclusion on the Senate agenda, if the members were acting consistently in a rational manner, what could one expect to observe in their behavior? Most extant models of rational choice (see, for example, Bazerman & Moore, 2009; Beach & Connolly, 2005; Gouran & Hirokawa, 1996, 2005; Janis & Mann, 1977), on the surface, do not neatly fit the sort of task on which I have chosen to focus. Bazerman and Moore (2009), for instance, have decision makers defining the problem, identifying criteria, weighting the criteria, generating alternatives, rating each one in relation to each criterion, and computing the optimum choice. Upon reflection, however, one can extend aspects of these sorts of models to such tasks as assessing the readiness of a piece of legislation for consideration by a body such as a university faculty senate. In the case at hand, one would expect to see the group using previously identified indices of readiness (for example, clarity of the report, completeness of the information, and conformity to approved guidelines for the preparation and submission of reports) to arrive at one in a range of possible judgments, including "Place on the agenda," "Place on the agenda but with specified modifications," and "Do not place on the agenda."

Despite the apparent simplicity in making a rational choice concerning the disposition of reports as to their readiness, members of the Senate Council do not consistently function in a manner that comports with the description, nor do many other groups with which you undoubtedly have experience or knowledge. It is in this sense that they are difficult. The fact that they are is what begs for explanation and is the matter to which I now turn my attention.

WHY SUCH GROUPS ARE DIFFICULT

Although the failure of the members of a decision-making group to function in a suitably rational manner relative to a recurrent task is undoubtedly attributable to a combination of a large number of factors, several appear to have greater significance than others. Particularly noteworthy in my estimation are ignorance of task requirements, misunderstanding of protocols and roles, pluralistic ignorance, ego involvement, status differences, and failures in leadership. Within the framework of this volume, these factors best relate to the category of rational process, the deficiencies in which I trust will become clearly evident as I discuss each in order.

Ignorance of Task Requirements

In *Crucial Decisions: Leadership in Policymaking and Crisis Management,* Janis (1989) notes that a common failing among decision makers is their relative inattention to the issues to be resolved (see also Hirokawa & Rost, 1992). I encounter this problem frequently among students in an introductory course involving group decision making that I regularly teach. For instance, a group that is supposed to be discussing a question of fact such as, "How serious is the problem of climate change?" can easily go off point and focus its attention on what to do about it (a question of policy). This is reminiscent of my earlier observations concerning members of the Senate Council who sometimes lose sight of precisely what they are being called on to do, namely, to assess the readiness of reports for others' consideration, not their agreement with the contents.

It should be fairly obvious that if the members of a group do not understand the requirements of the task they are performing, the likelihood of making an appropriate decision is rather small, but the confusion often does not become apparent to them until late in the process of interaction—sometimes much too late for any corrective influence to become operative. The fact is that far too many of us fail to check early enough on our understanding of what we are supposed to be accomplishing as members of a group, with the unfortunate consequence of wasting time or making decisions that go well beyond what we are responsible for.

Misunderstanding of Roles and Protocols

In their familiar typology of roles, Benne and Sheats (1948) identify three categories: task, relational, and self-centered. Those enacting the first two types tend to function positively in moving the members of a group in the directions their tasks require. In the case of self-centered roles, however, enactment often functions disruptively, not so much because those involved are attempting to perform with malicious intent, but because they see themselves as having the responsibility to control outcomes in a way that serves the interests not of the group and what it is supposed to be accomplishing but those external to it and whom they may see themselves representing. Multiple group memberships, we know, often lie at the base of conflicts within particular groups in which a person's loyalty to other groups unduly influences how he or she behaves in the one having the responsibility to serve larger collective interests (see Folger, Poole, & Stutman, 2009).

The phenomenon I have just noted is, I believe, often operative in the Senate Council at those times when members seem to be steering the body toward recommending that a report not be included on the Senate agenda out of concern that their constituents might find specific provisions or related actions objectionable in some sense. Although this process may lie outside the conscious awareness of the guilty parties, at other times they are fully aware of their motivations. For example, I once participated in a group at another institution appointed to determine whether or not an outside member should be a requirement for the composition of dissertation committees. One of the members made it clear at the outset that he was present to ensure that the committee did not endorse such a policy because those he represented (specifically, the graduate faculty in his department) did not want outside members serving on their doctoral candidates' dissertation committees. However, the committee members had not been appointed to represent their academic units, but rather to determine what was in the best interests of the institution. Despite that, this particular individual took it upon himself to promote the position his departmental colleagues favored independently of its merits, which, in turn, hampered the work of the rest of the group substantially.

Pluralistic Ignorance

Despite the superiority sometimes attributed to groups as compared to individuals and the professed virtues of "collective wisdom" (for example, Surowiecki, 2004), there is a good deal of evidence that groups can and do perform ineptly. When this is the case, especially as related to behaving nonrationally, if not irrationally, one can trace the problem, in part, to what Schanck (1932) long ago identified as "pluralistic ignorance," or as Shaw (1981) notes, the tendency of group members who disagree with what other members are deciding to see themselves as the only ones who do and to think that expressing their opposition "would serve no useful purpose" (p. 444). (See also Harvey, 1974, for a variation he refers to as the Abilene paradox, and the discussion of subgrouping in Chapter One.)

Operating on assumptions like those implicit in the concepts of pluralistic ignorance and the Abilene paradox, those members of decision-making groups who sense that their fellow members have a different understanding of the task but are apparently doing the task correctly (because no one seems to object) may well engage in the sort of self-censorship that Janis (1972, 1982) portrays as contributing to groupthink. Especially vulnerable in the case of the Senate Council would be those newly elected members who, in the absence of indications to the contrary, are likely to presume that those "who have been around know what they are doing" and refrain from checking on the accuracy of their perceptions. This is similar to what Asch (1951) reported discovering in interviews with those taking part in his studies of conformity.

One group of participants experienced *judgmental distortion,* as opposed to *perceptual distortion;* that is, even though they saw other group members as being in error during the performance of a perceptual task, they questioned the accuracy of their own judgments and went along with those making the wrong matches.

Ego Involvement

Citing the work of Festinger (1957, 1964) and his associates, Janis and Mann (1977) point out one of the interesting aspects of decision making: the tendency people have to bolster choices they have previously made even if those decisions prove to be of questionable merit. For example, when members of the Senate Council who have stated their inclinations to exclude items from the Senate agenda have been challenged, they have displayed a level of defensiveness that seems to be out of proportion and certainly out of keeping with the dictates of rational choice.

According to Janis and Mann (1977), participants in the decision-making process may also bolster their preferences both by magnifying their attractiveness and diminishing that of the alternatives. I cannot recall the number of times I have heard a highly ego-involved fellow Senate councilor desirous of keeping an item off the Senate agenda offer some observation such as "I am confident that if this goes forward, our colleagues will almost certainly vote it down," or, in the case of an endorsement, one like, "This is a very important piece of legislation, and we cannot afford to fool around putting off enactment until next year." In such cases, readiness does not seem to enter into the defense of the recommended action under consideration, when in fact that should be the paramount concern.

The sort of behavior I have described surfaces in many decision-making arenas. I see it frequently in group discussions concerning who should be appointed as members of important committees—a responsibility often under the aegis of an organization's "committee on committees." It is not uncommon to witness a pattern of exchange such as "X would be absolutely perfect for this assignment!" followed by "I could not agree more." A person who questions the wisdom of the group under conditions of such unbridled enthusiasm may find himself or herself on the receiving end of some not-so-pleasant feedback, despite the fact that almost all of us can recall instances in which we endorsed the "obvious choice," only later to come to the realization that it was not such a great one after all. Our tendency to bolster, then, can overcome our desire to behave in a rational fashion—that is, to make logically and empirically warranted choices. A useful precaution is to act in line with Janis's advice (1982, 1989) to review all tentative selections or to have "second-chance" meetings for consequential decisions before proceeding to implementation.

Status Differences

Differences in status among the members of a decision-making group often contribute to interactions that run counter to the interests of rational choice in at least two respects. First, we tend to be more susceptible to the judgments of those who have higher status than we do, particularly when the differences are grounded in perceived knowledge and expertise. We tend to defer to the judgments of those we consider to be superior to us in these respects (see Torrance, 1954). Consequently, in the Senate Council, for instance, when someone of relatively higher status wants to keep an item off the Senate agenda, those of lower status, in an "all other things being equal" scenario, are more apt to accede to his or her wishes than they are to those of a peer. I have observed such deference many times when colleagues emphasize differences in knowledge and expertise (for example, "Twenty years of experience tell me that . . ."), even if an objective rendering would in fact show no genuinely salient differences between the individual doing the claiming and the targets of influence in respect to these two attributes.

Differences in status also lead members of groups to overlook, or at least perceive as less serious than it actually may be, deviant behavior of those having relatively high status (Wahrman, 1972). Status seems to afford some individuals entitlements that do not apply to the rest of us. Hence, even when members of the Senate Council are clearly aware that a high-status individual is not in fact assessing the readiness of a report, they are unlikely to mention that. As a result, they inadvertently contribute to some items' unwarranted exclusion from or inclusion on the Senate agenda.

I remember an occasion when certain members of the university administration were eager to have a piece of legislation advance to the Senate for consideration. When one councilor raised concerns about readiness, a more senior member commented that we could not afford to be indulging in "parliamentary niceties." This effectively preempted further consideration of the only issue that was germane at that point. It is difficult for me to believe that other members of the Council saw this conduct as appropriate. Rather, it appears to have been more the case that we were willing to let the behavior go unsanctioned because of the person's status.

Failures in Leadership

During my tenure as a member of the Council, the extent to which diversion from its stated agenda-setting responsibilities has been a source of difficulty has varied substantially on the basis of who has occupied positions of leadership, and more specifically that of chairperson. Ultimately, it is what chairs say and do in response to attempts to control what appears on the Senate agenda that is the critical determinant of whether or not decisions concerning what to include and exclude will be made rationally. Some chairs have been exceptionally tolerant of the sorts of deviant, nonrational behavior I have noted. Others have exhibited a much stronger and consistent tendency to intervene and call attention to the fact that guilty parties are not behaving in line with their charge. However, the distinction is not so simple as whether or not the chair displays laxity or firmness in this regard. How the chair or others who begin to function as leaders express concern is also important.

There is a substantial body of work in the area of leadership in groups and organizations indicating that mere occupancy of a formal position does not ensure that leadership will occur in ways that have desired consequences (see Bass, 1990). Given Northouse's definition of leadership as "a process whereby an individual influences a group of individuals to achieve a common goal" (2007, p. 3), far more critical than occupancy is who actually functions to exert influence—that is, which individuals are in fact responsible for movement toward a desired objective or outcome. We call such participants "emergent" leaders. Sometimes the designated or appointed leader and the emergent leader are one and the same. In other instances, actual leaders are other people. Whatever the case, and consistent with Northouse's definition, as Bennis (2007) observes, "[L]eadership exists only with the consensus of followers" (p. 3). Some individuals seem to be more adept in achieving such consensus than are others.

In the case of the Senate Council, my observation has been that chairs who have been most successful in keeping the members focused on the readiness of items for Senate agendas have manifested the sorts of personal qualities that Zaccaro (2007) has recently identified. These include, among others, such attributes as "cognitive complexity, cognitive flexibility, metacognitive skills, social intelligence, emotional intelligence, adaptability, openness, and tolerance for ambiguity" (p. 10). They also seem to have a good deal of interpersonal skill when it comes to stressing the need to stay on task without becoming offensive. Those lacking such qualities have considerably greater difficulty striking a responsive chord.

WHAT ONE CAN DO TO FACILITATE WORKING WITH DIFFICULT GROUPS

For the tendencies in decision-making groups to become inadvertently caught up in patterns of interaction that contribute to their functioning in a less than rational manner, there clearly is no single solution or panacea. However, there are actions you can take to prevent the difficulty or to counteract it when you begin to sense the unwanted directions in which one or more of the participants are taking a group. These include clarifying the objectives, task, and procedures to be followed at the outset of a discussion; enacting the role of reminder throughout; and, if necessary, becoming a procedural champion or advocate for following appropriate means to the desired ends. Let me briefly touch on each of these measures.

Clarifying the Objectives, Task, and Procedures at the Outset

As much of the earlier part of this chapter reveals, the assumption that those who belong to a decision-making group, merely by virtue of their membership, somehow have a firm grasp on their responsibilities and how they should behave is often a highly questionable one. Rather than operate from that assumption, even in groups having a history of making routine decisions, you are probably well advised to take the precaution of verifying that everyone taking part understands what it is that the group seeks to accomplish, what the task entails, and how the members are to perform it. We know that there is a moderate to strong correlation between the quality of procedures a decision-making group employs and the outcomes it achieves (Herek, Janis, & Huth, 1987; Gouran & Hirokawa, 2005). Hence, such an ounce of prevention, as Seibold and Krikorian (1997) suggest, can yield substantial dividends as the members work their way through the process by establishing boundaries within which participants are apt to remain.

In the Senate Council, on occasions when the chair announces at the start the purpose of the discussion, as well as what does and does not constitute pertinent commentary, it has been clear that the members do a much better job of discharging their responsibilities. There is evidence from different venues suggesting the effectiveness of this sort of tactic when a group has not achieved a very high level of maturity (see Hersey & Blanchard, 1993).

Enacting the Role of Reminder

Despite success with preventive measures, such as the one mentioned in the previous section, one cannot afford to rely exclusively on them for keeping a group on track. It was this recognition that led me some years ago to conceive of leadership largely as a form of corrective action to which I attached the label *counteractive influence* (see Gouran, 1982, 2003b). This form of influence consists of communicative acts that serve to restore movement onto a group's goal path under conditions in which members are departing from it. Such acts are often necessary in substantive, relational, and procedural spheres. For purposes of this chapter, however, it is the procedural sphere that is of the greatest interest.

A particularly pertinent form of counteractive influence involves the simple act of reminding group members of their roles and responsibilities when they are behaving in ways that are not in line with expectations. This form of *procedural enactment* (see Gouran, 2003a) is a corrective measure. In a study of decision-making groups that include members trained to offer such "reminders," digressive tendencies were much less pronounced (Schultz, Ketrow, & Urban, 1995). In comparison to groups lacking such individuals, the former functioned much more effectively and at a qualitatively superior level.

I have witnessed the same outcomes in meetings of the Senate Council in which particular individuals took it upon themselves to function as reminders—sometimes diplomatically (for example, "I think that we may be a little off point here") and other times bluntly (for example, "We are supposed to be assessing readiness, not our personal likes and dislikes regarding this item"). It has been interesting to me that both types of behavior have typically had the same consequence, namely, getting the Council to return to doing what it was supposed to be doing all along.

Becoming a Procedural Champion

Poole (1991) has noted that the members of groups are frequently averse to following procedures for any number of reasons, but primarily because they see them as a source of interference or hindrance that complicates rather than facilitates the performance of tasks. The negative comment I mentioned earlier regarding "parliamentary niceties" is illustrative of the point. Overcoming such perceptions and inappropriate attendant behavior, in Poole's judgment, requires the presence of "procedural champions"—that is, participants who have respect for systematic ways of examining issues and who are willing to insist on conformity among the members of a group to agreed-on approaches to the performance of their tasks. I am inclined to agree with him.

Becoming a procedural champion is not without its costs, as the person is likely to come across as an irritant to some of his or her fellow group members. When an individual has been too conspicuously functioning as a procedural champion in meetings of the Senate Council, he or she is sometimes on the receiving end of such responses as, "I think that you are just nit-picking," "I am sure that X is going to call me on the carpet for saying this, but this is a terrible piece of legislation," and "I know, I know, we are not to be discussing content, so save your breath." Alternatively, personal costs can be avoided by bringing in a group facilitator who is not a member of the group and whose formal role as procedural champion is legitimized by the group. The personal costs or, in the case of hiring an outside facilitator, the organizational costs seem a rather small price to pay when the procedural champion succeeds in keeping others from indulging their impulses and forcing them instead to behave in line with what their participation, if it is to yield positive outcomes, requires of them. My experience has been that the presence of procedural champions in meetings of the Senate Council, and other venues as well, has precisely this consequence more often than not.

CONCLUSION

In this chapter, I have attempted to indicate (1) the senses in which such groups as the one about which I have written can be difficult, (2) why they are difficult, and (3) what one can do, facilitatively speaking, to surmount the problems they pose for participants who want to make good decisions and others whose well-being they may affect. Exhibit 8.1 is a summary of the specific topics addressed in the chapter.

As the exhibit shows, decision-making groups can be difficult in many different ways when they fail to behave in a rational manner, including members' failing to satisfy task requirements in situations involving consequential

Exhibit 8.1
Suboptimality in Decision-Making Groups, Why It Occurs, and What One Can Do

How Decision-Making Groups Can Be Difficult

- Failing to satisfy task requirements
- Making inappropriate decisions
- Creating intragroup tensions
- Complicating the lives of others external to the group
- Adversely affecting their own members' credibility

Contributing Factors

- Ignorance of task requirements
- Misunderstanding of roles and protocols
- Pluralistic ignorance
- Ego involvement
- Status differences
- Failures in leadership

Remedies

- Clarifying the objectives, task, and procedures
- Enacting the role of reminder
- Becoming a procedural champion

choices, making inappropriate decisions, creating tensions among the members, complicating the lives of others, and adversely affecting their own lives by diminishing their credibility. As to why groups become difficult in these respects, six contributing sources of influence are often operative: members' ignorance of task requirements, misunderstanding of roles and protocols, pluralistic ignorance (or the misperception that other members have formed judgments and are agreed concerning what constitutes appropriate action when that in fact may not be true), members' level of ego involvement in the matters to be resolved in the decision-making process, undue influence resulting from differences in the status of members, and failures in leadership to ensure that members are on and remain on the goal path. Even though such sources of influence can be powerful, the members of groups—especially those who seek to play a facilitative role—are not without recourse. One can mitigate their impact by routinely clarifying objectives, task requirements, and procedures; reminding members of their responsibilities when they seem not to be fulfilling them; and becoming a procedural champion, or the person who emphasizes the need for progressing through a decision-making task that optimizes the prospects of the members' choosing appropriately.

One does not have to experience the sort of frustration that Senator Browne or the senator who decided not to stand for re-election do in the fictitious scenario at the beginning of this chapter. Groups do not set out to be difficult, and they need not become so if one is aware of the intrusion of unwanted sources of influence and has a clear sense of how to address them. To that end, I hope that this chapter proves to be instructive.

chapter
NINE

Working Without Rules: A Team in Need of a Different Picture

Ann Lukens

The ten-member team provided infrastructure support for the organization across the country. The team was described as having had a difficult working relationship for a few months, stemming from a disciplinary issue with a staff member outside the team who was a relative or friend of several team members. The circumstances were subsequently discussed at a departmental social event, where all team members were present. Strong views were expressed both in support of and against the person's actions, and because of the personal relationships involved, the event triggered stress and illness in the team, so two team members had been off work, and were about to return. Productivity had been affected in the interim.

Management asked for support to help manage the return to work and to maximize the potential for resolution and closure with this team. They wanted the team to regain its effectiveness and credibility, and to be able provide support for extensive organizational changes.

INTRODUCTION

When I'm asked to mediate or facilitate a session for a team to help them through some difficult changes, I'm often given a snapshot of what's happening at a particular point in time. These pictures usually come from someone in management or the human resources department, and the stories this person tells are about short-term issues that need a quick fix. Almost as often, I find that the real story has a more complex set of issues that has developed over a far longer period of time. The first meetings with the team and the individuals and those first experiences of their interactions with me and with each other expand the frame of that story. I begin to understand their issues and start to identify what the process must provide to support them through change.

I share here my experience of working with a team that had struggled for a number of years, and how I used affirmative conflict communication approaches alongside other facilitation and mediation techniques to enable the team to "create positive stories, and tease out hidden positive resources within negative stories" (Barge, 2001, p. 96). Although there were some difficult moments along the way, the methods helped the team find ways to explore their resources and capacities with optimism and enabled them to take some risks, moving away from their despairing pattern of accepting and holding on to their problems and damaged relationships.

I'll relate their original story and analyze their difficulties, and highlight my thoughts about the techniques and processes that would enable them to understand their issues. I'll describe the processes that worked with this group and that I've used on other occasions in working with groups in conflict.

In addition, I'll touch on what we as facilitators and mediators bring to the frame, and what impact our values, beliefs, "constellation of theories" (Lang & Taylor, 2000, p. 69), and resulting choices of methods and tools have on results.

HOW THE GROUP WAS DIFFICULT

The Team's Story—First Impressions

I began my assessment of the situation by meeting with the whole team. I explained my thoughts on the overall process and that I would be meeting with each team member individually. This initial group meeting added another level of understanding about the group and told a new piece of the story. Each person came into the room and chose carefully where and with whom he or she sat. Some team members turned their chairs and sat with their backs to others. The meeting was brief—no one wanted to ask questions or open any discussion in the room. They all agreed to meet with me individually, with cynicism expressed about the possibility of any positive outcomes. They showed "behavior patterns, beliefs, rituals, and ways of doing things" (Wilson, 2002, p. 12) that clearly affected their ability to communicate. These patterns seemed much more entrenched than something that had begun as a disagreement at a social event a couple of months earlier!

The Team's Story—Individual Perspectives

I then met with the individual team members. After seeing negative and ineffective team interactions in the introductory meeting, I wanted to build some trust, enable interactions (Kouzes & Posner, 2002), and encourage a spirit of inquiry and openness (Chasin & Herzog, 2006). The participants understood that these initial sessions were confidential, and so were able to speak openly about their views. During these individual interviews, my understanding of the conflict broadened. The individuals spoke of problems that had existed for *years,* not just months, with recent events signifying simple examples of what was wrong. Of the ten members, four were connected by family relationships or had been friends since secondary school; they were the core part of the team and had worked together in different capacities for nearly fifteen years. They supported each other and were extremely loyal; this support and loyalty had extended to the other staff member who had left and were part of the reason for the damaging conversation at the social event. Interestingly, they all seemed to understand that event as a very small piece of a much bigger set of issues. This group of friends and family within the team expressed confusion about the oversensitivity of several of the other team members and their inability to become part of the team and the organization.

Team members with less tenure described themselves as isolated and excluded. One team member, who was looking for a new job, noted that it was really difficult being "the new kid" and that he just never fit in. He said this with sadness and a real sense of failure. I asked how long he'd been on the team and was surprised to learn that he'd been there for three years—I had thought months! Another said, "It's just a job; if I keep my head down and do what I'm told, nobody gives me a hard time." She enjoyed parts of the job, but limited her team interaction to avoid criticism and problems. Personal and professional relationships were blurred. This caused feelings of exclusion and favoritism, setting up a system of rivalries and competition. The system "put a premium on special relations" (Armstrong, 2004, p. 19), and this dynamic was letting the team down. Many team members noted that criticism and negative comments were often disguised as humor by those handing them out—and in the open plan office, they were aware that many other teams heard and were unhappy about this behavior.

All nonmanagement parties raised another aspect of the conflict: anger at management and the organization for allowing these behaviors to continue and for evading responsibility for changing things. Those with friends in middle management pointed further up the management structure, while those on the "outside" of the friendship circle pointed firmly at the team manager and her direct line manager. The middle managers who led the team and were involved in the process expressed disbelief at the behaviors of the team and a sense of defeat at both understanding and having any impact on changing them.

Each individual and the team as a whole communicated defensively, using variations of evaluative, superior, certain, or controlling language; the behavior patterns, working habits, and beliefs and rituals (Folger, Poole, & Stutman, 1993) trapped them in a cycle of conflict. It was difficult for team members to perform their tasks or to pursue career development without thinking about the repercussions of any action. They operated socially rather than professionally, and this meant that their individual and team achievements at work were not recognized. The team knew that their interactions were poor, but blamed the poor behaviors of others. They knew the *team* needed to change, but didn't take any *individual* responsibility, and avoided looking at the impact this had on the team's work. The "history of wrong-doing of the 'other' preserved their own self-esteem—by holding on to the other's faults, parties are able to overlook their own" (LeBaron, 2002, p. 107), thus escalating the conflict and undermining collective possibilities.

No one agreed to joint mediation with other individuals, which was offered to most of the participants as a first step in the process to help build individual relationships and clear the air. Each felt strongly that this implied personal guilt, so those processes for exploring some of the more difficult individual relationships more safely were rejected. It was clear that the group wanted change, but in opening up the discussion they were "afraid of it—fearing that it will upset a precarious but important set of power relationships" (Mayer, 2004, p. 94).

On the positive side, the team members recognized the team's strengths and skills and knew that collectively they had the ability to perform well and access the resources they needed. They understood the tasks and knew that their contribution was important to the organization overall. They were not worried that they couldn't do the jobs; they were concerned about who would get the "plum" ones, who would be in charge, who would bear the brunt of the workload, and who would be thanked. They were concerned about how people would behave toward them and how they were perceived.

WHY THE GROUP WAS DIFFICULT

How had the team arrived at this point? What was the organization's role in the enabling of the behaviors of this team? And what part did each team member play in keeping the conflict going?

The request for support from management occurred at the same time that the need for this team's work had increased, due to their reorganization. It was apparent that management's awareness and need to address the problems had been heightened by a business circumstance (Wilson, 2002)—their need for the team's "product" had increased, and the ineffectiveness and difficult communication within the team had been noted and highlighted outside the team, perhaps for the first time.

In my conversations with the team members, it was clear that the organization had changed dramatically in recent years. Although it had always been part of a national group, it had been a small regional office operating quite independently. It had recruited locally and had developed a strong "family" atmosphere. As time passed, this office was being relied on to support functions nationwide. As an organization, it had failed to recognize the impact of the changes on the internal workings of the office. For this team in particular, the old ways of working and the new requirements were at odds; the team's issues had their origins in this changing organizational context.

Aside from a couple of team members, the team had little knowledge or perspective about structures, roles and responsibilities, and its place in the larger organizational context, and so had no "clear sense of how to achieve goals, a sense of progress, the freedom to participate, be valued and welcomed" (Wilson, 2002, p. 239). This lack of framework and structure allowed "individuals to exercise personal power or otherwise manipulate each other to get things done" (Jacques, as quoted in Armstrong, 2004, p. 21), leading to regular "debate about who should do what, suspicions about whether the distribution of workloads was fair, and irritations caused by apparent interference" (West, 2004, p. 174).

The initial conflict, firmly founded in the organizational context, had led to a conflict now more centered on factors of structure and process, with emphasis on a relational perspective. The process would need to help the group address members' behavior toward each other and to understand and work with their differences and conflicts more effectively in order to support the stronger cohesion and delivery that were needed from them.

WHAT HAPPENED NEXT—THE PROCESS

Analysis and Design

With only two days available for the group to address these issues, I needed to identify clearly what would give the team the best chance of moving forward, and meet the client's need for the team to become more productive. I had asked each individual as we finished our one-to-ones about what goals he or she had for the facilitated sessions that could be shared with the team, and compiled a list.

As shown in Table 9.1, I put together the rational objectives (Stanfield, 1998) for the process based on the goals and needs expressed by the organization, team, and individuals. These were the practical goals, and reflected the outputs the process would try to achieve. Then I worked on the experiential aims and objectives—the impact of the process on the group, the experience the group would have. In this workshop, with relationships and communication difficult, I felt that these experiential objectives would be critical to getting the process moving.

The team's need to develop different relationships and new ways to communicate meant that the processes I used needed to encourage buy-in from the group and help alter the structure of their interaction. They needed an experience of what it *could* be like, and to try out new behaviors to support a long-term chance of working together. They needed ways to communicate and engage

Table 9.1

Formulating the Conflict: Analysis of Goals and Interests

Organization Interests	Team Interests
Explicit • Help manage return to work (safety) • Maximize the potential for resolution and closure with this team (move past this) • Help team regain its effectiveness and credibility (get the job done professionally) **Underlying** • Manage reorganization effectively • Avoid further employment complications • Stop complaints from other areas	• A need for clarity and understanding about the reorganization and their roles and responsibilities both as team members and in the organization as a whole • A team structure that was balanced, fair, and efficient • Openness about decision making • A sense of direction from management • Individual and team professionalism—accomplishments understood and recognized • Changed communication—making the shift to professional and appropriate behaviors from the personal and difficult behaviors that had become the norm • To feel okay about coming to work in the morning • To trust their teammates and move past the issues they'd been having

Process Needs—Rational Objectives—What the Team Needed to *Do*

- Begin to rebuild team relationships
- Find ways for the team members to engage—with the issues and with each other
- Strengthen the team's ability to carry out the work
- Support the team in developing future actions, defining roles and responsibilities
- Support information required from the organization: decisions outside the team

Process Needs—Experiential Objectives—How the Team Would *Feel*

- Experience the power of positive, affirmative communication
- Find the resources and the successes of the past
- Find positive images and energy and the common ground in those stories
- Feel lighter, less burdened, more hopeful
- Shift the picture of the team from despair and blame to hope and responsibility

with each other positively, so an early part of the process ahead needed to bring humanity back to their interactions—to work with a set of beliefs and a vision of how to proceed (Mayer, 2000).

I felt that reviewing issues and problems too early would result in a very difficult and potentially damaging session; the high emotion in the team had already resulted in staff members' taking time off from work because of stress. I needed the group to feel safe and supported and to build trust and momentum, enabling the group to experience different ways of communicating and to "find places of understanding" (Weeks, 1992, p. 97). I didn't want to open anything we didn't have "time to work with and resolve" (Bunker, 2000, p. 553), and needed methods and approaches that addressed the conflict at levels that were workable for the team (Fisher, 2000) and that encouraged all parties to "accept responsibility for their lives and their choices" (Cloke, 2001, p. 30).

I knew that at some point the parties probably needed to address what had happened and the emotional impact—so that the issues would be named and cleared—but wanted to choose when and how much negative emotion to release (LeBaron, 2002), ensuring it could happen constructively and in a balanced way. It seemed that the way to begin this process was to look at how their stories were told, to encourage an affirmative view of past experiences, and to find a new way of looking at what had happened, opening the doors for a more optimistic "what could be."

I felt that a limited Appreciative Inquiry approach would be helpful in opening up that type of dialogue, finding more complete and balanced memories of the past, and enabling the imagination to explore new futures. As shown in Figure 9.1, Appreciative Inquiry comprises four stages: Discover, Dream, Design, Deliver. In this case, I felt it would be most useful to concentrate on the Discovery and Dream stages through paired interviews. It would help remind the participants what had been good in the past, creating memories and history that they'd lost (LeBaron, 2002). The parties could use these memories to understand their needs, build on the positive, and envisage a future "enriched with detail" (Kouzes & Posner, 2002, p. 119).

Both Appreciative Inquiry and visualizing techniques help create images that will "determine the current or direction of behavior" (LeBaron, 2002, p. 112). Images evoke auditory and kinesthetic modes of experience and connect us to the essence of new ways forward; "positive images evoke positive possibilities" (Kouzes & Posner, 2002, p. 325). By using methods that demonstrate these

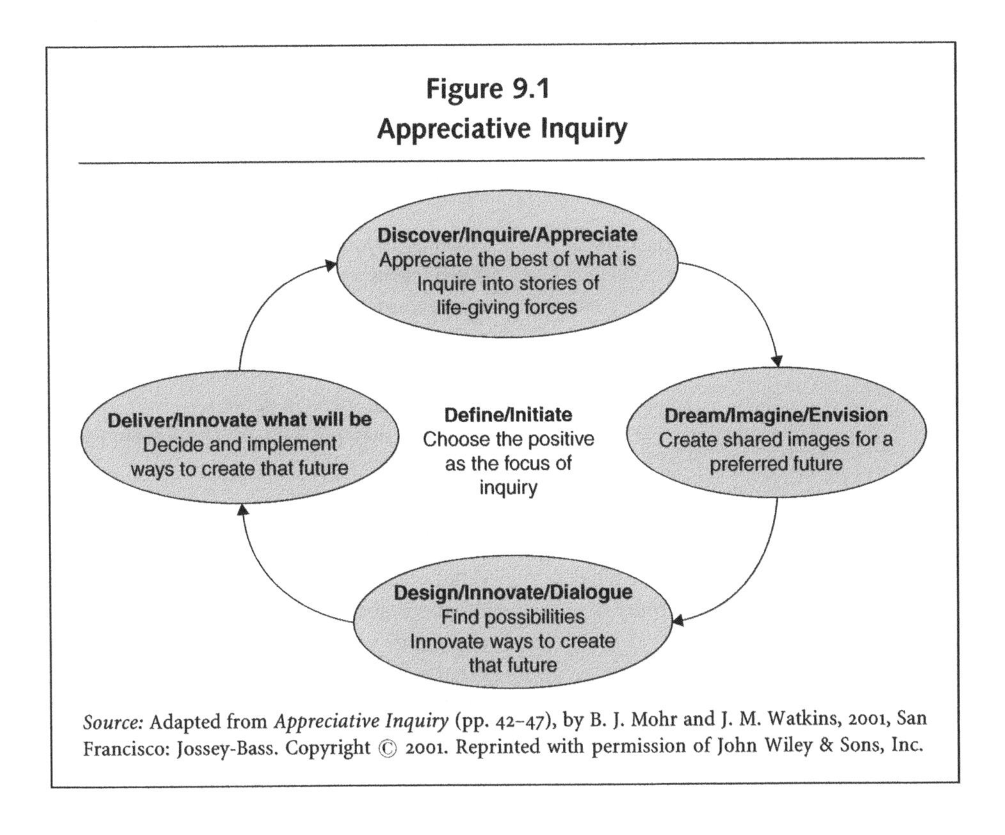
Discover/Inquire/Appreciate
Appreciate the best of what is
Inquire into stories of
life-giving forces
Deliver/Innovate what will be
Decide and implement
ways to create that future
Define/Initiate
Choose the positive
as the focus of
inquiry
Dream/Imagine/Envision
Create shared images for a
preferred future
Design/Innovate/Dialogue
Find possibilities
Innovate ways to create
that future

Figure 9.1
Appreciative Inquiry

Source: Adapted from *Appreciative Inquiry* (pp. 42–47), by B. J. Mohr and J. M. Watkins, 2001, San Francisco: Jossey-Bass. Copyright © 2001. Reprinted with permission of John Wiley & Sons, Inc.

principles, I felt that the long-standing communication and relationship issues that the group experienced could be transformed at both conscious and unconscious levels with long-lasting effect (Mohr & Watkins, 2001).

Appreciating the Past—Remembering What We Know That Has Worked

After initial introductions to the day and the process, the team began with an Appreciative Inquiry (AI) exercise to "choose the positive as the focus of the inquiry" and as a starting point for engaging the participants in "building the kind of organization . . . they want to live in" (Mohr & Watkins, 2001, pp. 56, 58). The questions, listed here (derived from "An AI Mini Experience," Mohr & Watkins, 2001, p. 59), enabled individuals to interview each other in pairs and remember and enjoy past team experiences. The pairs then joined together in small groups to draw pictures of those experiences. Building on that exercise, they next identified the key criteria that made good, effective teams. The stories they related about past successes served as a base for generating a new script for steps to take in the future.

Appreciative Inquiry Questions

Invite participants to "see the past" to be objective, find memories.	• Looking at your entire experience in working in teams, recall a high point, a time when you felt that you and the team were operating at your best, when you felt most excited about what you were doing. Describe the scene in detail. • Who else was involved, and how were they significant?
Invite them to hold on to the good feelings from that good experience.	• How did you feel during that experience? • How do you feel talking about it now?
Invite them to analyze and identify what's important to them that this memory evoked.	• What made it a peak experience? • What is it about your work in teams that you value? • What is the single most important thing it has contributed to your life? • What do you think are the core values of teamwork at its best?
Invite them to look at how they bring this into their present and future.	• What are three wishes or dreams you have for yourself as a continuing member of this team or for the team in general that would help all of you work at your best? (This would lead to a visioning exercise)

After building pictures together, the small groups presented their ideas to each other, and were surprised and pleased that so many ideas were similar—humor, accomplishment, teamwork, and recognition appeared across the groups. In working together in the small groups to produce the pictures, they acknowledged each other's talents in drawing and humor in creating some poems and limericks about teamwork. The woman who "keeps her head down" doing her work showed her talents as a great cartoonist, and held her head high, receiving the right kind of recognition. A team member whose negative humor was cited as a problem had used that humor positively in identifying her experiences in a sports team. The atmosphere lightened a bit; they started to see that they weren't so far apart in what was important to them. Their differences began to be more balanced on a scale with their similarities—their common ground. The stories, even of past experiences, became positive stories, shifting the view of teamwork from impossible to possible, and putting a very different, positive frame on their stories.

Identifying What We Want—Using Our Past Experience to Build a New Future

We used these wishes and dreams as a starting point for a workshop to build a vision of where they'd like this team to be in a year's time. The ICA Consensus Workshop method was used. It allows for individual thinking and sharing ideas in small groups (Stanfield, 1998), then building consensus by grouping those ideas together and naming them to identify insights and develop meaningful high-level practical pictures of what the group wanted for the future. It creates "shared images for a preferred future" (Mohr & Watkins, 2001, p. 37). I asked them to visualize:

What do we want our team to look like in a year's time?

I asked the team members to imagine that they were having lunch with a new employee who had not yet been placed in a team and would probably be given a choice among a few teams in which she could work. I asked them to imagine that they wanted her on the team and needed to take this opportunity to explain why their team was a good place to work. Using the past positive experiences they'd just identified, what could they show her? What would the team look like? What would the new employee see and hear between team members that would highlight why it was a great place to work?

The individual ideas were identified, but they triggered some tensions. Defensive patterns of behavior were still strong, so the person identifying "a polite, quiet environment" was challenged by one of the more extroverted members of the team, who felt that the comment was directed at her joking and banter. "Everyone doing his or her bit" had been seen by another as an accusation of slacking off. The team manager heard "career development" as a challenge that she didn't support the people in developing skills. In each case, the initiators of the ideas explained that that was not the case—that it was an extension of what they'd enjoyed on teams in the past—so these concerns were alleviated to some degree. Even so, it was apparent that the team's patterns of blame and defense were hard to shift. We continued to work on naming and finding the common intent of the ideas, with resulting themes including structure and development opportunities in place, professionalism, good team bonding, and positive recognition.

Reaffirming Strengths and Resources, and Identifying Where the Blocks Are

I felt that the group needed to generate some positive energy again, so next we did a simple exercise to highlight the strengths and resources they already had in place to help them achieve their vision. The team was again very clear about what they were good at, but there was still tension, still comments about how *they* could do the job, that it was somehow "others" who still posed problems. It seemed that until the team had the opportunity to name and clear those issues (LeBaron, 2002), the deep mistrust would continue to pop into even the most positive of pictures they could paint.

So I facilitated a session to identify those issues in order to clarify what the group felt would prevent them from achieving their vision. I posed the following question:

What will block our team's path to the vision?

This approach worked in the same way as the vision exercise, inviting individual brainstorming of the possible issues they faced in achieving what they wanted. I asked the group to think about the big picture—the blocks at organizational and team levels, highlighting things that they felt might be external—and also to think about what they personally might be doing that might prevent them from achieving the vision.

Several individuals noted different working styles, methods, and personal priorities. We grouped these together, and someone suggested that we name this group Intolerance, triggering bristling in the room and more blaming and defensive comments. I challenged the group to talk about what was happening, and suggested that diversity in the team seemed to be an issue. At first, the team strongly denied that "diversity" was the issue—that diversity was about different cultures, religions, and ethnicity. I asked them if diversity could apply to their differences in personal work style and approach. As they explored the concept, they began to see the issues and each other differently, using some understanding they'd always reserved for traditional concepts of diversity to become more aware and accepting of their colleagues' differences in style, and to recognize the impact of their own style. One of the key concepts they discussed was the use of humor—that it could be great when everyone was tense and needed some relief, but could also feel like bullying when it became personal. This discussion enabled the group to complete the exercise, and as the first day was drawing to a close, we needed to look at what would happen between this meeting and the next.

Taking Small Steps

There had been many positive "light bulb" moments during the day, amid other more difficult ones. I knew that it would be important for the team and individuals to identify "next steps" they could take to gain some individual commitment and responsibility. Also, I knew that these steps needed to be achievable: small steps so that during the interim period between this meeting and the next, their small successes would be building a new story. I asked the team to self-select to work in smaller groups on specific categories of blocks, in areas where they felt they could really make a contribution. Many actions identified were individual actions centered on behaviors, which reflected awareness that their behaviors (and judgments of others' behaviors) had real impact on the team. Management made commitments to clarifying the reorganization and personnel issues impacting the team. Finally, the group agreed to gently remind each other if they were not following through on their commitments. As the team reflected on the process, they felt that they had some things to look at and work on. There was still skepticism, but after only a day, it was unlikely that they completely believed in their own and each other's ability to change. They had become more human for each other, they better recognized their common goals and needs, and they had successfully worked together in different ways throughout the day.

Reflect, Review, Affirm What Has Worked

I was glad that they had agreed on these actions, as it took more than two months to bring the group back together to finish the process. Because it had been so difficult to arrange the next meeting, I feared a change in the level of commitment to resolving the issues. As the team came into the room, though, I noticed a change in their relationships to each other and the ease with which they found seats and chatted before we started. And as we moved through a review, it became clear that the "resistance" to setting up the meeting was really only logistical—a big project delivery and holidays—rather than resistance to the process itself.

We began with a review of the last session's action plan. The review identified that the team had really moved forward, and many external pressures on the team due to the reorganization had been clarified. Everyone was able to clearly identify changes that were already in progress. They had delivered a huge project for the organization, and had worked hard to ensure that that work had been handled fairly for the team. They had several team meetings to get information on the reorganization, to plan the workload, and to discuss as a team who was best placed to do the work. The middle management had made a concerted effort to ensure that the team was up-to-date on organizational information, and the team was now clear about their position in the new framework. They also related that they had stuck to their personal actions and had been pretty successful. They had begun to experience some new ways of working together for real.

Their reflection on the last two months at work was their new positive story. Taking the time to reflect on their recent successes as a group brought the positive energy back into the room and created a sense of accomplishment and the beginnings of trust.

Affirm Each Other's Contributions, Identify Needs, Make Requests

Two months before, I had asked the group to concentrate on the future and take positive action. For this new session, I put together a process to look at some of the interpersonal issues that had affected the team, and on seeing their energy and sense of success, I felt that the exercise would work and that they would be able to look at some of their past difficult experiences and emotions in a constructive way.

To begin, I asked the team to review the qualities of great teams that they had identified in their Appreciative Inquiry, how they had developed those into a vision for this team, and how successful they had been recently. I asked them to use these positive images to write two cards: one, to encourage them to identify what they really appreciated about each other, was an appreciative statement for each person in the team; the other was a request—what they needed the other person to do or do more of that would help achieve the vision or help the team. I asked them to avoid requesting that someone stop doing something, inviting them instead to think about what it would be like if a behavior or activity stopped and what behavior or action would be in its place. There was a collective gasp as a wave of nerves flashed around the room, but they all set to work, writing two cards for each other person in the room. During the process, I checked in with everyone to help if they needed support in using that positive language, but everyone seemed to find it possible.

When everyone had completed his or her cards, we began a "speed-dating" process to ensure that everyone in the room was able to share his or her cards.

It was quiet at first, and I moved around the room to help with any difficult discussions. A buzz started in the room—by the end there was laughter and a huge sense of relief. The affirmative language they were using was intoxicating; the positive strokes they gave each other enabled them to speak together in ways they hadn't experienced in years. I asked the participants to identify some personal actions that they might take away from those conversations, and invited them to share those actions and how they felt about what they'd learned. Everyone chose to share, and as they reflected on what it had been like, the participants noted that they felt they couldn't have done this exercise or anything like it when the process began. They agreed that it was "scary" at first, but it had given them the chance to be honest with everyone on the team. They were surprised at how easy it was and were also surprised by what people had said to them, and they were clear that the positive, affirmative way they spoke to each other made a huge difference. They all chose to make their personal actions part of the overall plan so that the whole team was aware of their commitment to making them happen. They understood that they still had struggles ahead, but all felt that they now had a way forward and a way to ask each other for things in the future.

Although the session continued for a few hours longer as they built a more task-oriented, specific action plan for upcoming projects, the main aims of the workshop had been achieved. Their conflict was no longer the driver—their day-to-day work was, and they knew they had to work on their relationships as part of the day-to-day. They were clear that this intervention didn't solve everything, but they now had positive experiences they could draw on to support their work—successes in delivery, communicating honestly in affirming ways, and constructing their positive stories together—past, present, and future.

THE FACILITATOR'S PRESENCE—SETTING THE POSITIVE FRAME

As facilitators, we are trained to affect process, not content. I think we sometimes assume that this means our influence on how the team progresses is minimal, but our choice of process and approach, and our own core values and behaviors (Schwarz, 1994) will influence the group profoundly. I believed at the outset that the group could work differently. With this optimism, I worked to generate an "atmosphere of co-operation and trust" (Goleman,

2004, p. 30). Choosing an affirmative communication approach instead of a problem analysis approach set guidelines for communication both in the session and back in the office. "High expectations lead to high performance—if we believe people can create their own future and move past their conflicts, and our words and behaviors identify this, we enable our clients to work at their best" (Kouzes & Posner, 2002, p. 323). "The effectiveness of our interventions arises not from their forcefulness but from their authenticity. When our actions—whether they are directed at mundane questions or questions that go to the heart of the matter—communicate a high degree of genuineness, presence and integration, even the gentlest interventions may produce a dramatic result" (Bowling & Hoffman, 2003, p. 37)."

This was not a gentle intervention, but one based on the strong belief that this team had the power and knowledge to change. Putting a process in place to support this enabled them to see a new picture of themselves, to replace a story of cynicism, despair, and blame with a new picture they built together that was based on hope, taking responsibility, collaborative working, and affirmative communication.

chapter TEN

Interaction Archetypes: Keys to Group Difficulty and Productivity

Steven Ober

A group of executives and managers met to forecast company productivity for the coming quarter. The company made its projections in terms of the exact number of product units they would manufacture and sell. They had a long record of productivity and profit. They also had a history of making, and achieving, ambitious, optimistic forecasts. Statements like "We can do it," "We always get the job done," and "We achieve the impossible" were their bywords. Failure, not meeting the numbers, was unthinkable. In recent quarters, however, company accountants had adjusted the books by prerecording sales projected for early next quarter in order to make it appear that they were meeting their highly optimistic projections. Meanwhile, their market was shrinking. In this particular forecasting meeting, a key member of the

Special thanks to David Kantor, Ph.D., of The Kantor Institute, Cambridge, Massachusetts. His groundbreaking work in structural dynamics created the foundation on which this chapter stands.

team suggested yet another very optimistic number for the next quarter. Following the company's proud tradition, everyone in the room voted for the projection. In later conversations, *every person in the meeting acknowledged that they endorsed the forecast even though they knew it was not a real number!* At the end of the quarter, the company did not make its quota. Furthermore, it was no longer able to borrow units against the future via the accounting process; the well had run dry. For the first time, the company registered a loss rather than a profit. Over the next week, its stock price plummeted.

A group of key government executives and senior engineers conferred several times about whether or not to move forward with a highly publicized launch. On the one hand, they all knew that there was significant danger of O-ring failure if the launch-day temperature fell below acceptable levels. They also knew that O-ring failure could result in disaster. The weather forecast did not look promising; lower than normal temperatures were projected. On the other hand, key executives felt intense political pressure to move forward with the launch. Their budget and reputation for success were at stake. The agency had a proud history of making outstanding contributions to the nation, a reputation that it needed desperately to uphold. In the decision-making conversations, key executives advocated strongly for going ahead with the launch. Senior engineers stated that they were fearful about the O-rings; but the executives, citing political and budgetary realities, pushed back hard. The senior engineers felt stifled by the aggressive executives and the surrounding political pressures. The group decided to proceed with the launch. Those who were concerned about the O-rings left the conversations with a sinking feeling. A few days later, the launch occurred on a cold morning; temperatures were lower than acceptable. Key O-rings failed, and the *Challenger* exploded, resulting in the worst disaster in the history of United States space exploration (D. Dwoyer, director of research at NASA Langley Research Center, personal communication, September, 1998).

Groups often make decisions that have monumental consequences. In the examples I've cited here, there were overwhelming reasons to support different decisions than the ones made. Yet, in one instance, people sat on their knowledge; in the other they didn't push it hard enough. In both cases, the results were disastrous. Why do these kinds of situations happen? Why do intelligent, reasonable people, when they become part of a group interaction, often behave in ways that are clearly not in the best interests of the organization, the group, and the individuals within it? Why does group-based decision making sometimes become groupthink (Janis, 1972), which stifles productivity, and results in decisions that are far less than optimal? When these kinds of incidents occur in your client groups, what can you, as facilitator, do to help turn the tide?

This chapter offers some guidelines for effective facilitation in these kinds of tough situations. It provides a simple language that will enable you to help groups get unstuck and make dramatic shifts in favor of openness, learning, and productivity. The chapter makes four key points that, when fully understood and applied, can move your client group to a new level of performance:

1. Groups engage in repetitive, observable sequences of interaction that dramatically influence their ability to create results. Some of these interactions support productivity; some of them get in the way.
2. You can learn to track these sequences of behavior and see their impact on results. Furthermore, you can help the group shift its behavior in favor of results by helping members see and change their own behavior.
3. Entrenched, repetitive, nonproductive interaction sequences are always rooted in or reinforced by underlying ways of thinking and broader organizational forces—by both individuals' mental models and the social context.
4. You can track how these ways of thinking and organizational forces inhibit a group's ability to produce, and you can help group members create shifts in these deeper (individual) and broader (organizational) forces so that they support rather than hinder group productivity. When the group shifts these structural and contextual forces, they can more easily make—and sustain—needed behavioral changes.

THE FORCES INFLUENCING GROUP EFFECTIVENESS

To increase your client groups' ability to make effective decisions and create outstanding results, you need a language for group functioning that answers three questions:

1. What are the forces that impact group performance?
2. How, specifically, do these forces influence groups' ability to make decisions and create results?
3. What can I, as facilitator, do to help groups shift their behavior and dramatically increase their productivity?

In this chapter, I present such a language and provide specific guidelines for using it.

As discussed in the Introduction to this volume, there are three high-order factors that influence group performance. They are a group's *context* (environmental variables), *structure* (formal and informal aspects of group design), and *process* (interaction variables—behavioral exchanges before, during, and after group meetings). Difficulties in groups are due to some combination of these context, structure, and process attributes.

The variables that impact group productivity are very much interrelated. Each influences and is significantly influenced by the others. For example, behavior in a group is influenced by how members think. What happens in group interactions can, in turn, influence both future thinking and organizational direction. Each set of variables, when fully understood as part of a group's *system*, can be used as a lever to significantly enhance team productivity (Ober, 2000).

To support effective systemic observation and facilitation, a useful way to think about these factors is in terms of their point of origin and, therefore, their level of visibility to group members and facilitators:

Group structural and process forces are the variables that originate in the group. They include the tasks the group performs, how the group organizes itself, conversations the members have, and interactions necessary to get the work done. Most group-level forces are visible to group members—for example, a set of interactions or the group following an agenda in a meeting.

Contextual forces are the broader organizational, business, and environmental variables impacting the group. Contextual forces include the reward system, the power structure, cultural norms, customer demands, and the pressures of the marketplace. They are less directly *visible* than in-group structural and process variables, but nonetheless they significantly influence group decision making and productivity.

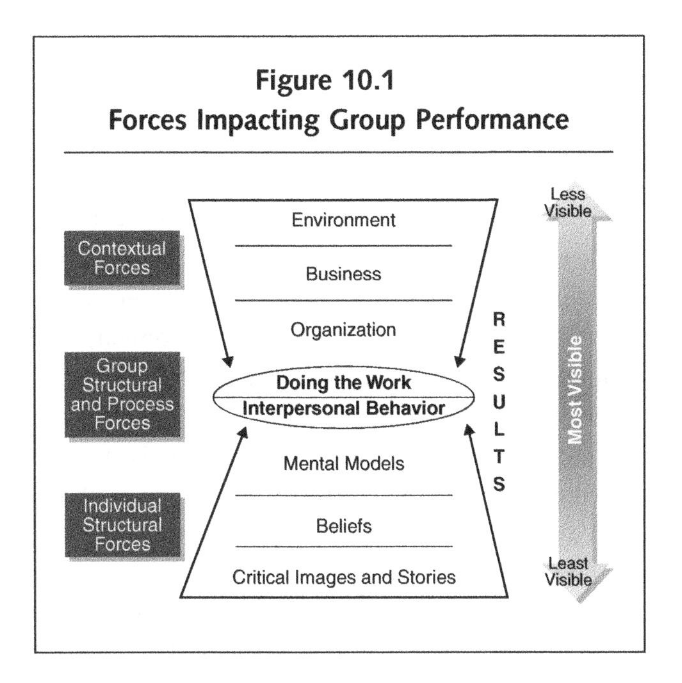

Individual structural forces are the thoughts, feelings, and deeper beliefs that each individual brings to the table. Even though they are, by definition, the least visible of the forces at play, they exert a powerful influence on individual and group behavior. In the framework of this book, these forces are included as part of structure. In this chapter, these individual structural forces are highlighted.

Following this logic, the factors influencing group performance are illustrated in Figure 10.1 (Ober, Kantor, & Yanowitz, 1995).

All of these forces, visible, less visible, and least visible, are at play in every group. Part of the facilitator's role is to make the invisible and less visible forces more visible so that rather than being controlled by them, the group can manage them to increase its effectiveness.

A POWERFUL WAY TO INFLUENCE GROUP EFFECTIVENESS

Interaction sequences in a group are an excellent entry point for enhancing group productivity. Interaction sequences (Ober & Kantor, 1996) are a very good place to begin because they are

1. Among the simplest, clearest, and most visible of variables

2. Easy variables in which to make quick changes and see results
3. A powerful entry point into seeing and shifting broader contextual forces and deeper individual forces

A group's interaction sequences are, in a very real sense, the media through which the invisible and less visible forces—mental models and deeper beliefs; organizational, business, and environmental variables—exert their influence on the group's ability to perform. In the group context, interactions are reminiscent of John Muir's observation: "When we try to examine a little piece of nature, we find that it is connected to the whole universe." A given sequence of interactions in a group, especially if it is a repetitive one, is intricately connected to and influenced by group members' thoughts, feelings, and values as well as by contextual forces from the organization and environment (Ober & Kantor, 1996).

In short, interaction sequences are an excellent entry point for seeing, intervening in, and shifting key process, structural, and contextual forces impacting group effectiveness.

The Kantor Four-Player Model

The Kantor 4 Player System (Kantor & Lehr, 1975), an empirically based model of interactions (aside from the content) in human systems, provides a simple but powerful framework for seeing and shifting group behavior. Specifically, careful observation indicates that when we strip complex interactions to their bare essence, four types of actions make up the sequences of interactions in groups:

- A **Move** initiates a sequence of interactions.
- A **Follow** supports one of the other actions.
- An **Oppose** challenges another action.
- A **Bystand** observes the interactions in ways that help the group move toward desired results.

All interactions in groups, no matter how complex, can be observed and mapped as combinations of these four actions.

Each of the four actions performs an important function in effective groups.

- A **Move** provides direction.
- A **Follow** enables completion.
- An **Oppose** creates correction.
- A **Bystand** offers perspective.

In an effective group, all four actions are enabled; that is, the group system allows and encourages the actions to perform their functions successfully. (Note: The actions do not always occur in the listed order, and a repetitive interaction does not necessarily contain all four actions.)

SEEING AND SHIFTING GROUP BEHAVIOR

In my years of working with executive teams and other groups, I have noticed recurring patterns of these four behaviors, apart from content. These patterns, which I call *interaction archetypes*, are structural dances that occur in teams; that is, they are repetitive behavioral sequences that significantly impact groups' ability to produce results. Groups can learn to observe and shift their interaction sequences in ways that dramatically increase their effectiveness. In addition, they can learn to see how their behavioral sequences are reinforced by specific ways of thinking and feeling, by the nature of their work, and by forces in the organization, and they can shift or influence these broader and deeper forces in ways that support group productivity.

Some of the more common interaction archetypes that occur in groups are discussed in the next sections. The discussion of each archetype includes

- An example
- The key actions in the sequence
- A description of the behavioral sequence—what it looks like, how it plays out
- The impact of the sequence on the group's ability to create results
- How the behavior tends to be reinforced by individual and contextual forces
- What facilitators can do to help a team break out of the nonproductive dance and move forward
- How facilitators can use identified interaction sequences as doorways into intervening in deeper and broader forces that help or hinder group productivity

Point-Counterpoint

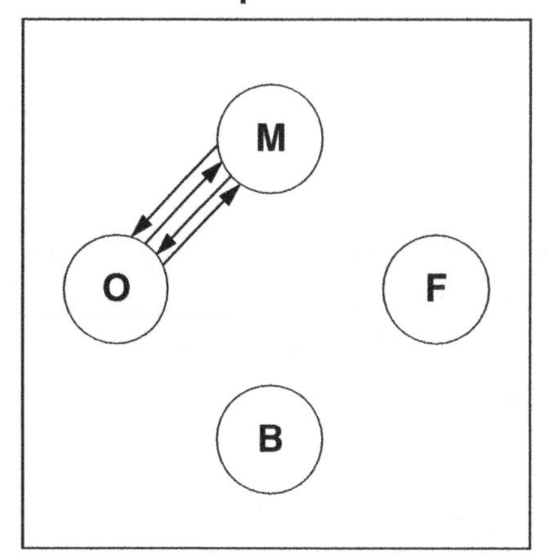

Example The VP of manufacturing says, "I think we should purchase a new MRP package."

"We don't have enough money in the FY96 budget," retorts the CFO.

"But we need the new package in order to complete the upgrade of our manufacturing process so that we can increase revenue," says the manufacturing VP.

"That's all well and good, but we cannot continue to bypass our budget planning process, especially for large purchases like this. I simply won't allow it!" answers the CFO.

The other members of the executive team sit and listen in frustration, thinking things like "Here they go again. Ted and Bill always get locked in these conflicts, and we never get anywhere. I suppose I should say something, but it won't do any good. Besides, I don't want to get yelled at." The interaction continues in this vein; no resolution is reached.

Key Behavioral Sequence Move-Oppose. (Often, there are other interactions also occurring in the group. The key sequence is the one that determines the outcome of the interaction.)

Description A point-counterpoint sequence is exactly as the name suggests. Someone makes a move, and the next person opposes that move. The next action opposes the previous one, followed by another opposition, and so on. The conversation becomes a behavioral tennis match in which each protagonist continues to advocate his or her opinion. Following and bystanding are either absent or ineffective in bringing perspective or closure.

Impact on Results A point-counterpoint structure is incapable of producing closure or results in terms of, for example, a decision about an important topic. The outcomes of a move-oppose structure are frustration, energy drain, and a feeling of being stuck.

Relationship to Other Forces Often, groups characterized by highly entrenched point-counterpoint sequences exist in organizations that have powerful histories, organizational processes, and business processes that encourage competition—for example, highly competitive divisions, reward systems that encourage competitive rather than collaborative behavior, and leaders who pit people against one another. There are often deeply held mental models in the culture about the win-lose nature of the business and the necessity of win-lose behavior to be successful. Point-counterpoint sequences can also occur in groups facing scarcity of resources, which helps create a zero-sum-game mentality among group members.

What Facilitators Can Do

1. Bystand (help the group reflect on its process) by asking group members what they see happening. If necessary, point out to the group, in a non-judgmental way, what they are doing and the impact it is having. Ask the group how they see it, so that they start learning to bystand on their own behavior and eventually break out of their move-oppose cage. For example, "It seems we're doing something we do a lot. Ted and Bill are in an overt conflict, and the rest of us are sitting silently. There may be something we can do to get ourselves out of this trap. How do other people see it?" (Bystand)

2. Help the group use the move-oppose conflict as an opportunity for learning and correction. "I think Ted and Bill both have some good points. Let's see what we can learn from the two positions and then see if we can reach a compromise." (Move)

3. Enable the silent bystanders. Most of the time, a significant number of the silent team members see exactly what is going on, but they are uncomfortable pointing it out. For example, "I believe we can all contribute to helping us move forward. I'd like to hear from those of you who are not saying anything. What do you think is going on?" (Move/Bystand)

4. Draw out the followers. "I know that some of you support Ted's or Bill's position. I'd like to hear your thinking." (Move)

5. Establish and enforce specific ground rules to mitigate the move-oppose behavior—for example, "We will not oppose a suggestion without improving on it or offering a better alternative." (Move)

6. Help the team reflect on and change their underlying ways of thinking. For example, point-counterpoint is rooted in a win-lose mental model. Raise this possibility and suggest an alternative: "Perhaps we can find a way in which Ted and Bill both win in this situation." (Bystand)

7. Encourage the organization to adjust the reward system so that more collaborative team behavior is reinforced. Work to establish organizational norms of openness: saying what's on your mind will not be punished; it's not only OK but encouraged. (Move)

8. The protagonists may be so entrenched in the point-counterpoint structure that they see any behavior on your part, even a bystand, as an action that they must oppose. Therefore, attempts to change the pattern become just another element in the move-oppose popcorn popper. In situations like this, do off-line one-on-one or pair coaching for the protagonists, affirming their good intentions and helping them see their behavior and its impact on the group. (Move/Bystand)

Courteous Compliance

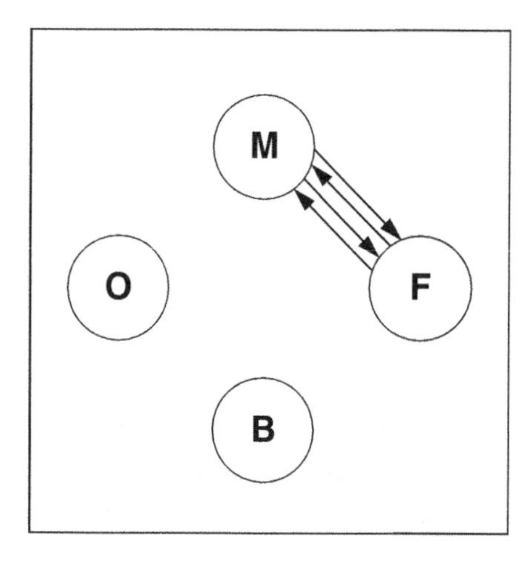

Example A group comes together with a stated agenda: to discuss whether or not they should purchase a small competitor. The CEO makes the opening move by saying, "It's very clear that we have to buy Acme to increase our market share. Let's figure out how we want to go about it."

One group member says, "Well, we could start by putting out some feelers through our informal contacts."

Another member says, "Yes, and in parallel we should assess their fair market value and the benefits to our firm."

The conversation continues in the same vein. Toward the end, the CEO sums up suggestions and identifies the steps they will take.

Key Behavioral Sequence Move-Follow

Description Someone makes a move, and the rest of the team courteously follows. The conversation is characterized by polite, rational conversation within the box they were handed. There is no controversy or push-back. Also, no one points out to the group what is happening. Often the person making the initial move is the formal leader of the group.

Impact on Results Courteous compliance produces results within the parameters of the initial move. A decision is reached; an issue is resolved. However, creative opposition, exploring a wider range of options, and learning about the group's functioning (through bystanding) do not occur. People may politely, but not deeply, support the outcome. The quality of the decision, people's commitment to it, and the team's ability to fully implement it are usually lower than they would have been had the group explored a broader range of options. Courteous compliance results in "doing things right" (regarding the position of the initial mover) rather than in "doing the right thing" (creative exploration of a broader array of choices).

Relationship to Other Forces Courteous compliance often happens in traditional, hierarchical cultures where immediate acceptance of direction from the formal leader is the norm. In a pure courteous compliance structure, people don't overtly, or even covertly, resent the fact that more options were not examined. Thinking outside the box they are handed simply does not occur to them. In groups with entrenched courteous compliance sequences, there are often very deeply held mental models about team play and loyalty—which behaviorally look like going along to get along. Opposers are seen as "disloyal" and not team players, and are often ostracized. These mental models are sometimes reflected in organizational and business processes that smooth conflict, sweep unpleasant data under the rug, and avoid exposing the truth about negative issues.

What Facilitators Can Do

1. If a leader in the group tends to be the initial mover in a courteous compliance pattern, help her notice and change her behavior. Encourage the leader to start the conversation with a true inquiry into the issue rather than with a conclusion or narrow framing. (Move/Bystand/Move)

2. Bystand and point out to the group what it is doing and the potential impacts of the behavior on results. Ask the group how they see it, thus helping them learn to observe themselves. "It seems that we always operate within the nine dots we are given rather than exploring issues more broadly. We may be inhibiting our ability to have rich conversations and make the best possible choices. How do you see it?" (Bystand)

3. Strengthen the creative opposition and bystander functions in the group. Encourage people to offer creative alternatives. Ask members to point it out when they see the team limiting itself by not exploring a wider range of options. Suggest that the team set a norm that "loyal opposition" is not only OK but also a creative contribution to the work. (Bystand/Move)

4. Modify organizational and business structures, norms, and processes that support the courteous compliance structure. Answer questions like "Do we really tell each other the truth in our project reviews, or do we just courteously say what we think people want to hear?" "Do our deeply held norms of loyalty and team play have an unintended consequence of excluding creative opposition?" (Bystand)

Covert Opposition

Covert opposition resembles courteous compliance on the surface. However, in courteous compliance, people are simply not thinking beyond boundaries they have been handed. In covert opposition, there is very real, but hidden, opposition to what has been proposed.

Example The chief operating officer of a pharmaceutical company is championing a major change project intended to flatten the organization, further

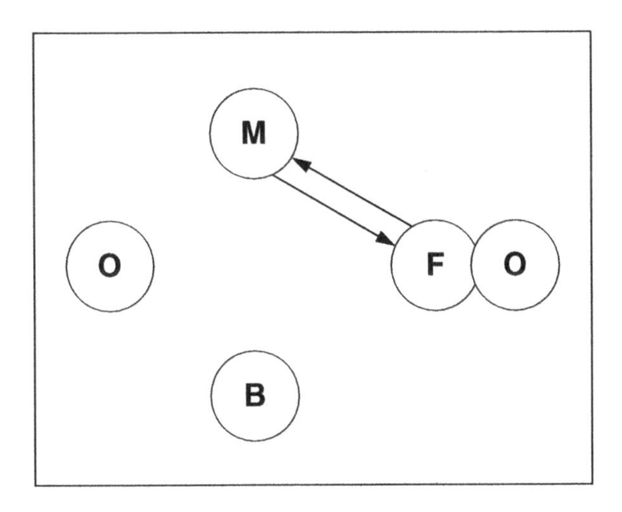

organizational learning, and more effectively integrate marketing, strategy, and product development. The steering team for the change effort consists of the division managers, because their organizations will be most directly affected. In a steering team meeting, the COO says, "The design team members for our change initiatives will come from your organizations, and the job will take 30 percent of each team member's time." Division managers listen, and some nod their heads. "Since team members will come from your organizations," the COO continues, "you need to go back and negotiate priorities with your line managers so that their people's time can be freed up. As far as I'm concerned, this change effort is priority one." A lengthy conversation ensues about the negotiations for design team members—how they will be selected, what questions they will be asked, how long the selection process will take, how the work they have to put aside will be handled.

Several of the division managers are thinking, but not saying, "My managers will never go along with this. Everything is priority one around here. Freeing up 30 percent of someone's time is a joke!" However, only one person voices his concern about being "beaten up" by his subordinates. The division managers leave the room having overtly agreed to complete the necessary negotiations within three weeks. One month later, at the next steering committee meeting, the COO asks for progress reports on negotiations and freeing up people's time. "Let's have a progress report. What has happened?" he asks. As the conversation unfolds, it is clear that nothing has happened.

Key Behavioral Sequence Move-Follow/Oppose

Description Someone makes a move, and people publicly, overtly follow. Underneath their overt following, they are actually skeptical of or against what is being proposed. Some may even be very upset by it. Yet there is very little, if any, open opposition. Back in their own areas, people passively or actively resist the mover's initiative. All the while, the initial mover believes that the team supports his move. Lots of time, money, and effort are expended on an initiative, but very little happens. Concerns, legitimate or otherwise, are never surfaced and worked through. Therefore, they fester and create behavioral logjams that stifle change. The initial mover's credibility is undermined, people develop a deep-seated skepticism of change efforts, and innovation becomes more and more difficult.

Impact on Results Results may be partially achieved, but widespread commitment to them never develops. Sometimes organizations go through the motions of change, establish committees and project offices, but none of the activity means very much; little if any *real* change occurs. Implementation is at best spotty. In the extreme, results are totally undermined by the covert opposition, and the effort disappears into the organizational woodwork.

Relationship to Other Forces Covert opposition sometimes occurs in hierarchical systems where it is not OK to oppose openly. It is present in organizations that tend to avoid direct conflict for other reasons—for example, "nice" cultures with "make nice" norms. Covert opposition also occurs in highly relationship-oriented cultures in which people believe that they cannot be successful if they alienate anyone; maintaining cordial relationships with all players is a priority at all costs. Hence public opposition is swept under the rug of overt geniality. In all three cases, underlying mental models include "It is in my self-interest to publicly support; it is against my self-interest to publicly oppose" and deeply held fears about what will happen to the opposer if he surfaces a real difference of opinion publicly. Finally, covert opposition often occurs in large, complex bureaucratic systems subject to numerous, competing forces that are out of most individuals' direct control. In these kinds of systems, a frequently held mental model is "I don't like this initiative, but why should I risk opposing the boss's favorite project openly? In all likelihood, things will return to normal in a few months anyway. This too will pass. And, in case it doesn't, I can still jump on the bandwagon because I haven't alienated anyone by opposing openly." Covert opposition is a terrible sequence for creating business results. It is a great way to achieve survival.

What Facilitators Can Do

1. Bystand and help the team see the structure and how it impacts their ability to produce results. "In your meetings, everyone agrees to the next steps. Then very little happens. Do people agree with this perception? What do you think is going on?" (Bystand)

2. The facilitator can help the initial mover legitimize the covert opposition. She or he can ask people to feel free to voice it in the interest of providing creative input. "I know that a number of you probably have serious doubts about the initiative I have proposed. I understand, given the history of our system, why you would want to keep that to yourself. However, I'd like to invite you to say what you really think. I believe that is the only way we can move forward." (Move)

3. Teach movers how to receive opposition as creative input. Teach opposers how to offer it as such. Reinforce interactions in which overt, clean, creative opposition occurs. "Bob, I think Susan was legitimately trying to enrich our thinking by proposing an alternative. Can you entertain her suggestion in that context?" (Move)

4. Explore underlying mental models about conflict, opposition, and the futility of fighting the system. "What are people's underlying beliefs about creating change in your system. Is it possible? Is it worth the effort?" Then, "Are there other ways to think about the system? What are the risks of not acting?" (Bystand)

5. Suggest that the group establish ground rules that encourage opposers to speak up. Call the group back to the ground rules when it gets stuck. "Remember your agreement that for each major decision, you will explore at least one very different approach. Who can suggest one?" (Move)

6. The overarching stance in shifting covert opposition is to help the group members *reframe how they see and experience opposition*—from a dreaded, destructive, or useless act into a caring, creative act of learning.

The Hall of Mirrors

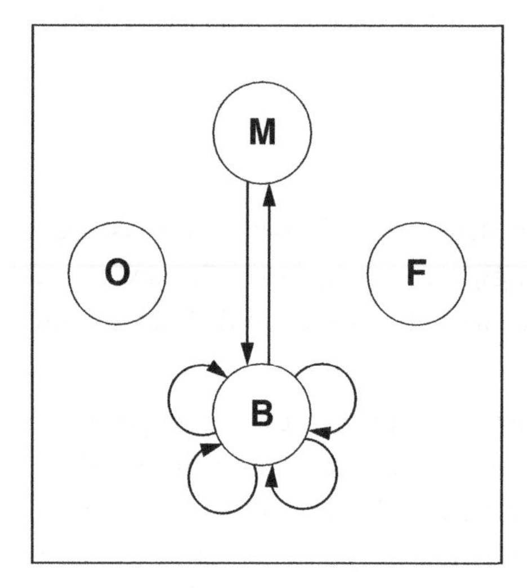

Example An executive team of an engineering consulting firm meets for the third time to decide whether or not to undertake a new line of business. In their two previous meetings, they were unable to come to closure. "We're here to discuss again whether or not to get into the business of environmental projects," says the president. "They have been very profitable for our two major competitors."

"Haven't we been trying to have a conversation about this complex issue without doing our homework?" asks a senior VP. "Shouldn't we spend a few minutes reviewing Joe's report to get us all on the same wavelength?"

"It might be a good idea to spend time reviewing the report," offers another VP, "but I wonder if that would cause us to get too detailed too quickly. We often do that. Then we can't seem to make a decision."

"It seems to me that we can't make a decision because we don't stay focused on the data," says another executive.

"Maybe we should back up for a second," offers the president. "It seems that we do tend to get too detailed to quickly, and then we get stuck. Why don't we spend a few minutes discussing the general lay of the land and then look at the report and organize the data?"

"Didn't we decide to review the report first? It seems like we always start something and never stick to it," says a senior engineering consultant.

"Wouldn't we be better off creating an agenda to guide us?" asks another member.

"I'm lost!" mutters another.

"We're doing what we always do," says the marketing director. "We get too many things going at once. Maybe we should stop and get organized."

"Don't you think that happens because we're all so technically oriented?" reflects yet another member.

"What happened to the idea of creating an agenda?" asks the COO.

The conversation continues in this vein, and the team never reaches closure.

Key Behavioral Sequence Move-Bystand-Bystand-Bystand

Description Initial move(s) are followed by bystanding. Then someone bystands the previous bystand, and the next person bystands that bystand, and so on.

The group gets lost, and stuck, in a hall of bystanding mirrors—process on process on process. People literally forget exactly where they are in their conversation and how they got there. The longer the team is stuck, the more members make additional bystand moves to get unstuck. However, these additional bystands add to the confusion. People feel as though they have lost control and can't get it back; frustration and anger increase.

Impact on Results The hall of mirrors structure does not produce results; it produces only more and more process and, ultimately, high frustration.

Relationship to Other Forces The hall of mirrors structure is usually created by team members who are intelligent and reflective, people who by temperament prefer to observe and comment on the action rather than to be in the center of the action. They usually have mental models about the importance of thinking things through very carefully before doing, and they sometimes believe that full understanding is actually more important than the imperfect world of action. Further, they tend to believe that bystanding is the most powerful role they can play in a group. For groups who engage in the hall of mirrors sequence, organizational and business processes (for example, strategic planning) can take inordinate amounts of time, because each step gets caught in a kind of paralysis of bystanding analysis.

What Facilitators Can Do

1. Encourage pure move, oppose, and follow behavior. Ask people to support reasonable, albeit imperfect, moves with clear following. Strengthen the positions of movers and followers in the team. Encourage people to make simple, straightforward statements like "I think we should do X," "I don't think Y is a good idea for these specific reasons," and "I agree with Jim. I think we should do Z." (Move)

2. The hall of mirrors is a difficult pattern to change. In most sequences, a first action of choice is to bystand and help the group bystand on itself. However, in the hall of mirrors structure, the group is choking on its own bystanding. A bystand intervention will typically become just another confusing mirror in the hall, in response to which someone else will bystand, adding to the confusion. An action of choice in a hall of mirrors structure is to reestablish direction through clear moves. You can encourage most teams to learn by reflecting, to learn to use bystanding to get themselves out of stuck patterns—"Don't just do something, sit there and reflect." In contrast, you encourage teams caught in the hall of mirrors structure to learn by doing and then reflect later—"Don't just sit there and reflect, *do something*!" (Move)

3. Establish clear organizational and business processes (for example, strategic planning, budgeting) with real deadlines, and stick to the deadlines. Also, structure participation carefully to allow people to have input without being personally involved in every step of the process. Limit direct participation in each step to those who really need to be there. (Moves)

SUMMARY—GUIDELINES FOR FACILITATORS

The interaction archetypes are very powerful tools for seeing and enhancing group performance. At the same time, it is important to remember that they are guides to inform your understanding and action, not cookbook prescriptions or easy answers. A particular group situation may resemble, but never look exactly like, one of the archetypes. Further, this set of interaction archetypes is not necessarily complete. Once you learn the four-player language and understand how group interaction reflects other forces impacting effectiveness, you can begin to identify patterns of behavior, mental models, and organizational influences particular to your client group.

The following are some general guidelines for action:

1. Learn to use the four-player language to map your group's interaction sequences.
2. Start by looking at your own behavior. Do you inadvertently contribute to the group's nonproductive patterns? Your most powerful instrument is yourself. How can you shift the patterns by changing your own behavior and ways of thinking?
3. Enable the bystanding function in your client group. Help the group learn to look at itself from the balcony and gain perspective on how it operates.
4. Help the group turn opposition into a creative force. First, encourage members to make it OK to oppose. Then help the group learn how to offer and use opposition as creative, corrective, learning opportunities.
5. Learn to see how interaction sequences are reinforced by underlying ways of thinking and by forces in your client's organization, business, and environment. Learn to use the archetypes as "fractals," as reflections of and entry points into broader and deeper (contextual and structural) patterns that contribute to nonproductive behavior in groups.
6. If you really want a change to last, help your client make aligned shifts in *at least three levels* of in the system. For example, help your group modify nonproductive move-oppose behavior (group level), think together about how to create win-win solutions (thinking and interaction levels), align the goals in team members' job plans so that they are motivated to work in the same direction (individual and organizational levels), and reward people accordingly (organizational and individual levels).

In summary, interaction archetypes are powerful doorways into seeing and changing a group's process, context, and structure. By applying these guidelines, you can help your group engage in ongoing learning for continually enhanced performance.

chapter
ELEVEN

Virtual Teams: Difficult in All Dimensions

Thomas A. O'Neill
and Theresa J. B. Kline

Team D was characterized from the beginning by little communication, few goals for the project, and very little feedback. In what could be interpreted as a sarcastic reply, one member wrote "reply reply reply reply reply" in response to another member's request for a reply if his message was received. The first of several messages indicated a lack of understanding of the project and the lack of task goals. In an early message, one member asks "what the heck" they are supposed to do. The same individual repeated the question one week later. The members of the team showed great reluctance to take on individual responsibility and be proactive. There was only one instance of positive feedback where a member thanked another for providing leadership. The leader completed the final assignment alone and submitted it from "Team D" without mentioning inactive members. (Jarvenpaa, Knoll, & Leidner, 1998, pp. 49, 50)

INTRODUCTION

Many organizations have responded to the increased pace of change and globalization by assuming dynamic and distributed structures described in the literature as virtual, network, or cluster organizations (DeSanctis & Poole, 1997; DeSanctis & Jackson, 1994). Smaller forms within these organizations are virtual teams (VTs). VTs can potentially give organizations increased flexibility and responsiveness, permitting geographically dispersed experts to rapidly form cohesive units to work on urgent projects. This is the most positive outcome of such an arrangement. However, for a number of reasons, VTs do not always live up to their potential of effectiveness (see a review by Kline & McGrath, 1999).

Following Hackman (1990), we define effective VTs as those whose (1) productive output meets the standards of relevant stakeholders; (2) work processes enhance the team's viability; and (3) ongoing experience contributes to group members' personal well-being. We also follow Kline and McGrath's typology (1998), which considers team performance as a function of problem solving, quality of work, workload allocation, meeting objectives, and displaying a team attitude. In this chapter, we will discuss why VTs experience difficulties in meeting these criteria for effectiveness, and provide some avenues for coping with VTs and their unique issues. The difficulties we discuss have been documented in research that has compared face-to-face (FTF) and VTs and has found them to be particularly salient in VTs, as are the remedies we recommend for overcoming them.

The most important difference between VTs and traditional FTF teams is that phenomena that are often implicit in FTF teams *must* be made explicit in VTs. This fundamental difference gives rise to a host of issues that make VTs particularly problematic (Hackman, 2002). Each of them can be described in terms of the matrix of factors (context, structure, and process) outlined in the Introduction to this volume. Refer to Figure 11.1 for a road map of what our chapter covers with respect to each factor. With regard to all three factors, we find the relational and rational perspectives on group effectiveness to present specific difficulties for VTs. In addition, for the process factor, difficulties are found also in the political and empirical perspectives. The specific difficulties VTs face, organized in terms of the model, are presented in Table 11.1.

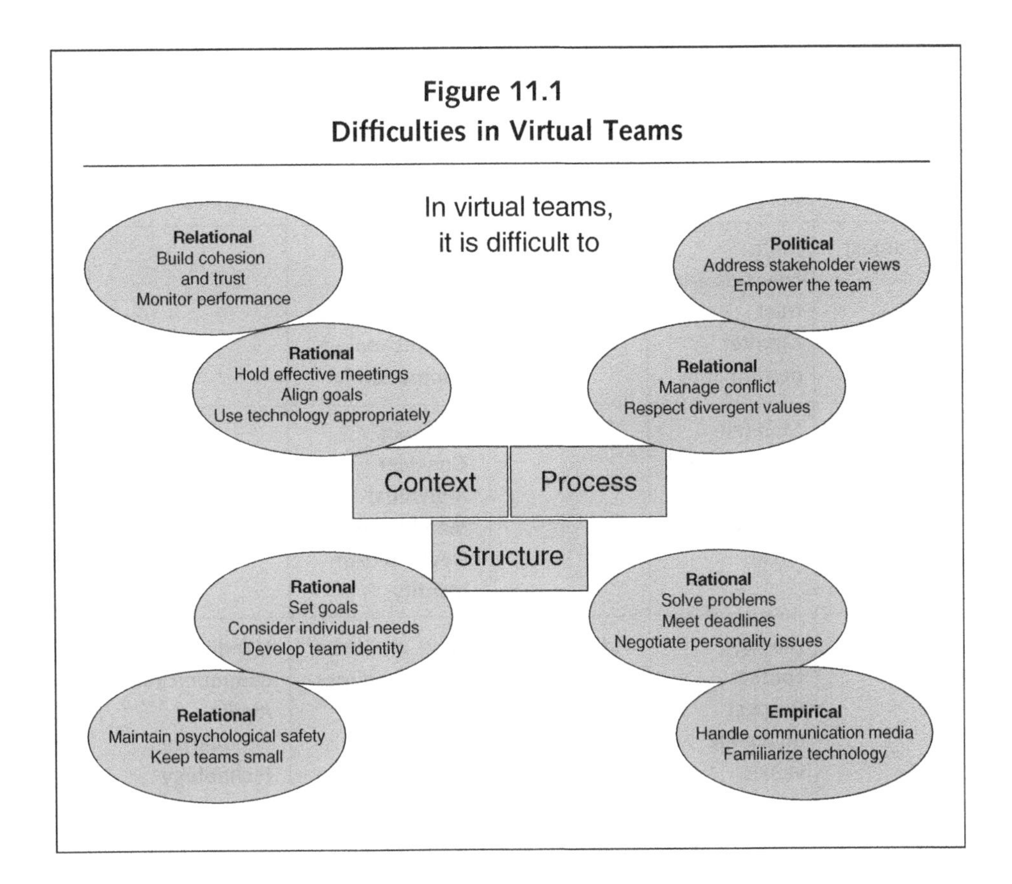

CONTEXT

The context of any team is the overall environment in which it finds itself. Most FTF teams are embedded in a single organizational, societal, and cultural environment. This is not the case for most VTs. Because VTs by definition are composed of members scattered across geographical areas, they may exist in multiple organizational, societal, and cultural environments—not to mention different time zones. This creates the potential for problems in developing effective relationships between members and conducting the rational work of the team.

Relational: Build Cohesion and Trust, and Monitor Performance

Cohesion and trust between members are typically developed by FTF interactions between members. There is a free flow of information between members, which includes dialogue about not only work tasks but also the team members themselves. They have ample opportunity to describe or

Table 11.1
The Special Difficulties Presented by Virtual Teams

	Relational	Political	Rational	Empirical
Context	Build cohesion and trust Monitor performance		Hold effective meetings Align goals Use technology appropriately	
Structure	Maintain psychological safety Keep teams small		Set goals Consider individual member needs Develop team identity	
Process	Manage conflict Respect divergent values	Address stakeholder views Empower the team	Solve problems Meet deadlines Negotiate personality issues	Handle communication media Familiarize technology

demonstrate their skill sets to each other, to give and take ideas while respecting members' rights to speak and be heard, and get to know one another at a personal level. This occurs naturally when members do a variety of things, such as ask each other about their weekend activities, discuss each other's children, and talk about the latest gossip. In short, they develop a sense of being a collective just by interacting with each other on a regular basis and getting to know one another at both professional and personal levels.

This does not typically happen spontaneously with VTs. For VT members to develop mutual trust, they must complete their team-related work on time and with the expected level of quality (Jarvenpaa et al., 1998; Jarvenpaa & Leidner, 1999). That is, trust is not between the members as individuals, per se, but between members as part of a working unit. Members learn they can rely on each other because they consistently fulfill their duties.

Cohesion (working together to form a unified whole) in VTs is characterized by formality, politeness, and professionalism directed at task performance.

Rarely does it take on the more informal cohesion of FTF teams. For example, our own research conducted in collaboration with other colleagues has found that short-term FTF teams are more cohesive than short-term VTs (MacDonnell, O'Neill, Klien, & Hambley, 2009). This is likely due to the limitations inherent in the capability of computer-based communication technologies to transmit emotional and humorous information. However, it is likely also due to people's relative inexperience with interpersonal work arrangements that do not include FTF contact. Indeed, several researchers have suggested evolutionary-based models, where team members get better at using non-FTF communication methods for person-focused discussions over time (for example, Kock, 2004; Walther, 1992). Keep in mind that VTs can and do develop trust and cohesion—it just takes longer than in FTF teams.

On the organization's side, one related issue is the use of electronic performance monitoring (for example, monitoring e-mail content, keypresses) to supervise employee productivity. This controversial practice has been linked to stress, decreased physical health, and the avoidance of using monitored tools (for example, Aiello & Kolb, 1995; Markus, 1983). In addition, if trust is damaged, citizenship behaviors, job satisfaction, and in-role performance will decrease, whereas counterproductive behaviors will increase. Not surprisingly, leaders may be more likely to monitor performance when they expect a particular VT member's productivity to be lacking (Alge, Ballinger, & Green, 2004). We suggest avoiding electronic performance monitoring in general, however, because of the negative consequences of this practice. If it is needed, allowing member input to the program and how it is used (for example, for feedback purposes), and using openness and sensitivity in its application will help increase acceptance.

What you can do. How does one build trust and cohesion in VTs? It starts with everyone on the team being clear on the task. This includes the expectations for the quality of the work, the timelines and budget for the work, each person's role in the work, and putting into place a way to monitor team members and team progress on a regular basis. Particularly at the beginning of the task, team members' making and keeping milestones will ensure that they develop trust and cohesion. Regular conference calls, videoconferences, and e-mail exchanges can facilitate the process. If at all possible, the team should get together FTF for a "kick-off" meeting so that members can put faces with names, e-mail messages, and voices on the phone. This helps personalize the team members to each other (Cascio & Shurygailo, 2002; Hambley, O'Neill, & Kline, 2007b).

Rational: Hold Effective Meetings, Align Goals, and Use Technology Appropriately

It was noted earlier that meetings are an important part of developing team trust and cohesion. However, holding effective meetings for VTs is difficult due to many factors. First, there is a lack of socioemotional cues between members. For example, the impoverished environment of e-mail makes it difficult for the proper "tone" to come across to other team members. One member may be making a joke, but another might interpret the joke as a serious remark and possibly react in a counterproductive way. This is particularly problematic when VT members are from different cultures; language barriers and local communication norms can impose an added layer that may contribute to misunderstandings.

What you can do. Even between members of FTF teams, meetings are often viewed as time wasting. In order to have effective VT meetings, agendas should be sent out in advance, with enough time for all members to review pertinent documents and information in order to be prepared to contribute to the meeting. A protocol for interacting in the meetings should be agreed on beforehand. This should include instructions that (1) each person is expected to put forth his or her views on the agenda items; (2) each person is allowed to complete his or her thoughts without being interrupted; (3) members should build on prior contributions, and not review or rehash old issues; (4) minutes of the meeting are sent out within twenty-four hours of completion of the meeting, with action items highlighted for each member to complete, providing documentation of the members' expectations of each other; (5) the next meeting time is agreed on; and (6) follow-ups are conducted to ensure that action items were completed, and if not, the reasons why. Following this process helps align member expectations, which ultimately allows members to predict future team member actions and adapt behavior accordingly (that is, develop a "shared mental model"; see Fiore, Salas, & Cannon-Bowers, 2001). For other ideas on VT meeting effectiveness, see checklists provided by Bradley and Beyerlein (2005).

Another rational issue is that all teams perform better when their goals are aligned with those of the organizations involved (Kline, 1999a). Because VTs often represent geographical or functional differences in the organization, it is even more difficult for VTs to align themselves with large organizational goals. There may even be cases where the goals of one part of the organization conflict with the goals of another part of the organization. If members of the VT come from these different units, superordinate goals have to be generated so that the VT members can work together and share a meaningful direction. For dealing with this issue (and many others), team leadership is crucial. The VT leader provides the link between the VT and the rest of the organization. An important role for the leader is to ensure that VT members are working on tasks relevant to the organization, that the primary team goal is authoritatively delivered to team members, and that the exact means of reaching that goal are left to the team to decide. If these conditions are met, then the VT will have a better chance of performing effectively for the organization (Hackman, 2002; Wageman, 2003). This should hold regardless of whether the leadership role is formally assigned or naturally emerges.

Finally, VT members will have different needs and familiarity with different technologies. It is important that all members are comfortable with the various technologies used for communicating (Kline, 1999a). Some collaboration tools to keep the team coordinated, organized, and on track toward its goals are instant messaging, e-rooms, collaborative space, data-sharing applications, electronic bulletin boards, collaborative authoring programs, and project forums, to name a few (for many others, see Bradley, 2008). Simply having workshops on technology use for all team members will go a long way toward solving technological issues that may seem simple but that get in the way of effective work. It should not be assumed, however, that team members have the needed technological skills simply because they are familiar with the communication software and hardware. At team start-up, norms around what collaboration tools will be used for what purposes must be made explicit, and revised accordingly thereafter. One suggestion is to stick to richer mediums early to help the team develop shared expectations, and gradually shift to leaner methods once everyone is on the same page (O'Neill, Lewis, & Hambley, 2008).

STRUCTURE

In the previous section of this chapter, we discussed how some of the environmental contextual factors may impact the effectiveness of VTs. In this section we turn to the structure of the VTs themselves to understand how best to facilitate VTs from this perspective.

Relational: Maintain Psychological Safety and Keep Teams Small

Teams work well when their members feel they are working in a "psychologically safe" space (Edmondson, 1999). This means that team members feel free to provide honest opinions without fear of retribution by the other team members. Such an environment fosters creativity and openness in the members (Gibson & Gibbs, 2006). For VTs this is can be particularly problematic, as nothing is "off the record." In fact, almost everything discussed can be captured on some sort of recording device. Thus members should be cautioned to keep discussions focused on team tasks and not on office politics. Humor should be used, but with care that no individual or group is being singled out as the subject of that humor. Although this may seem stilted, it does ensure that the VT is perceived by its members and by others to be professional in its interactions.

Another structural issue that plagues many teams is size. Frequently members are added to teams for politically expeditious reasons—members are there to represent a constituency. This hinders FTF teams from working effectively and can be debilitating for VTs. It is difficult enough to find times for integral VT members to meet virtually, let alone try to accommodate members who may be tangential to the task at hand. Thus VTs should be used on short-term projects where the task is clear and the members of the team are all active contributors to the team's work, either in terms of expertise they bring to bear or the skill sets they have to complete the work. As is the case with FTF teams, smaller is better in terms of team size for VTs (Kirkman & Mathieu, 2005).

What you can do. Recently, Walther and Bunz (2005) identified six rules for virtual groups that facilitate the development of trust, cohesion, and performance. First, the group should start on task work immediately, as virtual work tends to take longer than work done FTF, and VTs tend to put off task work longer. Further, research has clearly documented a procrastination effect in teams; that is, teams tend to delay substantive work until about the midpoint of the team's life cycle. Whereas that strategy may work in FTF teams, VTs who follow suit will probably fail to reach their objectives on time. For the second rule, Wather and Bunz stipulate that communication must be very frequent, as some team members may need information before continuing their tasks or may need to be made aware of something and adapt their work accordingly. Third, the team should multitask, getting organized and working on action steps simultaneously. Planning and strategy formation can take a significant amount of a team's time—even more so in virtual space. This means less time for task work. Tasks must be assigned, and may later be modified at the same time as strategy is developed. The last three rules are fairly self-explanatory but nonetheless deserve mention: members should overtly acknowledge that they have read one another's messages; members need to be explicit about what they are thinking and doing; and they must set deadlines and stick to them. These six rules represent norms or standard operating procedures that should be made explicit if virtual teamwork is going to be effective and the virtual climate is going to be trusting and cohesive. Keeping teams small will facilitate the development of a psychologically safe structure.

Rational: Set Goals, Consider Individual Member Needs, and Develop Team Identity

The fulfillment of leader roles is probably the most important structural issue to impact the day-to-day operation of the VT. One of the most salient roles for the leader is the establishment of goals for the team. Because VT members do not have the luxury of FTF discussions about their goals, and because VTs need to move forward as quickly as possible with substantive task work, it is often best to have goals assigned. Goal-setting theory, one of the most widely accepted theories in organizational research, suggests that as long as the assigned goals are accepted and committed to, a participatory discussion about the goals is not needed (Latham & Marshall, 1982). Accordingly, goals should be set such that tasks are concretely understood and the project is of such duration that members can see it through to completion.

What you can do. Although the purpose and direction of the team should not be up for debate, we recommend a participatory approach to setting the smaller goals that will lead to attaining the overarching missions of the team. A participatory approach might involve the leader suggesting a short-term goal and allowing the VT members to provide feedback. In this way, the goal can be revised and negotiated to ensure feasibility, acceptance, and commitment. Throughout the goal-setting process, it is critical to demonstrate confidence in team members' abilities, as this should increase the difficulty of goals selected and the quality of the resulting performance. Ultimately, it will be helpful to outline what goals are expected to be completed by certain times so that the team stays on track with regard to its expected work (in other words, set deadlines and stick to them).

Although individual goals are needed, it should be clear that team-level goals are important too. Again, the superordinate mission should be set by the team leader or project manager. To get VT members on board with the team's purpose, a team identity should be established. When team identification is high, team members internalize the values, needs, and beliefs of the group (Ellemers, De Gilder, & Haslam, 2004). Essentially, the team's values and purpose become, at some level, those of the individual members. When team identification is high, and the team looks as though it is set on a trajectory for success, motivation to contribute toward the team effort (that is, the superordinate goal) will be highest.

The best ways to get team members to identify with the team are to (1) show confidence that the team can accomplish its task, (2) provide the resources needed, (3) demonstrate how the superordinate goal or purpose is an important one, and (4) link the superordinate goal to smaller, short-term team and personal goals that are doable (O'Neill, Lewis, & Hambley, 2008). Another role for the leader is to ensure that each member feels that he or she is contributing to the task. This means assigning tasks to members that they can complete, providing them with the resources needed to complete their work, and ensuring that everyone is rewarded and recognized for his or her contributions. This is not an easy job for leaders of VTs. It takes time and energy to check in with each member on a regular basis to determine if there are problems with which the member needs assistance in order to complete his or her section of the task. Nevertheless, this is time well spent by VT leaders, as it ensures that the team members are all working together effectively toward a common end, and it shows that the leader is considerate of each individual's unique challenges and constraints. VTs should be recognized not only for their task accomplishments but also for their capability of working across distances and time zones. This balanced approach to the assessment of VT member performance is exhibited by the best VT leaders (Hambley et al., 2007b).

PROCESS

The final factor to be examined regarding VTs is that of the internal processes of the team in conducting its work. Process issues have an impact on all the aspects of team performance outlined in the Introduction. This is not surprising, as process issues are really how the team accomplishes its work, and such variables set the stage for future team functioning and performance (Ilgen, Hollenbeck, Johnson, & Jundt, 2005).

Relational: Manage Team Conflict and Respect Divergent Values

One thing that is impossible to avoid in teamwork is conflicts of opinion. Dealing effectively with group conflict is especially difficult in VTs because of (1) the limited time members can spend interacting to resolve conflicts, (2) the increased time needed to manage such conflicts using virtual means, and (3) the fact that conflict is likely to be perceived as negative and aggressive in VTs. Meta-analyses show that group conflict is almost certainly detrimental to group performance (De Dreu, 2008). It is important to determine how conflicts will be resolved in the team *before* they happen.

What you can do. If a set of principles for making decisions when members have different perspectives on an issue is established ahead of time, then this protocol can be observed when the conflict occurs. Perhaps the team agrees that they must meet FTF when conflicts arise. Perhaps a set of alternatives is suggested with pros and cons of each, circulated to members, and a virtual meeting devoted to the resolution of the issue is scheduled. Whatever the approach, it should be viewed as fair by all team members. This will ensure their continued support for the team and its tasks.

Even with conflict management norms in place, conflict may still occur. This is bound to happen in teamwork, as people just don't always agree with each other, no matter what the ground rules are. But in VTs, the impact of the technology might make conflict more likely. To address interpersonal conflicts, we suggest employing the tried-and-true methods based on the organization development literature. One approach, called role negotiation (Harrison, 1972), asks each VT member to list what he or she expects of the other members. The group can then meet with a facilitator or coach to review this information and jointly clarify and negotiate each member's role. A second method involves bringing in an independent third party to help the group move through the real issues that underlie the conflict. The intervention should aim to (1) prevent ignition of further conflicts, (2) constrain the current form of conflict, (3) help the team cope differently with sources of conflict, and (4) resolve the issues on which the conflict is based (for more, see Walton, 1969).

One final suggestion for mitigating conflict is to take the time to develop formalized channels for dealing with problems. This is particularly important for VTs, as the team leader may not be the members' direct supervisor, meaning it may become unclear who should manage complaints. A good starting point would be to have the VT members consult the team leader. If the VT leader fails to effectively manage the problem, however, members should know where the problem can be reported. Whatever the appropriate channel is, making a plan in advance and communicating it to the team provide members with appropriate avenues for dealing with conflict and ways to go around the leader, should the case warrant such an approach.

Whereas many teams may have conflicting views about how to carry out their work, VTs are more likely to suffer from value incongruence between members because they are more likely than FTF teams to be made up of members from different countries. Drawing on the work of Hofstede (1980) and results from project GLOBE (for example, Javidan, Dorfman, de Luque, & House, 2006), we know that different cultures have different views about power distance, individualism, masculinity, uncertainty avoidance, and long-term orientations, to name a few. These can sometimes get in the way of the VT accomplishing its tasks. For example, in India, paternalistic and authoritative leadership is often preferred. However, for people in the United States, participative leadership is typically most important for performance (Dorfman & House, 2004). The best way to deal effectively with these and other value differences is to identify them in advance and make a determination of whether or not they will be a hindrance to the VT's work. At these junctures, plan on having several virtual meetings, and anticipate a slowdown in the team's work until the issue is resolved.

Political: Address Stakeholder Views and Empower the Virtual Team

Obtaining adequate representation from all the relevant stakeholder groups is problematic for VTs. VTs must be small to work effectively, but may miss out on some major perspectives in completing their work if a particular stakeholder group is left out. Furthermore, FTF teams may get accolades from their organization for a "job well done" and accrue scarce resources for the team as part of their reward. For VTs, however, team rewards are not easily obtained, and members do not easily build a sense of being an empowered team. These challenges have negative consequences for working together in the future and for the work satisfaction of team members (Kirkman, Rosen, Gibson, Tesluk, & McPherson, 2002).

What you can do. One way to manage stakeholder views is to include all relevant stakeholders when setting up the VT's primary goals and work plan. This way their perspectives can be conveyed to the VT members before work commences. However, the various stakeholders do not have to actually conduct or oversee the VT's day-to-day work. Interim reports to stakeholders on the team's accomplishments, and meetings of the stakeholders with the team leader are efficient ways to keep stakeholders "in the loop" as well as to take advantage of their perspectives.

Encouraging and supporting VTs and their members may be accomplished by using participative leadership principles (for example, allowing members some discretion in their work) and showing individualized consideration (for example, paying attention to each member's special circumstances). Moreover, such relationship-oriented leadership behaviors may increase motivation and feelings of empowerment (see Avolio & Kahai, 2002). Empowerment is generally thought to hinge on intrinsic motivation, and is characterized by a sense of personal competence and the feeling that one's work has an impact, is meaningful, and involves choice (Pinder, 1998). Some of our previous suggestions are consistent with those that lead to empowerment: leaders should specify goals, but not the means for accomplishing those goals; instill confidence in the team; build a team identity; show individualized consideration; and communicate frequently. Putting these conditions into place should help the VT feel more empowered and intrinsically motivated, enabling it to perform excellent work.

Rational: Solve Problems, Meet Deadlines, and Negotiate Personality Issues

By setting up an agreed-on problem-solving process and setting problem-solving norms across geographical locations and time zones, teams will be better able to anticipate conflict and confront it before it happens. VT leaders need to ensure that team members do not avoid important task-related conflict when it arises, or use strategies that result in a compromise when that is not the optimal solution to the problem (see results from Montoya-Weiss, Massey, & Song, 2001). Indeed, those authors found that the lack of FTF contact necessitated either a more competitive approach to dealing with conflict, or a more collaborative approach where the most important points of each party are incorporated into the final solution (see also Kline & Sell, 1996). Other methods that did not work included avoiding, compromising, and accommodating. Thus, the VT leader must oversee the use of one conflict management strategy over another and step in when needed to determine whether one particular group member's suggestion is best (competitive), or an additive sum of several members' ideas should be formed (collaborative).

Regardless of the approach used, ensuring the most effective problem-solving and conflict-resolution processes may not always leave members feeling equally satisfied. When this happens, team members need to know whom they can go to for support. Developing appropriate, formalized channels for dealing with conflict, usually beginning with the team leader, then including other parties from there, will help mitigate this problem. People often feel better if they at least know someone cares if they feel slighted and if they know they have an opportunity to complain if necessary.

One proposed problem-solving decision-making method that we think would be useful in VTs comes from Witte (2007). The author proposes the following problem-solving steps. First, an individual-oriented, structured technique aims to capture each team member's arguments around possible decisions. This circumvents well-known motivational losses usually called loafing and free riding, as well as biases such as group conformity and the sharing of information that is common (instead of unique) to each team member. These arguments are supported by the individual's own logical presumptions. All individual information is then shared anonymously—usually a facilitator or group leader will be needed. The anonymous sharing of information will preclude many subjective (and potentially biased) judgments that hinder problem solving. Finally, the group works to integrate the individual ideas to come up with the best approach possible. Witte's approach should be particularly effective in VT environments, where motivation losses and personal biases may operate at their strongest. On the upside, problem solving is generally more effective in VTs as personal issues can be set aside, and optimal task completion is of primary importance. For example, Jonassen and Kwon (2001) found that problem-solving VTs were more satisfied with the process and saw their solution quality as superior compared to FTF teams. The trick is to follow effective conflict management strategies outlined in this chapter and to keep the group focused on the task-related issues and not interpersonal ones.

Another work process issue that can plague VTs is that work may not be completed on schedule. It is easy to let work associated with VTs "slide" in the face of other tasks that are more salient to the members. To keep the VT's work at the attention of team members, a reminder schedule should be set up that automatically alerts members that work deadlines are approaching. These reminders can be sent through e-mail, collaborative workspaces, or desktop widgets, among other means. In addition, sanctions for members who do not complete their work and rewards for members who do complete their work should be set up to establish a culture of meeting deadlines. These consequences must be made clear to all team members, however, and they must be enforced, or else trust and cohesion may be threatened.

Finally, when it comes to the selection of VT members, the personality factor of conscientiousness is likely to be helpful, particularly in the area of following through on commitments (English, Griffith, & Steelman, 2004). People who are conscientious do their work well and get it done on time. Regarding other traits, Hertel, Konradt, and Voss (2006) found that performance ratings from VT leaders were higher for those members high in cooperativeness. This makes sense, as uncooperative team members are unlikely to contribute to the VT's mission. Elsewhere, Kline (1999b) refers to a trait known as *predisposition to be a team player.* Essentially, people high on that trait tend to enjoy working in teams, which was found to be predictive of team performance in a recent empirical study (MacDonnell et al., 2009). Finally, extroversion is likely to be important for VT members, as those who are more sociable, friendly, and talkative are likely to keep in better touch with other VT members and be more satisfied with working virtually (O'Neill, Hambley, Greidanus, MacDonnell, & Kline, 2009). When it comes to leaders, however, there may be a more important aspect of extroversion needed. The dominance-assertiveness facet of extroversion may be particularly important, as individuals high on this trait will probably be more explicit in directing VT members and making sure everyone on the VT is clear about his or her roles and responsibilities.

Empirical: Handle Communication Media and Familiarize Technology

It has long been known that the communication media used have an effect on VT effectiveness. They can hinder effective group interaction because they do not capture and replicate the entirety of a FTF exchange. In videoconference, for example, there is typically a time lag between the movement seen on the screen and the voiceover that accompanies it, making communication more challenging (Hambley, O'Neill, & Kline, 2007a). In e-mail, the environment is completely impoverished, with little to no allowance for emotion, tone, or nonverbal body language to assist in interpreting the meaning of a team member's statements.

What you can do. To combat these problems, team members need to become familiar with using the technology. They should have time to be trained in how to use it and also how to repair it should the need arise. That way, the members are not dependent on technology staff to assist them with their VT interactions. In addition, simply having experience with these newer technologies is a great asset for VT members. Making time for trial runs and training sessions can assist in making VTs interact more effectively. But recall also that norms around communication must be set up so that team members are on the same page in terms of how best to communicate different types of messages: richer methods earlier on, followed by leaner, more efficient ones later. The choice of medium also depends on the purpose of the message. If the message is a motivational one from the leader, then a rich method is needed; if the message is solely task related and relatively simple, and familiarity is high, then a leaner method such as instant messaging should work.

Meetings have to be held at unusual hours for some team members if they are geographically dispersed. The meetings should be held so that each member of the team is inconvenienced equitably by time zone differences (Hambley et al., 2007b). In the study cited, one leader referred to this practice as a "share the pain" mentality, whereby everyone takes a turn meeting at an inconvenient time. Finally, people must agree to be available during a certain set of core hours so that communication is not delayed more than it needs to be.

CONCLUSION

It is certain that VTs pose greater challenges to organizations than those faced by traditional, FTF teams. The plethora of academic and practitioner readings on the topic demonstrates both a fascination with VTs and the difficulties in making them effective. In this chapter, we provided some guidance to VT leaders about how they can improve team functioning. The suggestions were based on the research literature and, where that was sparse, on our own experiences.

Referring back to Figure 11.1, there appear to be two issues that underlie the challenges to VT effectiveness. Simply put, most of the difficulties can be described as hindering communication or motivation. For instance, holding effective meetings relates to communication, and building a team identity is a motivational concern. Furthermore, these overriding issues are deeply intertwined, as most attempts to enhance motivation include communication, and communication is often driven by motivational concerns. Thus, for VTs, keeping communication and motivational issues at the forefront can serve as a quick and easy heuristic for noticing potential problems before they arise. After identifying a threat to the team's performance or functioning, you can refer back to the specific strategies that were mentioned in this chapter. We trust that the topics covered will be helpful to current and future VT leaders and members. After all, virtual teamwork is an organizational issue that can only become more important in the years to come.

chapter
TWELVE

Politics of the Arts: Challenges in Working with Nonprofit Boards

Richard W. Sline and Anna C. Boulton

There was silence in the room as every head turned in our direction. We just sat there dumbfounded. Norm, the board chair, had opened the meeting by updating the new people about the history of our involvement with the Foundation and our agreed-on role with this project. He then turned the meeting over to us. Out of respect, rather than jump right into the planning process we had prepared to facilitate, we asked Kevin, the executive director, if he had any opening comments. To our utter amazement, Kevin informed those present that a smaller group including two new board members had convened a few days before, over wine, and had drafted a set of recommendations for this group to discuss. In that single statement, our entire process was sabotaged once again!

Working with the boards of directors of nonprofit arts organizations can be challenging for external facilitators. The very nature of a nonprofit arts organization influences the group dynamics and contributes to the potential for ineffective group decision-making processes. To illustrate *how* working with nonprofit arts boards can be difficult, we begin with a case in which we were contracted to provide external facilitation for the strategic planning initiative of a medium-size nonprofit arts organization. We then analyze the case using Schuman and Rohrbaugh's Competing Values Framework (in the Introduction to this volume) to explain, at least in part, *why* this group was difficult. In our analysis, we draw upon parallel experiences we have had in our respective positions working with other nonprofit arts organization boards.

Although grounded in theory and praxis of nonprofit board governance, the chapter is written as a "confessional tale" (Van Maanen, 1988) in which we retrospectively reveal our own culpability in the choices we made throughout the extended process of working with this nonprofit board. We then suggest what others can do to compensate for the political issues that can inhibit facilitator success.

HOW THESE GROUPS WERE DIFFICULT

Year 1: Our History with the Music Foundation Begins

Our seven-year history with the Music Foundation (a $700,000 per year organization hereafter referred to as "the Foundation") began when we were contracted to conduct an analysis of a conflict that had developed between the Foundation and its host community's Chamber of Commerce over the ownership of a successful three-day summer music festival that had been sponsored by the Foundation but essentially managed and heavily funded by the Chamber. It is important to note that the funds for this consulting intervention were provided by the festival's primary corporate sponsor. The corporate leaders were pleased with their sponsorship role but very concerned about the ongoing bickering between the Foundation and the Chamber, and had made it clear that the conflict had to be resolved.

After weeks of interviewing stakeholders in both organizations, we designed and facilitated a daylong "confrontation meeting" that allowed the major stakeholders to carefully examine the issues through a process that encouraged openness and perspective sharing (Beckhard, 1967; French & Bell, 1984). This particular meeting was one of those magical experiences that occasionally occur between external facilitators and clients (Sline, 2006). Two major outcomes from the facilitation were adopted: the Foundation's board was reconstituted and expanded to include several members appointed by the Chamber, and the founder of the Foundation was asked to step down as the organization's president and turn the leadership responsibility over to someone who could provide a fresh start to the newly constituted board.

Years 2–4: Growing Pains

We both continued working with the board for the next five years as pro bono organizational advisers. The organization began to achieve some stability during this period, although it did so with considerable staff and board member turnover. Much of this turnover could be attributed to underlying tensions among board members and staff leadership created by their differing relationships with the founder and their opinions about his level of involvement.

Our roles with the Foundation expanded when we were each asked to serve on different Foundation committees as non-board members. We also facilitated a successful board and staff retreat, attended board meetings, and participated in ongoing communication.

These years were turbulent ones for the board and staff leaders, characterized by the resignation of a very competent festival director and the hasty hiring and almost immediate termination of a new festival director. However, the most embarrassing event was an emotional public conflict involving two of the Foundation's leaders, Craig and Mick, who served respectively as chair and vice chair of the board. After the new hire was terminated, Craig agreed to step down as board chair so that he could serve as the interim festival director to get the organization through the festival. Mick, in turn, stepped up to serve as interim board chair. Although the festival was successful in the eyes of the audience, it lost a lot of money. Even worse in the minds of many, Craig and Mick created tremendous turmoil among board members, staff, and community volunteers; their conflict culminated on the last night of the festival, where, in the front rows of the audience (occupied by festival donors), they engaged in a public shouting match and physical altercation.

Shortly after the dust settled, we were contracted by the board to conduct an investigation and analysis of this conflict. Interviews with board members revealed beliefs that egos, hidden agendas, and power struggles for control were the source of much of the problem. Many were justifiably concerned about public image because too much alcohol consumption contributed to the festival outbursts.

After this intervention, a continuing pattern of leadership turnover ensued, including the hiring of a new board chair and a new festival director, who only remained in the position for eighteen months. This was due in part to the redefinition of the festival director position to Foundation executive director, with greater responsibility and authority. This established the structure to allow for a more appropriate division of board and staff roles and responsibilities, a change for which we had been advocating for some time.

Year 5: The Beginning of Our Problems

Kevin, a young energetic man with a marketing and sales background, was quickly hired as the new Foundation executive director. Immediately he began to look for ways to create a development position responsible for fundraising. He approached the festival's primary corporate sponsor with a proposal for a three-year capacity-building grant of $60,000 to help defray the salary for this position. The corporation representatives clearly stated that due to the Foundation's turbulence over the past five years, they were only interested in making this investment if we were willing to help facilitate a long-range planning process to increase the organization's sustainability. In essence, we became a condition of the grant, a condition, we subsequently discovered, that Kevin did not wholeheartedly accept.

When we first met with Kevin to discuss our facilitation proposal, he seemed visibly stunned at the level of board member involvement and number of hours we projected. However, he included our estimated hours in his grant proposal and put off finalizing the details of our work until after the grant was formally approved. He subsequently submitted and received the grant to hire a part-time development director; the grant provided (this grant also included funds) for our facilitation of a sequence of four interconnected task force projects to be completed by fall 2006.

Year 6: A Year of Frustration

In January of our sixth year working with the Foundation, Norm, an experienced business leader, began his term as board chair. At about the same time, Kevin hired a part-time director of development for the Foundation. Whereas we expected that the long-range planning process would quickly get under way, it was delayed. We made numerous attempts throughout January and February to contact both Kevin and Norm about beginning the planning process, but with no success. Finally, Norm responded to explain "the unavoidable nature of these delays."

He explained that the Foundation had been in discussions with the International Association of Music Educators (IAME) about partnering with the Foundation to host IAME's annual weeklong summer institute. Even though the financial terms of this partnership had not been agreed on, when Kevin attended IAME's annual convention in New York, he allowed himself to be introduced to over seven thousand delegates as a representative of IAME's new partner organization. At this time, he presented the IAME leaders with a symbolic check for $1 million. This seemingly premature million-dollar pledge that had not been formally authorized by the Foundation board became a huge concern and, over the course of several months, consumed many hours of the board and its legal counsel.

The next several months presented a continual struggle to schedule the first two task force facilitations. The first task force, charged with developing a fundraising plan, did not meet until October. We hoped that the success of this meeting would serve as a catalyst to move the process along more quickly, but this was not the case. Kevin finally scheduled the second task force, charged with focusing on the future of the music festival, to meet in mid-November, despite the fact that some key board members could not attend. We were very surprised when in fact *no* board members were in attendance! Instead, only Kevin, two of his staff members, and a person Kevin was recruiting to join the board (whom he referred to as "someone of like mind") arrived with a written agenda of issues that he and Kevin wanted to address. Because no board members were in attendance and no decisions could be made, we decided to remain silent, let the meeting run its course, and then reschedule for another date. We communicated our concerns to the board chair, Norm, who led us to believe that these problems would be rectified. If they were, we couldn't tell from what happened next.

Year 7: The Final Straw

Our efforts to convene the next task force meeting continued to be difficult, complicated by scheduling issues and changes in the composition of the task forces to suit Kevin's needs. Then, at the meeting described at the beginning of this chapter, we were dumbfounded when Kevin once again undermined the agreed-on facilitation process. Once again, we felt strategically circumvented, disconfirmed, and disrespected.

From this series of events, it appeared quite obvious to us that Kevin was not happy with the process that he and Norm had agreed we would follow. This led us to seriously question the level of commitment that the Foundation truly had to create a long-range plan for the organization's sustainability. After lengthy discussion, we concluded that major changes were needed in order for us to continue as facilitators of this project.

WHY THIS GROUP WAS DIFFICULT

Competing Values and Nonprofit Arts Boards

The conceptual framework for working with difficult groups presented in the Introduction provides a useful template to examine the factors that made our work with the Foundation so problematic. Rohrbaugh (2005) argues that in the Competing Values Framework as applied to groups, an appropriate balance needs to exist among relational, empirical, political, and rational values within a group's context, structure, and processes in order for the group to achieve optimal effectiveness. Yet our collective experience working with many nonprofit organization boards suggests that such an optimal balance rarely occurs—making the facilitation of such groups particularly challenging. Our experience summarized in this chapter serves to illustrate how an overemphasis of some of these competing values can create chronic group impairment. Although there were problems associated with the relational, empirical, and rational perspectives in the framework, all but one of the issues that made this group difficult were within the political domain. These issues are summarized in Table 12.1 with their corresponding indicators, identifying factors, and effectiveness strategies.

Political Context: Struggles for Legitimacy

The Foundation was preoccupied with gaining legitimacy in the eyes of external stakeholders. Examples of this preoccupation included its drive to be recognized as one of the most prestigious music festivals of its genre in the world and its continuing attempt to bolster its legitimacy in the eyes of its community Chamber of Commerce by increasing tourism revenue. We believe these were the Foundation's major motivations for jumping into a partnership with IAME to host its

Table 12.1

Nonprofit Indicators, Identifying Factors, and Strategies for Group Effectiveness

Domain	Nonprofit Indicator	Identifying Factors in Case Study	Effectiveness Strategies
Political—context	Struggle for legitimacy	Foundation's partnership with IAME	Recognize this need for legitimacy in planning and group processes, by using specific activities such as environmental scanning, SWOT, and so on.
		Status as a tourism draw with the Chamber of Commerce	Clarify your role and possible impact up front with the group.
		Need for involvement with corporate sponsor	
		Position of facilitator with the state arts agency	
Political—context	Drive for adequate resources—money and time	Continuing focus on financial survival	Recognize the need for concise processes, and plan appropriately when possible
		Reactive, time-starved leadership and other group members, especially board members	Fully explain why specific processes need additional time
		(Reactive, time-starved leaders and board members.)	Offer suggestions for possible resources to fund an effective process.

(*Continued*)

Table 12.1
(*Continued*)

Domain	Nonprofit Indicator	Identifying Factors in Case Study	Effectiveness Strategies
Political—structure	Struggle for leadership and authority	Dual authority structures, unclear board and staff roles	Become familiar with the organization's history and current structure as outlined in the bylaws.
		Founder's syndrome	Clearly define who the client is and specify that in the contract.
		Frequent leadership turnover and restructuring	Recognize board turnover as you plan a lengthy process and provide continuity activities.
Political—process	Controlling stakeholder input	Resistance from executive director, delays and excuses	Be specific with deadlines, time lines, and so on in the contractual process and hold to them.
		Strategic inclusion and exclusion of participants	Ensure that stakeholder interests are represented in the group.
Relational—structure and process	Destructive conflicts	History of conflict, personal animosities	Probe and interview to fully understand driving forces behind conflicts.
		Expectation that member are above discord in nonprofits	Address possible conflict when developing the process plan; suggest that the organization establish a conflict management plan.
		Confusion with regard to who is the "client"	Allow time to gather input from all stakeholders.
		Perceived trust	

annual summer institute, even before knowing whether it could financially support this partnership. A third example was the Foundation's continual focus on retaining legitimacy in the eyes of the seven-year corporate sponsor of its annual music festival. Finally, a contributing factor underlying its struggle for legitimacy was one of the author's (Anna's) position with the Utah Arts Council, a state government agency. Her perception of the organization's legitimacy had the potential to influence its chances of receiving state, regional, and National Endowment for the Arts (NEA) grants to support its programs.

Political Context: The Drive for Adequate Resources—Money and Time

Nonprofits are values driven, not profit driven, and often this factor contributes to ineffective group functioning (Carver, 1990; Howe, 1995; Larson, 2008). As the Foundation developed and its programs grew, a myopic attention was focused on how to raise more money from sponsors, donors, and grants, as evidenced by the need for a capacity-building grant to pay the salary of a development director for the Foundation.

Another resource deficiency of nonprofit arts boards is adequate time to effectively perform their functions. Board members of large arts organizations are often people from upper socioeconomic levels with multiple motivations for participation. Many are indeed arts patrons, but others only possess a drive to gain and retain legitimacy in the eyes of other members of their social circles. These board members often hold simultaneous positions on several nonprofit boards and are seated more for their financial connections than for their expertise. Hence, nonprofit arts boards are frequently reactive and time-starved, without "adequate time to complete all group work" (Rohrbaugh, 2005, p. 454). Typically volunteer boards are always in a rush. There's never enough time to thoroughly prepare for making decisions about sophisticated, complicated strategic planning or to efficiently schedule such activity (Carver, 1990; Larson, 2008; Robinson, 2001). This problem is exacerbated because nonprofit board members are not compensated for their time and frequently are busy professionals with multiple commitments.

Political Structure: Struggles for Leadership, Authority, and Control

The locus of legitimate group leadership is a common problem with nonprofit boards (Carver, 1990). Depending on the organization's stage of development and size of staff, legitimate leadership and authority are often predicated on the relationship between the board chair and the executive director. These two individuals set the tone and can avert potential problems or, conversely, create a "we-they" climate that limits the group's effectiveness (Wolf, 1999). With the Foundation, we experienced a continual fluctuation in this perception of legitimacy from both the internal and external stakeholders. Board chairs often overstepped their role and involved themselves in administrative tasks and programmatic decisions that should clearly be an executive director's responsibility. This was most evident in the earlier growth period of the Foundation, when the leadership was transitioning from the founder to the festival director and eventually the Foundation director (Kimberley & Miles, 1980; Simon & Donovan, 2001).

For quite some time, the Foundation was clearly experiencing what is often referred to as *founder's syndrome.* Nonprofits are very prone to becoming dependent on the person or persons who initially started the organization. Founders tend to be dynamic, visionary, and charismatic, all of which are strong assets beneficial to getting the new nonprofit off the ground. As the organization grows from an entrepreneurial stage to a more established one, however, some founders have difficulty changing the way they lead and manage the organization. Often, the founder becomes anxious and defensive, which can lead to the formation of alliances and factions, and to passive-aggressive behavior by both the board and staff (McNamara, 2008; Kimberly & Miles, 1980, Simon & Donovan, 2001; Wolf, 1999). Board members will frequently tolerate this untenable situation far longer than they should, sometimes putting an organization at risk and "almost always undermining the morale of those connected with it" (Wolf, 1999, p. 135).

In the case of the Foundation in 2000, the founder had been asked to step aside as the chair of the board due to conflicts with other members of the board, but he remained on the board as a lifetime ex-officio member. As a visionary, he represented the passionate "heart and soul" of the organization and had his followers. However, over time his passion was overshadowed by board members and leaders concerned with the business aspects of the organization. His influence over the organization waned, which contributed to his exhibiting anxious, defensive, and passive-aggressive behavior that further marginalized him from the board.

Another factor common in nonprofits that contributed to the struggle for legitimate leadership, authority, and control in the Foundation was the rapid turnover of leadership of board chairs, staff festival directors, and board members. In the seven-year period of our involvement with the Foundation, there were no fewer than eight chairs and six festival directors! Frequent turnover also strains staff relationships with board members, illustrated by the repeated need of executive directors to seek affirmation and legitimacy.

Political Process: Controlling Stakeholder Input

Kevin had a high need to control both the process and outcomes of the strategic planning process. As evidenced by who was invited and present at the meetings, we perceive that he attempted to involve only new board members who were "of like mind"—that is, who agreed with his vision for the organization. Even though there is strong evidence that participative management will lead to more effective organizational outcomes, Kevin, like many organizational leaders, resisted stakeholder involvement, and as Block (1981, p. 123) writes, "When we get resistance, one good guess why is the manager feels he or she is going to lose control."

Also, it seems quite apparent that Kevin resisted our involvement as Foundation stakeholders. Our respective roles as cofacilitators went far beyond the normal external client-facilitator relationship. We had a long-term dual relationship as advisory nonvoting members of the Foundation and as consultants. We were members of foundation committees, had open invitations to attend board meetings, and received minutes of all meetings, yet we were not officially members of the board. In essence, we were not a part of the board system but, rather, resource inputs to that system. We were considered longtime stakeholders in the organization, and our relationship with the organization was predicated on our perception that we were trusted and would be dealt with in trustworthy ways.

In addition to his behavior undermining our planned facilitations, there was other evidence that Kevin resisted our involvement in the project from the beginning. The inordinate amount of time it took to launch the project and the huge gaps in time between different segments of the project can be viewed as a form of resistance. As Block (1981, p. 115) cautions, "The whole time issue, [which] we all face every day, is most often resistance against the client's having to tell you how he or she really feels about your project."

Relational Structure and Process: Destructive Conflicts

The final explanation for why this organization was a difficult group is best viewed within the relational domain of the Competing Values Framework. Relational values, overlapping the structure and process factors influencing group effectiveness, made working with these groups very difficult as well. The Foundation had a long history of ineffective management of internal conflict resulting from both structural and process influences. Ineffective conflict management is particularly common in nonprofit organizations due to the expectation that members are above discord because they are "good people doing good work" (Angelica, 1999, p. 4), dedicated to the values of the organization. Many nonprofits do not have clear conflict resolution procedures, and the Foundation was no exception (Boulton, 2005).

From a *structural* perspective, many conflicts within the Foundation were destructive and based on personal animosities between people who were disrespectful of and sometimes deceitful with one another. A litany of examples of conflicts between the founder and board and staff leadership occurred over our seven-year tenure with the Foundation. The public altercation between Craig and Mick, and Kevin's passive-aggressive behavior with us are other examples of destructive responses to conflict (Wood, 2007).

From a *process* perspective, many of the interventions with which we were asked to become involved were a result of the organization needing to rely on third parties to work through conflicts. However, many other conflicts were often simply avoided, which added to the defensive climate within the group (Gibb, 1961).

Kevin's unwillingness to confront us about his internal conflict with our role in the organizational sustainability project undermined our trust in him. The unwillingness of the board leadership to address Kevin's dysfunctional behavior had a similar effect on our trust in them. Much has been written about the importance of external facilitators and consultants building a trusting relationship with clients (Bell & Nurre, 2005; Block, 1981; Dannemiller, 1988; DeWine, 2001; Hunter & Thorpe, 2005; Rodas-Meeker & Meeker, 2005; Schwarz, 2002). However, trusting relationships are mutual, and very little is written about how external facilitators and consultants should respond when clients behave in nontrustworthy ways.

We approached our role as cofacilitators of this project embracing the key values from the International Association of Facilitators' Statement of Values and Code of Ethics for Group Facilitators, particularly those dealing with respect, safety, equity, and trust. However, these values were not reciprocally exhibited by the client. In hindsight, one explanation for this may be that the exact identity of our client was unclear. We believed that the Foundation board of directors was our client; however, this was probably not the view in the minds of the project leaders, Kevin and Norm. The financial sponsor of our project was the corporate sponsor of the music festival, the entity that granted funds for the Foundation's sustainability project. The corporate sponsor had practically mandated that the Foundation use our services in order to receive the overall grant. We are not sure whom Kevin and Norm viewed as our client, but their behavior suggests that they may have believed that the sponsor was also the client, rather than the Foundation board of directors. Perhaps Kevin and Norm felt coerced by the corporate sponsor. As Schwarz wrote, "being the client means you get to decide whether you want to work with me as the facilitator" (as cited in Hunter & Thorpe, 2005, p. 552). It is conceivable that Kevin and Norm believed that they were not given the choice of whether to work with us as facilitators.

Although we believed that we engaged this project without any conflicts of interest (Hunter & Thorpe, 2005), in hindsight, it's possible that we were unknowingly caught in the middle of a conflict between Kevin's interests and those of the sponsoring corporation. We were well into the project before we learned that the sponsoring corporation had decided to end its contract with the Foundation at the end of the 2007 festival. This impending severance, which had not yet been announced publicly, may well have contributed to Kevin's apparent apathy regarding our work with the Foundation.

WHAT YOU CAN DO

We recognize our culpability in assuming mutual trust due to our long-term relationship with the Foundation. This assumption led to our overlooking a need for a written contract that specified who the client was and the role expectations for each party. However, this experience afforded other valuable insights into ways facilitators might compensate for the difficult nature of working with nonprofit boards.

The following are some issues, questions, and suggestions to consider:

1. *Saying no.* When you have a history with the group such that you might be making assumptions about each other's roles, expectations, and levels of trust, consider saying no to the engagement.

If you continue to work with the nonprofit, give careful attention to written contracts, formal communication, and methods of addressing concerns as they arise.

2. Agreeing on *realistic time.* Is the group willing to spend enough time and resources to fully explore issues and adequately facilitate your process design or intervention?

Be clear on actual costs in terms of both time and money. Even pro bono work requires adequate time and resources for the group to accomplish its goals and objectives. Do not agree to a smaller amount of time or money if it will undermine the process.

3. *Ensuring equitable participation.* Are all the key stakeholders who are needed to address all aspects of the problem invited to the table openly and wholeheartedly?

Nonprofit boards are usually made up of people with diverse backgrounds and skills. Explore whether the leadership is "stacking the deck" with board members and other stakeholders who are like-minded so as to further its own agenda. Become familiar with state nonprofit meeting rules and the group's bylaws regarding decision making.

4. *Seeking openness.* How does the group respond to outside stakeholders? Do the leaders (for example, the executive director, board chair, founder) share similar views of establishing legitimacy with the outside environment?

Understand the nature of the current environment and the group's knowledge about that outside environment. If it is limited, consider processes to raise awareness and create a more responsive agenda.

5. *Understanding organizational history.* What is the history of conflict management within the organization? Is the original founder still involved with the leadership? What is the nature of that involvement?

Negotiate for time to interview a microcosm of organizational stakeholders to obtain multiple perspectives during the assessment stage. By identifying factions or tensions, you can address these issues before they undermine or blindside you and others. Don't make inferences from limited data.

6. *Terminating with integrity.* Know when and how you will decide to walk away from a difficult group.

Establish your boundaries for continuing contractual relationships with groups, and openly share them with the client. If expectations are repeatedly not fulfilled after due warning, walk away, knowing that some groups are not ready for help. "When the pupil is ready, the teacher will come."

CONCLUSION

Shortly after we left the Year 7 "final straw" meeting, we received e-mail messages from the board chair, Norm, and the vice chair, Jack, asking to schedule next steps in the Foundation's strategic planning effort, something that was very rare for them to do. We responded (with copy to Kevin), that before we could continue to be a part of the Foundation's strategic planning process, we needed to renegotiate our roles as consultants-facilitators because the current relationship was not working for us, and we suspected that at least some of them felt the same. We then outlined the chronology of events that had occurred (or not occurred) that led us to this conclusion, emphasizing that it had been over two years since the capacity-building grant had been awarded and that we still had not completed even half the project! We told them that we needed assurance that a sincere commitment existed to create a real strategic plan for the Foundation, not just to see the project through to be able to say it was done. We also articulated our need to be actively involved in decisions regarding changes in the process agreed on by Foundation leadership. Further, we emphasized that we would need to withdraw from the project if the process continued to be undermined and redirected.

We closed by suggesting two options for next steps: schedule a time as soon as possible for all parties to discuss our future role in light of the points we had made, or accept our decision to withdraw from the project. One week later, Kevin asked that we submit our final invoice for services.

In this confessional tale, we have attempted to demonstrate the kinds of political and relational constraints that external facilitators can experience when working with nonprofit groups. Establishing trusting facilitator-client relationships is extremely important for both external facilitators and client groups. Such relationships are particularly difficult to create in the normally short time between requests for project proposals and the time of contracting. In this case we thought we could avoid this difficult relationship-building time due to our long history with the Foundation. We assumed that our seven-year relationship with the organization would insulate us from the politics that can undermine otherwise well-designed facilitations. We couldn't have been more wrong.

chapter THIRTEEN

Competitive Group Interactions: Why They Exist and How to Overcome Them

Taya R. Cohen, Brian P. Meier,
Verlin B. Hinsz, and Chester A. Insko

On November 5, 2007, the Writers Guild of America (WGA) went on strike against the Alliance of Motion Picture and Television Producers (AMPTP) because of failed contract negotiations over various issues regarding payment of writers for the use of their material on new media, such as the Internet and DVDs. The WGA is a labor union that represents the interests of writers working in television, radio, and film in the United States; the AMPTP is a trade organization that represents the interests of approximately four hundred U.S. film and television producers. The writers' strike lasted one hundred tumultuous days, finally ending on February 12, 2008 (Cieply, 2008). Relations between the WGA and AMPTP were quite hostile during the strike, and the public nature of the controversy allowed audience members everywhere to witness this hostility firsthand. Over twelve thousand writers joined the strike (approximately four thousand of whom ultimately voted on the contract proposals), and some economists estimate that the strike cost the Los Angeles economy as much as $2.1 billion (White & Fixmer, 2008) and cost writers and production crew members over $340 million in lost wages (Littleton, 2007).

Why were relations between the WGA and AMPTP so contentious? Why did it take so much time before the WGA and the AMPTP could negotiate an agreement? In this chapter, we review empirical evidence relevant to answering these questions, and discuss when and why group interactions are competitive or antagonistic, and how competition can be replaced with cooperation. Although the findings we review are drawn primarily from social psychology experiments, we will return to the writers' strike example as a way of illustrating the empirical findings. Throughout the chapter, and particularly in the final section, we provide suggestions that group facilitators, leaders, and members can use to promote cooperation in interactions involving groups.

THE INTERINDIVIDUAL-INTERGROUP DISCONTINUITY EFFECT

Over three decades of research comparing the behavior of individuals in one-on-one interactions to the behavior of groups in group-on-group interactions have revealed that interactions between groups are less cooperative and more competitive than interactions between individuals in mixed-motive contexts, or situations involving a conflict of interests between two sides (McCallum et al., 1985; Schopler, Insko, Graetz, Drigotas, & Smith, 1991; Schopler et al., 2001; Wildschut, Pinter, Vevea, Insko, & Schopler, 2003; Wolf, Insko, Kirchner, & Wildschut, 2008). The prototypical example of a laboratory-based mixed-motive situation, or social dilemma, is the prisoner's dilemma game (PDG; see Figure 13.1). The PDG represents a situation in which there is a conflict

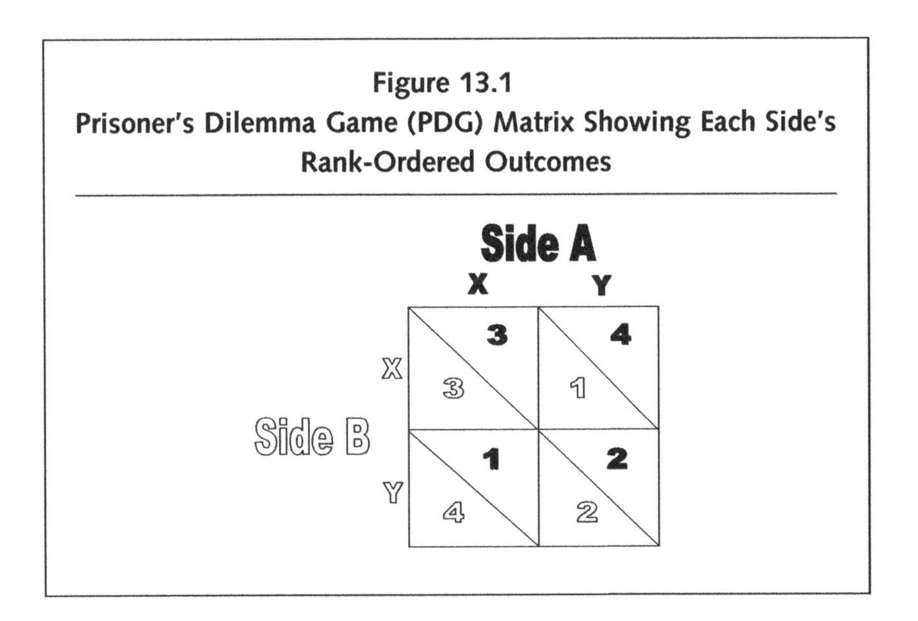

Figure 13.1
Prisoner's Dilemma Game (PDG) Matrix Showing Each Side's Rank-Ordered Outcomes

involving two sides. In Figure 13.1, these sides are labeled Side A (the bolded player) and Side B (the outlined player). Sides can comprise either individuals or groups. In the typical game used in experimental research, each side chooses one option, either X or Y. Each side's outcomes (for example, a monetary payoff) are determined jointly by its own decision (X or Y) and the other side's decision (X or Y). For example, if side A chooses X and side B chooses Y, side A receives $1 and side B receives $4.

The conflict inherent in the prisoner's dilemma is that each side can attempt to maximize its own outcomes (that is, receive the most money) by choosing Y (the competitive choice), but if both sides choose Y, they will both be worse off than if they had both chosen X (the cooperative choice). The game can be varied in a number of ways, including having players interact in one trial or over multiple trials, or allowing communication between the two sides or not. Put simply, "any situation in which you are tempted to do something, but know it would be a great mistake if everybody did the same thing is likely to be a prisoner's dilemma" (Ridley, 1996, pp. 55–56).

The PDG matrix was developed by game theorists in 1950, and its name comes from an anecdote about prisoners choosing whether or not to "rat on" their partner in crime. In the classic anecdote, each prisoner is faced with a decision to remain silent (choose X) or to give evidence against his partner (choose Y). The values in the matrix represent the severity of the sentence (4 = the most favorable sentence; 1 = the least favorable sentence). Each prisoner can minimize his sentence by giving evidence against the other, but if both choose to do so, they will both be convicted of more serious charges (resulting in the lower right-hand cell of Figure 13.1) than had they both remained silent (resulting in the upper left-hand cell of Figure 13.1). (For more on the history of game theory and the PDG, see Colman, 1995; Poundstone, 1992.)

Over one hundred experiments have compared group with individual behavior in the PDG and in PDG-like situations (Wildschut et al., 2003). Typically these studies compare the behavior of two interacting individuals to that of two interacting groups (groups are typically composed of three members). These studies have established that intergroup interactions are much less cooperative than interindividual interactions; that is, groups are more likely to choose Y, whereas individuals are more likely to choose X. John Thibaut, one of the first researchers to study this phenomenon, labeled it the *interindividual-intergroup discontinuity effect* because there was a discontinuity or disconnect between how individuals behaved toward each other versus how groups behaved toward each other. Although the majority of studies of the discontinuity effect have investigated differences in how groups and individuals behave in the context of the PDG matrix, the effect has also been found with nonlaboratory methods, such as diary studies (Pemberton, Insko, & Schopler, 1996); among various cultural groups, such as the Dutch (Wildschut, Lodewijkx, & Insko, 2001) and Japanese (Takemura & Yuki, 2007); and in different contexts, such as in negotiations that have a prisoner's dilemma structure (Morgan & Tindale, 2002) and situations involving intergroup aggression following a provocation (Meier & Hinsz, 2004).

Most of the studies on the discontinuity effect have compared group-on-group to one-on-one interactions, but several studies have examined the effects of interacting as a group versus interacting with a group (Meier & Hinsz, 2004; Morgan & Tindale, 2002; Pemberton et al., 1996; Wildschut, Insko, & Pinter, 2007; Winquist & Larson, 2004). Overall, these studies have established that the greater contentiousness of intergroup behavior is due both to acting as a group and to interacting with a group ("the actor effect" and "the opponent effect," respectively; Wildschut et al., 2007).

Writers' Strike Example

Throughout the writers' strike, it appeared as though both the WGA and the AMPTP were primarily concerned with maximizing their own outcomes with little regard for the other side. The length of the strike might have been extended because of the group-on-group nature of the interaction. In support of this idea, the WGA's strike against David Letterman's company was resolved in fifty-four days as opposed to one hundred (Carter & Cieply, 2007). Why was Letterman's company able to work out a cooperative agreement with the WGA in nearly half the time that it took the AMPTP? One possibility is that Letterman owns his company, and that the WGA was thus able to negotiate with representatives concerned primarily with satisfying the interests of only one person (David Letterman). With the AMPTP, in contrast, the WGA was negotiating with representatives concerned with satisfying the interests of many different parties. Of course, this is unlikely to have been the only reason that the WGA's strike of Letterman's company was resolved in half the time, but research on the discontinuity effect suggests that it may indeed have been a contributing factor.

Implications for Working with Groups

Businesses, corporations, and organizations are replete with groups (for example, management, research and development, marketing, information technology). These groups often interact in order to facilitate day-to-day operations. The discontinuity effect suggests that organizations could avoid creating difficult group situations by allowing individuals from groups to work and interact with individuals from other groups rather than allowing group-on-group interactions. In some ways, this interindividual context would mimic the one-on-one condition of the discontinuity research, which is marked by cooperation rather than competition. However, competition is not likely to be completely eliminated by this approach because individuals serving as group leaders or representatives are often just as competitive as the groups themselves, possibly because they feel a responsibility to advocate for their group's interests (Pinter et al., 2007). As we will discuss in more detail later, group representatives or leaders may need some independence or reduced accountability from their group to allow them to act as cooperatively as individuals.

WHEN ARE GROUP INTERACTIONS COMPETITIVE?

Fortunately, not all intergroup interactions are characterized by competitive behavior. In situations where there is little or no perceived advantage to acting competitively or selfishly, intergroup interactions will be just as cooperative as interindividual interactions (Wolf et al., 2008). In the PDG, there is a negative relationship between the two sides' outcomes: what is good for side A is generally bad for side B, and vice versa. Intergroup interactions become increasingly more cooperative as the relationship between each side's outcomes becomes more positive (Wolf et al., 2008) or less negative (Schopler et al., 2001). Competition is rare when both parties' interests are aligned. That is, cooperation will trump competition when "what is good for one is good for the other and what is bad for one is bad for both" (Kelley & Thibaut, 1978, p. 12).

In an empirical demonstration of this idea, Wolf et al. (2008) compared intergroup and interindividual interactions in a context in which there was a strong negative relationship between the two sides' outcomes (a prisoner's dilemma game) and a context in which there was a strong positive relationship between the two sides' outcomes (a bargaining game involving coordination). Whereas intergroup interactions were much less cooperative than interindividual interactions in the game with a negative relationship between the two sides' outcomes (cooperation rates were 59 percent for groups and 100 percent for individuals), intergroup interactions were just as cooperative as interindividual interactions in the game in which there was a strong positive relationship between the two sides' outcomes (cooperation rates were 98 percent for groups and 97 percent for individuals). These results have the encouraging implication that intergroup relations can be made less contentious if the context of the interaction is changed so that the mutual advantage of cooperation is clear.

Although thoughtfully structured situations can reduce competition, one should also recognize that people are often influenced more by their perceptions of the situation than by the actual situation (Fisher, Ury, & Patton, 1991; Kelley et al., 2003; Kelley & Thibaut, 1978). In *Getting Past No,* William Ury (1993) relates an anecdote that captures this phenomenon quite well. The story involves a man discussing with his nephew what he learned at Harvard Law School:

> You know Bill, it has taken me twenty-five years to unlearn what I learned at Harvard Law School. Because what I learned at Harvard

> Law School is that all that counts in life are the *facts*—who's right and who's wrong. It's taken me twenty-five years to learn that just as important as the facts, if not more important, are people's *perceptions* of those facts. (p. 18)

This anecdote highlights the importance of perspective taking and understanding how the other party perceives the situation. Even if you think your interests are aligned with the other party's interests and that you both should act cooperatively, the other side might view the situation differently. Cooperation can be encouraged not only by changing the situation itself but also by changing how the situation is perceived.

Writers' Strike Example

Research on the domain of the discontinuity effect (Schopler et al., 2001; Wolf et al., 2008) suggests that both the WGA and the AMPTP likely perceived the contract negotiation that preceded the strike as a situation with a strong conflict of interests—a situation in which there was a negative relationship between the two sides' outcomes. At the outset of the conflict, the writers believed that they should strike instead of accepting the contract specifications. Likewise, the producers believed that they should remain strong and allow the writers to strike instead of yielding to their requests. The length of the strike might have been abbreviated had both the writers and producers realized sooner that it was in their mutually shared interest to each relinquish some of their less pertinent demands in order to achieve an integrative agreement that satisfied their mutual underlying interest of getting back to work and making money.

Implications for Working with Groups

In attempting to resolve conflicts and promote intergroup cooperation, group facilitators, leaders, and members would be wise to highlight compatible underlying interests, the benefits associated with mutual cooperation, and the costs associated with mutual competition. Focusing groups on the advantages of mutual cooperation and the disadvantages of mutual competition can change how they perceive the situation and can help them recognize that their own outcomes may in fact be positively related to the other side's outcomes. Altering group members' perceptions in this way increases the likelihood that both sides will choose to cooperate, which will benefit them over the long term. We revisit this idea in the section that focuses on reducing intergroup competition.

WHY ARE GROUP INTERACTIONS COMPETITIVE?

There are two main reasons why intergroup interactions are less cooperative than interindividual interactions in mixed-motive contexts: fear and greed. Compared to interindividual interactions, intergroup interactions are characterized by greater fear or distrust of the other side and greater greed or support for behaviors that help one's own side or hurt the other side (Insko, Schopler, Hoyle, Dardis, & Graetz, 1990; Schopler et al., 1993; see Wildschut & Insko, 2007, for a review). In the PDG, groups are more likely to choose the competitive choice because of greater fear of receiving the lowest possible outcome (either in an absolute or relative sense) or because of a greater desire to receive the highest possible outcome (either in an absolute or relative sense). The greater fear and distrust of groups may arise from a stereotype or schema of groups that suggests that groups are competitive, untrustworthy, hostile, and abrasive (Hoyle, Pinkley, & Insko, 1989; Pemberton et al., 1996) or from the personal connection or empathic concern that individuals tend to feel toward each other but that groups do not (Rea, Insko, Wildschut, & Cohen, 2009).

The greater greed that characterizes intergroup interactions can arise from multiple sources. These include (1) the anonymity or reduced identifiabilty that comes from acting as a group member instead of as an individual (Schopler et al., 1995); (2) the explicit and implicit social support that group members provide for the competitive pursuit of selfish or group-serving behaviors (Insko et al., 1990; Schopler et al., 1993; Wildschut, Insko, & Gaertner, 2002); (3) in-group-favoring norms that encourage group members to "take care of their own" or do what is best for their own group despite potential harm or costs to others (Cohen, Montoya, & Insko, 2006; Wildschut et al., 2002), and (4) altruistic rationalization—the justification that selfish, competitive behaviors are being pursued in order to help one's fellow group members (Pinter et al., 2007). Wildschut and Insko (2007) provide a detailed discussion of these motivations. What they share in common is that they all exacerbate or foster the tendency of groups to engage in greedy group-serving behaviors.

Writers' Strike Example

The hostile relations between the producers and writers may have resulted from several sources, but the distrust between the AMPTP and WGA during the writers' strike was palpable. On the one side, the AMPTP distrusted that the WGA was willing to negotiate in good faith, and on the other side, the WGA feared that the AMPTP would exploit them. The following quote captures the animosity and tension felt by many of the writers: "This is not over. Nor is it close . . . . On the streets, on the net, I say reason is for the 'moderates.' Remember what they've done. Remember what they're trying to take from us. FIGHT. FIGHT. FIGHT" (Whedon, 2008).

Whedon's statement was posted on a blog, presumably in an effort to garner social support for the WGA's decision to strike—the competitive choice in that situation. Statements such as these fostered greed and fear motivations by providing social support for pursuing competitive and antagonistic actions toward the other side. In the next section, we discuss ways in which competition motivated by greed and fear can be reduced.

HOW CAN INTERGROUP COMPETITION BE REDUCED?

Research on intergroup relations and the discontinuity effect has revealed four ways to make intergroup interactions more cooperative (see Cohen & Insko, 2008, for a review).

- Encourage or teach groups to consider future consequences of competitive behavior (Insko et al., 1998, 2001; Wolf et al., 2009).
- Promote independent leadership (Pinter et al., 2007).
- Increase empathy toward opposing groups (Cohen, 2008; Stephan & Finlay, 1999).
- Change the situation (or group members' perception of the situation) to one in which cooperative behavior yields more attractive outcomes than competitive behavior (Wolf et al., 2008).

Consideration of Future Consequences

Research on the consideration of future consequences has revealed that intergroup competition can be reduced by having groups think about how their own competitive actions will affect the other side's future actions. In a straightforward demonstration of this technique, Wolf et al. (2009) had groups of three participants answer a few short questions prior to repeated interactions with another of group of three participants in a PDG matrix similar to Figure 13.1. The questions asked groups to consider what the other side would likely choose on trial 2, if their group chose Y on trial 1, and likewise, what the other side would choose on trial 2 if their group chose X on trial 1. These simple questions led groups to report less distrust of the other group and to compete less with the other group compared to groups who were not asked these questions. Other research has revealed that future-oriented thinking can also be promoted by using a tit-for-tat strategy to interact with opposing groups (Axelrod, 1984; Insko et al., 1998) and making it salient that there will be multiple interactions with the other group, as opposed to just one (Insko et al., 2001). Overall, findings from these experiments suggest that an effective way to promote intergroup cooperation is to help group members understand that the long-term costs of competition are often far greater than the potential short-term benefits.

Group facilitators, leaders, and members could easily put this strategy into practice. In most organizations, interactions between the same groups occur in multiple settings, not simply in one-shot encounters. Thus an effective way to reduce intergroup competition in organizations may be to make it salient to group members that they will be interacting with the other group again in the future, and that any competitive or antagonistic behavior in the present will likely be intensified in future interactions. In addition to highlighting the potential for repeated interactions with the other side, leaders and facilitators could also ask group members to consider how their present behavior could affect the other side's future behavior. These reminders and considerations will likely facilitate cooperation because group members will be motivated to avoid future conflict and the costs associated with it.

Independent Leadership

Group leaders often struggle with the dilemma of having to satisfy their constituency of loyal group members while still enacting cooperative agreements with those outside the group. Politicians have to deal with this dilemma quite often when they are forced to reconcile moderate or centrist statements made during general election contests with more extreme left- or right-leaning statements made during primary election contests. Research on leadership suggests that one way to make intergroup interactions more cooperative is to allow group leaders to have some degree of independence from or reduced accountability to the members of their group so that they have the freedom to cooperate with those toward whom their more extreme base might prefer to compete (Pinter et al., 2007). This statement needs qualification, however, because not all leaders will act cooperatively when they are unaccountable. Unfortunately, reduced accountability allows less ethical leaders to pursue their own selfish goals. But if it is known that a group's leader is a moral or ethical person, a certain degree of independence is likely to be quite helpful for negotiating cooperative deals with other groups. Group facilitators, leaders, and members might be able to avoid difficult group situations by allowing ethical and trustworthy group leaders to have some degree of autonomy when representing their group's interests and desires.

Empathy

A third strategy for improving relations between groups is to foster empathy for members of the opposing group (Stephan & Finlay, 1999). This strategy is often employed by peace workshops seeking to resolve protracted intergroup conflicts throughout the world (Malhotra & Liyanage, 2005). Empathy is an important variable in predicting cooperation and helping behavior (Eisenberg et al., 2002; Graziano, Habashi, Sheese, & Tobin, 2007). Empathic individuals are able to consider and imagine others' feelings, making it more difficult for them to commit antisocial behavior.

In a laboratory study of empathy and intergroup conflict, Cohen (2008) found that group members with high scores on a measure of dispositional empathy were more likely to cooperate with an opposing group in a prisoner's dilemma game. Moreover, those with low empathy scores were swayed to cooperate when they were instructed to consider the feelings of opposing group members. This latter finding is important because it demonstrates that empathic concern can be activated in people who are not empathic by nature, and can increase their tendency to cooperate in intergroup interactions.

A second study by Cohen (2008), however, revealed that empathy for opposing groups can sometimes backfire. The same empathy intervention that promoted cooperation in the prisoner's dilemma game increased intergroup aggression when groups were provoked by the other side. These somewhat contradictory results suggest that feeling empathy for opposing groups may increase cooperation in some intergroup interactions, but in situations where there has been a prior provocation, considering the other group's feelings may lead to retaliation instead of forgiveness.

People seeking to avoid difficult group situations could use empathy to promote cooperation. For example, group-on-group interactions could be preceded by simple empathy-enhancing exercises that require group members to imagine the feelings that members of the opposing group are experiencing. This activity might make cooperation between the groups more likely, especially if the group members are unaccustomed to feeling empathic concern for others.

Change the Situation

Changing the situation or group members' perceptions of the situation is another way of reducing intergroup competition. We discussed this idea earlier when summarizing Wolf et al.'s study (2008) that found that groups were as willing to cooperate as individuals when there was a strong positive relationship between the two sides' outcomes. Changing group members' perceptions of the situation by highlighting compatible underlying interests is an effective strategy for reducing conflict. The difficulty with this tactic is conceptualizing how to change the situation into one in which cooperation is perceived to be more valuable than competition. Rewarding cooperation but not competition might be one method for enacting such a transformation. For example, the possibility of cooperation could be strengthened with the promise of positive rewards, such as increased profit sharing, for behaving cooperatively or reaching mutually beneficial agreements.

Other methods for enacting cooperative transformations are discussed by Fisher, Ury, and Patton (1991) in their classic book on principled negotiation, *Getting to Yes.* Gaertner and Dovidio's research on the Common Ingroup Identity Model (2000) also offers some insight into how competitive situations can be changed into cooperative ones. They suggest that intergroup relations will be improved when members of opposing groups recognize that despite their differences, they share many things in common (for example, all work for the same organization, all want their organization to succeed)—and if nothing else, they are all members of the human race. Highlighting intergroup commonalities instead of differences is one way to change a situation so that cooperation is viewed as more attractive than competition.

Writers' Strike Example

The WGA's strike against the AMPTP ended on February, 12, 2008, when 92.5 percent of 3,775 writers voted to terminate the strike and return to work (Cieply, 2008). As noted earlier, the strike lasted one hundred days, and it concluded when a three-year contract was agreed on by both parties. Resolution of the conflict was precipitated by the recognition by one or both sides that it was in their mutually shared interest to settle the dispute so that the writers could go back to work, production could resume, and both sides could continue making money. This recognition may have encouraged the two parties to make their contract proposals more reasonable so that the other side could potentially accept them. Shortly after the strike ended, Patric Verrone, president of the WGA's West chapter, discussed how the WGA had achieved most, but not all, of its goals: "Giving up animation and reality was a heartbreaking thing for me personally. But it was more important that we make a deal that benefited the membership, the town as a whole, that got people back to work and that solved the biggest problems in new media" (quoted in CNN, 2008).

Verrone's statement suggests that by the end of the strike, he perceived cooperating with the AMPTP as, overall, more beneficial for his organization than competing against it. Verrone's recognition may have occurred because the consequences of protracted mutual competition were realized: The strike had cost the writers and producers millions of dollars in lost wages and revenues. These lost wages and revenues may have led both parties to consider the long-term costs of a failure to resolve the conflict. Thus a consideration of future consequences likely contributed to each side's decision to ultimately end the dispute and ratify a contract.

The fact that Verrone seemed to be an independent group leader is important because his ability to see the long-term benefits of cooperating with AMPTP may have allowed him to help the WGA negotiate a contract, which would not have been possible if the opinions of some of the more extreme members of the WGA were heeded. Take, for instance, WGA member Harlan Ellison's response (2008) to the final contract proposal:

> You may have heard my name. I am a Union guy, I am a Guild guy, I am loyal. I f*** in' LOVE the Guild. And I voted NO on accepting this deal. My reasons are good, and they are plentiful; Patric

> Verrone will be saddened by what I am about to say; long-time friends will shake their heads; but this I say without equivocation. . . . THEY BEAT US LIKE A YELLOW DOG. IT IS A S*** DEAL.

It seems unlikely that WGA leaders, such as Verrone, would have been able to negotiate any agreement with the AMPTP had they not been given at least some degree of independence from those with opinions as strong as Ellison's.

Overall, it seems that the WGA and AMPTP were ultimately able to cooperate and agree on a contract because one or both sides realized that cooperation was more advantageous than competition, considered the future consequences of a failure to cooperate, and allowed their group leaders to have some independence from group members with more extreme positions. These factors, among others, are likely to have worked in combination to bring about the strike's conclusion.

CONCLUSION

Organizational operations often require group-on-group interactions. Group facilitators, leaders, and members should be aware that hundreds of experimental studies reveal that group-on-group interactions are more competitive than one-on-one interactions in situations characterized by a conflict of interests between two sides. Fear of the opposing side and greed related to maximizing one's own outcomes are two causal factors. Although this tendency for groups to act competitively is robust and apparent in many group interactions, it can be reduced by a number of different strategies. These strategies include encouraging consideration of future consequences, promoting independent leadership, fostering empathy toward opposing groups, and changing the situation or perceptions of the situation so that the mutual benefits of cooperation and the mutual costs of competition are highlighted. It is our hope that this chapter will allow individuals who work in or with groups to achieve some insight into how to manage difficult group situations.

chapter FOURTEEN

Active Facilitation: How to Help Groups Break Through "Mutual Stalemate"

Celia Kirwan and Wes Siegal

The "Boost Joint Sales" event brought together sales, marketing, and operations representatives from several businesses within a single financial services company. The purpose was to help sales and operations managers from the businesses agree on how they could better integrate their offerings for three shared market segments. In the past, joint-selling efforts had been frustrated by a lack of contact and collaboration between the businesses.

During the event, three sales teams, each focused on a particular market segment and including representatives of the affected businesses, were tasked to develop plans to increase the pipeline—and close more deals—in the months ahead. A fourth team for marketing communications was also engaged to provide support. Over the course of two days, these four teams were to develop integrated plans for immediate execution.

HOW THE GROUP IS DIFFICULT

At first, the atmosphere on the teams was workmanlike, with most participants displaying a blasé attitude. This surprised the facilitators, who had understood the challenge to be very ambitious and so expected more innovation and creativity. But by the end of the first day, the workshop seemed to be headed for a stalemate. The atmosphere had degenerated, and each function and business was blaming others for its inability to progress—the very patterns that had prevented effective collaboration in the past.

The sales teams were declining to build anything beyond the most generic action plans. These uninspired plans included such items as "identify potential customers, distribute market materials, follow up and act as needed." They claimed they could not develop these plans further until the marketing communications team gave them the material they needed to describe their proposition to customers. The marketing communications team, though, had similarly vague contributions to offer: its work plan included generic steps such as "receive product and market specifications from sales teams, develop materials, produce and distribute, supplement with a promotional campaign."

All four teams' proposals were to be presented to a small panel of senior executives at the end of the second day, and they were expected to carry approved ideas directly into implementation. Everyone sensed the inadequacy of what had been done so far. Tensions escalated to the point of outright name-calling. The conflict was familiar. Marketing and communications expected a full description of the target customers and the joint service offering—in response to which it could develop and execute a campaign. And the members of the sales teams had habitually attributed poor performance to the absence of strong marketing materials.

Each was holding out, waiting for another team to develop a perfect solution. A sense of resignation set in, and people started to murmur that they might have to report on this stalemate to the executives. They started to criticize the workshop design as out of step with their organizational realities.

This case describes a familiar situation: groups that are encouraged to behave in innovative ways will often use ongoing conflicts with other groups (with which they are ultimately interdependent) to explain their inability to progress.

Organizations in every sector around the world are recognizing the competitive urgency of innovation and are exhorting their employees to continually develop new ideas to improve margins and market performance. Although employees can often generate a variety of innovative ideas, execution often breaks down—frequently because the many groups whose collaboration is required are not included. And even when the right variety of groups is included, participants are often unable to break the patterns of mutual blame and inactivity that impede innovation.

We call this pattern—in which two or more groups each abdicate its responsibilities until another group makes a first move—*mutual stalemate.* In our experience, mutual stalemate occurs surprisingly often, especially in publicly held companies that tend to fully allocate their employees' time in the drive to meet quarterly and annual targets, leaving no time for creative experimentation or innovation. Mutual stalemate is also common in matrixed organizations, where accountability for strategically important results can be divided or unclear. Despite the theoretical agility of both publicly held and matrixed organizations, we have found them to be some of the more difficult environments for stimulating innovation. It can sometimes appear as though everyone's main objective is to survive meetings unscathed and unnoticed—and leave as quickly as possible so that they can return to the commitments they already have.

There are three hallmarks of mutual stalemate. First, individuals within the affected groups avoid risk-taking or public commitment to new activities that might contribute to the task at hand. Second, there is poor tolerance of conflict or divergence within each affected group. Finally, there is a rancorous atmosphere of blame and recrimination between two or more groups that need to work interdependently with one another to develop or execute a solution.

Martinez-Moyano (2006) presents a model of intergroup collaboration which suggests that the productivity of interdependent groups improves as each one successfully meets commitments, learns about the other group's role and capabilities, and builds trust. In this model, collaboration increases as parallel virtuous cycles—experienced by each group—contribute to shared success and to the development of mutual confidence in the other group's capabilities.

Mutual stalemate describes the absence of these patterns. When groups lack confidence in their own or a partner group's capabilities, they defend themselves by uniting to scapegoat the other group as the cause of any breakdowns in productivity. Each group colludes with the other to construct a shared reality that offers everyone refuge from the difficult work of changing behavior.

Groups frequently express some initial resistance to a manager's challenge that they change or improve. Most facilitators are quite able to create a climate that helps group members examine varying individual reactions and gradually increase their receptivity to a management request. But mutual stalemate is an extreme form of resistance—in which groups strongly limit the abilities of their members to take risks and experiment with collaboration. The group's attachment to a narrative that holds another group responsible for the absence of progress is so strong that the dynamic can be especially intransigent.

A number of organizational factors can contribute to the emergence of mutual stalemate; we describe these in more detail in the next section.

WHY THE GROUP IS DIFFICULT

Examples of productive collaboration between groups are very common. Sales will welcome Marketing's analyses and materials. Partners in a joint venture will make the adjustments needed to service one another's legacy customers. But a mutual stalemate between two groups, like that described at the opening of this chapter, can be attributed to a number of contextual, structural, and process factors. Contextual factors refer to the social, organizational, and task environment within which the groups in question are operating. Structural factors refer to the dynamics arising from the participants themselves, and the skills they bring to the situation. Process factors describe the groups' strategies for handling conflict and working together.

Contextual Factors

Three contextual factors regularly contribute to stalemate:

- Measurement of group performance is poorly attuned to the changes that must take place.
- Priorities shift frequently, or are diluted during a series of handoffs.
- Challenging new demands are conveyed to fully allocated people or groups with no adjustment in priority.

Performance metrics are rarely adjusted when two groups must collaborate to achieve a shared outcome. For example, it is typical to evaluate a service department on the average time it takes to generate a contract. But this measure might create incentives to delay production of a small number of complex contracts, and emphasize instead the vast majority of cookie-cutter contracts. If the neglected contracts are for customers in a strategically important niche, some adjustment in performance metrics will be required. Another common example of this type of maladjustment occurs when an organization tries to manage performance of end-to-end processes, but the metrics of the participating functions remain focused on internal efficiency rather than on the efficiency of the overall process.

When organizational priorities shift frequently and management demands action on various crises "du jour," a learned cynicism often takes hold. Groups will search for legitimate delays that can excuse the hard work required. Group members have learned that as these delays accumulate, chances are good that management attention will drift to other issues. Another group's lack of performance can offer the ideal excuse for inaction, because it can explain delays in progress, with no direct repercussions.

A third contextual factor that contributes to mutual stalemate is an organizational tendency to overload resources with unreasonable demands—without adjusting priorities. This tendency creates a psychological environment ripe for scapegoating. As tensions about achieving targets increase, organization members search for someone who can be held responsible. Groups bond together and search for outsiders whose (actual or constructed) malfeasance can explain their own lack of progress. Thus mutually dependent groups can turn against one another if they have not had some consistent guidance on the importance of their collaborative undertaking and how it rates in comparison to their other responsibilities.

Structural Factors

Several factors related to the composition of the groups are at play during mutual stalemate. Perhaps the most important of these is based in the fact that none of the groups alone possesses the skills required to successfully respond to a management directive. The contextual factors described in the preceding section can lead groups to focus on their partner group's contributions rather than their own. Furthermore, in mutual stalemate, group identities typically remain with the preexisting groups. Another group's capabilities can become the fuel of resentment. "If they are so critical to making this happen," group members might wonder, "why isn't it their responsibility?" Anxieties about being able to contribute—and about having that contribution recognized—can be mutually projected onto the "other" groups, creating a situation in which another group's possession of valuable skills can be perceived as a threat rather than an asset.

Process Factors

Finally, the groups' own methods for structuring work and resolving conflicts contribute to the condition of mutual stalemate. Habitual clinging to preexisting group boundaries can reinforce the false hope that each participating group might be able to complete its contribution independently. So the groups parcel work according to preexisting concepts of how it should be done, with no allowance for the collaborative learning and exploration required to discover new approaches.

In our example, these contextual, structural, and process factors played heavy roles. Joint sales to the target client base had been advocated for some time, but the managers of the different businesses and functions had not delivered a unified, consistent demand to their respective groups. Nor had they created performance measures that would hold the groups accountable. As a result, the group members felt more comfortable scapegoating one another for lack of progress than they did challenging one another to take the risks needed to respond to their shared assignment.

WHAT TO DO?

Many facilitators believe that groups cannot move into a collaborative mode with other groups until they have developed their own motivation to do so. A common strategy when facing a conflict is for the facilitator to provide feedback about group behavior in the hopes that one or more group members might break ranks with his or her colleagues, suggest a compromise, and thus move the group forward. But this approach underestimates the power of the group dynamics that regulate individual behavior when mutual stalemate occurs.

But to break through the strong norms that accompany mutual stalemate, facilitators need to confront the pattern very actively. As Schwarz (2002, p. 61) states: "You are partial about what constitutes effective group process because that is your area of expertise. As a skilled facilitator, you know what kind of behavior is more or less likely to lead to effective problem solving and other important group outcomes—and you convey this knowledge through your actions as a facilitator."

The fundamental challenge is to break the patterns of mutual blame and inactivity and to enable shared accomplishment. The shared experience of successful execution, even on a small scale, can become the catalyst to subsequent trust and collaboration (Martinez-Moyano, 2006). We outline here a model of what we call *active facilitation*, which can be used to create this sense of shared accomplishment and break through mutual stalemate when it is encountered.

Active facilitation is more a mind-set than a behavioral prescription. There are five important guiding principles: focusing on results, ensuring that managers demand improvement, encouraging productive conflict, providing structure for group outputs, and creating time urgency (see Figure 14.1).

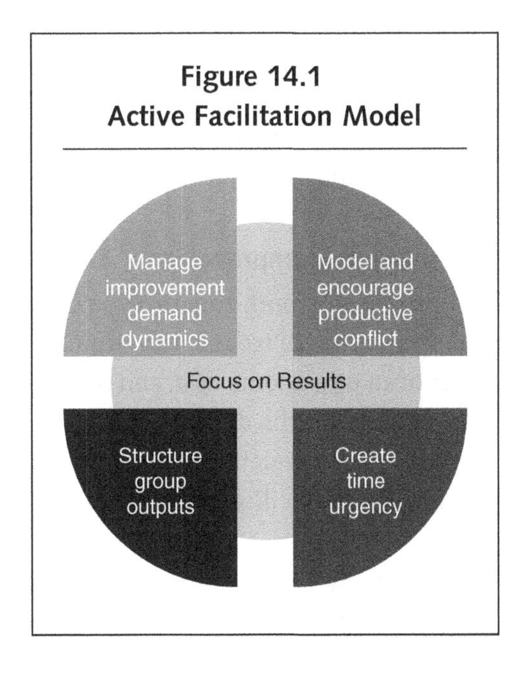

Figure 14.1
Active Facilitation Model

Focus on Results

Many facilitators are trained to focus on process, not content. It is true that facilitators usually cannot and should not be content experts. In fact, much of a facilitator's value can come from bringing a naïve, external perspective to the group. But a facilitator can serve a group most effectively by committing to help it achieve a tangible, observable result—preferably an unambiguous "hard" business achievement—or a direct contribution to it.

Active facilitators push the groups they are working with to help them appreciate the difference between a focus on activities and a focus on results. Compare the following three goal statements for a company looking to improve sales performance:

1. Complete sales training and implement sales force software.
2. Perform joint sales calls.
3. Increase sales by 20 percent.

The active facilitator would point out to the group that only the third statement is focused on results. The first statement is activity focused; the second focuses on preparatory milestones. (Of course, both statements one and two may well be key implementation *activities* to achieve the *result* of increasing sales by 20 percent.) Helping the group differentiate between the results finish line and the activities or means to get it there is key to the active facilitation approach. This focus on results, rather than activities, requires some engagement with content.

Ensure That Managers Demand Improvement

Often facilitators will be engaged both to convey an assignment and then to help a group respond. This is where trouble can begin. The facilitator is easily isolated as the deliverer of an unwelcome task, and becomes a flashpoint for the group's resistance. Symptoms of this dynamic can include repeated requests that a facilitator restate or interpret the group's objectives or, even worse, challenges from the group for the facilitator to defend the rationale and value of a particular assignment.

To make matters worse, many senior managers consciously or unconsciously avoid directly expressing demands for improvement that might be seen as unreasonable or challenging, and this further complicates the facilitator's position. Facilitators who are eager to be seen as value-adding partners will quickly take on an assignment, assuming that participants will understand what is expected and its importance (Schaffer, 1991). This pitfall is even harder to avoid in cross-business and cross-functional situations, where demands must be aligned across several working units in order to be effective.

A facilitator may be in the best position to understand the potential gains that can be realized with improved collaboration. Many well-meaning facilitators take it upon themselves to encourage people to take advantage of these possibilities. But this encouragement alone is insufficient to break the patterns of mutual stalemate. Expressions of impatience for change and improvement must come directly from managers and key opinion leaders of participating groups. The facilitator must be seen as a resource that helps groups respond to a management directive—not as an agent who communicates on management's behalf.

In the active facilitation mind-set, the facilitator helps managers strengthen their skills in communicating demands for change and improvement, and then helps group members respond to those demands. By following these steps, facilitators can take an active role in ensuring that demands are communicated:

- Help identify the manager or managers who must express demands for improvement.
- Help managers specify the importance of results, the minimum results expected, and the speed with which those results must be achieved.
- Help those managers communicate their expectations clearly, while also delegating responsibility and allowing freedom to innovate.
- Help the groups who receive demands respond to them productively.

Managers need to convey not only the strategic or competitive importance of improving but also the need to do so quickly. This is where mutual stalemate can be avoided. As in the Boost Joint Sales case, groups will typically respond to a demand for improvement by pointing out the long-term issues that must be resolved before improvement can be expected. But when groups are challenged to demonstrate some new level of breakthrough performance, perhaps for a limited time or in a pilot area, they must behave as if these improvements were already in place.

One of the key elements of this principle of active facilitation is to coach managers not only to communicate aggressive demands but also to allow group members to respond to a challenge innovatively. For example, a requirement to "update all large customer information in the CRM system by mid-quarter" is an activity, so it will achieve less traction than a result-oriented challenge along the lines of "double the sales pipeline of potential customers for our large enterprise solution." The first challenge is an activity that is a means to an end, whereas the second is a result-oriented challenge that can stimulate creative and holistic thinking within the group about all the components of a system. Hackman (2002) describes these types of challenges as specifying the "what" but not the "how"—and therefore setting the stage not only for the most efficient use of the group's human capital but also for advancing its capabilities.

An additional benefit of this approach is that groups that have been given a stimulating challenge will perceive the facilitator as a valuable resource. Instead of banding together against the facilitator who is conveying an unwelcome assignment, group members look to the facilitator for help in responding to the demands that have been placed on them.

Encourage Productive Conflict

The facilitator plays a key role in "making conflict safe" for the group. Unfortunately, many facilitators choose to make conflict safe by unconsciously helping the group avoid it. Others may simply let the conflict run without intervention, leaving the process and outcome to existing group norms. Some facilitators may intervene to resolve the conflict in an effort to improve relations, rather than drive toward a needed result. Active facilitation, though, requires that conflicts be interpreted in terms of a required outcome. Before intervening, an active facilitator uses inquiring language to test whether a conflict has direct impact on people's abilities to deliver a result.

Reframe the Conflict in Terms of the Results Needed In our Boost Joint Sales example, group members were getting frustrated with one another because no one that felt he or she had the information needed to go to market with a new service model. Some facilitators would respond to this conflict by revisiting team ground rules about respectful communication, or by putting the issue of marketing materials and product features into a "parking lot" to be addressed at some later time. An active facilitator, in contrast, would make the group's result paramount, and reframe the conflict in those terms—for example, "What is the minimum product information we need to take a concept to market and get some initial feedback from our customers?"

Fractionate Conflict The active facilitator can take cues from Fisher's insights (1964/2008) into the value of "fractionating" conflict. Fractionation involves breaking a larger, entrenched conflict into smaller issues that, when resolved, lessen the overall severity of the conflict, shift the climate between the aggrieved parties, and build each group's hopefulness about the possibility of reaching a mutually agreeable solution. An active facilitator will suggest ways of fractionating entrenched intergroup conflict, and prompt people to work on this more specifically defined issue.

In the case of the Boost Joint Sales event, the experience of mutual stalemate had recalled long-standing patterns of mistrust and name-calling between the sales and marketing teams. The facilitators responded to this situation by challenging each sales team to agree during the workshop with the marketing communications team on just two things: (1) the profile of its target customers and (2) the predominant product features that would appeal to that group. Even this small advance shifted the climate between sales and marketing from impasse to initial agreement, laying the foundation for successful collaboration experimentation.

Model Accountability-Seeking Behaviors In mutual stalemate, requests for action or commitment can exacerbate conflict. Both the individuals and the groups involved need some support to develop their accountability-seeking skills. Accountability-seeking skills are those behaviors that allow groups to productively make requests of one another—and to link those requests to commitments.

Active facilitators can model accountability-seeking behaviors in groups by directly asking "impolite" questions that firm up commitments (Sole, 2006). These can include, "Who will do that? Can it be done by the end of next week?" Similarly, facilitators can help extend the group's comfort with confrontation about the quality of its work by asking such questions as "Is this going to satisfy our sponsor? What else would people like to see included in the proposal?"

By reframing conflicts in terms of results, fractionating conflicts to build a foundation of confidence and trust, and modeling accountability-seeking behavior, a facilitator can help a group develop its ability to host productive confrontation and conflict.

Structure Group Outputs

Another element of active facilitation involves specifying interim deliverables for interdependent parties to create. These progress markers should be built into the design of a meeting or workshop. By specifying outputs and making group members accountable to one another for the creation of those outputs, a facilitator can build trust and confidence, and help groups structure important discussions.

The following are examples of concrete deliverables that teams can be tasked to create on a schedule—either during a workshop (for example, Ulrich, Kerr, & Ashkenas, 2002) or over the course of a longer-lasting implementation period:

- Short lists of options or preliminary ideas
- Specific descriptions of goals, success metrics, and key activities
- Well-developed work plans with concrete task assignments
- Specific requests for permission and resources
- Prototypes
- Intermediate products, such as an updated database, a new training manual, or a written policy statement

Interim deliverables like these focus the group more on its product than on its process, more on agreeing about what it wants to create than why it is difficult to create it. They can help groups move beyond a priori assumptions that breakthrough results require significant investment or redesign. Completing these tasks on time helps build a group's sense of confidence in its own ability to deliver—and the abilities of other groups to collaborate. And they ensure alignment within the group about what is being proposed and the work involved. Finally, interim requirements once again position the facilitator as a resource who helps the groups complete the assignment appropriately.

Create Time Urgency

The earlier discussion of demands highlighted the need for groups to understand why action on an issue is urgent. The facilitated event itself should reinforce this need for rapid resolution of issues. Pressing time demands can help spark a different level of collaboration in groups. The challenge is to set aggressive but realistic deadlines that challenge people to eliminate extraneous discussions and focus on the heart of the matter, creating a "tyranny of the clock."

Time urgency can also be created with a workshop design that challenges participants to respond to demand makers quickly with an actionable solution. For example, facilitators can ask demand makers to "top" and "tail" a workshop. During the kick-off session, or top, they convey the need for quick action to the group and their intention upon their return at the tail to hear proposals that meet a minimum expectation.

Time urgency ameliorates mutual stalemate in several ways. It allows facilitators to map out tasks and discussions so that they fit within an assigned time frame. It makes the group less likely to resist being pushed forward when it is stuck in a corollary discussion or to revisit familiar patterns that delay decision, accountability, and action. Most important, it gives group members permission to challenge themselves and one another to leave unproductive behaviors and conversations behind.

OUTCOMES

In the case of the Boost Joint Sales event, many active facilitation principles helped turn the group dynamics around and break the stalemate. The facilitator team called an emergency meeting to revisit its assumptions and redefine its role. Facilitators agreed on shared templates for deliverables from the three sales teams and the marketing team. Early on the second day, a senior sponsor dropped into the workshop to clarify demands: he expected a "rough draft" of both the product and service description and the high-level marketing plan, from each of the sales teams. The facilitators reframed the conflict between groups' members as a conundrum, and asked the members for a public commitment to deliver their first drafts of their service offerings and marketing messages simultaneously. Having made this commitment, the sales teams had to identify the critical elements that must be contained in any service offering. One facilitator hosted a series of three one-to-one work sessions between marketing communications and each sales team to review its initial work and identify next steps for improving the alignment of each group's product.

As the second day proceeded, the energy and optimism began to increase. People started to develop a tangible product where only excuses had existed before. By midday, all four teams were prepared to meet with executives from the three affected businesses to review not only their proposals but also detailed timelines for implementing them. As the teams moved into implementation, they built on these breakthroughs, holding one another accountable for delivering on the work plans to which they had agreed. And today, these businesses are seeing their shared pipeline for these offerings grow dramatically.

You may interpret active facilitation as being more focused on results than relationships—or more basic than developmental in focus. In reality, active facilitation addresses both results and relationships. But active facilitation turns on its head the common assumption that relationships must be developed *before* results can be achieved. Indeed, the active facilitation model creates a context where experimentation with relationships is easier because group members share interest in achieving a well-defined, common result. For this reason, the approach is well suited to breaking through the change resistance pattern that we have called mutual stalemate.

chapter
FIFTEEN

Mediating History, Making Peace: Dealing with the "Messy" Stuff in the Conciliation Process

Dagmar Kusa, Adam Saltsman, and Philip Gamaghelyan

After a year of the Turkish-Armenian dialogue, when participants were almost in harmony and friendly with each other, there was a "hot session." It was the first time the group did not have a facilitator; somebody became agitated, the others got provoked, the facilitator wasn't there to challenge the group, and everybody suddenly became either a hard-line Turk or a hard-line Armenian, throwing at each other the usual accusations, screaming and almost hitting each other. Armenians became aggressive, accusing their Turkish friends of all possible sins. Turks who always said there was a genocide, were now screaming that there was none and that Armenians were all jerks and liars. Everyone had suddenly started repeating the mainstream stereotypical lines, hating each other and believing it. Then one of the participants stopped, with the intent to walk out, offering to continue only when there was a facilitator. The group stopped; looked at each other, shocked; and asked her back. They decided that they couldn't rely all their lives on a facilitator; they had to find a way to sort this out on their own. Everyone was embarrassed at how he or she had behaved. They realized that whenever they were pushed to a corner and attacked, they tended to adopt a rather radical position and felt a need to be patriotic and to defend their own side, even if they did not believe in what they were advocating.

During the first trip to Phnom Penh, community members from Svay Rieng province—most of whom had never been to Cambodia's capital city—mixed dialogue and reflection with memorializing activities. A group of eighteen villagers, staff from the ICfC, and support staff from a local mental health organization toured the genocide memorial museum and former Khmer Rouge detention center, Toul Sleng; and the killing fields, Choeng Ek, located on the outskirts of the city.

While at the museum viewing the exhibit of photographs of some of those who were detained at Toul Sleng and then killed at Choeng Ek, one community member found a photograph of a relative thought to be long missing. Such a sighting sparked dialogue among the visitors: "I knew people who were killed during the Khmer Rouge," said one villager, "but I did not know exactly how they were killed. Now I know." Another community member said, "When I go back to my village, I have stories to tell. I wish the children in my village were able to see these pictures. Then they would believe me." Later at the killing fields, upon seeing some monks wandering the grounds, the group of villagers requested a Buddhist ceremony to honor the dead.

These experiences proved cohesive not only for the group of villagers on the trip but also for the community members who remained at home. With the conclusion of the trip came new dialogues and activities that included youth and elders, men and women. As one villager who had been on the trip shared, "Lots of people asked me about my trip to Phnom Penh. I told them all about it. The children are more likely to listen to my stories now after they knew that I went to see Toul Sleng and the killing fields."

IDENTITY-BASED APPROACH TO CONFLICT RESOLUTION

Israel and Palestine, Turkey and Armenia, former Yugoslavia, Northern Ireland, Cambodia, Rwanda—all are places where people are divided by conflict with roots embedded in the histories of their country or region. Conflict resolution approaches in these settings are quite diverse—as they have been for many years—and they meet with varying levels of success. However, most of them have one thing in common, the "let the bygones be bygones" approach, with its stance that messing with official versions of history hinders the development of positive relationships and stands in the way of peace.

Approaches presented in this chapter are based on experience with identity-based conflicts such as those mentioned above. Our approaches are grounded in academic research related to history, memory, and identity. Quite interdisciplinary, we call on the fields of sociology, psychology, political science, conflict resolution, and family therapy. These approaches put history at the forefront. We believe that by addressing the proverbial elephant in the room—that is, painful memories that frame conflict relationships in identity-based conflicts—we can help build deeper, more stable, and longer-lasting relationships, thus providing a firm basis for peace that is not just on paper, but finds its way into people's minds and hearts.

Historical conciliation, the term that sums up the philosophy behind our method, is not a substitution for other conflict resolution strategies. Rather, it builds on these approaches and enriches them, especially during the initial engagement of the conciliation process, but also throughout.

In this chapter, we describe the philosophy of historical conciliation, developed over the years by the fellows and associates of the International Center for Conciliation (ICfC). This approach centers on the role of historical memory in the resolution of identity-based conflicts, particularly those marked by stories of widespread mass violence and trauma. We illustrate our methodology with two cases, one of Turkish-Armenian dialogues (ethnic conflict) and another of community dialogues in remote villages in Cambodia (healing a community that is crippled by a deep historical trauma).

HOW THE GROUP IS DIFFICULT

Conflicts addressed by historical conciliation are rooted in the conflicting identities of the people involved. Whether the identity at stake is the people's ethnicity, gender, religion, or culture, the process of historical conciliation requires a comprehensive approach that takes people's needs, hopes, fears, and concerns into account. People's identities are related to their sense of dignity, feelings of security, and perception of their status. "Identity-driven conflicts are rooted in the articulation of, and the threats or frustrations to, people's collective need for dignity, recognition, safety, control, purpose, efficacy. Unfortunately they are rarely framed that way" (Rothman, 1997, p. 7). Underlying needs held by individuals are not always transparently placed on the table; oftentimes we have to feel around for them. In order to identify these needs, we often have to start the search in the past, because one's history (or what one selectively remembers from it) forms a crucial part of one's image of who he or she is.

Identity-Based Versus Resource-Based Conflicts

Identity-based conflicts often manifest themselves in the form of resource-based struggles. (In the conflict resolution literature, resource-based conflicts are often labeled as "interest-based conflicts." We prefer the first term, because "interest" covers a wide range of meaning from the most tangible to the most abstract and thus is too vague to be useful.)

The distinction between identity-based and resource-based conflicts is often not immediately visible and not clear-cut: all identity conflicts have tangible components, but not all resource-based conflicts contain disputed identities. In Table 15.1 we identify some distinctions between these two types of conflicts. However, the longer any conflict continues, the more likely it will develop into an identity conflict as more people connect their dignity and memories with the dispute. Conflict analysis before the initial engagement is crucial in order to develop the right approach to conciliation. Traditional conflict resolution techniques, developed for dealing with resource-based conflicts, can sometimes exacerbate identity-based conflict, as they tend to avoid dealing with the "messy" issues of emotions, memories, values, belief systems, and so on that are at the core of identity-based conflicts.

Relational Conflict

Conflicting identities are also a basis for relationships gone awry. In a relationship riddled with conflict, people often feel threatened, humiliated, angry, and resentful (Petersen, 2002). They perceive the situation as an assault

Table 15.1
Resource-Based Versus Identity-Based Conflicts

	Resource-Based Conflict	Identity-Based Conflict
Center of the dispute	Tangible resources, clearly defined stakes over finite goods or services	Intangible, existential needs (collective need for dignity, recognition, safety, control, purpose, efficacy, and so on) that are rooted in abstract dynamics of history, culture, and belief systems
	Concrete desired outcomes	Abstract and complex goals
Conflict management/ negotiation approach	Involves resource-based and mixed-motive bargaining	Interactive dialogue about needs and values, which promotes voice and recognition
Goal of the negotiation	Address the tangible, practical resources being competed for	Create space for a long-term conciliation

Source: Adapted from *Resolving Identity-Based Conflict in Nations, Organizations, and Communities* (p. 17), by J. Rothman, 1997, San Francisco: Jossey-Bass.

to their dignity, and the blame for the situation and their negative feelings falls on the other side. All of this leads to blind spots in understanding who these individuals are in relation to the other in a nonexclusive way. Compassion and dialogue that promotes empathetic feelings are crucial in overcoming the impasse and managing and resolving the conflict. "Contemporary ethnicity is . . . a highly conscious, political, and new mode of interest-articulation and conflict, which nevertheless also retains its quality of sacredness. Ethnic groups are simultaneously primordial and modern, because in social life tradition and modernity are not necessarily mutually exclusive, nor is their interplay a zero-sum game" (Rothschild, 1981, p. 30).

Recent studies in psychology and neurobiology have found that relationships—connection with others and a sense of belonging—are more central to our emotional and mental health than experts previously assumed. Humiliation is a violation of this essential human need, and is likened by some researchers to a social pain, triggering the same receptors in the brain as physical pain (Hartling, 2005). As a result, a lingering sense of humiliation can lead to a decrease in self-regulation of behavior, to self-defeating and risky behavior, and all the way to open violence. This is true not only for individuals. It is also to a large extent applicable to groups. Overcoming humiliation, humanizing the other, and establishing a sense of dignity for the participants are among the main tasks of the initial stages of the conciliation process (see, for example, Hicks, 2002).

A sense of humiliation, anger, resentment, fear, or rage toward the other side, together with mutual distrust and blame for the conflict and current situation, are all factors that accompany identity-based conflicts. They are the outcomes of previous conflicts, reinforced through patterns of strained relations that can lead, in a vicious spiral, to escalation and further conflicts. Participants arrive with a problem-saturated conflict story that is based on the popular beliefs and representations of the conflict in their ethnic or religious group, and are often unable to distinguish between the other side and the conflict itself. Because people ultimately experience identities on an individual level, the conflict does not only relate to the groups; it is personal and intimate for the participants, and runs to the core of their beings. Often emotions run high and erupt throughout the process.

Two Examples

Unfortunately, examples of large-scale and violent identity-based conflicts around the world are in abundance. For an illustration of both the nature of the conflict and the possibilities for overcoming it, we highlight the case of long-term community dialogues and action development related to issues of transitional justice in postgenocide Cambodia, designed and launched by the chapter coauthor Adam Saltsman, and the case of Turkish-Armenian dialogue groups, led by the coauthor of this chapter Phil Gamaghelyan along with his colleague Ceren Ergenc. The first case relates to communities wounded by memories of a traumatic event or era in their past; the second case illustrates situations in which two historically hostile groups seek conciliation. Before examining each case in detail, we provide an introduction to each and explore their underlying causes.

Communities That Do Not Talk or Trust: Cambodian Rural Villages As a United Nations–backed tribunal begins the prosecution of the top surviving leaders of the Khmer Rouge regime, those deemed most responsible for one of the world's most gruesome genocides in the 1970s, Cambodians may have an opportunity for the restoration of their torn social fabric. Yet the tribunal's proceedings, meaning, and outcomes are widely unknown to the Cambodian public, especially in remote areas beyond the reach of radio news. Many also question the tribunal's legitimacy. Moreover, the tribunal staff have little to no knowledge about the rural population's concerns and interpretations regarding the court or what Cambodians actually need in order to glean a sense of justice.

In Cambodia, the ICfC designed a community social justice and history outreach program to serve as a connecting link between the tribunal and rural populations. The ICfC assists in interpreting local and international concepts of justice for the court and for the ICfC's Cambodian beneficiaries. Most important, through a participatory methodology, the ICfC offers some healing mechanisms to the communities divided by the trauma of the genocide, a trauma people rarely discuss.

In a society where discussion of the past has been taboo for many years, Cambodian villages face multiple relational and structural difficulties. Silence and politically manipulated narratives dominate the discursive terrain of history. Despite the fact that nine out of ten Cambodians lost a close relative during the Khmer Rouge regime, individuals' stories remain unknown beyond the closest of kin, if that, due to an active political repression of public discussion of history. Young people often have trouble believing the stories their parents and grandparents tell them, as they have not heard them anywhere else—neither in their schools nor in the media. In addition, there is a deep sense of mistrust as village chiefs and political and other leaders are sometimes from the ranks of the former Khmer Rouge or subsequent violently repressive regimes in a society where authority plays a crucial role. Such factors render the average Cambodian—particularly one living in a rural area far from the urban centers of information dissemination—disempowered and alone when it comes to dealing with his or her past.

Reaching out to the Enemy: Turkish-Armenian Dialogue Group History is central to the conflict between Turks and Armenians. The central disagreement in the present-day Turkish-Armenian conflict is whether the mass killings of Armenians in the Ottoman Empire during World War I constitute genocide. For nearly a century, Armenians have overwhelmingly been on one side of this dispute and Turks overwhelmingly on the other. Armenians argued that one-and-a-half million Armenians were subjected to genocide by the Ottoman Turkish state during World War I. Turks argued that the Armenian allegations are baseless or exaggerated. This dispute is not merely academic; what happened in 1915 has shaped the identities of the Turks and particularly the Armenians and continues to have profound consequences for relations between the two nations. Turkey and Armenia, two neighboring countries, have no diplomatic relations; the border is closed, and they routinely lobby other countries to support them against one another. When Turks and Armenians meet abroad, they avoid each other, resort to a direct confrontation, or, if they befriend each other, try not to discuss any controversial issue.

In September 2005, a number of Turkish and Armenian students and young professionals living and studying in Boston decided to break this cycle and engage in a long-term dialogue to try to understand each other and find out if there is any room for reconciliation between the Turks and the Armenians. Although the work with this and similar groups provides the example, the methodology is applicable to other conflicts that involve ethnic groups that live in different countries (such as Serbs and Croats, Armenians and Azerbaijanis) or in the same country (Arabs and Jews in Israel; Protestants and Catholics in Northern Ireland). What all these groups have in common is the condition conducive to their segregation and isolation from one another during their upbringing and education. Such dialogue groups are difficult, as the participants are often from societies deeply divided by years and often decades of continuous or repeated violence. The members of these social groups tend to evaluate their in-group positively in contrast to the out-group, which is seen negatively. This creates fertile conditions for the development of deep-rooted stereotyping and extreme—often perceived as "primordial"—hostility.

WHY THESE GROUPS ARE DIFFICULT

There are multiple and complex reasons for the groups involved in identity-based conflicts being difficult to work with. The people involved in ethnic or religious conflict grow up with a strong sense of mistrust and hostility toward the other and tend to have profound negative stereotypes about them as well. They are often isolated from and harbor strong mistrust toward the other, and are not used to interacting with members of the other group beyond a superficial level, if at all.

In addition, identity-based conflicts represent personal struggles for involved participants. As mentioned earlier, group identity is embedded in and experienced through the individual person and is therefore something quite intimate. It is a powerful mobilizer, as memories that form one's identity come with emotional anguish and potentially more serious psychological problems. This interconnection between personal sentiments and group identity engenders stakeholders who are deeply invested in their conflict. In these instances, rational analysis of the situation and the identification of possible solutions are not immediately feasible goals.

We now proceed to describe these two cases in more detail.

WORKING WITH GROUPS PLAGUED WITH INTERNAL HISTORICAL TRAUMA: VILLAGE DIALOGUES IN RURAL CAMBODIA

> *If the law let me do what I want, I would beat the [Khmer Rouge] leaders vigorously with a club.*
>
> —Community member and dialogue participant, Takeo province, Cambodia

Beneath the veneer of daily subsistence, residents of rural villages in Cambodia divide on at least four levels. First, systematic and institutionalized gender discrimination manifests itself in a pervasive sense of unequal power relations between community men and women. Second, a growing gap in traditions, values, and experiences between old and young forms generational polarities. Third, membership in different political groups that were once engaged in armed conflict with each other and remain violently opposed to one another pits an opposition minority against an autocratic majority and leaves the moderate center intimidated. Fourth, former Khmer Rouge cadre who at one point terrorized the Cambodian population during the 1970s and 1980s now live in villages with victims of the brutal regime, though they deny ever committing any crimes. In order to maintain the uneasy village peace, village leadership pushed residents to decide that it could only do harm to talk about the past. Thus, on a deep emotional and historical level, enmity from the years of the genocidal, ultra-Maoist Khmer Rouge rule dissects communities, filling residents with suspicion and a decades-old silence that perpetuates a thick blanket of mistrust.

These four levels of division interact with and sustain each other, creating a seemingly unending cycle of conflict, disempowerment, and mistrust. In attempting to engage residents from six Cambodian villages in community dialogues, the ICfC ran into enormous relational, political, and rational obstacles, summarized in Table 15.2. In our initial project design, we wrote that we would make three preparatory visits to each village to pitch the idea of a dialogue, meet interested participants, and build some trust and comfort between participants and facilitators. We would then make two to three more visits to conduct one- to two-hour dialogues per trip. Follow-up visits would come subsequent to the dialogue, and we would be able to evaluate our pilot method.

Table 15.2
Obstacles to the Initial Design for Community Dialogues in Rural Cambodia

	Context	Structure	Process
Relational	Deep historical grievances and silence about the past, along with painful memories, cause severe mistrust.		Lack of ownership of the process leaves participants without sufficient incentives to engage in dialogue.
Political		The gender divide and political tension deny some participants the feeling of being well represented.	Participants felt disempowered by process and did not feel comfortable making decisions.
Rational			Facilitators made only day trips to the villages, so restrictions on the time scheduled for dialogue sometimes made it inconvenient for villagers.

At various times during the first few dialogues, we found that men talked far more than women or refused to engage when many women were talking; the opposition party members (who are a vast minority in any village) were silent when sitting in a circle with a village chief from the dominant political party; and youth expressed disinterest and disbelief at Khmer Rouge survivors' stories of the past as elders used stories of suffering to scold the bad behavior of village youth and fill them with guilt. Most egregiously, former Khmer Rouge cadre denied their participation in the regime's atrocities at the same time that victims cried out for justice and an end to impunity.

Facilitators quickly recognized that the initial approach was not productive; the only thing participants claimed to gain from the dialogues was the recognition that a group from outside the village made an effort to provide them with emotional support. Although our dialogue project was already unique in Cambodia for spending as much time as we did eliciting conversation from relatively small groups of people, we needed to change the way we went about making initial contact with participants, designing the dialogue structure, and facilitating the process. We realized that underlying all the aforementioned obstacles was the fact that participants did not feel any sense of ownership of the entire process, from planning to dialogue implementation. We decided to place greater emphasis on the collaborative coconstruction of problem identification and strategies for moving forward.

WORKING WITH CROSS-CONFLICT GROUPS: THE TURKISH-ARMENIAN DIALOGUE GROUP

In addition to the reasons cited earlier in the section Why These Groups Are Difficult, groups from societies divided by decades of hostility present a number of additional, less obvious difficulties.

First, the conversation in such groups usually focuses on the matters central to the conflict, yet the two sides usually have very different underlying assumptions about the context and background of the conflict. Each group has its own problem-saturated story that tells the conflict story from a heavily biased and selective perspective. Many assumptions are taken for granted by each side as "common knowledge" that should be shared by the other side and the facilitators. These assumptions are normally rarely discussed and frequently lead to miscommunication.

In the Turkish-Armenian groups, the discussions and disagreements are centered on the massacres of the Armenians in 1915; Armenians refer to these massacres as genocide, whereas Turks usually dispute the applicability of the term. The context of the events is rarely discussed, yet can explain the attachment of both sides to their respective positions. Armenians see 1915 in the context of centuries of occupation and discrimination by Turks, culminating in the Genocide in 1915 and the subsequent Turkish policy of denial. That it happened during World War I is considered only as a convenient pretext for a plan to exterminate Armenians that could be carried out without getting much attention from the international community. The context, as seen from the Turkish perspective, is entirely different. For them, the Ottoman Empire, even if not perfect, had for centuries the best record among the empires with regard to minority rights and religious practices. The Turks consider that these minorities, particularly Armenians, betrayed them during World War I and became the "fifth column" during the most difficult periods of Ottoman history when the empire was losing a war and was in the midst of collapse. The killings are seen in a context of a civil war imposed on the empire by the Armenians, rather than deliberate massacre.

There is another, methodological difficulty of working with groups such as these. The conflicting perceptions of the past that are often the unspoken driving force of the conflict constitute "baggage" that hinders the progress of the dialogue if these perceptions remain unaddressed. A practice of discussing and handling historical discussions during interethnic dialogue becomes crucial, as otherwise such questions are still brought into the open but are often mishandled, leading to a bigger conflict that damages the dialogue. In the Turkish-Armenian case, the conversation usually develops into a cycle of mutual accusations: Armenians accusing Turks of a genocide and subsequent cover-up, the Turks accusing Armenians of betraying them and of exaggerating and manufacturing a "false" history to hurt Turkey.

WHAT YOU CAN DO

As a group facilitator, how can you help the group work more effectively through the messy parts of a conciliation process? Overcoming humiliation, feelings of anger, hatred, resentment, and rage related to the memories of violent conflict, and feelings of victimization is a key goal of historical conciliation, particularly in the phase of initial engagement in the conciliation process. The parties need to find a way to relate to each other on a universal human level: to rehumanize the other. Empathy, an honest, heartfelt experiencing of the other's story from the other's point of view (without necessarily agreeing), is the path toward building relationships based on trust and understanding, on which the process can move forward using already widely established conflict resolution techniques (Halpern & Weinstein, 2004). Acknowledgment of the validity of the other party's narrative and of their emotions facilitates empathy and lends dignity to both parties. It goes a long way toward establishing trust and willingness to work together on solutions.

Empathy building with parties stuck in historically rooted and identity-based conflicts begins long before face-to-face discussion between opposing sides can take place. By the time conflicting parties can speak with each other, much "rehumanizing" work has already been done.

First, participants in a historical conciliation process need to decide for themselves that they are willing and committed to what may be a long and painful series of meetings with an "other" who embodies a whole series of culturally resonating negative collective memories; that is, an other who may unwittingly bear the burden of generations of pain, anger, suffering, and humiliation. This willingness to engage with the other at all signifies the opening of a possibility to build a new relationship based on empathy rather than hate.

Second, participants must be able to see some possible benefit—there must be a concrete, forward-looking goal—to a conflict resolution process that seeks to delve deeper than the resource-driven tension that may lie on the surface and that may be the most immediately relevant issue with which parties wish to deal. This is to say that conflicting individuals or groups must see for themselves the benefit of a deeper, identity-based intervention even when it appears that the problem can easily be fixed with a resource-based mediation procedure.

Third, it is essential that participants be empowered to contextualize any conflict resolution intervention into their own local discourse, ensuring that the process is ontologically resonant. This puts the participants' unique expert knowledge into the dynamics of their community; something that can be instrumental in figuring out how to get people to the table, how to elicit narrative, and how to work with those narratives to move toward empathy and acknowledgment. Once parties see for themselves—in their own terms—the possible benefits of deep mutual engagement, they are truly present and committed.

Historical conciliation borrows heavily from narrative mediation methodology and adapts it to work with stories based in collective memories. Although narrative mediation originates from family therapy, it has been applied in other areas as well. Narrative mediation offers tools to foster empathy and acknowledgment through working with the conflict stories that the participants bring to the table. Its foundation in social constructivism and its focus on validating people's experiences and feelings render the approach very useful in working with identity-based conflicts. "Mediators who use a narrative orientation are interested in the constitutive properties of conflict stories. In other words, whether a story is factual or not matters little to the potential impact it has on someone's life. Our emphasis is on how the story operates to create reality rather than on whether it reports accurately on that reality. Stories therefore are not viewed as either true or false accounts of an objective 'out there' reality" (Winslade & Monk, 2001, p. 3). Stories are viewed as constructing the world rather than describing the world as independently known. Acknowledgment in this setting therefore relates to the validity of one's perceptions and feelings stemming out of the conflict story rather than to the factual basis of that story.

In ethnic, religious, and other identity-based conflicts, multiple stories form groups' collective memories, the building blocks of their identity. "Narratives are implicated in the onset, escalation, and maintenance of ethnic conflict. However . . . it is important to recognize their potential in de-escalation as well, because narratives can and do evolve over time" (Ross, 2007, p. 44). A narrative approach helps the participants deconstruct their problem-saturated stories, find the source of their strong emotions, and "externalize the conflict"—separate it from the people who came together to resolve it, and thus create the possibility of moving on and working toward solutions together.

Ross (2007) focuses on narratives that foster peace processes on a national level. Those narratives "arise when there are connections made between culturally available references and events on the ground. . . . Changing the narrative frame can also facilitate de-escalation when it helps people caught in conflict to envision alternatives to ongoing confrontation. In order for this to happen, each side must appreciate the perspective of the other, and learn that there is someone to talk to on the other side and something to talk about." The same is true in dialogue settings at the local level when we work with groups of students, villagers, and various other stakeholders.

This process does not necessarily lead to creation of a shared narrative that everybody can agree on. Although groups sometimes coauthor shared narratives or broaden and diversify each other's points of view, this process is not seeking one ultimate "truth" as the outcome. Rather, the focus is on acknowledging the other's experience, validating its authenticity, and honoring the other's dignity needs—and by doing so, building lasting relationships.

There are numerous practical ways of navigating through this process. In the next section, we will look at the use of participatory village dialogues in rural Cambodia.

RESHAPING RURAL COMMUNITIES OF CAMBODIA THROUGH LONG-TERM DIALOGUE

> *It is not easy for us to talk about our past experiences because we feel great pain. However, we notice the relief of tension and stress that we feel inside ourselves after talking.*
>
> *After I cry, I feel fresh.*
>
> —Community members during dialogue, Takeo province, Cambodia

Our case study in Cambodia speaks primarily to the early stages of historical conciliation: establishing a foundation of collaboration that can lead to the coconstruction of conciliation strategies uniquely suited to each village.

In an effort to design a forward-looking and open dialogue process for a community unaccustomed to discussing the past or dealing with deeper-level conflicts, we sought an approach that would create space for community members to decide for themselves the extent and nature of their need and interest in engaging in a process of historical conciliation. We realized that this approach would not be possible if (1) we were seen as enigmatic outsiders—causing suspicion among villagers—and (2) if the villagers did not feel a sense of investment in and ownership of the process. Our approach became rooted in the belief that community members and conflict resolution practitioners must work together to create an empowered space where beneficiaries can voice their needs and strategize on the best way to deal with problems facing their community.

The five-stage strategy that we developed to actualize such a belief is grounded in elements of what development practitioners call *participatory action development*—known more commonly by the social science terms *participatory action research* (Cornwall & Jewkes, 1995; Fals-Borda, 1991), *participatory rural appraisal* (Chambers, 1994), *critical collaborative research* (LeCompte, 1995), and *feminist participatory action research* (Reid & Frisby,

Figure 15.1
A Five-Stage Strategy for Sustained Dialogue

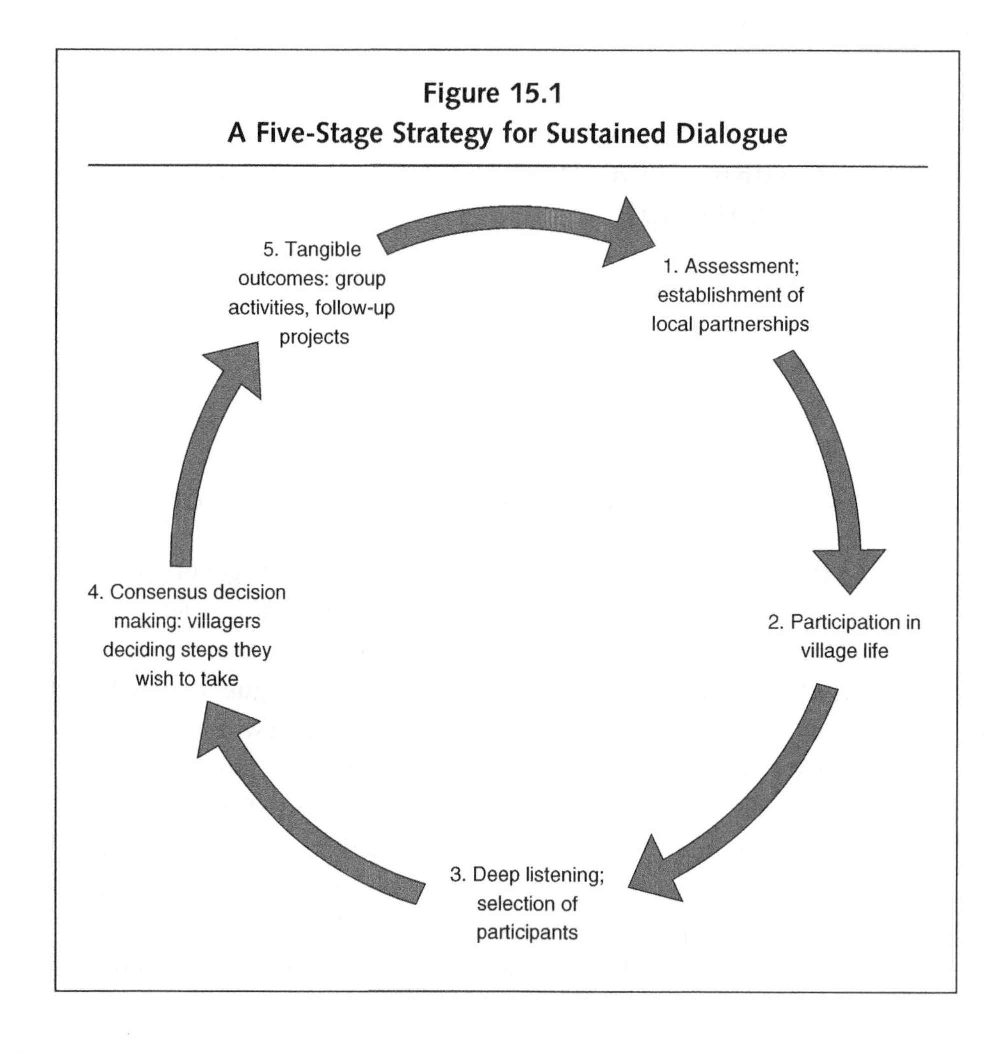

2008). Also included are elements of *sustained dialogue* (Saunders, 2001). The approach is illustrated in Figure 15.1 and described here.

Assessment and Establishment of Local Partnerships

We recognized the benefit of long-term stays in the villages where we planned to conduct dialogues; we recognized that authentic collaboration requires a foundation of familiarity and trust. However, due to constraints of time, funding, and commitment, it was not possible to stay for months or even weeks at a time. In an effort to expedite the work of trust building and also to ensure some continuity for whatever gains might be made from the dialogues, we found villages in which community based organizations (CBOs) worked and maintained positive and empowering relations with residents. Often these organizations were focused on community development, helping villagers set up sanitation systems, rice banks, and sustainable animal husbandry programs.

We approached these organizations, asked about social tension within the village, and offered to partner with the CBO in addressing these tensions. They agreed to help introduce us to the village leadership—a crucial step to gaining the privileges of sleeping in the village and of free access around the village. They also introduced us to all the villagers, informing them of the partnership between the CBO and the ICfC. We agreed to provide conflict resolution training for the CBO staff with the intention of eventually cofacilitating the dialogues and ultimately handing over the dialogue project to them. When village residents saw that we had the "blessing" of the CBO that they knew so well and trusted, they welcomed us into their village.

Participation in Village Life

After partnering with the local CBO, we arranged to stay with village families. We ate with the families and gave assistance to villagers as they farmed rice paddies, constructed houses, cared for their animals, and cooked meals. As we were inexperienced with some of this work, the villagers became our teachers. Becoming a regular sight around the village normalized our presence there. Our interactions with village residents became casual: we joked, discussed politics, and talked about our families.

By participating in so many aspects of daily village life, we found ourselves in a position to observe interactions between village residents and to locate the strengths and weaknesses in their relationships. Although the divisions noted earlier in this chapter did exist, we saw in place systems of reciprocity binding households to one another in the struggle for subsistence. Often people did not know of others' experiences with the Khmer Rouge, but they knew that they had helped each other survive since the end of the armed conflict.

Deep Listening and Selection of Future Participants

In addition to participating, we tasked ourselves with both casual and "deep" listening. Rather than bringing up social tensions in the village, historical divisions, or memories of suffering, we paid attention to which village residents raised these issues and how they came up in everyday conversation. We took copious field notes over the course of our stay in the village. After an initial assessment, we began to seek out and engage in casual conversation those individual residents who talked most often about the Khmer Rouge years, current injustice, conflict, and the need for peace. We referred to these people as "high priority."

After one or two weeklong village visits, we gathered together the group of high-priority residents and presented some of the results of our assessment. "We recognize that you all have raised certain issues quite often in casual conversation," we told the residents, "and we are wondering if we can help you deal with these issues in some way."

Consensus Decision Making: Villagers Deciding the Steps They Wish to Take

Once we presented community members with a summary of the results from our active listening and observations, both we and the community members decided on the next steps. In each village, most of the approximately twenty-five residents we brought together said they would like to do something to deal with their pain from the past and with current social tensions, but it proved difficult to transform this desire into a particular action. We assisted community members by providing them with a list of potential activities, which included dialogues; visits to Phnom Penh—Cambodia's capital city—to see the genocide memorial museum and the court currently trying the former leaders of the Khmer Rouge; and the establishment of village memorials. In each village, community members decided to engage with all three of these activities. We discuss these various activities in the next section.

In setting up the dialogue, it was the community members who decided on the time, the venue, and the dialogue agenda. Community members strategized with us about the best way to deal with suspicious village authorities. In some cases, community members wished to involve the chief to dispel any suspicions; in other locations, villagers preferred to keep the activities free from the chief's influence. When the chief did come, participants would divide into small groups partway through the dialogue so that the chief would only be able to influence a fraction of the overall number of participants. We sought to have an equal number of men and women participating as well as a large number of youth. This was not counter to the wishes of the community members, though in the future, facilitators might leave it entirely up to the villagers. The youth, respecting their traditional roles in the village, remained quiet when it came to making decisions. However, the increased level of trust and sense of purpose brought greater equality between male and female participation, aided by the presence of several outspoken women who felt some ownership in the process.

Tangible Outcomes: Group Activities and Follow-Up Projects

As mentioned in the previous section, community members in most of the villages where the ICfC worked expressed an interest in initiating dialogue; visiting Phnom Penh, the Khmer Rouge tribunal, and the genocide museum; and building a memorial in the village. Such collaborative decision making toward concrete actions reflects the extent to which community participants felt a sense of ownership over these activities; the manner in which community members and facilitators carried out activities was a product of the community participants' interests and needs.

The cumulative effect of the dialogue and the visit to Cambodia's capital was empowering and provocative, as many who had never deeply revealed their stories with those outside their nuclear families began to see that despite historical divisions, they shared with others the experiences of pain, loss, and injustice. This opened a door for victims and perpetrators to hear each other's stories. It also gave the opportunity to the young people to hear the stories for the first time on a community sharing level; youth were hearing about the past not as a tool of parental scolding but as an important part of their own story. This helped open up space for intergenerational bonding and healing. During the dialogues, facilitators worked hard to highlight the many empathy-rich moments that lay just beneath the surface by verbally drawing attention to them and mapping them for the villagers. Facilitators did this by taking notes during the dialogue sessions, compiling the comments they identified as important, and then relaying this list of points back to participants for reflection and further discussion. Depending on the flow of conversation, it sometimes made sense for facilitators to revisit these empathy-rich moments during the dialogue sessions, whereas at other times facilitators waited until the next gathering.

In this project, the participatory methods lay the groundwork for sustained dialogue that fit the needs of the community members. Facilitators elicited historical narratives and employed them in dialogue in a way that helped make space for public discussion of history in the community. Table 15.3 provides a useful comparison with Table 15.2, which illustrates the obstacles to this dialogue work. It also highlights the ways in which our changes to the project's approach affected the role of the dialogue and how it functioned within this specific context. This should not suggest that all the

Table 15.3
Reframing the Dialogue Design for Community Dialogues in Rural Cambodia

	Context	Structure	Process
Relational	Empowered village residents feel incentives to engage in a dialogue process that belongs to them.	Empathy increases sincerity and trust.	Facilitators work to highlight "empathy-rich" moments to connect village residents' seemingly disparate stories of the past.
Political	Empowerment of villagers ensures that the time and space of the dialogue fit participants' needs.	Empowerment and sense of ownership among participants create an equal forum for decision making.	Lengthy assessment, trust building, and process of familiarization help make each participant feel well represented.

aforementioned community divisions disappeared. Rather, this intervention represents an initial effort to ground historical conciliation practices in the local discourse so that historical empathy can play a generative role in building positive relationships that make it more possible to deal with current dilemmas and deep tensions. Much more work needs to be done in these communities and in others like them.

AN HISTORICAL TIMELINES APPROACH IN CROSS-CONFLICT DIALOGUE GROUPS

The "historical timelines" approach was developed by Ceren Ergenc and Philip Gamaghelyan. Ergenc is from Turkey; Gamaghelyan is from Armenia. Together they have facilitated Turkish-Armenian dialogue groups, and trained facilitators, journalists, and educators working in a wide range of conflict situations. They have researched extensively the role of history and collective memory in conflict and its resolution and found practical applications of their findings in groups divided by ethnic conflict.

The methodology derives from the assumption that historical memory is at the core of ethnic identity of the group and the driving reason behind the hostile feelings and the conflict itself. It builds on the premises that history is often a divisive topic and that it is often not possible to find the "truth." However, the popular perception of history—the collective memory of it—has to be addressed, and its role in the conflicts can and should be understood if the parties to the conflict ever want to achieve real reconciliation. The understanding of the process of collective memory, its forms and agents of transmission, by the participants can help transform the relations between the conflicting parties.

The reason for engaging historical memory, from the conflict resolution perspective, is not to establish all the facts with regard to who was right or wrong, or "who did what to whom when." Instead, the aim is to see the difference between the history as it happened and the memory of the history, how it has been transmitted differently by the two societies in conflict, how it generates hatred and stereotypes, how it creates conflicts, and how this awareness can be used to resolve conflicts. The historical timelines methodology allows us to analyze the underlying reasons for the "historical hatred" and also outline solutions to the conflict.

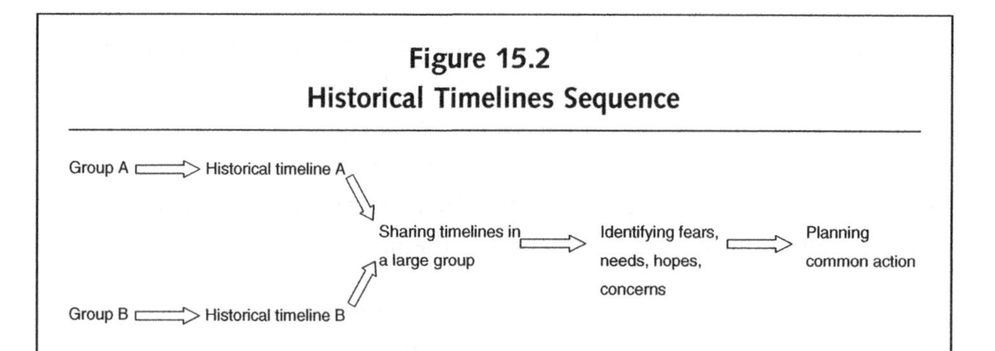

Figure 15.2
Historical Timelines Sequence

As shown in Figure 15.2, the two groups representing the two sides of the conflict are asked to write two simple timelines, each group from its own perspective, recording the important events they remember from history that impacted the relationship with the other side. The groups work on the basis of consensus—only events that are familiar to and deemed important by all members of the group make it onto the group timeline. Each group then explains its timeline to the other; then the timelines are discussed in detail and analyzed. This process can take a number of days to complete; usually at least two days are needed for discussions to run their course.

The timelines are then placed next to each other, and the participants are asked to view and analyze the two stories through the eyes of an independent observer. Our experience with one Turkish-Armenian and two Armenian-Azerbaijani groups showed that the two narratives are usually less contradictory than they are different. Our documented timelines from these workshops showed that out of ten to fifteen events chosen by each group, only one or two events out of the entire timeline coincide in a contradictory manner. In their entirety, however, the stories look as if they were not even related to the same conflict. (One participant exclaimed that these countries could be on the opposite sides of the planet, as they have almost nothing in common.) Analyzing the narratives invariably demonstrated that the groups in conflict selected and emphasized very different events in their history, with different values and meanings attached to them, and consequently constructed very different identity stories. Even when the events do directly contradict one another, the timeline illustrates the possibility of having multiple perspectives on one single moment. Highlighting this during the workshop can be used to reinforce the need to work away from finding one "true" history and working toward a kind of acknowledgment. Such realizations

- Lead to empathy by facilitating the understanding of one another's identity needs.
- Help break the "us versus them" dichotomy in the construct of the identities by visually showing that, in important ways, the narratives are different, rather than contradictory as is often assumed. This discovery makes it easier to give the other's account a chance, to acknowledge its validity for the other side.
- Help identify and understand stereotypes by indicating the patterns in the group memory that constitute the foundation of negative stereotyping.
- Provide ground for working with group perceptions for researchers and policymakers who are committed to large-scale reconciliation projects.
- Provide context for the core views and positions held by the other side that otherwise are seen as unreasonable demands.

The process brings the dialogue group to a place where looking into the present and the future is a lot more feasible and productive. The learning that results from the historical timelines experience enables the group to share a higher degree of mutual trust and understanding. From this point, facilitators lead the group through the process of identifying current fears, needs, hopes, and concerns; identifying solutions for overcoming obstacles; and planning common or individual follow-up activities designed by the participants.

Our experience also shows that a large percentage of participants who have shared this experience tend to be engaged long-term in follow-up activities. Because the timelines approach involves undergoing a profound learning experience about people's perception of what their identity means and where it comes from, participants' investment in the process after the end of the dialogue remains high, as they wish to share the gained insight with others.

CONCLUSION

Approaches utilized within historical conciliation may vary widely. Some are set up in a traditional dialogue setting, some are designed as interactive retreats combining outdoor and dialogue elements, others have elements of community participatory action development. What they share is the philosophy that navigates the process toward the desired outcome: transformed relationships that build on deep trust, empathy, and understanding. Collective memory is recognized as the humanizing force that leads to that end result. Even though the first days are invariably difficult, messy, emotional, and even explosive, they provide participants with the platform to speak in their own voice; to understand not only the other side but also their own story and its place in the conflict and to see a wider context; and to connect on a universal human level, experiencing the stories from the teller's point of view. The process can result in a peace that is deeper and longer lasting, and in relationships that lead to cooperation between the participants well beyond the duration of the conciliation engagement.

chapter
SIXTEEN

Deep Democracy: Multidimensional Process-Oriented Leadership

Stanford Siver

A Middle East desert expedition peace project set out from Jerusalem, traveling to Tripoli, Libya, by truck, foot, and camel with a goal of demonstrating that they really can get along despite their enormous differences. The group included eight designated participants, chosen for their diverse and extreme experiences, and a small army of support staff that included four documentary filmmakers, three drivers, two organizers, one Tibetan Lama, a doctor, a photographer and various media people who would come and go, an Egyptian security officer, and me, the staff conflict facilitator, all crammed into three overloaded trucks.

The eight participants—from Afghanistan, Iran, Iraq, Israel, Palestine, the former Soviet Union, and the United States—had not met before. Despite their extremely diverse views and personal histories, they began the trip with a common belief in their solidarity: *we all get along; it's our governments who don't get along.*

With the pace and the stress of cramped conditions and long days traveling, it was no surprise that the group's difficulties included all of the tensions that exist in life everywhere and Middle East politics in particular: gender politics, conflicts among the support staff and organizers, and participants who projected their conflicts onto government leadership and swore that they all got along despite obvious disagreements and escalating tensions.

In an earlier peace project, the same organizers had brought four Israelis and four Palestinians to South America, sailing across the Strait of Magellan and Drake Passage to Antarctica. They climbed a previously unscaled mountain together and named it Friendship Mountain as a symbol of joint Palestinian and Israeli friendship.

On camera, it had been an inspiring undertaking that grabbed the attention of major media and over five hundred million viewers around the world. Off camera, things were rather complicated.

By the time they reached the mountain, one of the participants refused to be seen in photos with some of the others, and other rifts were evident along lines of gender, ethnic identity, and race. Problems that exist globally tend to be mirrored within organizations, and peace projects are no exception. It was because of these complications that the organizers' executive team had decided to include a conflict facilitator in the second expedition.

The first days of the journey went well. The participants believed in their mission and made inspiring speeches for the media and filmmakers; the staff were busy working to keep things rolling; and the tensions that arose rarely flared for long. Still, despite the obvious tension, there was a clear "no" to deeper dialogue. There was a line beyond which neither staff nor participants were prepared to go until several weeks into the journey when a man from Afghanistan suddenly decided to leave in the middle of a small Egyptian city. Even worse, the project organizers didn't ask why, but were politely saying good-bye while thanking him for having come this far. People should feel free to leave, but I felt that we were failing if we didn't at least try to finally have a deeper and more meaningful interaction. I decided to join him, amplify the reason for leaving, and occupy the role more clearly: "Fine! If he's going then I'm going! If he's not important to all of you, then this project isn't important to me. Fine that he goes, but not without our working together to understand why, to hear his frustrations, and to see if there is something we can do together to make this work for everyone."

It was a chaotic hot spot. The film crew ran for their gear. One organizer was stunned; the other was furious. But everybody gathered around. And then there was a moment of silence. For the first time, the group could see that something wasn't working. It isn't only our governments that don't get along. Something had shifted, and people understood that they needed to work together.

We traveled just far enough to escape the city noise and gathered in a circle on the desert sands of the eastern Sahara. Not certain where to go or what would happen, I dropped the role I'd taken on and spoke briefly as a facilitator and invited the man from Afghanistan to speak first. He talked about his country, about the U.S. invasion, about differences between East and West, between Judeo-Christian culture and Arab culture. And then he said, "It feels like there is no room for my experience. You all believe that it is only our governments, that we are all the same, but I feel so put down by your attitudes."

A chaotic group process erupted as the Iraqi man joined with the man from Afghanistan in speaking against U.S. invasions, imperialism, and the CIA. The men from the United States reacted and spoke about the horrors of 9/11 and the great things that the United States is doing and the beautiful ideals for humanity in the background, and countered that when they had told their stories they didn't feel that the Afghani man had listened. People talked about suffering and love and horrible things that had happened to them, their families, and their countries.

There was a moment of silence and tears. Realizing the shared humanity of suffering often brings people closer together. And then one woman spoke about her vision for humanity, that we can demonstrate that we really can get along, that we can demonstrate peace. There was another moment of silence, but it felt like the air being let out of a balloon. The peace she described felt oppressive. Peace is people being real, open to chaos, open to diverse experiences, working together on difficult issues without picking up guns, saying the kinds of things we don't often say to people who don't agree with us, trying to find the other in themselves, learning to discuss extremely hot issues without recreating war, and learning to understand ourselves and others.

As I thought back to the earlier days of the project, the signals of someone's leaving were there all along, as were the signals of a deeper, more disturbing dialogue waiting to emerge. People *left* by keeping their real feelings and thoughts about other cultures, countries, and religions to themselves, preferring to support the friendly group atmosphere of camaraderie while gossiping privately about their views. In a sense, they hadn't showed up yet.

The Afghani man did leave. Not everyone wants to stay and work it out with others. Some love it. Some prefer to hit and run. Others prefer to avoid any confrontation. Over time, each group will find its own way to work with the diverse experiences that arise once it finds the courage for deeper dialogue.

DEEP DEMOCRACY

Deep Democracy is a psycho-socio-political paradigm and large group facilitation and change management model that integrates concepts from quantum physics, psychology, and anthropology. The basic methodology involves the use of dual awareness and an attitude of inclusiveness to cocreate group cohesion. The first awareness focuses on the group's content and surface dynamics. The second awareness focuses on microsignals; self-organizing tendencies; subjective experience; and the facilitator's own experience, which is organized by the same forces that organize the group and is a meaningful mirror of the group's process. Introducing and practicing these concepts are difficult because Deep Democracy is not a set of rules about how to run groups. It is a set of tools and principles that can help the group discover its own path by noticing itself and embracing an atmosphere of inclusiveness.

Deep Democracy was developed by Arnold Mindell (1992), the founder of Process Work (also known as Process Oriented Psychology; see www.aamindell.net and www.iapop.com). Deep Democracy has been further developed into a multidimensional process-oriented leadership model by Max and Ellen Schupbach, cofounders of the Deep Democracy Institute and partners in MAXFXX, an organizational consulting group.

Arny Mindell (2000), originally a physicist and Jungian analyst, has researched and written extensively on how awareness creates reality, how we perceive experiences on different levels, and how this creates different frameworks of reality. This idea follows discoveries in quantum physics, chaos theory, and the symbolic thinking of Jungian psychology, and also stems from ancient spiritual traditions such as Taoism and indigenous philosophies.

In the late 1980s, Mindell began formulating his ideas as a political principle that he called *Deep Democracy:* Unlike "classical" democracy, which focuses on majority rule, Deep Democracy suggests that all voices, states of awareness, and frameworks of reality are important. Deep Democracy also suggests that the information carried within these voices, awarenesses, and frameworks are all needed to understand the complete process of the system. Deep Democracy is an attitude that focuses on the awareness of voices that are both central and marginal (A. P. Mindell, 1992).

The focus on voices that are both central and marginal refers to the voices of various states of consciousness, subjective somatic (bodily) experiences, synchronicities, and experiences associated with rank dynamics. Developing our ability to notice, understand, and use the information contained in these voices can help us improve our ability to facilitate complex interactions. It isn't easy to see how our limited awareness is creating a problem when we are in the midst of working with a difficult group. The difficulty seems painfully real, and we may think it obvious that a particular person or group is the cause of the problem. Unfortunately, this narrow assessment rarely helps relieve the tension. It doesn't work.

The greatest difficulty is often our inability to understand and appreciate events in terms of their underlying processes. One way that our limited awareness may serve to cloud our understanding is through an unconscious attachment to our own agenda, which is often expressed through an implicit expectation that a group *should* be easier to work with, which really means that "they should follow me." Groups may be seen as difficult when conflicting leadership efforts are not supported through facilitation, resulting instead in chaotic and painful authority fights.

Facilitators can capitalize on group disturbances and improve their ability to understand a difficult group's dynamics, facilitate more effectively, and transform disturbances by understanding the patterns that structure group dynamics and individual behavior. These patterns appear as signals that are critical for understanding difficulties, recognizing and supporting emergent leadership, and helping groups find more creative and sustainable solutions. Deep Democracy and a multidimensional process-oriented view of leadership provide a framework for understanding these patterns. Mindell defines *process* as a constant flow of information—which we experience through signals, body symptoms, relationship experiences, and other channels of information flow (1989) and refers to a *group process* as an event where people work together to bring awareness to the tensions, roles, ghosts, and dynamics that pattern the group's dynamics.

PROCESS THEORY

Process work theory says that the psychology of the facilitator and the group are organized by the same forces. These forces create a *field,* similar to an invisible electromagnetic field, that pulls people in various directions. These varied directions appear as *roles,* which are the viewpoints or functions within a field that are occupied by various people or subgroups at different times—for example, the leader, the worker, the helper, or the troublemaker.

Although any given role may at times seem to be located within a given individual, roles are actually dynamic *timespirits.* Timespirits are roles that change with time, sometimes quite rapidly, and often move from one individual or group to another. For example, while speaking angrily against tyranny, I may inadvertently tyrannize others, at least momentarily. Timespirits are part of the field's self-organizing pattern.

Groups are most difficult when the structural elements of the field's pattern are not seen and addressed. These elements include the tensions and feelings that exist between various roles and *ghost* roles. Ghosts are roles that are somehow felt to be present but can't quite be located. For example, sexism is a common ghost role in organizations. People may feel its presence, and although no one speaks in favor of sexism directly, it persists.

Group difficulties tend to escalate when key signals are not addressed because the underlying roles remain invisible—like ghosts that are felt and that effect the group but aren't directly expressed or spoken to. Also, groups tend to become frozen when one *polarity* (two central but opposed roles) is given too much attention and when groups lack the *fluidity* (an ability to consciously shift between different roles and to avoid being grabbed by a role) that comes from understanding roles as dynamic timespirits rather than static positions. Understanding roles as timespirits means that any one person or subgroup is not the role but also changes and needs awareness of and access to other positions as well. Groups tend to be more cohesive when disturbing subgroups and individuals are seen as momentarily occupying emergent roles that are asking to be welcomed to interact with the group's dominant views and individuals.

Welcoming disturbing roles and behaviors is difficult because people are often opposed to certain roles and at times enjoy *winning* by defeating and silencing others; and positional leaders and designated facilitators often feel threatened by the emergent, momentary leadership of others and don't always support the group's direction as opposed to their own agenda.

The following sections describe methods for tracking the *process structure*—the patterns that organize the information in terms of the rank, roles, and polarities and the tensions that exist between them and that therefore organize the group structure—and lay the foundation for the section on multidimensional leadership. Group structure is patterned by process structure, and thus by the same organizing forces. In this sense, the terms *group structure* and *process structure* are synonymous in this chapter.

TRACKING

If process is a constant flow of information, then signals are a constant flow of symbolic indicators, which indirectly inform us about various competing processes. These underlying processes are evident in signals and their *structure*—the patterns in verbal and nonverbal communications, movement, roles, emotional cues, and somatic experiences. But we often marginalize the signals because we don't understand their meaning. Signals often seem chaotic, and confusing signals are often ignored. For example, in moments when you might expect someone to attentively listen, signals that don't go along with attentive listening (gazing out the window, fidgeting with a cell phone) will usually be ignored until their strength (either through an increase in intensity or repetition) exceeds a certain threshold. Below that threshold, their informational value is lost, and our ability to learn from complex situations is limited.

The root of the word *learn* is *leornian,* arising from a Proto-Indo-European word meaning "to follow or find the track" (Harper, 2001). *Tracking* is the root of learning. Tracking means to notice the signals and discover how they fit together, revealing a path that leads forward. The first step is to notice signals that don't seem to go along with the normal flow of communications and to track those signals.

Groups become difficult because these signals and fledgling processes are often ignored, and they are often ignored because they conflict with other processes, and so the cycle continues. It takes a change of attitude to understand that those signals that we might prefer to ignore can be used to discover an emerging tendency that is crucially deserving of support rather than a troublesome obstacle to be overcome.

Tracking isn't meant to be a reductionist exercise in conducting an increasingly detailed analysis of signals and their patterns, but is meant to uncover the meaning behind the signals. By tracking signals and unfolding the meaning hidden within their patterns, facilitators can begin to understand the underlying processes that organize the group dynamics and individual behaviors. Process structure is the symmetry between the signals, their informational patterns, the underlying processes, and the way they manifest in terms of individual behavior and group dynamics. Understanding structure is the key to understanding difficulties, recognizing and supporting emergent leadership, and helping groups find more sustainable and creative solutions.

PROCESS STRUCTURE

Central to understanding the structure of a group's processes is an ability to understand the *roles* that are present. Roles perform specific functions within groups, not all of which are popular. Some less popular roles include the disrupter, the slacker, the sexist, the critic, and the oppressor.

People tend to avoid certain especially unpopular roles in order to prevent being scapegoated or being identified as, for example, the troublemaker in a group. These roles are often *unoccupied,* meaning that no one wants to be seen or to see themselves in this way, but are somehow noticeable in a group. They are like ghosts that appear as tensions in the atmosphere, or you may hear people speaking about them by listening to the group's gossip in the breaks. Understanding these ghost roles and their impact on a group is an important part of helping a group deal with its problems and develop its creativity and power.

A group can be viewed as a field or a collection of roles (formal, consensual, ghost, and otherwise) that pull in different directions, polarizing individuals and groups into conflicting viewpoints. Roles grab us to play their parts. A given role could grab anyone, but if I have a particular affinity for that role, then I may be easier to grab than someone else. You might find yourself in a boring meeting and suddenly act like a rebel or be in a chaotic meeting and suddenly stand for rules and structure. The field pulls you into the roles where your own personal development lies. The more emotional affect you have, the less understanding of the role you have and the less access you have to fluidity. For example, developing greater understanding of my own exuberant rebelliousness can help me notice my tendency to react against a boring or otherwise unproductive meeting and to use the tendency in a more positive way. I'm no less rebellious; I'm just better at using it constructively.

One common ghost role is *the learner* (one who doesn't know but is open to learning). It is difficult to be a learner candidly within an organization that values *knowing*. The assumption is that if you are open to learning, then you must not know. It is often more career enhancing, and thus more common, for people to be in a role that says, "I know." Behind this knowing there is a lot of creativity and power, but also there is frequently a lack of relationship awareness in the way that the knowing is expressed (often as a putdown of others) and in the way that it marginalizes learning personally, in others, and within the organization:

Example 1

We should do X.

No! X won't work. We should do Y.

This is very different than

Example 2

I know you've given it a lot of thought. I'm thinking that maybe we should do X, but what do you think?

Wow . . . yes, X. X definitely looks promising. We tried something similar; we may not have had it right, but when we tried it, this is what happened. How could we have done it better or ensure that this same problem won't happen again here? Can we explore that together? And also, we were wondering about Y. What do you think?

The relationship *metaskills* (feeling skills and an ability to consciously choose when to be sensitive or tough, for example; (A. S. Mindell, 1995) demonstrated in example 2 communicate some of the same information as example 1, but also communicate concern for the other and exhibit a style of relationship and organizational teamwork that is important. What you say is informed by your awareness of which role you are in, your feeling connection with others, and an ability to demonstrate fluidity while caring for others. Arnold Mindell (1992) calls this quality *eldership*. Speaking as yet another force countering the other's leadership may not be as effective as eldership: caring for others and for the whole system by speaking first as an enthusiastic supporter before introducing other ideas. Everyone knows this, but we forget, especially in difficult situations, and this adds to the difficulty. Example 1 could be viewed as *leader versus leader*, example 2 as *(follower + leader = elder) versus (follower + leader = elder)*.

Another problem with a leader versus leader interaction, even when it works, is that my inner critic knows it is only half working. I got the slam dunk, but I downed a team member, created an enemy, and disrupted the group's ability to work together. My inner critic says this wasn't so good, but my everyday personality says, "I won't be downed by this criticism, and anyhow, the team needed my strong leadership." Then the elder in me thinks, "OK. Get through this. Relax. Just notice the roles and the tensions . . . critics, power, leadership. Hmmm. Power messes everybody up." The learner is waking up, learning how to do it better next time. "OK. Maybe I can help turn this around."

The next section introduces concepts from physics that have been shown to mirror dynamics in psychology, organizational dynamics, and process structure (A. P. Mindell, 2000).

SPIN

One of the remarkable discoveries in quantum physics is *spin*. Spin is a property of particles, sometimes loosely described as the rotational inertia of the particle's magnetic field. Spin has two possibilities, nominally described as either *up* or *down*. Pairs of particles are coupled, meaning that if one particle's spin is up, then the other's is down. The remarkable thing is that if the spin of one particle is changed, then the spin of the other particle changes simultaneously regardless of the distance between them. The particles are *entangled*, and the change is instantaneous. This phenomenon mirrors relationship patterns that we all experience (Mindell, 2000). The first relationship pattern is the tendency to polarize:

I propose X.

No, Y is better.

Oh no . . . not you again.

This doesn't mean that people shouldn't polarize. By themselves, polarities have an enormous creative potential. If we can polarize consciously and maintain a relationship connection with others and use a deeper set of skills to facilitate the polarities and tensions between the roles, polarizing consciously can help a more creative and sustainable process emerge. A tyrannical leadership style might seem easier and justified, considering that it takes time, skill, and effort to foster Deep Democracy. But it's easy to constantly polarize a group into an exhausted state of chronic ineffectiveness or submission and difficult to follow a deeper path toward developing a meaningful, creative, and sustainable organization. Overall, following the self-organizing process structure is the path of least effort.

Another relationship pattern that entanglement mirrors is related to the connection that changes the other particle's spin. Have you ever left a meeting after a relationship conflict, eventually found some resolution or ability to understand the other person, and then gone back only to find that he or she had also changed? Because of entanglement, relationship is a complex dance of roles and states of consciousness. We work on ourselves and the other person changes, and a fluid dance-like *rotational symmetry* emerges that moves us in and out of various roles. The dance stops, and the other side will not change if you are not fluid or are not facilitating the roles effectively. And if you think the other side will never change, you are finished as a facilitator.

Difficult groups are difficult because there is no *facilitator function* present helping bring awareness to the roles, polarities, tension, and visions of the team members. Facilitation doesn't have to come from a formally designated facilitator. The facilitator *function* is ontologically built in to all groups. It just isn't always used. It is often unoccupied, but anyone can help bring it out. The facilitator is a role, and you don't have to be the designated leader, extroverted, or abnormally charismatic to help bring awareness to a group. You only have to trust in your own experience and want to find a way to help the group that is supportive of others. Unfortunately, noticing and trusting in our own experience are not always so easy. There is only one problem a person can have in a group: not knowing the deepest part of himself or herself and not bringing it out and making it more transparent. The group needs this from its members for its own self-organizing development. Groups also need to learn and develop their own ability to notice, track, and process things and understand how entanglement and rotational symmetry are part of the process structure of a group's role dynamics.

RANK

Discussions of *rank* are challenging because rank is so precious and so complex and so threatening. When rank is mentioned, some may hear a Marxist ghost in the winds reminding us of those who want to use their own power to down others in a vain attempt to eliminate rank differences. Deep Democracy supports rank as well as power and leadership. We can support rank by acknowledging it and understanding it so that we can use it better. Among the many factors that can make a group difficult, rank problems lay toward the top of the list. People generally don't know how to use power well, so they use it to get at each other rather than to benefit the organization.

Organizational theories generally view rank in terms of formal hierarchical and informal organizational rank. Social theorists tend to view rank in terms of class, gender, and race. There are many dimensions of rank, some earned (such as educational rank) and others not (such as appearance-based rank or rank that stems from health differences) (A. S. Mindell, 1995). Three additional dimensions of rank are

Psychological rank	This is a sense of ease that someone has, even in difficult situations, that comes from knowing that she will be able to engage in a tense scene while also protecting herself. This includes an ability to track and believe in her own experience and remain fluid when under attack.
Spiritual rank	Some people have an ability to ground themselves in something that comes from beyond space and time, giving them access to an inner sense of meaning.
Street power	This is an ability to be comfortable in a group that gives you intense negative feedback.

Group difficulties often emerge as reactions against inappropriate use of rank. Helping the group members become aware of their rank and its effect on others helps them develop an ability to use rank better but also helps the group develop an ability not to rely on rank so heavily. Psychological, spiritual, and street power ranks are less central in most organizations than more normally acknowledged hierarchical ranks. Rank has a lot to do with centrality (an ability to gain access to resources or status). Tensions that derive from rank differences effect cognition and change our sense of our IQ. For example, I'm heading a meeting and feel as though things are going great. My boss walks in, and my IQ drops twenty points. Suddenly I get attacked, and it drops to single digits.

Rank is a contextual and relativistic concept because rank doesn't exist in and of itself. For example, people don't inherently have more rank based on gender or race; only within a sexist or racist context do these create rank differences, and these particular differences are only meaningful as models of gender- or race-based oppression.

Rank affects our abilities to think, speak, and stand for change, and it impacts our health (Morin, 2002). If there is a rank problem between two people, it exists because neither of them understand his or her own rank well enough. If they did, they would be able to understand the tensions, facilitate the conflict, and defuse the conflict. Rank problems can ultimately foster greater understanding and learning for the individuals and the group. For example, if you have a rank problem with someone of lower rank than you, you will notice it through her or his feedback. You say something the person doesn't understand or doesn't know much about, and he or she may look down or signal discomfort in some other way. If you have a rank problem with someone of higher rank, you may experience a constant irritation in the background.

If the organization has a culture where these problems can be addressed directly, great! This is the best. If not, you can work on yourself to understand what it is about the way that the person uses her rank that is disturbing. Generally, the most disturbing thing about rank is that people don't know they have it. If they knew they had it, they would use it in a more conscious way. Your challenge is to find a way to help the person see that she has it. To do that, you have to love her rank. You have to think, "This person does this and this and this, and she can't see it and can't love it yet. That's why it is so irritating." If you can love it in the other person, great. Then you can praise it and congratulate her for it and encourage her to use it more consciously. You have to momentarily be her therapist even though she has more rank. Eldership is learning to love every signal (Schupbach, 2004), which also means learning to love that you hate certain things.

There's something shamanic in the role switching involved in noticing my experience as a subordinate, understanding the scene with my superior, shape-shifting momentarily into being the coach or the therapist, making an intervention, and then returning to being the subordinate, all the while checking feedback carefully to make sure I'm on track. Is awareness enough to change the world? Is it enough to notice that my boss could use his rank better? Or does the world need a little push from time to time?

What does it mean to use your rank consciously? Let's say you have enough rank that one word from you can stop anything. When do you use that word? Before you use your rank battery, think, is there another way to go? For example, imagine that a subordinate makes an insensitive remark. A classic approach to dealing with the situation would be to immediately reprimand the subordinate. An alternative approach is to directly support the power and developing leadership behind the remark and suggest that the individual consider the advantages of transforming his or her power into something creative, useful, supportive of the leadership of others, and respectful of rank. It isn't possible that the remark is only negative. There is also something emerging that can benefit the relationship and the organization.

MULTIDIMENSIONAL PROCESS-ORIENTED LEADERSHIP

The main leadership paradigms all agree on certain basic principles: the leader has to have a vision and hold on to it while working to improve communications and to push power down by developing other leaders. From a process-oriented view, business, like everything, is driven by psychological and emotional profit margins. Because financial success is a by-product of these profit margins, the community aspects of the organization are as important as leadership and team development. Difficult groups are groups where the psychological and emotional profit margins are in the red and the community is failing to develop the team and its leadership (Schupbach & Schupbach, 2008). Multidimensional process-oriented thinking can help leaders, designated or not, turn this around.

Three distinct leadership models are an authoritarian model (an individual person leads), a systems model (people lead by consensus), and a chaos-driven, self-organizing model (where leadership is nonlocal—it can't be definitively located in any one person or group but is distributed throughout the field). These three models are very different. Similarly, there are three levels of human experience that need to be acknowledged and appreciated in order to help facilitate a group's development, as shown in Figure 16.1.

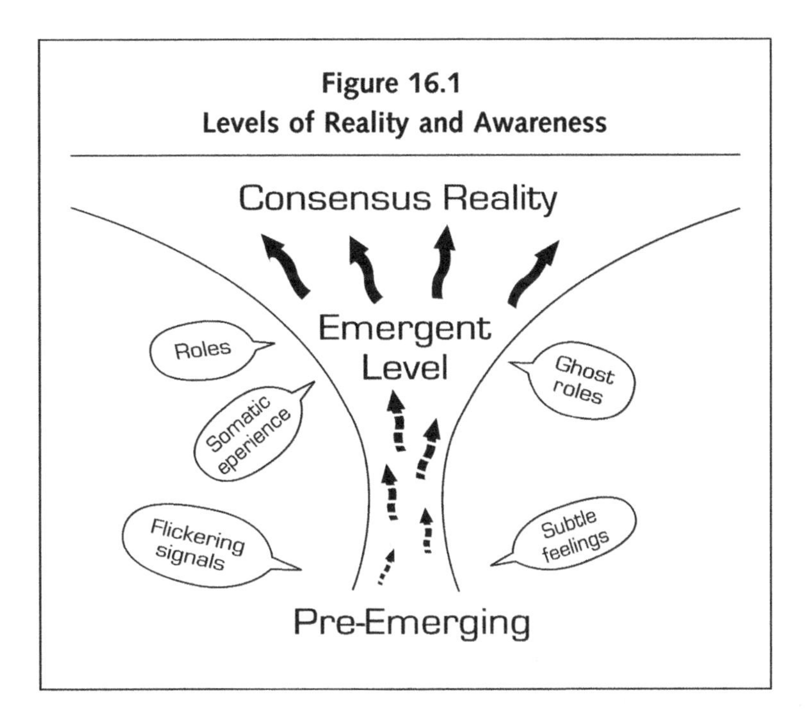

Figure 16.1
Levels of Reality and Awareness

Consensus Reality (CR): Consensus reality includes experiences that we tend to agree on; it includes focus on rules, structure, and objectively measurable outcomes and is based on an assumption that we can control events.

Emergent Level (EL): Emergent experiences are subjective, not measurable, and not in our control. They include group and relationship issues, experiences of rank differences, somatic experiences, roles, and our assumptions about each other.

Pre-Emerging (PE): The pre-emerging level is something that is sometimes barely noticeable, like an atmosphere or the most deeply held values that we can't quite articulate. It is an indescribable yet sentient essence, like a feeling, a tension, or something joyful.

For example, I'm working with an organization and notice that, over time, the routine CR details seem to be going well, but initiatives for new programs are blocked for reasons that only partly make sense. There is a mood, an atmosphere, that I can at times barely notice. It is a flickering signal mirroring a PE essence. As I observe my experience of the mood over the course of a few interactions, I notice two roles emerging: one is something like a creative revolutionary in the field who wants change; the other is something like a traditionalist who wants structure and supports things as they are.

These levels are based on what Arnold Mindell calls *consensus reality, dreamland,* and the level of *sentient essence* in clinical work. Schupbach and Schupbach (2008) and Schupbach (2007) use Mindell's levels in a change management context, and in this context call them CR, EL, and PE.

Awareness of each of these levels is an important aspect of the facilitation of groups. The solution to a problem in one of these levels lies in the other levels. Mirroring western culture's focus on CR details, organizational interventions often focus solely on the CR level and ignore the importance of working with EL and PE experiences. When Einstein (1931) said that we need a substantially new manner of thinking if we are to survive, he was referring to this shift in awareness away from hypnosis to objectivity and verifiable phenomena: "The most beautiful experience we can have is the mysterious . . . the fundamental emotion which stands at the cradle of true art and true science."

Some problems need to be worked out in CR; others can't be. The good news is that you don't have to *solve* these problems at all—at least not in the ordinary engineering sense of the word. You only have to support the self-organizing tendencies that are already present by facilitating the experiences in each of these levels to help complete the processes in the background. Notice what is already happening and help it complete (that is, emerge more easily). For example, I couldn't solve the relationship and political conflicts with the peace project, but by following the tendencies that were already emerging, I was able to help a more constructive dialogue take place.

The tendencies that drive everything appear at first as briefly flickering PE experiences and later appear as EL experiences with more defined signals, roles, and process structures. PE and EL control CR, but we can only follow PE and EL. We can help facilitate processes to complete, but we can't control them.

However, we do often try to control CR. When this works, we feel like heroes; we don't admit that we were just in the right place at the right time but really don't know why it worked. When it doesn't work, we feel like losers. Trusting in PE and EL experiences means believing that they will help guide us toward sustainable solutions to CR problems.

When PE experiences first appear as brief, flickering signals, we tend to overlook them, ignore them, or actively discount them. We aren't sure what to do. They are tiny microsignals that seem to flirt with us. We might suddenly notice a colleague and wonder if something signaled opposition to our proposal. What was it? Did her head move away almost imperceptibly? Did his eyes really narrow when I looked at him? Did I really see that? Does it mean what I'm thinking it means?

Chances are that these flickering signals will grow stronger down the road until the opposition has congruently developed into a full-scale roadblock. Noticing the signals early on gives us the chance to help complete the process in the background. But there's a problem. We don't always know what the signals of others mean, even if we think we do. Sometimes we are right. Often we are wrong. Western culture doesn't yet support us to work together on this level. It's too intimate. But we must. Our collective misunderstandings of these signals and their meanings, and our collective inability to facilitate deeper dialogues ultimately lead to war. What to do?

It is a very intimate thing to say something like, "I noticed while I was making this presentation that you were looking out the window, and I wondered if you might have some hesitations about the project. If so, I'd love to hear what they are so I can address them directly." Helping the hesitations emerge earlier is important so that they can be related to directly.

It's more common to feel relieved that the hesitations didn't emerge and to hope they will go away. Groups become difficult when the hesitations remain hidden, experienced as brief signals that don't coalesce as clear roles that can be interacted with. It can help to introduce this as a role play: "Imagine someone who would be against this proposal. What would that person say?" This allows people to speak more freely without fear of getting stuck in a role or being seen as negative. This freedom is the basis for empowerment, which plays a big part in helping a difficult group develop its ability to track its own experience.

There is a simple way to empower people. Anything that you see has meaning for the organization, although frequently the meaning isn't clear.

Empowerment happens through understanding the meaning of the person, event, or signal and reframing it in terms of its meaning to the group and to the organization as a whole.

Imagine being in a meeting where someone interrupts another person. Behind the interrupting may be a role that says, *I know better than you.* A facilitator might reframe this: "Two things are happening at once. Great. I hope that both will get to be completed."

Or imagine being are in a meeting where one person doesn't speak. Someone says, "There is Bill. How come he never says anything?" The roles are *Verbosity is better. Those who speak know more* and *He who says nothing doesn't know, and knowing is better than learning.* It's basically a put-down that comes from misunderstanding Bill, misunderstanding the function and dynamics of the group, misunderstanding creativity, and overvaluing centrality. A facilitator might reframe this: "I like what Bill does here. So many good things are being done here that we barely have time to listen. When I look at him, it reminds me to listen too. I think we're missing something because we don't take more time to listen and learn more."

FIRST AND SECOND TRAINING

The facilitator's first task is to notice and explore verbal content and nonverbal signals, but the second and more important task is to follow the signals toward something unknown and intimate and mysterious. This isn't a trivial distinction. Self-organizing forces can't be controlled.

Mindell refers to developing mastery in these two tasks as the *first training* and the *second training,* emphasizing the complexity and enormity of each of them. The first training is developing mastery in noticing and tracking signals, forming structural hypotheses from the patterns, creating interventions from these, and carefully noting the feedback from the group, which will either confirm the hypothesis or suggest another direction. The second training is developing mastery in following something mysterious and intimate, even when it can't be described by signals and structural patterns. It is ineffable, but it leads to the core of a group's self-organizing tendency and is always something intimate.

chapter
SEVENTEEN

Authentic Relationships and Collective Psychological Capital

Füsun Bulutlar

The most stressful period of my life was when I worked with a group of English lecturers in the preparatory school of a university. There was a lot of conflict in the group, and not a single day passed without a serious crisis. The coordinator of the group claimed to be very relationship oriented and to have a deep concern with everybody's problems. She also defined herself as a softhearted person who never wanted to hurt others' feelings. However, as she was generally overloaded with work, she had the habit of being engaged with something else (writing a report, giving orders to others, and so on) while listening to our problems. She always underlined the importance of justice and truth, and thereby wanted to be sure that we were just and truthful to the students.

At the time of a financial downturn, the coordinator kept layoffs secret and assured us that we would not be affected. Afterwards, when we asked her why she misled us, she said, "I told you so because I did not want you to be unhappy and suffer from unnecessary stress while waiting for who was to go. It was for your own good." We later learned that the top management had asked her to keep the downsizing a secret in order to prevent requests of favor from powerful outsiders and lobbying activities of insiders.

After the layoffs, the level of conflict among the lecturers increased considerably. We lost our trust in the coordinator and became skeptical, which led us to become very pessimistic about the future. The coordinator thought that this was due to the low morale resulting from the layoffs and that it would pass after a while. But as time passed, the conflict continued to spread, and we began to have problems with students, resulting in an increase in the number of complaints. The coordinator, who had waited silently and had not attempted to solve problems, decided that now it was time to intervene. We thought that she started to take action because she did not want top management to be aware of the situation, which would lead them to think that she was unsuccessful. Contrary to our thoughts, she claimed that the reason for her not trying to resolve conflicts was to let us solve our own problems because she thought we were mature and rational people. At a meeting, she said out of blue, "You have acted like infants. I have lost my confidence in you. I will not let this go on." As a result, one day she held a meeting and declared that if the complaints from the students went on and if we could not settle disputes among ourselves, she would be obliged to take strict measures that would not be to our benefit.

This speech had a disastrous effect on the self-efficacy of the group. We all began to think that we were useless people who could not do our jobs well. After a period of complete silence, conflict and stress exploded. Everybody had problems with each other, and we all together had problems with the coordinator and her in-group. This chaotic situation reached a peak when two of the lecturers literally had a fight and the coordinator dismissed them both. The internal problems were also transmitted to the students; hence they became more and more dissatisfied with the school, and the school's external prestige and reputation were negatively affected, which in turn resulted in a decrease in admissions.

In the case I've just described, it seems that everybody suffered and that the measures taken only worsened the situation. Now let us consider the situation if the coordinator had

- Really listened to people's problems and showed her concern by asking questions
- Acted as she talked—that is, told the truth about layoffs and acted in accordance with her own deeply held values instead of yielding to external pressures
- Told the truth about her genuine motives in keeping secrets from lecturers—or not kept any secrets
- Collected and interpreted self-related information impartially—in other words, interpreted the things that she heard about herself in an unbiased manner
- Been open, sincere, and intimate
- Established mutual trust in her relationships
- Verbally expressed her confidence in the group members instead of accusing them of infantile behavior
- Inspired and motivated the lecturers
- Been a good role model who enhanced the psychological capital (self-esteem, hope, resiliency, optimism) and authenticity of her followers
- Provided training opportunities that increased the group's self-efficacy

If she had behaved as such, she would have been an authentic leader. The authentic leader's transparent and intimate relationships would build trust both in the leader and in groupmates. Further, because authenticity is contagious, group members themselves would become more authentic and thereby would be able to understand better their own values, norms, and ambitions. They would act as they thought and would build transparent relationships that would reduce misunderstandings and misinterpretations. Moreover, if the leader were able to enhance the psychological capital of the group, then the group members would be hopeful, optimistic, and resilient enough to change. They would have high self-efficacy, thus experiencing lower levels of stress. There would be no hidden agendas; the leader and the group members would have a clear idea of their "selves." Last, because their actions would match their thoughts, there would be less conflict.

As can be inferred from the case I've described, working with groups is not an easy job. However, despite the difficulties of managing groups, internal and external forces lead more and more organizations to adopt team-based structures that will enable them to be more flexible and creative (Webber & Donahue, 2001; Wright, Barker, Cordery, & Maue, 2003) and help them achieve sustainable competitive advantage and success. When important decisions have to be made, contemporary organizations often refer to groups, accepting that groups may outperform individuals in terms of the quality of the decisions they reach (Ilgen, 1999; Homan, van Knippenberg, Van Kleef, & De Dreu, 2007). Also, it is claimed that working with groups results in increased productivity, innovation, product quality, performance, and employee satisfaction, and reduced absenteeism and turnover (Batt, 2004; Glassop, 2002; Frankforter & Christensen, 2005). However, simply adopting a team-based structure or establishing work groups does not guarantee success.

Working with groups is a challenging and difficult job in itself; moreover, not all groups are easy to manage. Managing groups is an "ambidextrous" task, given that issues related to groups are nearly always bipolar. For example, conflict can be a problem and an opportunity at the same time. On the one hand, it is constructive, inasmuch as it avoids groupthink; on the other hand, it can be destructive, decreasing performance and breaking down cohesion. In the management of groups operating in a volatile environment that is subject to frequent change, we can see that facilitators, team leaders, and organization development specialists will confront difficulties in establishing a fragile balance between these tendencies. Coping with these issues is not an easy job; there seems to be no standard manual available to guide managers. To organize the context, structure, and processes of groups effectively from a relational perspective, I suggest a framework that would distinguish situational and cultural factors and provide a useful guide to managers, leaders, and facilitators. Further, I assume that to cope effectively with conflict, becoming an authentic leader (or facilitator), building authentic relationships, and adding to the psychological capital of the group will produce valuable results. However, before I discuss how these actions might help, a brief explanation of these concepts should contribute to a better understanding of the relation between these issues and coping with difficulties related to groups.

POSITIVE EFFECTS OF AUTHENTICITY AND PSYCHOLOGICAL CAPITAL ON INTRAGROUP RELATIONS

Leaders or facilitators play a vital role in groups. They provide direction and facilitate the processes that enable groups to achieve their goals and objectives. Leaders who have integrity are said to be more successful in providing direction and helping individuals find meaning in their work (Gardner, Avolio, Luthans, May, & Walumbwa, 2005). They also play a very important role in shaping the behavior of individuals and their relationships. Leaders and facilitators are expected to help group members get along with each other and resolve problems that might arise due to lack of effective communication, unclear role and task expectations, interdependent tasks, and various other reasons. Leaders can achieve this through formal and directive methods (Bierhoff & Müller, 2005). However, these tactics will not enable the group to solve its problems permanently, because if the true causes of problems are not revealed and removed, they will tend to recur in another form. For example, consider two members of a group, one of whom continuously behaves rudely to the other. In this case, the leader may interfere and tell the one who is behaving badly not to do so, using his coercive power in order to influence the group member. Under these circumstances, the person might monitor his behavior and try to be kinder to the other, but this behavioral change might create some cognitive dissonance that in turn might lead to distress. In fact, even the person himself might not be aware of the true reason for behaving in such a way. For instance, he might be cruel to the person just because she reminds him of an individual about whom he had developed negative feelings in the past. To be able to reveal the true reasons behind the problems, both the leader and the followers should have high self-awareness. In other words, they should be aware of the assumptions and values they hold and aware of their source. This will also reduce conflict, especially relationship conflict (annoyance among group members due to personal incompatibilities), which is deemed to be detrimental to the functioning of groups (Greer, Jehn, & Mannix, 2008). Further, not all groups have unanimity; some of the members may have different opinions from the rest of the group. Bass (as cited in Schminke, Wells, Peyrefitte, & Sebora, 2002) pointed out that generally the deviant members move closer to the group. However, when this fails to happen, other members may reject the deviants. Then the leader's role becomes very important in achieving conformity (Schminke et al., 2002). Raven (1959) noted that individuals are more likely to show conformity if they are given the opportunity to express their ideas freely. Consequently, it is the leader's duty to facilitate communication and to create a climate in which differing opinions can be freely expressed; and members show respect to each other's ideas, listen to them without prejudice (Schminke et al., 2002), and make unbiased contributions.

To sum up, in order for a group to be effective, both the leader and the group members need to be aware of their values and beliefs, the way they think and behave, and their strengths and weaknesses. If they are aware of their true selves, behave as they think, are open and transparent, and have high moral values, then there will be fewer misunderstandings and less bias, which will be helpful in reducing conflict and negative emotions and will result in increased effectiveness. It is here presumed that if the leader is authentic, she will be able to develop authentic relationships, and the followers will also become authentic through the contagious effect of authenticity, and thus the group's efficiency will increase. The model proposed here also encompasses increased psychological capital (efficacy, optimisim, resiliency, and hope), which will be enhanced through these authentic relationships and have a positive effect on group dynamics. Psychological capital (hereafter referred to as PsyCap) is especially important in the sense that it is both an antecedent of authenticity and also an aid in developing authentic relationships between all parties. The proposed model of increased group effectiveness, shown in Figure 17.1, has three major components: authentic leaders, authentic relationships, and their effects on a group's authenticity and PsyCap. The next sections explain the meaning.

Figure 17.1
Positive Effects of PsyCap and Authenticity

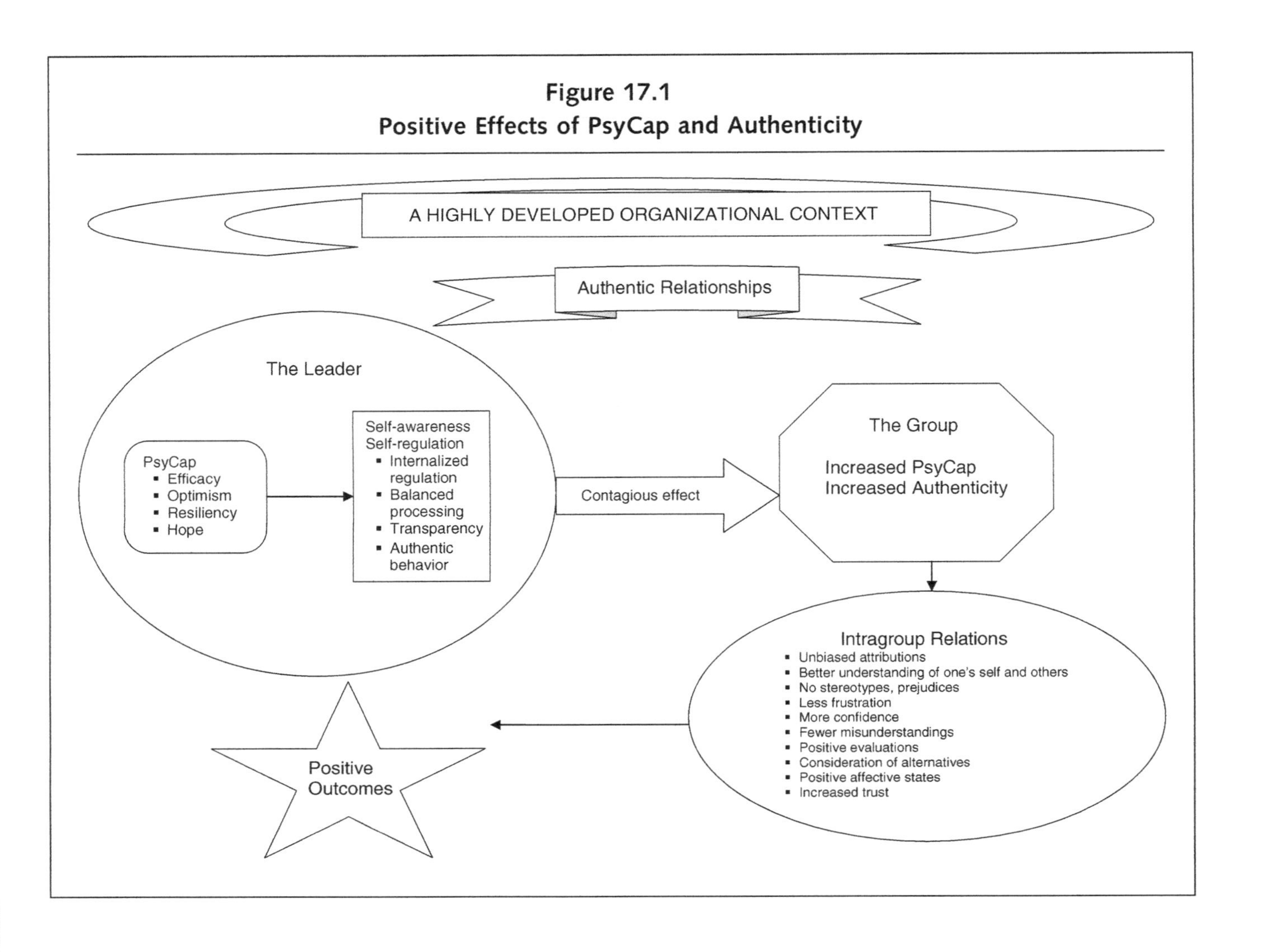

What Is Authentic Leadership?

The first component of the model is the leader. A leader's authenticity will not only have a positive effect on group dynamics but also enhance the group's authenticity through its contagious effects. Authenticity is an abstract concept that can be difficult to understand; however it can be simplified as *acting as you think.*

Whereas authenticity can be defined as *being the true self,* the definition of authentic leaders is more complex, as seen here:

> those who are deeply aware of how they think and behave and are perceived by others as being aware of their own and others' values/moral perspectives, knowledge, and strengths; aware of the context in which they operate; and who are confident, hopeful, optimistic, resilient, and of high moral character. (Avolio, Luthans, & Walumbwa, 2004, p. 4, as cited in Avolio, Gardner, Walumbwa, Luthans, & May, 2004)

In other words, a leader's authenticity refers to "owning one's personal experiences, be they thoughts, emotions, needs, wants, preferences, or beliefs, processes captured by the injunction to *know oneself,* and authenticity further implies that *one acts in accord with the true self,* expressing oneself in ways that are consistent with inner thoughts and feelings" (Harter, 2002, p. 382). Thus authenticity not only embraces being aware of one's personal experiences, which comprises personal values, thoughts, emotions, and beliefs, but also requires acting in accordance with one's true self—in other words, *expressing what one really thinks and believes, and behaving accordingly* (Harter, 2002).

The definition implies two major components: (1) knowing oneself and (2) acting in accord with the true self; these are identified as *self-awareness* and *self-regulation* in the model presented in Figure 17.1. Self-awareness is being aware of one's own emotions and cognitions regarding identity, values, motives, and goals (Gardner et al., 2005). To explain more thoroughly, self-awareness can be associated with self-reflection. The core values of authentic leaders that are in accordance with their identity, emotions, motives, and goals are elucidated through introspective self-reflection. To gain self-awareness, leaders need to try to understand how they derive and make meaning of the world around them. They should be aware of their own hypotheses and self-schema. In order to do this, they should direct their attention to some aspect of their selves. In other words, they should continuously try to find an answer to the question "Who am I?" (Gardner et al., 2005).

PsyCap is assumed to be an important element in identifying who you are. In other words, determining how hopeful, optimistic, and resilient you are and knowing the level of your self-efficacy help you identify your self (Jansen & Luthans, 2006; Luthans & Youssef, 2004). This subject will better be understood when PsyCap is thoroughly discussed later in this chapter.

The authentic leader should also look back and analyze past events as well as look forward to the future. This practice may recall memories about the same event, which will bring out a deeper understanding (Avolio & Luthans, 2006). Avolio and Luthans (2006, p. 80) advise "focusing on just one area at a time to learn self-awareness." As an example, they suggest trying, each morning, to answer the question, "How positive am I and why?" If leaders are highly self-aware, they will understand not only their own feelings and emotions but also those of others; in other words, their emotional intelligence will also increase. Further, self-awareness will enable them to increase their self-acceptance and autonomy, establish more positive relationships, and develop environmental mastery.

As can be seen in Figure 17.1, the second major component of authentic leadership is identified as self-regulation, which means that behavior is concordant with the true self and with inner thoughts and feelings (Endrissat, Müller, & Kaudela-Baum, 2007). It is the "ability to exert self-control by setting internal standards, evaluating discrepancies between such standards and potential or actual outcomes, and identifying possible means of rectifying such discrepancies" (Gardner & Schermerhorn, 2004, p. 272). In short, self-regulation is the process through which authentic leaders align their values with their intentions and actions.

There are four components of self-regulation: internalized regulation, balanced processing of information, relational transparency, and authentic behavior.

A person capable of *internalized regulation* sets and adheres to internal standards (they can be existing or newly formulated) rather than being driven by external forces or expectations. For example, the moral standards of the company may not be high, and using information gathered unintentionally about competitors could be accepted as ethical. However, the leader may set higher moral standards and may think that she should warn the competitors about the information leak.

For *balanced processing,* the leader has to collect and interpret the information regarding her in an unbiased way, even if the information is negative. Therefore, the leader must be sure that she is genuine and does not distort, exaggerate, or ignore relevant evaluations of the self. The leader in this case takes criticism seriously and considers correcting her fault instead of trying to justify behavior or just not listening. If she is told that she is stubborn, she engages in objective self-evaluation rather than denial.

Authentic behavior, as the name implies, involves actions that are in line with the leader's true self. In other words, they are actions that reflect his core values, beliefs, thoughts, and feelings. The leader should not change his way of acting according to environmental contingencies or pressures from others. An authentic leader, therefore, will not go hunting, for example, as a means of establishing good relationships with powerful individuals if he says he likes animals.

When a leader exhibits *relational transparency,* she is open, sincere, and intimate and establishes mutual trust in close relationships. The authentic leader is transparent in cases of failure; she admits the failure and tries to find the antecedents in order to make corrections, rather than finding excuses, making external attributions, or blaming others. In the aforementioned case, the coordinator should have told the truth about the layoffs instead of keeping them a secret.

All in all, the authentic leader is the one who knows who he is, has internal standards, takes the information about himself seriously and makes necessary corrections, behaves in accordance with his values and beliefs, and is open and honest in relationships. Although authenticity is not an either-or concept—that is to say, there can be varying degrees of authenticity—it is possible to identify some leaders as authentic. For instance, Gandhi and Nelson Mandela can be regarded as examples of authentic leaders (Cooper, Scandura, & Schriesheim, 2005). Let us turn now to the factors that help create an authentic leader.

Development of Authentic Leadership

Authentic leadership develops as a consequence of personal history, trigger events (past experiences or moments that matter, whether they are positive or negative) (Avolio & Luthans, 2006), comparison of the actual self and the possible self, and increased PsyCap. Educational and work experiences, challenges encountered, and influences of the family and various role models constitute the personal history of the leader. Trigger events are dramatic or even minor changes that affect personal development (Gardner et al., 2005). A highly developed organizational context together with positive PsyCap serve as leverage in developing authentic leadership. This context not only promotes greater self-awareness but also fosters self-regulated positive behavior on the part of leaders and associates, which in turn enhances positive self-development (Luthans & Avolio, 2003). A highly developed organizational context is one in which there is a high level of support; open communication and open access to information; and a caring, strength-based, and ethical climate. Shamir and Eilam (2005) specified four components in the development of authentic leadership:

1. Development of a leader identity as a central component of the person's self-concept
2. Understanding one's attitudes, values, and behavior more clearly. Development of self-knowledge and self-concept clarification, including clarity about values and convictions
3. Development of goals that are in accord with the self-concept
4. Increase of self-expressive behavior, namely consistency between a leader's behavior and the leader's self-concept

They also argue that development of authentic leadership is achieved through the development of the leader's life experience. They say that the answers to the questions Who am I? Who was I? Who might I be? lie in the leader's life history, convey the teller's identity, and are generated as a result of the relationship between life experiences and the recollected accounts of these experiences.

Shamir, Dayan-Horesh, and Adler (2005) found that leaders' personal accounts of leadership development are organized around four core concepts, all of which serve as bases for authentic leadership. These narratives reveal that leadership may be developed through a natural process, out of struggle and hardship, by finding a cause, and as a result of a learning process. As an example of leadership development as a natural process, one of the individuals interviewed by Shamir et al. stated that the tendency to become a leader was inherent in him, that he could not function without leading. Nelson Mandela can be regarded as an example of an authentic leader who developed out of struggle and finding a cause.

Avolio and Luthans (2006) suggest that leaders may compare their actual self with their possible self as a means of moving forward. They also highlight the importance of trigger moments, and argue that although genetics plays a role, leadership can indeed be developed, with trigger events facilitating the development of authentic leadership by making it possible to move from the actual self to the potential self. Shamir and Eilam (2005) propose the use of self-narratives as an effective way to reveal these trigger events, because such narratives serve to organize life events and the relationships among them across time.

Luthans and Avolio (2003, p. 251) propose a model for the development of authentic leadership and give examples of questions to be asked at every stage. The questions in Exhibit 17.1 are based on this model. These questions

Exhibit 17.1
Questions That Will Help

1. Think about your life experiences and try to define your past, where you came from.
2. Evaluate yourself; find out who you are. To what extent are you hopeful, optimistic, resilient, or confident? If you evaluate yourself poorly according to these criteria, try to find out why, and think of ways to improve.
3. Define the context in which you are working. Find out how your context is shaped and framed.
4. Think about your organization and evaluate how you are supported.
5. Think about triggering events, your experiences, landmarks in your life.
6. Think of yourself—evaluate your identity, ambitions, and emotions; be aware of and frank about your strengths and weaknesses; and try to expand your set of values so that you can regulate and develop yourself.

can help promote the development of authentic leaders and facilitators—individuals whose authenticity will prove contagious, so that group members will also develop authentic behavior.

In accordance with Avolio and Gardner's point of view (2005) and the fact that authenticity has a contagious effect, I propose that authentic leaders promote their followers' authenticity through increased self-awareness, self-regulation, and positive modeling. In other words, the followers of authentic leaders also increase their authenticity by observing the leader. The increased authenticity of followers results in heightened performance brought about by a decrease in misunderstandings and conflict and an increase in trust among leaders and peers. Building authentic relationships, which is the second component of the model, plays a very important role in fostering followers' authenticity, because leaders can help their followers in understanding their personal and social identities only if they can build authentic relationships (Eagly, 2005).

Building Authentic Relationships

Being a truly authentic leader is the first step in building authentic relationships. Afterward the following stated steps should be taken in order to build authentic relationships. First, building authentic relationships not only requires self-awareness but also requires awareness of others. Leaders should know their followers as individuals. In order to know the followers better, the leader should sometimes have a "chat" with them and try to learn about their personal values, ambitions, interests, and backgrounds (Cranton, 2006). They should seek frequent feedback from followers to be able to clarify misunderstandings. Leaders or facilitators must develop a style that is comfortable for them and congruent with their values, beliefs, and philosophy of leading (Cranton, 2006). For example, if the leader values being a transformational leader, he should act likewise and try to inspire the followers. If he values the autocratic style, then he should not restrain himself from acting in line with this belief; otherwise he will lose authenticity. Second, contextual factors, such as policies, procedures, and strategies pursued by the company, may influence authentic relationships. Exhibit 17.2 lists some strategies proposed by Cranton to overcome the difficulties related with these contextual factors.

Eagly (2005) identified two components of authentic relationships. The first is endorsing values that promote the interests of the larger community and

Exhibit 17.2
Strategies to Overcome Contextual Difficulties

1. Become familiar with written and unwritten policies and procedures, and question those that seem to have the potential of interfering with good relationships.
2. Find out how policies are established, and become a part of the policymaking procedures.
3. Discuss institutional norms and expectations with colleagues; have a critical voice in questioning those norms.
4. See yourself as an advocate for followers rather than an enforcer of institutional rules.

Source: Adapted from "Fostering Authentic Relationships in the Transformative Classroom," by P. Cranton, 2006, *New Directions for Adult and Continuing Education, 109*, pp. 11–12.

conveying these values to followers; the second is followers' personal identification with these values. The authentic leader does not need to force or even use soft influence tactics to convince followers; his authentic values, beliefs, and behaviors serve as a model in developing associates, and the associates themselves in turn become authentic leaders (Luthans & Avolio, 2003).

As shown in Figure 17.1, PsyCap not only plays an important role in developing authenticity and authentic relationships but also positively affects intragroup relations. Gardner et al. (2005, p. 345) explain how PsyCap helps in developing authenticity and authentic relationships: "authentic leaders draw from the positive psychological states that accompany optimal self-esteem and psychological well-being, such as confidence, optimism, hope and resilience, to model and promote the development of these states in others."

Psychological Capital

Whereas PsyCap plays a very important role in the development of authentic leadership, authentic leaders in turn play a vital role in cultivating the authenticity of their followers. PsyCap is an antecedent to authenticity; and increased self-efficacy, resilience, hope, and optimism are instrumental in heightening the self-awareness and self-regulatory behavior of the leader

(Luthans & Avolio, 2003). In the same way that PsyCap is an antecedent to authenticity, developing followers' PsyCap will have a positive effect on their development. We can presume that both PsyCap and authenticity will have a positive effect on group dynamics; however, prior to discussing how they can improve group effectiveness, let us look at the components of PsyCap.

Luthans, Youssef, and Avolio (2007, p. 3) define PsyCap this way: "PsyCap is an individual's positive psychological state of development and is characterized by: (1) having confidence (self-efficacy) to take on and put in the necessary effort to succeed in challenging tasks; (2) making positive attributions (optimism) about succeeding now and in the future; (3) persevering toward goals and, when necessary, redirecting paths to goals (hope) in order to succeed; and (4) when beset by problems and adversity, sustaining and bouncing back and even beyond (resiliency) to attain success."

Bandura (1982) identified four main sources of self-efficacy: enactive mastery (success experiences), vicarious learning (modeling), and verbal persuasion (coaching and encouragement), and managing physiological states (reducing the emotional threat of failures). Individuals who have high self-efficacy prefer challenging tasks and endeavors, have high motivation and exert considerable efforts to achieve their goals, and keep trying even if obstacles arise (Luthans & Youssef, 2004).

Optimism, the third component of PsyCap, has a positive effect on individuals' self-esteem and morale, because optimistic people attribute internal and permanent causes to positive events, and external, temporary, and situation-specific causes to negative events. This attitude results in high self-esteem and morale (Luthans & Youssef, 2004).

Goal-directed determination (agency or will) and the capacity to develop successful plans that will lead to goals (pathways or ways) are the two dimensions of hope. In other words, hope is the will and ability to achieve goals. As the will (agency) of individuals urges them to achieve their goals, they are ready to exert high levels of energy in order to fulfill this purpose. They also have high motivation that stems from beliefs in their capabilities to find alternative pathways to obtain desired results; hence they do not give up easily (Luthans & Youssef, 2004).

The last component of PsyCap, resiliency, is defined as the capacity to rebound or bounce back from adversity, uncertainty, conflict, failure, or even events that can be considered as positive, such as increased responsibility

(Luthans et al., 2007). For example, a person who is promoted to be a general manager may be overwhelmed by the vast amount of responsibility connected with the position. In this case, if the person is resilient, he might employ highly competent people and delegate his responsibilities. Hence, the person in this case is resilient enough to reduce the risk factors associated with the job.

The Impact of Authentic Leadership on Followers' PsyCap and Authenticity

Verbal expressions of confidence by the authentic leader will, because the leader is trusted, promote self-efficacy of the individual. Authentic leaders will also provide followers the emotional and cognitive support they need while performing the job. The authentic leader as a role model has a positive effect on efficacy through vicarious learning. Once the task is completed effectively, it will be a successful experience that will enhance efficacy.

Avolio and Gardner (2005) suggest that the authenticity of followers will be evoked through vicarious learning. For example, leaders will be role models to followers, and through their demonstration of self-awareness and self-regulation, followers will learn and their authenticity will increase. This increased authenticity will then contribute to their well-being and performance. Moreover, followers will believe in the integrity of the leader because they recognize that the leader's acts and deeds are congruent, that she is aware of herself, that she does not deny when she has experienced defeat or has acted in a wrong way, and that she is committed to the core ethical values.

The authentic leader's positive PsyCap, together with her capability for self-awareness and self-regulation, promote the development of these psychological capacities in her followers. As these are statelike capacities, they are open to development and change so that they can be effective tools for developing individuals, groups, and organizations to achieve sustainable prosperity.

COPING WITH DIFFICULTIES THROUGH AUTHENTICITY AND PSYCAP

When two or more people come together, differences in ideas, opinions, and values are inevitable. These kinds of differences may also trigger emotional reactions. According to the affective events theory (Weiss & Cropanzano,

1996), organizational events reveal affective reactions that have an important impact on employee attitudes and behavior. The disagreement, be it related with tasks, processes, or relations, will provoke negative emotions such as anger, frustration, and anxiety. These emotions, if not approached properly, might further be escalated by managers. In addition, there is the probability that emotions could be contagious and be produced as a result of any type of conflict that initiated emotional responses. The group's affective climate, and the totality of its members' emotions, will have an impact on the group's attitudes and behavior as a whole. An authentic leader, who has high self-awareness and thereby high emotional intelligence, will understand the feelings and emotions of the members and therefore be more effective in managing any kind of disagreement. Further, as authenticity is contagious, group members' self-awareness and emotional intelligence will also be high; they will understand each other. The ability to redirect goals will reduce the frustration emerging from any kind of negative event; making positive attributions will prevent anger, and being flexible will result in the search for alternatives. To express this in another way, increased PsyCap will prevent group members from experiencing negative affective states. In addition, self-awareness and the unbiased processing components of authenticity should lead to increased self-acceptance.

It is important for groups not to consider their own goals ahead of organizational goals. An authentic leader and the resiliency and hope dimensions of PsyCap will enable a group to redirect its goals toward overall organizational goals in the event that the goals are not in accord. As mentioned earlier, hope involves goal-directed energy and pathways (plans to achieve goals), and resiliency is the ability to bounce back after encountering obstacles. Therefore, if the organization's and the group's goals are not congruent, then the authentic leader needs the energy required to find alternatives that will result in satisfaction for both the organization and group members. An authentic leader sets goals that promote the interests of the organization and conveys these values to followers. High-hope individuals can develop alternative pathways to achieve their wishes. Hence they can find ways to achieve both their and the organization's goals. The authentic members of the group who have increased positive PsyCap can realign their actions and behavior in accordance with organizational goals. As they are resilient, they will not have difficulty in bouncing back. Further, group efficacy is positively related with performance because it is closely related with individual and collective beliefs about capabilities for performance. Group members' confidence results in seeking challenging jobs and exerting more effort due to higher motivation. They have higher motivation levels because they believe that their effort will lead them to the expected performance. Therefore, groups with a high level of group efficacy outperform groups with a low level (Guzzo, Yost, Campbell, & Shea, 1993; Shea & Guzzo, 1987; Sargent & Sue-Chan, 2001; Sosik, Avolio, & Kahai, 1997).

Authenticity will be a shield against taking incorrect or excessively risky decisions, because the individuals in the group will be aware of the underlying causes of their decisions. They will not only be aware of their own prejudices, biases, stereotypes, and underlying motives but also make balanced evaluations of the information they have.

As a result of their positive mind-sets, authentic leaders fully value followers and continuously try to reveal their performance potential. In other words, they are aware of themselves, and they make unbiased processing, which means that they can make unbiased evaluations. This ability, together with high levels of hope and optimism, make them recognize the positive traits of followers. An authentic leader who has high levels of PsyCap is able to find alternative ways to make an employee work hard who might otherwise be labeled as lazy by another manager.

For example, one of the members of the group might not be working as hard as the others and could normally be regarded as lazy in an ordinary group. A group member who is not authentic may not be aware of the true reasons for his behavior, or he may not confess the reasons even to himself and might therefore give false reasons when asked. Other members of the group would get angry with this person, his excuses would not be listened to, and he would be alienated. However, if the leader were authentic, the group members, through vicarious learning, would also be authentic. In that case, the less industrious person would confess the actual reason for his inaction, and the resilient leader and group members would be able to find alternative ways to make him work.

As a result, authentic leadership and increased PsyCap are expected to produce positive outcomes by producing a better understanding of oneself and others, consideration of alternatives, unbiased attributions, positive affective states, and positive evaluations, thus increasing confidence and trust, and decreasing frustrations, misunderstandings, stereotypes, and prejudices.

chapter
EIGHTEEN

How Leaders Can Make Diverse Groups Less Difficult: The Role of Attitudes and Perceptions of Diversity

Astrid C. Homan and Karen A. Jehn

A new product development team was put together to design a new cell phone. The team consisted of two engineers, both female, who were responsible for the technical aspects of the product; and two art designers, both male, who were responsible for the attractiveness of the product. The two engineers developed an exciting new software program, and the artists designed a very beautiful and functional phone. However, the specific technical aspects of the phone could not be produced using the look that the designers developed. Unfortunately, the team members experienced their professional and gender differences negatively and developed a perception of themselves as subgroups within the team, creating an unconstructive team climate. Meetings were characterized by conflicts and distrust, which made it very difficult for the engineers and art designers to communicate their vision and ideas to each another. They were unable to combine their great ideas into one working, satisfying end-product.

HOW THE GROUP IS DIFFICULT: PROBLEMS IN DIVERSE GROUPS

Diversity is a ubiquitous feature of society, and work group diversity is an inherent central aspect of organizational life. It is also a key concern for theory and practice in organizational behavior. Groups in organizations have become more diverse in terms of their demographic composition over the years and will continue to become more diverse in years to come (Williams & O'Reilly, 1998; van Knippenberg & Schippers, 2007). Further, organizations increasingly make use of cross-functional teams, thereby introducing more functional diversity in work teams. Whereas diversity can potentially boost team functioning, it has also been dubbed a double-edged sword and a mixed blessing (for example, Milliken & Martins, 1996), which speaks to the difficulties that may arise when working in teams whose members have diverse characteristics or attributes (see also Chapters Six and Seven for more on the effects of diversity on team processes and functioning). We define team functioning in terms of important organizational outcomes such as team performance, information exchange and processing, commitment, organizational citizenship behavior, conflict, and worker morale (for example, Kozlowski & Bell, 2006), and we propose that whether diversity hinders or boosts team functioning depends on the perceptions team members have of their diversity.

Diversity refers to differences between individuals on any attribute that may lead to the perception that another person is different from the self (Jackson, 1991; Williams & O'Reilly, 1998). Although this definition stresses the importance of *perceptions,* most research on diversity has focused on actual diversity (for example, number of males and females in a group, variance in age) rather than on the perceptions that team members have of their diversity (for example, van Knippenberg & Schippers, 2007). This is unfortunate, because the processes that supposedly underlie diversity effects are largely based on the idea that people see and experience their differences. In this chapter, we address this issue by proposing that diversity perceptions are the critical determinant of success or failure of diverse collectives and of whether the team is "difficult" or not. Moreover, we propose that team leaders have a central role in influencing the perceptions that team members have of their diversity and are thereby capable of making diverse teams less difficult.

A team can be defined as a group consisting of unique and interdependent members (Kozlowski & Bell, 2006). Teams are almost inevitably diverse, and previous research has shown that diversity has powerful effects on group functioning and performance (Milliken & Martins, 1996; van Knippenberg & Schippers, 2007; Williams & O'Reilly, 1998). However, these studies have produced inconsistent results: diversity has been found sometimes to enhance group functioning and sometimes to hamper group functioning (for example, Horwitz & Horwitz, 2007; Webber & Donahue, 2001). Of course, the potential negative sides of diversity are the core interest of this book, and it is crucial to understand how these difficulties can be addressed. The functioning of diverse groups is hindered when groups experience stereotypes and biases that can arise when people perceive their differences as problematic (for example, Milliken & Martins, 1996; van Knippenberg, De Dreu, & Homan, 2004). We will elaborate more on these underlying processes in the next section of this chapter.

Although diverse teams potentially have all the means to function effectively, oftentimes they are hindered by negative group processes. Diverse teams have been found to process less information, experience more conflicts, report less trust and more negative team climate, and perform worse than homogeneous groups (for example, Jehn, Northcraft, & Neale, 1999; van Knippenberg & Schippers, 2007; Williams & O'Reilly, 1998). As an illustration, in our opening story the new product development team consisted of males who were art designers, and females who were engineers. Although the team members were required to work together, their differences stood in the way of effective team work. The males could get into conflict with the females due to different working styles; or the language spoken by the engineers was not understood by the art designers, and vice versa. These types of difference-based frictions make effective team work less likely. If a team as a whole is incapable of working together, it will most likely come up with suboptimal advice and solutions.

Based on the conceptual framework described in the Introduction to this volume, we examine group functioning from an empirical perspective. This perspective holds that in order for a group to function effectively, its composition should be characterized by an appropriate pool of necessary skills, abilities, and expertise. Furthermore, to aid effective group functioning, communication between group members should be supported so that they can better inform and learn from each other. We propose that diversity has an impact on both the process factor (behaviors pertaining to exchanges before, during, and after meetings) and the structural factor (the design of the group) associated with group performance. On the one hand, the positive effects of diversity are predicted to arise from information elaboration processes (van Knippenberg et al., 2004). Because diverse groups often possess diverse perspectives, knowledge, and ideas, they are potentially capable of outperforming homogeneous groups. In order for diverse groups to benefit from these differences, however, they have to thoroughly exchange, process, and integrate this information.

On the other hand, the group's structure can impair these information elaboration processes when diverse teams experience subgroup categorization (for example, Tajfel & Turner, 1986). People use similarities and differences as a basis for categorizing the self and others into groups. The resulting categorizations distinguish one's own in-group from one or more out-groups. Moreover, categorization processes may promote subgroup categorization (that is, create "us" and "them" distinctions within the group), and give rise to problematic intersubgroup relations. People tend to like and trust in-group members more than out-group members and so tend generally to favor in-groups over out-groups (Brewer, 1979; Tajfel & Turner, 1986; Turner, Hogg, Oakes, Reicher, & Wetherell, 1987). This phenomenon has been called intersubgroup bias and is reflected in teams by higher levels of conflict, deteriorated relationship quality, and reduced trust (for example, Earley & Mosakowski, 2000; Pelled, Eisenhardt, & Xin, 1999; Thatcher, Jehn, & Zanutto, 2003). These negative group processes render the attainment of the potential benefits of diversity—that is, the elaboration of diverse perspectives and concomitant enhanced performance—less likely.

WHY THE GROUP IS DIFFICULT: PERCEPTIONS OF DIVERSITY

We argue that diversity is more likely to lead to negative group processes to the degree that group members perceive their differences in terms of subgroups. When diversity is construed in terms of subgroups, "us-them" distinctions are likely to occur, which negatively affect group interaction and processes such as conflicts, satisfaction, well-being, and trust (for example, Dovidio, Gaertner, Isen, & Lowrance, 1995; Levine, Prosser, Evans, & Reicher, 2005; van Knippenberg et al., 2004). Moreover, we propose that these subgroup perceptions rather than actual diversity will determine team functioning. In this respect, we define actual diversity as the objective, actual diversity constellation of a group. Actual diversity can be assessed by measuring the objectively existing variability between team members using statistical measures, such as proportion, standard deviation, Blau's index (1977; a common means of measuring variation in categorical data; cf. Harrison & Klein, 2007), and Fau (which measures alignment of diversity characteristics in teams; Thatcher et al., 2003). Perceptions of subgroups can be measured only subjectively by personally asking team members about the degree to which they perceive subgroups within the team. We believe that the relationship between actual diversity and perceptions of subgroups is not as straightforward as one might think.

Group members may not notice the differences within their team at all, they might perceive subgroups within their team, or they may even see differences that others—organizations, managers, or researchers—do not consider as such (Randel, 2002; Zellmer-Bruhn, Maloney, Bhappu, & Salvador, 2008; cf. Harrison & Klein, 2007). That is, actual diversity may only matter through the perceptions it instigates (Ashfort & Mael, 1989; see Harrison, Price, Gavin, & Florey, 2002). Supporting this idea, initial research findings showed that perceptions of diversity have a powerful impact on such outcomes as work group involvement (Hobman, Bordia, & Gallois, 2003) and helping behavior (Van der Vegt & Van de Vliert, 2005).

Data from a recent field study by Homan, Greer, Jehn, and Koning (in press) with actual work teams supported the idea that the relationship between actual and perceived diversity was not one-to-one; that is, teams with similar levels of actual diversity perceived it differently depending on the team members' attitudes toward diversity. In teams that were characterized by strong potential subgroups (in other words, actual diversity), teams in which members believed more in the value of diversity saw their team less as consisting of subgroups than did teams with members who believed less in the value of diversity. Moreover, perceived diversity was found to be more consequential for team processes than was actual diversity.

Going back to the example of the new product development team, the mere fact that the group consists of males and females and art designers and engineers can be a basis for subgroup categorization when the team members perceive their differences in terms of subgroups. This could lead the team as a whole to split into subgroups based on gender, professional or functional background, or both. These subgroup categorization processes can in turn increase conflicts and distrust within the team as a whole. Because the communication and collaboration between subgroups will be diminished, the team as a whole will make less effective use of task-relevant information that it needs to perform well.

In sum, teams that perceive subgroups are more likely to experience negative team functioning than teams that do not perceive subgroups (for example, Lau & Murnighan, 1998; Thatcher et al., 2003; van Knippenberg et al., 2004). It is important to note, however, that whether diverse groups will indeed experience subgroup categorization is determined by how salient or outstanding social categories are within the group (for example, van Knippenberg et al., 2004). To the degree that potential subgroups are easily distinguished within the team, team members are more likely to perceive these subgroups. Previous research on diversity issues has proposed that the salience of potential

Figure 18.1
A Schematic Overview of the Proposed Relationships

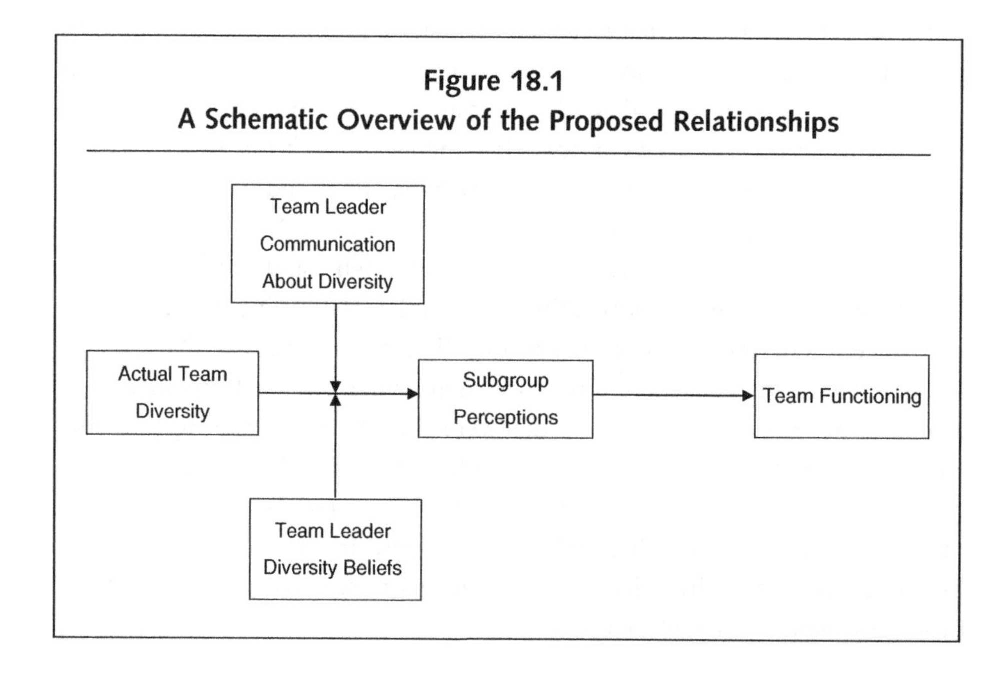

subgroups within teams can be affected by situational and contextual factors (for example, Homan, van Knippenberg, Van Kleef, & De Dreu, 2007a; 2007b; Homan et al., 2008; van Knippenberg et al., 2004). We argue that behaviors of team leaders can affect the degree to which subgroups will be perceived. More specifically, we propose ways in which leaders can decrease the salience of subgroups within teams and increase the level of team functioning. As shown in Figure 18.1, we propose that the relationship between actual diversity and perceptions of subgroups is determined by the team leader's communication about diversity and the team leader's diversity beliefs. The more the leader's communication stresses inclusion of all team members and the more positive the team leader's beliefs about diversity, the less that actual team diversity will be perceived as subgroups.

WHAT YOU CAN DO: THE ROLE OF LEADERS

Although leadership is one of the most examined topics in organizational research (for example, Chemers, 2000), research and theory on the role of leadership in the management of diverse teams is, remarkably enough, limited (see Chin, 2007). To date, there have been few studies that have explicitly examined the role of leaders in managing diverse groups (Kearney & Gebert, 2009; Shin & Zhou, 2007; Somech, 2006). These studies all focused on how leadership style affects the functioning of diverse teams—more specifically, directive and participative leadership (Somech, 2006) and transformational leadership (Kearney & Gebert, 2009; Shin & Zhou, 2007). Somech showed that participative leadership leads to more reflection and in turn more innovation in functionally diverse teams; Kearney and Gebert found positive effects of transformational leadership on functioning of informationally and demographically diverse teams. These effects related to the fact that transformational leaders increased information elaboration and the degree to which team members identified with their team.

However, research focusing on leadership styles is disparate, and results are inconsistent (for example, Chemers, 2000). The great number of different leadership styles frameworks and the overlap between one leadership style and another makes it difficult to really understand the potential effects of leadership styles on the functioning of diverse teams. For instance, consideration, participative, and person-centered leadership are highly similar to each other, just as initiating structure, directive, and task-centered leadership are (for example, Chemers, 2000). Which behaviors are really driving the effects that are found in these studies? Is showing considerate behavior enough to cultivate the potential of diversity, or are there specific things leaders can do to influence diversity perceptions? Similarly, the positive effects of, for instance, transformational leadership on team functioning are not limited to diverse teams, but have been found for teams in general (for example, Bass, Avolio, Jung, & Berson, 2003; Schaubroeck, Lam, & Cha, 2007). This questions the added value of these findings with regard to diverse teams. Finally, these studies all focused on effects of actual diversity rather than perceptions of diversity. In this chapter, we focus on specific leadership behaviors that one can exhibit to affect the perceptions that team members have of their team and thereby also affect team functioning.

Leader Communication About Diversity

We propose that the way in which team leaders perceive and address their teams will affect the diversity perceptions of the team members. As leaders are often seen as an important determinant of the success or failure of teams (for example, Bass, 1990), their behavior is very important for team members' perceptions and behavior. Team leaders guide teams using interpersonal communication (Stogdill, 1974), and this communication can shape the way team members perceive the world around them and thereby also the way in which team members perceive their diversity. In this regard, experimental research has made use of collective pronouns such as "we" or "they" to manipulate subgroup categorization (for example, Gaertner et al., 2000; Tajfel & Turner, 1986). We propose that leaders' use of these pronouns may affect team members' perceptions of the team's diversity. For example, leaders may communicate with a diverse team in terms of subgroups by saying, "Let the men make the PowerPoint presentation, they are more technical, and the women can then present the work, as they are better in communicating." Or less overtly, the leader might name certain team members, all of whom happen to be men, to work on a technical aspect of a task, and ask the other team members, all of whom happen to be women, to work on the communicative aspect of the same task. When a leader does this consistently, team members are likely to begin perceiving their team as consisting of (gender-based) subgroups. In contrast, the leader could also stress similarity within the team by saying, "You, as a team, are responsible for the development of the PowerPoint presentation and for presenting it at the meeting. You are all capable of doing this, so let's make sure that everyone works together on both tasks." This type of communication could decrease the perception of subgroups within the team. The communication of the leader will thus be an important determinant of the relationship between actual diversity and perceived diversity and thereby affect team functioning.

Leader Diversity Beliefs

Similar to our idea that leader communication can make particular diversity constellations more or less salient, leaders have also been found to impact the beliefs and norms of their subordinates (for example, Yorges, Weiss, & Strickland, 1999). Diversity beliefs can be defined as beliefs about the value of diversity to work group functioning (Homan et al., 2007a; van Knippenberg, Haslam, & Platow, 2007). People may hold beliefs about how group composition in terms of homogeneity or diversity affects group functioning. Especially for task groups, group composition may affect the extent to which the group is perceived as being a "good" group—where "good" is subjectively defined and may refer to actual or expected task performance as well as other aspects of group functioning. Some authors have noted that people may differ in their beliefs about or attitudes toward diversity (Hostager & De Meuse, 2002; Strauss, Connerley, & Ammermann, 2003) or that organizational climates and cultures may differ in the extent to which they value diversity (Ely & Thomas, 2001; Kossek & Zonia, 1993; Mor Barak, Cherin, & Berkman, 1998). That is, some organizations might stress the importance of having a diverse workforce, because this increases innovation and creativity, whereas other organizations put less emphasis on hiring diverse people. These studies have advanced the theoretical notion that beliefs, climates, or cultures valuing diversity are needed to harvest the benefits of diversity.

Beliefs about diversity inform responses to actual work group composition. The more that people believe in the value of diversity for work group functioning, the more favorably they respond to work group diversity (Homan et al., 2007a; van Knippenberg et al., 2007). Similarly, Ely and Thomas (2001) examined "diversity perspectives," which they defined as group members' implicit or explicit normative beliefs and expectations about cultural diversity and its role in their work group. On the basis of qualitative interviews and subjective reports of group functioning, they reported that when an organization's diversity perspective emphasized the value of cultural diversity as a resource for the organization, group members reported feeling more valued and respected, experiencing a higher quality of intergroup relations, and feeling more successful than group members did in organizations that did not value diversity. When individuals believe that diversity is beneficial for the task at hand, diversity is positively related to work group identification, whereas diversity is negatively related to identification when individuals believe in the value of homogeneity.

Along similar lines, research on the functioning of diverse teams has shown that pro-diversity beliefs can improve team performance because members of diverse teams are better capable of exchanging and processing task-relevant information (Homan et al., 2008; Homan et al., 2007a). Homan et al. (in press) showed that diversity beliefs also impacted the perceptions that people had of their team. The more team members believed in the value of diversity, the less they perceived subgroups when the team actually had strong demographic subgroups.

On the basis of these considerations, we propose that leader diversity beliefs may affect team members through two different processes. First, the leader's diversity beliefs might have an impact on the behavior of the leader toward the diverse team, which can indirectly affect the team's outlook on diversity. When a leader reinforces interactions among diverse team members, team members may develop a positive attitude toward their diversity. By contrast, when a leader ignores or discourages interactions among team members with different backgrounds, this may instigate negative attitudes toward diversity. Second, the leader can also explicitly express his or her diversity beliefs to the team members. To the extent that the leader succeeds in transferring his or her positive (or negative) diversity beliefs to the team, the team will be more likely to benefit (or not benefit) from its diversity (Homan et al., 2007a). Suggestive evidence for this second process is provided by Van Ginkel and van Knippenberg (2008). They found that when the leader had a positive outlook on diversity, teams adopted this attitude and in turn elaborated more information.

We propose that regardless of the underlying process, the more positive the leader's diversity beliefs, the less likely team members will be to perceive their diversity in terms of subgroups. In turn, these perceptions will have beneficial consequences for team functioning (cf. Homan et al., 2007a; Homan et al.,

2008). To summarize, leaders, through their actions and words, can make team diversity work by believing in the value of diversity and encouraging their teams to believe the same. Leaders should focus on setting norms that diversity is valuable and important for team functioning. This will make it less likely that the new product development team we described at the beginning of the chapter perceives subgroups based on gender or functional background and thus increases the likelihood that they can effectively use their differences.

CONCLUSION

Diversity can potentially create difficult groups because of subgroup perceptions and intersubgroup biases. This is unfortunate, because the potential benefits of diversity over homogeneity should be harvested. In this chapter, we gave a central role to team leaders as determinants of whether diverse groups will indeed be difficult. More specifically, we advanced the following propositions:

1. There is no one-to-one relationship between actual and perceived diversity.
2. The difficulties of diverse groups can be predicted from the degree to which team members perceive their differences in terms of subgroups.
3. Leader behaviors and leader beliefs moderate the relationship between actual diversity and subgroup perceptions.

We predict that two types of leadership characteristics can aid the effective use of diversity: leader communication and leader diversity beliefs. Through the leader's setting the norm that diversity is valuable and using inclusive rather than subgroup-promoting language, team members will develop positive perceptions of their diversity. The focus on leadership yields valuable insights that may be used by managers, consultants, politicians, school boards, families, and other professionals who frequently deal with diversity. We propose that leaders and policymakers should aim management strategies, diversity trainings, and human resource programs at managing diversity perceptions of teams, classes, and other types of groups. These strategies aimed at managing perceptions of diversity may prove to be a feasible, cost-efficient, and effective way to maximize the functioning of diverse teams.

chapter
NINETEEN

The Hero's Journey: Helping Inflexible Groups—and Inflexible Facilitators—Get Unstuck

Carol Sherriff and Simon Wilson

Even afterwards I couldn't really work out how I had got myself into such a situation or what else I could have done. I just got stuck in a position where one participant seemed to want a fight. Nothing I said reassured her that her voice would be heard. She kept on challenging me, twisting what I said. Every now and then, a couple of others joined in. We kept having breaks during which the senior management team disappeared to hatch up a new plan for handling "them." The other participants sort of huddled together for warmth. I didn't seem to have any option but to handle the challenges head to head, which didn't work no matter how hard I tried. Finally, we ran out of time and energy, and the group came to a sort of conclusion. I limped away defeated. Somehow I had become the bad guy.

—Carol

When Carol had stopped blaming "them" and the client for the whole debacle, she began to understand the critical role that she as facilitator had played in keeping the group stuck in a difficult position. She made a common error in such stuck situations: when what we are doing isn't working, we do more of the same with greater intensity (Maynard & Champoux, 1996). In our experience, facilitators and groups find it helpful but challenging to pause and reflect at those points where the group has become "difficult." The Hero's Journey provides a framework for such reflection and helps generate different options for moving forward that help group and facilitator become unstuck. Our intention in this chapter is to empower fellow facilitators to deal with some of the most challenging situations they get caught up in, not to blame or disempower. In that spirit, all the case studies cited in this chapter come directly from our own experience. We know how easy it is to become stuck and inflexible.

This chapter first reviews the idea that the group and the facilitator transfer their projections and mental maps onto each other. In terms of the framework of this book, it addresses the process and structure factors from the relational perspective. To understand the key points at which this is likely to happen, we use the framework of the three stages of the Hero's Journey and introduce the archetypal energies that are particularly active at each stage. As groups prepare to move on from one stage of the journey to the next, there are key transition points that are in themselves challenging for groups. If, however, the facilitator is facing the same transition, he or she may, through the process of transference, unconsciously hold back the group, creating the inflexibility we describe in our title. We look at examples and describe what facilitators can do in such situations. The chapter concludes with a facilitation process, *The Heroes' Journey*, which helps the group move through the transitions and helps ensure that the facilitator does not become stuck and inflexible.

WHY DO FACILITATORS EXPERIENCE GROUPS AS DIFFICULT, AND WHY DO THEY NEED TO BE FLEXIBLE?

Facilitators are, in our experience, resourceful individuals able to respond flexibly to the needs of groups. However, some situations and some groups seem to be particularly problematic. We notice from our own experience and that of other facilitators that the difficulties are not universal: different facilitators manage admirably in situations others find extraordinarily difficult. However, neither is the pattern totally individualistic: many of the "war stories" told by facilitators with a touch of pride and a lot of humor are strikingly similar. Nor are these difficult situations necessarily charged with negative emotion. Sometimes facilitators get stuck in situations that are experienced at the time as highly enjoyable or well ordered, and it is only clear afterwards that a difficulty was sidestepped or ignored by everyone, including the facilitator. In these stuck situations, facilitators can find it difficult to disentangle what went on and what they might have done differently, as Carol's experience demonstrates. Facilitators need to be able to learn from them, or there is a high risk that they will label certain types of situations or groups as difficult even in the face of evidence to the contrary. So the question is, How do you make sense of what is going on and remain flexible before and during a facilitated event?

TRANSFERENCE AND COUNTERTRANSFERENCE—THE ENERGETIC BOND OF THE GROUP

The idea that individuals unconsciously transfer or project hidden, repressed, or uncomfortable feelings onto others, particularly a perceived authority figure or a scapegoat, is a central part of psychoanalytic theories, particularly in Europe and to a lesser degree in North America. Bion (1961) and Hopper (2007), among others, have studied these patterns within groups and demonstrated how emotions transfer between group members, often increasing in intensity and sophistication. These transference patterns bind groups together and give different groups their character—what we describe as the energetic bond of the group. They can exert a powerful influence on the behavior of the group and on people with whom the group comes into contact.

Transference is not a one-way street, and therapists, authority figures, and facilitators countertransfer or project their own emotions and feelings onto groups. Heron (1999) identifies six patterns of transference for facilitators to pay attention to:

- Positive transference by one or two members of the group, which can lead to dependency on the facilitator
- Negative transference, which can lead to active resistance, denigration, sabotage, and rivalry, again on an individual basis
- Acute transference, in which these patterns for a short time become active throughout the group
- Chronic transference, in which the positive or negative emotions get fixed on the facilitator
- Universal transference, which "goes every which way, not just from member to leader, but from member to member" (p. 64)
- Countertransference, in which the facilitator projects unresolved or inappropriate emotions onto individual group members or the whole group

In our experience, each of the first four forms of transference, in which individuals or the group unconsciously project feelings and emotions onto the facilitator, are common. They may lead to problems, but normally facilitators, consciously or unconsciously, recognize these patterns of behavior and become adept at helping the group and individuals deal with them. Countertransference, the last on Heron's list, is also common, but as it is an unconscious mechanism, it is more difficult for facilitators to recognize. However, in most circumstances, the facilitator gets some feedback or insight that enables her to recognize and change her projection. In our experience, it is in situations of universal transference, when facilitators have become part of the energetic bond of the group through transference and countertransference, that facilitators become stuck and inflexible. In this territory, facilitators need a tool to help disentangle the energies that create the energetic bond and their attachment to it. For this we turn to the structure of the Hero's Journey.

THE HERO'S JOURNEY

The story begins with the hero, heroine, or band of friends in their home territory. They receive a call to action. It often takes them a while to recognize the call and to take on the responsibility of being the heroes. Inevitably something happens to force their decision, and they need to prepare for the journey. The transition between preparation for the journey and being on the journey can be swift, but it is a sharp divide. The heroes have left the known for the unknown. At the beginning of the journey, the heroes often face deprivation and suffering, but they also find love and friendship, a new depth to their relationships. They face challenges and enemies they need to overcome, and meet benefactors who bring gifts. The challenges and the gifts bring transformation and growth for the heroes. They then face the second transition point. They must return home, which means leaving behind the life of the road and taking on new responsibilities. Our heroes are often reluctant to leave a life they have come to enjoy. On the return, the gifts brought back need to be utilized to bring prosperity and stability to all. A new order is established, and for a time all is well. But any order can become stagnant, and needs renewal. This is the third transition point. It requires the heroes to set aside their certainties and established way of doing things, and heed the call to a new journey. Figure 19.1 illustrates the structure of the Hero's Journey.

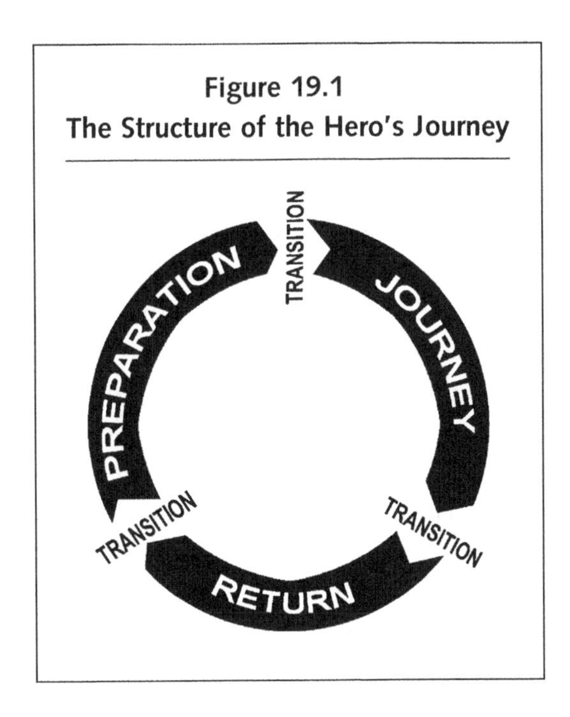

Figure 19.1
The Structure of the Hero's Journey

Research into the structure and power of stories (for example, Campbell, 1949/1993; Snowden, 2005) has found that fables, myths, and stories from around the world share this common structure, often referred to as the Hero's Journey.

1. Preparation: heeding the call and preparing for the journey
2. The Journey: confronting the challenges and accepting the gifts
3. The Return: bringing the gifts home to enrich and change the community

We have found that the Hero's Journey also works as a metaphor for group development.

Where Is the Group Now, and How Do I Recognize It?

A facilitator working with a group can use the structure of the Hero's Journey to make an initial diagnosis of the group's situation.

Is the group responding to some kind of call to develop its activities and relationships—for instance, is a new project to be undertaken? Do the group members recognize intellectually that they have to make changes but haven't really done anything? If so, they are in the Preparation stage. Has the group started to work together to explore changes, but faces challenges and hasn't yet found its strengths—for instance, are they exploring and assessing different options for program delivery? If so, it is on the Journey. Has the group gone through a period of change and reorganization, reevaluating strengths and weaknesses, and is it now trying to regularize new ways of doing things—for instance, developing operational frameworks? If so, the group is on the Return. Has the group worked together or separately as an established group, but on the horizon there is a change that will require new ways of doing things? Then the group is about to begin a new journey.

For facilitators it is important to recognize that progress from one stage of the Hero's Journey to the next always involves a transition—a time of uncertainty and change. It is often at these points that facilitators are called in to work with groups. These points can be very challenging. Transition points are like a chasm separating the group from the next stage. Groups (and facilitators) develop a range of tactics for dealing with the chasm: take one look and run away as fast as they can, decide that whatever is on the other side isn't worth the effort, or make solo attempts to bridge the gap. To find a way over or around the chasm requires the group members to pool all their skills and resources. For facilitators to help groups cross the transition, they need to delve a little deeper into the forces at work within the Hero's Journey.

The Hero's Journey and Archetypal Energies—A Framework for Group Development

Each stage of the Hero's Journey provides the foundation for the next. However, the transition between stages is not automatic. It requires individuals and groups to have learned the lessons of the stage they are in and responded to the call to the next stage. Pearson (1991) draws attention to twelve archetypal characters that appear in sequence during the three stages of the Hero's Journey. These are

1. The Preparation: the Innocent, the Orphan, the Warrior, and the Caregiver
2. The Journey: the Seeker, the Creator, the Destroyer, and the Lover
3. The Return: the Ruler, the Magician, the Jester, and the Sage

For there to be a successful transition to the next stage of the journey, all the archetypal characteristics for the current stage need to be actively expressed within the group, and no archetype (that is, pattern of behavior) repressed. Where a group finds itself stuck, one or more of the archetypal characters needed at the current stage are not being expressed.

These archetypes also help identify the patterns of transference and countertransference within the group and explain how facilitators may fail—and can succeed—in helping a group make a necessary transition.

Archetypal Energies at the Point of Transition—How to Recognize What's Happening in the Group

The archetypal characters help facilitators identify the energies that are an active part of the energetic bond of the group, and the ones that are being repressed or projected outside. At points of transition, when the group can be anxious and uncertain, the dominant archetypes can be expressed negatively as well as positively. The following sections describe what we have observed as the positive characteristics of each archetype and the symptoms of resistance to moving on to the next stage.

The Preparation Archetypes Four archetypal roles are grouped under the heading of the Preparation. They are the Innocent, the Orphan, the Warrior, and the Caregiver. Innocent and Orphan are a pair, as are Warrior and Caregiver. We focus more on the importance of the pairings in the next section.

Role	Positive Characteristics	Symptoms of Resistance to the Move to the Journey Stage
Preparation stage overview	*Taking responsibility for themselves within the group, exploring trust and interdependence with others, being able to stand up for what they believe to be right, equipping themselves for the journey ahead with realism and optimism.*	*Not wanting to move on, often blaming external forces for the need to; not recognizing personal impact on the group; splitting into factions and fighting among themselves; engaging in rescuing behavior and unnecessary self-sacrifice; generally denying the need to move forward.*
Innocent	Innocents want to be loved and be part of things. They trust others and can be a source of optimism and hope.	Denial of the need to change; superficial comments; friendly but unchallenging contributions to group exercises. Where the team is, is as good as it gets.
Orphan	Orphans try to protect us from being abandoned, hurt, or victimized. They recognize the importance of collective action.	Refusal to trust anyone outside the team; suspicion and the search for hidden motives on the part of anyone who may not be part of the group—including the facilitator.
Warrior	Warriors challenge everything that threatens the survival of their way of life. They are combative and competitive, with a strong team spirit, and are focused on winning current battles.	Assertiveness; not prepared to let the opportunity for a fight pass them by; competition between subgroups within the team; short-term focus on current goals.
Caregiver	Caregivers are prepared to sacrifice their own wishes to care for others. They are mutually supportive and team focused, and they look after the relational aspects of the group.	Inward looking and risk averse, they may display disempowered "victim" or inappropriate "rescuer" behavior. Members of the group may identify the facilitator as a threat, and the Caregivers within the group will seek to protect the members.

In our opening case study, the group had been called upon by changes in public policy and funding to work together in a new way. They had accepted, indeed some of them had welcomed, the change—the sign that a new Hero's Journey had begun. They had drafted a protocol between themselves on how to agree on local funding priorities. However, the closer they got to agreeing on the protocol, the more difficulties they experienced. In terms of the Hero's Journey, they were superficially preparing for the journey but hoped someone else might go in their place—a very common reaction. The closer they got to the transition—to starting the journey—the more they banded together fearing the worst (Orphan) and fought each other and outsiders (Warrior). The optimists in the group (Innocent) and those who considered the most important thing to be that the group members should support each other (Caregiver) were effectively silenced, and those energies were projected onto the facilitator. Carol felt the projection—being treated as naïve, caring, not living in the "real world." However, that was exactly what Carol feared most within her own transition. So she in turn repressed the uncomfortable archetypes, setting off a pattern of universal transference. She could have brought the Innocent and Caregiver energy alive within herself and the group by, for example, asking questions about the positive outcomes of working together, both for their constituents and their organizations.

The Journey Archetypes Four archetypal roles are grouped under the heading of the Journey. They are the Seeker, the Lover, the Creator, and the Destroyer. As before, these roles are paired: Seeker and Lover, Creator and Destroyer.

Role	Positive Characteristics	Symptoms of Resistance to the Move to the Return Stage
Journey stage overview	*Creating new meaning and value, building deep relationships, letting go of worn-out habits and procedures, seeking new ideas.*	*Identifying more areas that need exploring and new destinations of interest; obsessive creative activity; questioning and paring away at the nature of their mission. They may recognize the need to return, but it is clear that they are not yet ready to put down roots.*
Seeker	Seekers seek enlightenment and transformation.	Need for more information, desire to find out more. Keenness to set up new projects and visit new sites.
Lover	Lovers seek deep connection with themselves and others. They give of themselves but do not sacrifice themselves.	Enjoying the companionship of the journey, seeking more friends and connections.

(Continued)

Role	Positive Characteristics	Symptoms of Resistance to the Move to the Return Stage
Creator	Creators are interested in new creation and beginnings, facing the challenge as a new opportunity, receiving the gift as an opportunity to do something new.	More things to create, continuing idea generation, new options and models for action without a decision.
Destroyer	Destroyers know that you cannot create and recognize your gifts without being prepared to let go, to destroy in order to rebuild.	More challenges that need to be tackled, paring away at the current mission while resisting the need to move on.

> Working with this team was one of the most enjoyable experiences of my facilitation career. As a bunch of communications specialists in a national organization in the United Kingdom, they encouraged me to design highly creative events in which everyone let their hair down, had fun, and bonded. They did get some work done, but this was a team of mavericks, and they liked it that way. Their leader was a great guy—utterly committed to his people but very much part of the team. Sometime later, I was very surprised to discover that the team leader was being pushed out of the organization, and after his enforced resignation, his team all missed him a lot and were unhappy about the new unimaginative boss who made them fill in their time sheets.
>
> —*Simon*

This team and its leader were stuck in the Journey stage and had not paid attention to a change at the top of the organization, which signaled the need to deliver results—the Return. The time for mavericks had passed, but this team did not realize it. The missing archetype was the Destroyer, which would have required the group to take a critical look at its plans and consider what could be cut back and how to prioritize. This would have paved the way to a transition to the Return stage in which a more settled and structured approach could have been developed. Universal transference was also at work here. Simon supported the dominant pattern within the group because of his own personal preference for the Journey and because of his high Creative and Seeker energy, which led him to encourage continued exploration. The necessary Destroyer energy was projected outside the group and eventually brought into the group by the incoming senior management team. Distracted by his enjoyment of working with this group, Simon was not able to help the group recognize the call to change or to make the transition to the Return.

The Return Archetypes Four archetypal roles are grouped under the stage of the Return. They are the Ruler, the Magician, the Sage, and the Jester. Ruler and Magician are paired, as are Sage and Jester.

Roles	Positive Characteristics	Symptoms of Resistance to the Move on to the Preparation Stage
Return stage overview	*Creating a prosperous and healthy organization that benefits all.*	*Strong, often credible and authoritative commitment to the current rules and hierarchies; arguing that major change can be accommodated within the present way of doing things; recognizing that one day the call will come to begin another journey, but believing that the time has not yet come.*
Ruler	Rulers' goal is a well-ordered prosperous, healthy, and happy state of affairs.	Emphasis on rules and the current way of doing things; demonstration of status and power within a group event.
Magician	Magicians are interested in transformation, extending possibilities, and healing wounds.	Arguing that the new change is part of the existing transformation, not a need for a further transformation.
Sage	Sages are the wise ones who give trusty, knowledgeable advice.	Contradicting and undermining new forms of knowledge, using evidence to uphold the status quo.
Jester	Jesters make light of serious issues and thereby have the ability to speak truth to those in a position of power.	Inappropriate joking and wisecracking.

I facilitated a team event for a department in a governmental organization in the United Kingdom. This had recently been created as a merger of two organizations, and the department had moved over, largely intact, from the old organization to the new one, complete with its department head. The event was a nonevent. As a facilitator, I was trying to maintain my old rapport with the department head, but the event design did not signal that things had changed. In one of the coffee breaks, a member of the team I knew said to me, "If this new organization is all about innovation, why is this event exactly the same as all the old ones?"—and she was right.

—*Simon*

The department head still wanted the certainty and rules of the old world that had been established on his return from the last journey (the last organizational restructuring). All the event activities he wanted were about the rules and structures that were not yet in place. The group expressed high Ruler and Sage energy—producing the results of analytical surveys and setting up new program structures—without actually addressing the real issues. The key repressed energy in this case was the Jester—the ability to speak truth to power, point out that the emperor is naked, to make the case for change. Simon as a facilitator normally makes good use of Jester energy. But the group repressed the Jester energy it needed to move on, and projected it onto Simon as a negative characteristic—the Fool. He repressed his own strong Jester energy in an attempt to please the client, even neglecting the opportunity presented by the coffee break comment, which was a classic Jester moment. By not taking this opportunity, Simon helped the group remain stuck in the Return stage and miss the opportunity to make the transition to a new Preparation stage for which a new set of energies and ways of doing things would have been required.

What Can the Facilitator Do to Help? The facilitator's job is to understand the stage of the journey the group has reached, the energies actively expressed by the group, and whether there are any energies missing or projected outside the group. The next step is to help the group reconnect with the missing or projected energies and help them move on to the next stage of the journey.

As can be seen by our case studies, there is a critical need to be self-aware. The stage of the journey on which a group finds itself is underpinned by strong energetic forces. Facilitators called in to help support transition and change can find the full force of this energy projected onto them—in Heron's terminology (1999), chronic transference. Our examples show that facilitators counter-transfer archetypal energies and, if they are not aware of the effects particularly of their personal transitions, then they create a situation of universal transference in which they and the group become stuck and inflexible.

Understanding Your Own Preferences and Work on Your Projections So it helps facilitators to understand their own archetypal preferences. What characters do you most welcome into your own personal story? Do you regard any of the archetypes as bad, weak, inappropriate, something you do not do? These are the ones you are likely to repress or to project onto others (or both). As outlined earlier, the archetypal characters are paired. You are likely to use one energy in a pair more than the other. Many facilitators find Ruler energy challenging and favor Magician, with its emphasis on transformation. Yet sometimes the task facing a group is to set rules and standards. Equally, many facilitators love the Creator and frown on the Destroyer. Yet the Destroyer cuts back deadwood to make way for new growth and development.

In our experience, facilitators also have a preference for particular stages of the journey. Some facilitators have a preference for the Preparation: getting ready for the journey, getting to know the group and identifying all the data and information the group needs to begin its task. Some facilitators love the Journey with its creativity and exploration, and are reluctant to press the group to move to a return and closure. Others prefer the Return, which involves analysis, rules, procedures, and action plans, and they can be reluctant to see the need to move on to a new Hero's Journey.

Your preference is of course both a gift and a challenge. It is a gift because you are likely to have developed a sophisticated range of tools and approaches for that stage of the journey. It is a challenge because you may prefer to dwell in that stage and be reluctant to move on, even though that would serve the group better. Facilitating yourself through the process we call *The Heroes' Journey* is a good way of developing your own archetypal energies.

FACILITATING THE HEROES' JOURNEY

The most appropriate facilitation tool we have found for helping groups move forward is to use the archetypal journey as a facilitation framework—*The Heroes' Journey*.

Before the Event

The process works through a literal spatial separation of the three stages of the Hero's Journey, with space representing the transition from one stage to another. The archetypes also have their own spaces at each stage. Although the group may be in a transition from one stage to another, it is helpful for them to carry out all the stages. Divide the room into three "stages" to represent the Preparation, the Journey, and the Return. You can preprepare flip charts with the name and a brief description of each of the archetypes, using the information in this chapter, and display them at the relevant stage. You might want to think of individuals known to the group who exemplify archetypal characters from well-known stories or from organizational life.

Prepare a key question flip chart for each of the stages, perhaps including the following questions:

- The Preparation: What are the resources we need to build our team and prepare for the journey?
- The Journey: What are the challenges we will face? What are the strengths and gifts we will develop?
- The Return: What do we need to do to ensure that the community and group benefit from the fruits of our journey?

Setup

The purpose of the activity is to help the group make the transition successfully and easily from one stage to another. Introduce the idea of the Hero's Journey to the group. We use the frame of a band of friends traveling together. Ask the group members to discuss the nature of their journey. Depending on the group, you can keep the exploration close to its current experience or encourage the group members to explore the metaphorical and story aspects—is this journey a trek, a sea voyage, foreign travel? Is it a particular story, movie, or TV series? At this point you can personalize the archetypes: in the story of a sea voyage, who is the Innocent character? You can use your diagnosis of the dominant and repressed archetypes to help the group explore the positive contribution of the repressed archetypes and help the group activate them.

Depending on the number of participants, the group may either work as a single group or divide into three subgroups—three subgroups of four are ideal, as participants can take on the perspective of a particular archetype at each stage. In this case, two of the subgroups will begin already on the Journey or at the Return. This can seem counterintuitive to start with, but deepens the reflection. You can explain that many stories start in the middle and move backwards and forwards.

Explain that the groups will spend time at each stage. Their task is to discuss, picture, or act out what happens at each stage in their Heroes' Journey and note their key reflections on the question flip chart. Each person takes responsibility for making sure that the perspective of a particular archetype is taken into account. It helps to stand "in its shoes" and view the world from that archetype's perspective. The more the groups become absorbed in the story and act out the archetypes, the richer their insights.

Facilitate the Journey

Facilitate the activity so that the group or subgroups move from stage to stage, taking on the archetypal perspectives and identifying the issues for them at each stage of the journey. Encourage them to draw, note down, and act out the story of this stage. Give them a five-minute warning when they should note on the question flip chart their key insights and answers to the question. Just before moving on to the next stage, ask them to pay particular attention to what they feel and do as they move from one stage to another.

From your diagnosis of where they are on the journey and of the dominant and repressed archetypes, notice how the group and individuals representing different archetypes act. If the groups struggle with any particular archetypes, note that and also activate the archetype in yourself and move into the archetypal space of that energy. You can ask questions based on that archetype. Where an archetype is expressed negatively, you can encourage them to consider the positive aspects as well as the negative. The more you as facilitator can journey through all twelve archetypes, the greater your service to the group.

When the groups have visited every stage, call a break during which they are encouraged to tour their Heroes' Journey, noting the points made by other groups.

Reflection and Discussion

After the break and tour, invite them back together to discuss their responses to the key questions and their reflections, insights, and learnings, particularly as they transitioned between stages. Which archetypes were useful? Which did they find most challenging? Which parts of the journey and changes were most easy or most challenging? Which were the key transitions, and how did it feel to make them? What, on reflection, will they do differently? You will find that people want to get up and demonstrate their insights—encourage them to do this. You can lead the discussion into an action plan for each stage of their journey and in particular for the transition they are moving through.

CONCLUSION

Facilitators deal with many complex and potentially challenging issues and people, in the main with great flexibility and resourcefulness. However, there are times when the facilitator gets caught up in or responds inappropriately to the energetic forces at play within the group. Often this is the expression of archetypal energy resisting a necessary transition in both the group and the facilitator. Facilitators can help the group move on, but can also inadvertently make things worse. The framework of the Hero's Journey, an understanding of the different archetypal energies, and use of *The Heroes' Journey* can help facilitators respond more flexibly and effectively.

chapter TWENTY

Difficult Groups or Difficult Facilitators? Three Steps Facilitators Can Take to Make Sure They Are Not the Problem

Glyn Thomas

In the early stages of my development as a group facilitator, I experienced numerous difficult groups, but one particularly stands out in my memory. I was the designated leader for the educational experience, but only in title, because there was a small subgroup who clearly did not want to be there and had little respect for others or for the way I was trying to facilitate the group experience. However, their disruptive behavior was rarely explicit, and the lack of overt problems left me afraid to confront the subgroup's behavior. Unfortunately, I took it very personally, I felt a strong sense of rejection, I was tangled in their web, and my confidence with the whole group waned. I doubted my ability to provide a safe container to explore the cause of the unrest, and my responses to the subgroup became more defensive, causing my interactions with the whole group to deteriorate. The "voices in my head" had no trouble highlighting my ineptitude, and for me the experience could not end fast enough.

Sooner or later, most facilitators come across the "group from hell." With such groups, no matter what the facilitator does, the group can still seem to be stuck or, worse still, regressing. There can also be an uneasy tension caused by unresolved issues within the group or between the group and the facilitator (or both). Sometimes, groups are just hard work. Other times, we as the facilitators may be part of the problem, albeit unknowingly. It is not difficult for facilitators to get caught up in the group's issues and contribute to its ineffectiveness. If we are honest, most facilitators would acknowledge they have had experiences like the one I've described here, although we may try to repress such unpleasant memories.

A group facilitator's purpose is to help the participants achieve their individual and common goals. When a group encounters a difficulty, it can place considerable demand on the skills, knowledge, and experience of the facilitator to help the group find a resolution. Unfortunately, facilitators can also unknowingly contribute to the difficulties their groups experience if they lack the needed skills, knowledge, or experience. Hence, my underlying premise is that sometimes the source of the difficulties that a group may experience lies not with the participants but with the facilitator. I will highlight some examples of when this may occur, identify some causes, and suggest ways to address the problems.

The assertions I make are based both on my personal experience and on my research exploring the theories and practices of facilitator educators (Thomas, 2007). My study used interviews and participant observations with seven facilitator educators in Australia and New Zealand. The primary recommendation of the study was that to become effective group facilitators, the emerging facilitators should receive education and training focused on four areas: (1) technical facilitator education, (2) intentional facilitator education, (3) person-centered facilitator education, and (4) critical facilitator education (see Thomas, 2008a, 2008b, Thomas, in press). I maintain that participation in a comprehensive, balanced facilitator education program focusing on these four areas should produce graduates who are technically capable, intentional, perceptive,

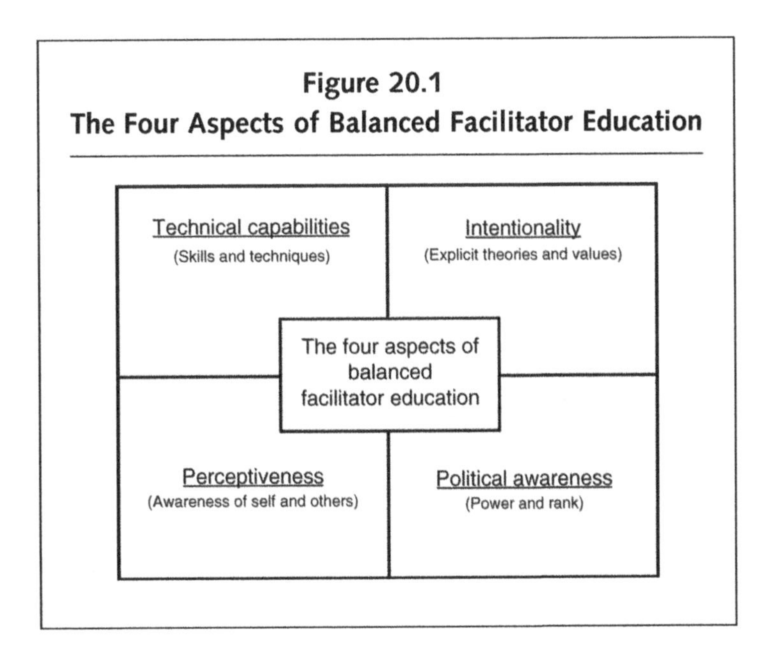

Figure 20.1
The Four Aspects of Balanced Facilitator Education

and politically aware, as shown in Figure 20.1. If a facilitator's overall education and training are unbalanced, he or she runs the risk of causing difficulties for groups. In the next section, I will focus on three avoidable, yet common, problems that groups experience that may be resolved through better facilitator education.

HOW THE FACILITATOR CAN CONTRIBUTE TO THREE COMMON GROUP DIFFICULTIES

Three common problems that occur in groups and that may be associated with ineffective facilitation are *unclear purposes and misaligned activities, defensive and overreactive communication,* and *abuses of power.* This is by no means a conclusive list of problems, but my study's findings indicate that these three problems warrant greater attention in the preparation of group facilitators.

Problem 1: Misaligned Activities

Despite high levels of activity, some groups are limited in their effectiveness either by their failure to rally behind a common purpose or by a lack of clarity about how to work toward that purpose. Consequently, such groups wallow in uncertainty and ineffectiveness, leading to dissatisfied and frustrated group members. When considering the group structure from the rational perspective, we know that goals, objectives, and tasks need to be clearly defined to enhance group effectiveness. If the facilitator does not help the group establish a clear purpose,

> everyone is obliged to assume the purpose—and assumptions are most likely to be different. Even mild differences about the purpose of a group can and will lead to misunderstandings. Facilitators or group members who say there is no time for setting a purpose do not understand the power of setting intention. (Hunter, 2007, p. 39)

Similarly, from the perspective of group process, the random or inappropriate use of tools, strategies, and activities by facilitators can have an equally detrimental effect on group effectiveness. The availability of facilitation resources (for example, Bendaly, 2000; Bens, 2005; Havergal & Edmonstone, 1999) is helpful but not sufficient to ensure that the facilitator will know how and when to best apply these tools, strategies, and activities. It is foolish for facilitators to collect skills, strategies, and tricks for their toolbox and think that they can effectively apply them in a formulaic manner without any clear understanding of their potential impact on a group's functioning (Weaver & Farrell, 1997). Schwarz (2002, p. 9) argued that facilitators

> not only need a set of methods and techniques but also an understanding of how and why they work. . . . you see the reasoning that underlies each technique and method . . . you can improvise and design new methods and techniques consistent with the core values.

Problem 2: Defensive and Overreactive Communication

Upon reflection, most group facilitators will be able to describe a time when they were not at their best when working with a group. At such times, some group participants seem to have an amazing ability to get under the facilitator's skin or press the facilitator's buttons, which can lead to defensiveness and inappropriate responses from the facilitator. When considering important group process factors from a relational perspective, there is no doubt that being triggered in this way lowers the facilitator's levels of *free attention,* which

Hunter (2007) described as "that part of your awareness not caught up with thoughts, feelings (emotions) and body sensations" (p. 51). The negative consequences when a facilitator gets distracted in this way are twofold: (1) he or she is less able to serve the group, and (2) some participants can be distracted from working toward the group's purpose by being drawn into conflict with the facilitator. Either way, the group is less able to achieve its desired outcomes.

Problem 3: Abuses of Power

A group facilitator, by virtue of his or her role, can have significant power or influence over participants and the group process. This power and influence can be used in a positive manner to assist the group to achieve its purpose, or they can be misused to service hidden agendas and to privilege certain interests. Facilitators can create problems in groups by mismanaging the power relationships between participants or failing to consider those whose views are marginalized. This may occur when a facilitator makes incorrect assumptions about participants and fails to acknowledge diversity, uses stereotypes or sexist language, or uses activities that do not allow all members to participate in a meaningful way. This mismanagement of power in groups is not always deliberate, but that does not justify the facilitator's action (or inaction) when such behavior occurs. If facilitators are unaware of the way they use or misuse their power or authority in a group, they may unintentionally contribute to the group's ineffectiveness, which is a good example of a structural problem from the political perspective.

WHY THE FACILITATOR MAY CONTRIBUTE TO THESE PROBLEMS

Why do facilitators contribute to these three problems? Of course, these problems may have multiple causes, and the discussion that follows does not imply direct single-cause relationships between these three problems and the facilitator's actions or inactions. However, my contention is that facilitators can contribute to (1) unclear purposes and misaligned activities if they *fail to ensure constructive alignment;* (2) defensive and overreactive communication if they *lack self-awareness*; and (3) abuses of power if they *mismanage their role.*

Facilitator Contributions to Problem 1: Failure to Ensure Constructive Alignment

The first problem, unclear purposes and misaligned activities, is often caused by a lack of *constructive alignment.* This term was coined by Biggs and Tang (2007) to describe the process of systematically aligning learning activities with desired outcomes in a higher education context. This structural problem has direct relevance to group facilitation contexts too, and it is not uncommon to see groups busy with tasks or activities that do not effectively contribute to the successful achievement of desired outcomes. Key tasks for a group facilitator include helping the group define its purpose and then selecting (or helping the group select) the best strategies to achieve that purpose. This process of strategy selection implies that there are some underlying principles or theories that can guide the group facilitator. However, the literature presents confusing perspectives on the relationship between the theory and practice of facilitation. For example, a puzzling comment in the preface of a book on advanced facilitation strategies reads, "while references are made throughout this book to the experts who have given facilitation its theoretical underpinnings, the strategies described in this resource represent practical techniques found to work in everyday situations" (Bens, 2005, p. xii). This could be taken to imply that theoretical underpinnings are not relevant to the effective practice of group facilitation.

In group counseling, the use of practices without a clear understanding of the reasons for using them is called *technical eclecticism* (Schneider-Corey & Corey, 2006). The view that good group facilitation can be realized by selecting activities without a clear rationale for how they will help the group was debunked by the facilitator educators in my study (Thomas, 2007) and discredited by other authors in the facilitation literature (Ghais, 2005; Hunter, Bailey, & Taylor, 1999; Jenkins & Jenkins, 2006). In the absence of some guiding underlying principles, it would be lucky if the strategies and activities chosen or recommended by a group facilitator lead to the successful attainment of a group's purpose. Facilitators who practice in such a manner increase the likelihood of contributing to a group's frustrations and ineffectiveness. This can be avoided if facilitators are careful to ensure that there is constructive alignment between the activities selected and the group's identified purpose.

Facilitator Contributions to Problem 2: Low Facilitator Self-Awareness

Leading a group is demanding. Among other things, the facilitator has to monitor the behavior and contributions of participants, listen deeply, and choose when to intervene to keep the group focused on achieving its purpose. A facilitator's ability to function effectively is partly determined by his or her ability to remain attentive, open, and awake to the group while attending to the sayings and advice from what Jenkins and Jenkins (2006) describe as the facilitator's *interior council*. Jenkins and Jenkins encouraged facilitators to be aware of the "voices in their heads" offering guidance and then to wisely select which ones to pay attention to and which ones to ignore. A facilitator who is unable to do this in real time while working with a group will find it very difficult to maintain high levels of free attention (Hunter, 2007) and to avoid becoming defensive when he or she encounters resistance or hostility.

There are numerous examples in the group facilitation literature lending support to the idea that leading groups is as much about who the facilitator is *being* as it is about what he or she is *doing*. For example, Hogan (2002) enumerated the importance of relationships and the need for group facilitators to be *fully present* and authentic with group members. Similarly, Ghais (2005) explained that no amount of brilliant skills and techniques will help a group facilitator if he or she lacks personal awareness, and "whether we're aware of it or not, our inner states, moods, attitudes, and thoughts are always on our sleeves" (p. 14). Jenkins and Jenkins (2006, p. 1) also concurred with this view:

> The most difficult thing any facilitative leader can do is master himself or herself. Every leader experiences doubt, anxiety, cynicism, and his or her own dark side. Facilitative leaders need to restore their personal energy, maintain respect for both colleagues and themselves, find new sources of ideas and inspiration, and battle the human propensity toward self-limitation, caution, mediocrity, and dependency.

Ringer (2002) explained that effective facilitation is "not about control of the group or dazzling with knowledge or skill, but simply maintaining your self fully present with the group and providing appropriate support for the group to achieve its goal" (p. 18). Ringer encouraged facilitators to pay close attention to their complex mix of feelings, thoughts, actions, and memories. Hence, according to these authors and the facilitator educators in my study (Thomas, 2007), effective group facilitators require high levels of self-awareness. If a facilitator lacks such awareness, he or she may unknowingly contribute to group problems. Effective group facilitators must be able to monitor their own reactions to group processes and group participants. Without this awareness and perspective, they can contribute to defensiveness and over-reactive communication.

Schwarz (2002) provided a useful conceptual framework to help facilitators understand what happens internally when they are faced with challenging situations with groups. His approach, based on the work of Argyris and Schön (1996), used the concept of *theory-in-action* to explore what guides a facilitator's interventions. According to Schwarz, *espoused theory* describes how a facilitator says he or she would like to act in a given situation. In contrast, *theory-in-use* is what actually ends up guiding a facilitator, and it can quickly and powerfully influence how a facilitator interacts with a group, typically outside his or her level of awareness. Facilitators are especially susceptible to this when they find themselves in an embarrassing or tough situation with a group, and they can unknowingly be guided by their theory-in-use when they feel threatened or uncomfortable. In such situations, facilitators typically become very controlling as they impose their perceptions of the group and attempt to minimize the expression of negative feelings to avoid conflict or further loss of control, while espousing the need for rationality (and, particularly, their version of rationality) (Schwarz, 2002). Facilitators' behavior becomes guarded, which can lead to misunderstanding, conflict, mistrust, limited learning, and reduced effectiveness and satisfaction. Hence, when a facilitator lacks the self-awareness to notice what is going on internally, he or she can be susceptible to controlling behaviors and overreactive communication.

Facilitator Contributions to Problem 3: Mismanagement of Power

Most group facilitators would not deliberately set out to misuse the power associated with their role. However, Kirk and Broussine (2000) warned, "Facilitation can become part of a system of oppression and perpetuation of dependant relations, with facilitators becoming unwitting agents of manipulation and managerialism" (p. 14). Protestations of neutrality show either naïveté or cleverness on the part of the facilitator; there will always be tensions around whose interests the facilitator should serve—the group's, the manager's, the organization's, or those of the person who contracted him or her (Kirk & Broussine, 2000). Similarly, Warren (1998) argued that effective group leadership requires facilitators to be more conscious of how their methods can advance or impede social justice. She is critical of facilitation training that focuses only on techniques, and she suggested that emerging facilitators must also focus on the "social and cultural backgrounds . . . and the way their locations in privilege or marginality affect how they teach and facilitate" (p. 23).

Kirk and Broussine (2000) identified four positions of facilitator awareness in which facilitators may find themselves when they work with groups. The articulation of these four positions was intended to help facilitators "consider and review continuously our efficacy, political engagement and our ethics in our work with groups and organisations" (p. 17). The four positions identified are *partial awareness–closed, immobilized awareness, manipulative awareness,* and *partial awareness–open.* The position most relevant to this section is the partial awareness–closed position, in which facilitators are unaware of or closed to the fact that their awareness of the group is limited and incomplete, are unaware of the interpretative lenses through which they see the world, deny the potential abuse of power, are unaware of group pressures on them as facilitators, and are unaware of the influence of the contracting party on them. In an acerbic critique, Kirk and Broussine claimed the "naïveté of such a position does not excuse its incompetence" (p. 18).

Mindell (1995) used the term *rank* to describe the "conscious or unconscious, social or personal ability or power arising from culture, community support, personal psychology and/or spiritual power" (p. 43). All facilitators have some form of rank, but some are more consciously aware of their rank than others, and Mindell's concern is that when a facilitator is "heedless of rank, communications become confused and chronic relationship problems develop" (p. 49). In terms of group structure, facilitators can contribute to the abuses of power when they are unaware of their rank or when they fail to acknowledge the political pressures they may be facing when working with a group. Some examples include when a facilitator panders to the agenda of some group members over that of others because of pressures he or she feels but doesn't acknowledge; when a facilitator makes assumptions about participants based on their ethnicity, race, gender, or other characteristics; or when a facilitator ignores the potential impact of his maleness or whiteness on female or nonwhite participants.

WHAT FACILITATORS CAN DO

The previous sections highlighted how and why facilitators can contribute to some specific problems that groups can experience. They can avoid these situations by participating in a comprehensive, balanced program of facilitator education. Specifically, intentional, person-centered, and critical facilitator education can help a facilitator avoid contributing to the three problems identified by helping them *facilitate intentionally, develop high levels of self-awareness,* and *increase awareness of power and rank.* Hence facilitators can (1) avoid having unclear purposes and misaligned activities by facilitating intentionally, (2) avoid defensive and overreactive communication by developing high levels of self-awareness, and (3) avoid abuses of power by increasing their awareness of power and rank.

Solutions to Problem 1: Facilitate Intentionally

Facilitators act intentionally when they are conscious of what they are doing and why they are doing it. They demonstrate this intentionality through the dialogue used, through an awareness of the group process, by making otherwise hidden processes explicit, by encouraging an awareness of personal stances, and by modeling desired behaviors (Brockbank & McGill, 1998). Robson and Beary (1995) explained that many theories underpin good facilitation practice, and those theories can be used to guide and justify a course of action and predict likely outcomes. The Skilled Facilitator Approach, developed by Schwarz (2002, 2005) is a good example of a theoretically sound approach to facilitation based on a set of core values, assumptions, and principles. His approach attempts to integrate theory and practice, and he argued that facilitators should be able to provide reasons for doing what they do. Using a skill or adopting a strategy without an understanding of the corresponding rationale is problematic—particularly when working with a challenging group. The proponents of explicit intentional facilitator education argued that practitioners who are unable to provide rationales for their practice are disempowered (for example, Brockbank & McGill, 1998; Schwarz, 2002).

The facilitator educators in my study (Thomas, 2007) agreed that there is a need for facilitators to be intentional, although there were differences in how they encouraged their emerging facilitators to practice in this way. One facilitator educator preferred the term *being purposeful,* because she argued the need for facilitators' interventions to be based on conscious purpose.

Others agreed that good facilitation is about choosing practices consciously, guided by values and principles, and that facilitators need to have good reasons for the actions they take with groups. Personally, I think the terms *intentional* and *purposeful* mean much the same thing, and the commitment to these principles demonstrated by the facilitator educators in my study was aligned with similar calls in the literature (Brockbank & McGill, 1998; Killion & Simmons, 1992; Robson & Beary, 1995; Schwarz, 2002, 2005).

In summary, the call for intentionality in the way facilitators lead groups is compelling, and group facilitators who fail to heed such advice may contribute to some of the difficulties that groups may experience. However, this does not rule out the possibility that intuitive processes can also guide a facilitator's practice at times; I have discussed this idea at length elsewhere (Thomas, 2008b). I concur with Claxton (2000), who suggested that intuition has the potential to be extremely useful but that the information it brings should be treated as a hypothesis. It is important to note that facilitators can be taught how to use intuition more reliably and perceptively, which means using intuition intentionally.

Solutions to Problem 2: Develop High Levels of Self-Awareness

Before people can facilitate groups effectively, they must be able to facilitate, or manage, themselves. Hunter (2007) considered the task of learning to facilitate oneself as the most important work facilitators must do. She described this process as "a life journey—a scary and exciting journey that will take you to places within yourself that will surprise, delight, inspire, as well as disturb, horrify and disgust you" (p. 46). Facilitators must learn to cope with the doubts and fears that plague them, and this requires an acceptance of their shortcomings and imperfections.

To varying degrees, all of the facilitator educators in my study focused on helping emerging facilitators develop greater levels of self-awareness and self-management. They maintained that facilitation processes, skills, and tools are built on this foundation because the facilitator is the instrument of effective group leadership. The facilitator educators were not prescriptive about the frameworks or tools emerging facilitators should use to develop their awareness, but they did acknowledge that this process of introspection may be challenging. However, the difficult nature of the journey was not considered an appropriate excuse for avoiding this important inner work. This stance is consistent with that taken by the group counselor education field, where experiential participation in group counseling sessions is a compulsory requirement despite the fact that it may be difficult or awkward for the trainees (Anderson & Price, 2001; Kottler, 2004; Yalom & Leszcz, 2005).

According to Schwarz (2002), most facilitators do not set out to be guided by their theory-in-use; it is what happens when they are stressed or when they feel threatened or out of control. When the facilitator becomes conscious of the values, assumptions, and strategies underpinning such actions, he or she can become aware of the flawed thinking that was previously driving his or her behavior. Fortunately, facilitators do not have to be slaves to their theories-in-use, nor are they forever destined to low levels of self-awareness. Schwarz recommended that facilitators develop an awareness of their internal functioning by slowly increasing the range and length of difficult facilitation situations in which they practice operating from their espoused theory. With appropriate reflection and guidance, emerging facilitators can get better at avoiding reliance on ineffective theory-in-use. Jenkins and Jenkins (2006) described the challenge for facilitators of managing their interior council as an essential discipline for the facilitative leader. They explained that developing such self-management entails becoming aware of the voices in their head and learning to choose the most creative and enabling voices when they are facilitating.

> When you begin to have a profound appreciation of these internal advisors, then you learn to ignore those who dehumanize you or others, and pay attention to the ones who give you courage to be more human. The ones you ignore are not those that you dislike, but those who are not furthering you on your journey. The ones you pay attention to are not necessarily those who you agree with, but those who increase your ability to serve, and offer you the wisdom, skills, and capacity to inspire. (Jenkins & Jenkins, 2006, p. 155)

So when facilitators encounter resistance in the groups with which they are working, they have some choices. They can choose to listen to the critical voice that highlights their inadequacies, imperfections, and shortcomings and that completely blames them for the problem. Typically, this leads to a defensive reaction from the facilitator, which is only likely to escalate the problem. Alternatively, the facilitator could choose to listen to different voices that consider alternative explanations for the resistant behaviors and that don't necessarily require them to take full responsibility for the problem. Advantageously, this allows the facilitator to remain open to the group and increases the likelihood of finding ways forward. This internal dialogue is difficult to monitor in real time, but is at the heart of what it means to develop higher levels of self-awareness.

Solutions to Problem 3: Increase Awareness of Power and Rank

A comprehensive, balanced program of facilitator education will seek to increase a facilitator's awareness of power and rank as a way to avoid problems associated with their misuse. The goal should be for facilitators to develop and practice what Kirk and Broussine (2000) refer to as the position of partial awareness—open. From this perspective, the facilitator is "aware of his or her own limited awareness, actively and openly works with what they think is going on in themselves, in the group and wider system. They will do this vigorously, but cautiously, realising their own partiality" (p. 20). It is important for facilitators to be aware that power and rank are not inherently bad, nor is their abuse inevitable. In fact, if facilitators are aware of their rank, they can use it to their own benefit and the benefit of others as well. In this regard, the objective of critical facilitator education approaches is not to help emerging facilitators transcend the influence of rank, but rather to help them notice their rank and use it constructively. As Mindell (1995) argued, "The facilitator's task is not to do away with the use of rank and power, but to notice them and make their dynamics explicit for the whole group to see" (p. 37).

Also, Mindell (1995) called on facilitators to engage in a special kind of inner work to transform them into "elders who can sit in the fire" (p. 33), which implies that they have developed the ability and self-awareness to cope with hot spots, or conflict in groups. Without this kind of development, facilitators may repress their awareness of group tensions and perpetuate the problems they experience in groups. Similarly, White (1999) argued that "good facilitators are . . . committed to empowering those who are weaker, more vulnerable, marginalised, oppressed or otherwise disadvantaged" (p. 9). At a more practical level, Kirk and Broussine (2000) provided some suggestions to help group facilitators practice with authority and confidence in the context of an increased political awareness. They encouraged facilitators to acknowledge, and be open about, their partial awareness. They also recommend that facilitators develop and practice *reflexivity,* which means "actively noticing in the moment, during the facilitation, what seems to be going on in themselves and in the group, and intervening or not as a consequence" (p. 20).

CONCLUSION

I have highlighted the potential for group facilitators to contribute to some problems groups may experience. Unfortunately, the problems described occur outside the facilitator's immediate level of awareness. However, this does not reduce the negative impacts of these problems or absolve the group facilitator of responsibility. My contention is that a comprehensive, balanced program of facilitator education that focuses on producing intentional facilitators with high levels of personal and political awareness will help counteract the problems identified. My research and personal experience suggest that a balanced emphasis on all four aspects of facilitator education shown in Figure 20.1, over an extended period, is critical to the development of effective group facilitators.

KEY TERMS

Note that the chapter in which the key term appears is displayed in parenthesis.

Accountability-seeking behaviors: Behaviors within a group in which members ask one another for clear commitments on intended actions, completion time frames, and explicit responsibilities. (14)

Acknowledgment: A public expression of the reality or legitimacy of another's status, claims, or grievances. (15)

Actual team diversity: The objective variation of social categorical, informational, and value-related characteristics within teams (for example, number of males and females in a group, variance in age, alignment of diversity attributes). (18)

Advanced interaction analysis (act4teams®): An instrument based on process analysis for coding group discussions. Individual remarks or sense units are classified by one of forty-four comprehensive categories. Discussions can be analyzed concerning positive and negative interaction. Research has linked assessments of discussions with act4teams® to such outcomes as satisfaction, applicability of generated solutions, productivity, and corporate innovation. (3)

Affective conflict: Disagreement and dissention among persons that largely relate to interpersonal or relational differences of an emotional nature. (6)

Affirmative conflict communication: An approach to communicating in conflict through a focus on affirmation rather than deficit-centered language, exploring the "best of what is," strengths, assets, and capacities, rather than problems and deficits. (9)

Alternative story: A story of cooperation that stands in stark contrast to the conflict-bound, dominant story. (15)

Appreciative inquiry: The art and practice of asking questions that strengthens a system's capacity to apprehend, anticipate, and heighten positive potential. (9)

Archetypal energies: The patterns that groups display in how they act, and the emotions that are sanctioned and not sanctioned by the group. Facilitators and other members of the group can often feel or tune into such energies. Associating them with an archetype makes the energies easier to identify. (19)

Archetypes: Models or stereotypes of characters and personalities that are very common in human stories, myths, and experiences. Jung argued that there were a number of universal archetypes. Joseph Campbell and Carol Pearson built on his work to identify the twelve archetypes in the *Hero's Journey*. (19)

Authentic behavior: Behavior that is in line with one's true self; actions that reflect one's core values, beliefs, thoughts, and feelings. (17)

Authenticity: Being the true self or acting as you think. (17)

Authentic leaders: Leaders who are deeply aware of how they think and behave and are perceived by others as being aware of their own and others' values and moral perspectives, knowledge, and strengths; aware of the context in which they operate; and confident, hopeful, optimistic, resilient, and of high moral character. (17)

Authentic relationships: Intimate and transparent relationships that are built on mutual trust. (17)

Balanced processing: The unbiased collection and interpretation of information regarding a person, even if the information is negative. (17)

Brainstorm: A process for a group to come up with a list of ideas quickly. All ideas are valid—no positive or negative comments allowed. Participants do not take time to discuss or debate the ideas until after the list is generated. (7)

Breakout groups: Smaller groups formed to encourage maximum participation and interaction. (7)

Bystand: An action in a group that observes the group as a system. A bystand provides perspective. (10)

Cognitive conflict: Task-focused dissonance arising from questioning and challenging assumptions, premises and conclusions, relationships among concepts, interpretations, and so on (cf. *affective conflict*). (6)

Collaboration tools: Mechanisms used to keep the team coordinated, organized, and on track toward its goals; these include instant messaging, e-rooms, collaborative space, data-sharing applications, electronic bulletin boards, collaborative authoring programs, and project forums. (11)

Complaining cycles: A pattern of complaining and support statements commonly found in group discussions. Complaining circles may be understood as a negative *group mood.* They have a strong negative impact on the discussion outcome and group member satisfaction. Moreover, they diminish team-level and organizational success in the long run. (3)

Confessional tale: A kind of ethnographic writing that goes beyond a realist tale focusing on what the authors think they know as their subject matter and often ignoring how such things came to be known. Confessional tales also take the author or knower as subject matter and attempt to share what it is that they know as a result of their fieldwork. (12)

Confrontation meeting: A meeting in which an entire management group works together to identify information about its major problems, analyzes the underlying causes, develops action plans to correct the problems, and sets a schedule for completed remedial work. (12)

Consensus reality: The level of our normal daily experience. Consensus reality includes experiences that we tend to agree on and focuses on rules, structure, and objectively measurable outcomes and profit. We assume that we can control events. (16)

Consensus workshop: A way to come to consensus in a short period of time through a collective integrated thinking process; the Consensus Workshop Method, one of the core methods of ICA Technology of Participation. (9)

Constellation of theories: A mediator's store of information and beliefs that shapes his or her understanding of people and experiences—made up of core beliefs and values, theories and abstracts, models and approaches, and facts and information. (9)

Constructive alignment: The process of systematically aligning learning activities with desired outcomes. (20)

Courteous compliance: The *interaction archetype* that consists of a *move* and a series of *follows*. Results are produced, but creative alternatives have not been explored. (10)

Covert opposition: The *interaction archetype* that consists of a *move* and a series of *follows* with a hidden *oppose* attached to the follows. The opposition, hidden in the room, is often expressed actively or passively outside the room. (10)

Cultural informant: Someone who is bicultural and either is from or has lived extensively in the culture you want to learn more about. (4)

Cultural markers: Identifiers of the basic areas of differences between cultures; identifying features that are distinctive. (4)

Decision making: The act of choice in which individuals and groups engage when they have a felt need to move from an existing, nonpreferred state to one that is preferable, as in the case of replacing a policy that is not serving intended objectives with one that shows promise of doing so. (8)

Deconstruction: The process of unpacking the taken-for-granted assumptions and ideas underlying social practices that masquerade as truth or reality. It is achieved by bringing to light the gaps and inconsistencies in a dominant story so that acceptance of the story's message or logic no longer appears inevitable. Deconstruction is less adversarial and more playful than critique or confrontation. (15)

Deep Democracy: An attitude that focuses on the awareness of voices that are both central and marginal. (16)

Deep-level diversity: Unobservable differences among people in regard to their opinions, attitudes, values, and so on (cf. *surface-level diversity*). (6)

Deep listening: Analytical listening for specific contents in conversations, taking into account the context and trigger, and operational mechanisms of the terms in the stories of the participants. (15)

Defensiveness: Behavior intended to protect oneself from threats known or unknown. (1)

Demands: Clear requests from leaders and managers for the achievement of measurable results in an improvement area. (14)

Developmentally and incidentally acquired characteristics: Differences among people that are a function of the normal maturation process or that are acquired through exposure to and experience in a given social milieu. (6)

Dialogue: Conversation intended to bring out multiple perspectives on an issue, sometimes with the intention of reconciling differences. (7)

Dignity needs: Essential human relational needs of belonging, recognition, self-determination, and security, which must be met for life in dignity, beyond mere survival. (15)

Discourse: A set of ideas embodied as structuring statements that underlie and give meaning to social practices, personal experience, and organizations or institutions. Discourses often include the taken-for-granted assumptions that allow us to know how to "go on" in social situations of all kinds. They are linguistic in nature (provided that language is taken to include nonverbal as well as verbal practices). (15)

Diversity: Human differences at a primary level (immutable characteristics, such as age and ethnicity) and a secondary level (relatively changeable dimensions such as socioeconomic status, knowledge, values); differences between individuals on any attribute that may lead to the perception that another person is different from the self. (7, 18)

Eldership: A role and a metaskill: an ability to care for others and the whole system simultaneously that includes an awareness of which role you are in, a feeling connection with others, and an ability to demonstrate *fluidity*. (16)

Electronic performance monitoring: The use of technology to monitor and supervise employee performance; examples include monitoring e-mail content, monitoring Web site visits, listening in on telephone conversations, and counting keypresses. (11)

Emergent leadership: An initial attempt to develop or express leadership, which is experienced in momentary signals of power, which—because they are not yet understood and may not be initially well directed—are often seen as difficulties, confusion, or a lack of respect for authority. (16)

Emergent level: Experiences that are subjective, not measurable, and not in our control. They include team work and relationship issues, experiences of rank differences, somatic experiences, and our assumptions about each other. (16)

Emotional contagion: In group research, a process in which one group member's mood, expressed through interaction, "wears off" on other group members. These others adopt the initial mood unconsciously or via conscious comparison processes, and follow with similar remarks. Emotional contagion can explain the development of *complaining cycles*. (3)

Empathy: The ability to see the world from the perspective of others and evaluate what they have done as a function of the circumstances in which they were operating. (15)

Entanglement: The symmetrical relationship between polar roles that lead people toward a fluid dance of *rotational symmetry*. (16)

Escalation of hostility: A sequence of events where interpersonally hostile acts in work groups begin to escalate into more severe bullying and persistent abuse (minor hostilities leading to extreme victimization). Often, a target finds himself or herself in a low-power position and is victimized to the point that he or she experiences severe strain and is expulsed from the work context. This pattern of events tends to occur if the group context is permissive toward hostility and no intervention is enacted to prevent escalation. (5)

Espoused theory: The thoughts, ideas, or principles that a person claims to draw on to guide his or her practice in a given situation. (20)

Ethnocentrism: A belief that one's own culture is central to reality. (4)

Ethnorelativism: A belief that culture is experienced in the context of other cultures. (4)

Everyday democracy: A national organization that provides materials and technical assistance to communities working to solve public issues by engaging its community in dialogue and action. (7)

Facilitator: A professional who designs and manages a process that helps a group accomplish its work while minimizing problems within the group. The facilitator(s) and group members share responsibility for progressing toward the goals of the group. A facilitator explains his or her role; sets a relaxed and welcoming tone; introduces herself or himself, but does not share personal opinions or push an agenda; does not take sides; makes everyone feel that his or her opinions are valid and welcome; does not use his or her personal experiences to make a point or to get people talking; uses probing questions to deepen the discussion; brings up issues that participants have not mentioned; and reminds participants of comments they shared in earlier sessions. (4, 7)

Facilitators: To design and manage a process that helps a group accomplish its work while minimizing problems within the group. The facilitator(s) and group member share responsibility for progressing toward the goals of the group. (4)

Facilitator education: The process by which facilitators develop the skills, knowledge, awareness, and experience to facilitate groups effectively. (20)

Facilitator function: A role that is ontologically built in to all groups that provides a natural tendency toward observation, facilitation, and emergence of awareness within the group. (16)

Field: A group of signals, tensions, roles, and tendencies. An emotional atmosphere or a felt sense of a particular shared a causal consciousness. (16)

First training: The development of mastery in noticing and tracking signals; forming structural hypotheses from the patterns; creating interventions from these; and carefully noting the feedback from the group, which will either confirm the hypothesis or suggest another direction. (16)

Fluidity: The ability to consciously shift between different roles and to avoid being grabbed by a role. (16)

Follow: An action in a group that supports one of the other actions (*move, oppose, bystand*). A follow enables completion. (10)

Founder's syndrome: Nonprofit organizations' tendency to becoming dependent on the person(s) who initially started the organization. As organizations grow from entrepreneurial to established, some founders have difficulty realizing the need for changing the way they lead and manage the organization. This can often lead to the founder becoming anxious and defensive, which can lead to passive-aggressive behavior and the formation of alliances and factions by both the board and staff. (12)

Fractionation: The process in which large, intractable conflicts are broken down into smaller emblematic ones, and through which the resolution of these smaller conflicts develops mutual trust and points the way toward resolution of the larger issues. (14)

Free attention: The part of our awareness not caught up with thoughts, feelings (emotions), and body sensations. (20)

Functional subgroup: An informal identity assumed by those who by their words and actions further the accomplishment of a group's task. (1)

Ghost role: A strong unoccupied role in a *field* that affects the group's dynamics but can't yet be directly interacted with. (16)

Group forces: Variables present in the group that impact their ability to produce desired results. (10)

Group mood: Synchronized moods of individuals. Group mood can emerge through verbal interaction between group members. The underlying process is *emotional contagion.* (3)

Group perspective on workplace hostility: A framework for understanding interpersonal hostility at work that illustrates how groups may precipitate and sustain high levels of hostility. This perspective advocates attention to hostility-promoting forces within the group processes (that is, communication patterns, conflict climate, identity, and emotions), group structure (that is, leadership, power distribution, work stressors), and group context (that is, harassment policies, appraisal and reward systems, expectations and training on respect). (5)

Group process: The sequence of planned and emergent actions by which collections of individuals who see themselves as constituting an entity perform tasks that have as their function facilitating the fulfillment of acknowledged goals, or moving from an existing state to a preferred state. A facilitated event where group members work together to bring awareness to the tensions, roles, ghosts, and dynamics that pattern the group's dynamics. (8, 16)

Hall of mirrors: The *interaction archetype* that consists of an initial *move* followed by a long series of *bystands*. Until the pattern is shifted, the group is lost in a hall of bystanding mirrors. (10)

The Heroes' Journey: An analytical tool and facilitation process, drawn from Joseph Campbell's work on one of the dominant structures of stories and myths, which helps groups identify and move through the transitions in their development. (19)

Highly developed organizational context: A context in which there is open communication, a high level of support, and open access to information. It is a caring, strength-based, and ethical climate. (17)

High-performing teams: Teams whose productive output meets the standards of relevant stakeholders, whose work processes enhance the team's viability, and whose ongoing experience contributes to group members' personal well-being. (11)

Historical conciliation: An applied conflict resolution approach that utilizes historical narratives to resolve conflicts, make peace, and maintain peace. Historical conciliation can involve many different methodologies and initiatives, including mediation, sustained dialogue, support of public commemoration activities, and public diplomacy to support adversaries' efforts to use their histories to resolve their conflict. (15)

Historical memory: Collective awareness of select historical facts, events, national myths, heroes, mission, and so on, transmitted via political leadership, education, and media systems; passed on within families and through opinion leaders; and so on. Historical memory is sometimes reflective and critical; oftentimes, however, it is shaped by personal, social, and intellectual factors that select facts out of the virtual infinity of facts. (15)

Historical timeline: A tool for analysis of the underlying reasons for the "historical hatred" of groups in conflict and also for outlining solutions to the conflict through a structured mediated discussion of events alive in the historical memories of the involved groups. (15)

Hot spot: A moment in a group process when there is a strong reaction. (16)

Identity-based conflict: Conflict revolving around values, beliefs, and needs that are perceived as fundamental to person's or group's existence. (15)

Immediate intervention for hostility: An intervention strategy that puts highest priority on the protection of stigmatized employees, hearing from all parties, mediation, and other immediate conflict resolution techniques. This process should be followed by the implementation of a long-term prevention strategy. (5)

Individual forces: Variables from individual group members—for example, thoughts, mental models, beliefs, feelings, and deeper critical self-images—that influence the group's ability to produce desired results. (10)

Informal subgroups: Silent coalitions that form around statements made in meetings. Subgroups remain invisible unless people choose to support or oppose one another or until someone asks an "Anyone else" question. (1)

Innate characteristics: Personal attributes largely determined by biology, comprising surface-level attributes such as gender, height, and skin color. (6)

Intentionality: The ability to provide a rationale or theoretical explanation for an action or practice. (20)

Intentionally acquired characteristics: Skills and knowledge deliberately acquired and developed. (6)

Interaction archetype: An observable sequence of actions that occurs repetitively in a group and has significant impact on the group's ability to perform. (10)

Interaction sequence: An observable sequence of actions in groups. (10)

Interindividual-intergroup discontinuity effect: The finding that group-on-group interactions tend to be more competitive and less cooperative than one-on-one interactions. (13)

Interior council: The voices, sayings, or advice that one hears in one's own head. (20)

Internalized regulation: The setting of and adhering to internal standards, rather than being subject to external forces or expectations. (17)

Interpersonally hostile work groups: Groups in organizational settings that are characterized by high levels of negative interpersonal actions that harm members of the group. These negative acts include behaviors that have been referred to as harassment, bullying, mobbing, aggression, emotional abuse, social undermining, and incivility, among others. These acts may be perpetrated by a single individual or multiple members, and may be directed at an individual or several members. They often become part of the group's norms, and targets may be victimized frequently over a long period of time. (5)

The Kantor Four-Player Model: An empirically based model of face-to-face interaction. (10)

Marginalized members: Group members who do not see that they belong or matter, or perceive that others care; such marginalization may be due to race, ethnicity, nationality, socioeconomic background, or language. (4)

Mattering: Our belief, right or wrong, that we matter to someone else. (4)

Media richness: The ability of a medium to carry information along primarily two axes; data carrying capacity refers to the ability of the medium to transmit information, and symbol carrying capacity refers to the medium's ability to carry information about the individuals who are communicating. Videoconferencing is an example of a rich medium; e-mail is an impoverished medium. (11)

Minimal intervention: The least action required to help a group stay focused on its task. (1)

Mixed-motive situation: Situation containing a mixture of competitive and cooperative incentives. These situations typically involve a conflict of interest such that what is best for one side conflicts with what is best for the other side. (13)

Move: An action in a group that initiates a sequence of interactions. A move provides direction. (10)

Multiattribute utility (MAU): A quantitatively based, structured modeling approach in which potential alternatives are assessed against weighted, and hierarchically ordered, utility functions. (6)

Multiculturally sensitive facilitation: Facilitation that intentionally considers differences in the knowledge and meaning systems of group members and the implications of those differences for facilitation. (4)

Mutual stalemate: A condition in which two or more groups, interdependent with one another to achieve a common goal, defer responsibilities for progress and adaptation to the other group(s). (14)

Narrative mediation: A mediation approach (originating in the field of family therapy) that works with the stories of people in conflict and uses mediated storytelling as a tool for facilitating conflict resolution. (15)

Nontraditional diversity: Diversity defined specifically in regard to the mission-based needs of a group or an organization. Within this perspective, a diverse group would be one that collectively encompasses differences in knowledge, perspective, and the like that are salient to a group's tasks. (6)

Oppose: An action in a group that challenges one of the other actions (*move, follow, bystand*). An oppose offers creative correction. (10)

Parking lot: A list maintained as a way of "storing" issues that may be off topic for the particular session. By placing an issue on the parking lot, the facilitator can move the group forward while giving the participant confidence that the issue will not be forgotten. (7)

Partial awareness–open: A state in which the group facilitator is aware of her own limited awareness, and actively and openly works with what she thinks is going on in herself, the group, and the wider system—while also recognizing her own partiality. (20)

Participatory action development: A process in which the participants in a long-term dialogue or project arrive at consensus on what activities they wish to undertake as a group and what actions will come out of the entire process. (15)

Perceived team diversity: The subjective view that people have of the composition of their team on any potential social categorical, informational, and value-related characteristic. (18)

Point-counterpoint: The *interaction archetype* that consists of a series of *moves* and *opposes*. Unless the pattern shifts, no results are produced. (10)

Polarity: Two opposing roles. (16)

Pre-emerging level: Experiences that are sometimes barely noticeable, like an atmosphere or the most deeply held values that we can't quite articulate. It is an indescribable yet somehow sentient essence like a feeling, a tension, a joy. (16)

Prevention of hostility: A long-term prevention strategy that addresses each of the precipitating and sustaining forces for hostility illustrated in the *group perspective on workplace hostility.* This involves ensuring that the organizational context and supporting group structures are appropriate before attempting to change interpersonal processes through task and conflict coaching. (5)

Prisoner's dilemma game (PDG): A *mixed-motive situation* in which two people can each attempt to achieve better outcomes (for example, more money) by competing instead of cooperating, but in which mutual competition is detrimental to both people. (13)

Problem-saturated story: The story that a party presents to a mediator in which the conflict is so dominant that there at first appears little sign of an alternative story. (15)

Process: Process is defined as the constant flow of information, which we experience through signals, body symptoms, relationship experiences, and other channels of information flow. (16)

Process structure: The patterns in verbal and nonverbal communications, movement, roles, emotional cues, and somatic experiences, and the symmetry between the signals, their informational patterns, the underlying processes, and the way they manifest in terms of individual behavior and group dynamics. (16)

Projection: Attributing to others unconscious aspects of oneself. The ascription or projection of one person's or the group's thoughts, emotions, and mental attributes onto another person or group. In classical psychology, projection is seen as a defense mechanism. More recently, it has become regarded as an important element of social interaction and empathy. (1, 19)

Psychological capital: Self-efficacy, optimism, hope, and resiliency. (17)

Psychologically safe space: In the context of teams, an environment where team members feel free to provide honest opinions without fear of retribution by the other team members. (11)

Psychological rank: A sense of ease that someone has, even in difficult situations, that comes from knowing that she or he will be able to engage in a tense scene while also protecting herself or himself. This includes an ability to track and believe in one's own experience, stay awake, and remain fluid when under attack. (16)

Rank: The conscious or unconscious social or personal ability or power arising from culture, community support, personal psychology, spiritual power, or a combination of these. (20)

Rational and experiential objectives: The intent or practical goal of an event or facilitated session; the practical product—what the group needs to know, understand, plan, produce, do, or decide (rational objective). The inner impact and overall experience of the group; the mood and tone (experiential objective). (9)

Rational choice: A set of conscious actions that have the greatest perceived or demonstrable likelihood of achieving desired outcomes relative to other sets of actions that may be available to those deciding. (8)

Relational transparency: The capability of being open, sincere, and intimate and establishing mutual trust in close relationships. (17)

Resiliency: The ability to keep going and bounce back when one is beset by problems and adversity. (17)

Resistance to change: A state of affairs that people who want to do something ascribe to those whom they consider reluctant to go along. (1)

Resource-based conflict: Conflict that revolves around distribution, access to, and control over tangible resources or services. Also often referred to as interest-based conflict. (15)

Rotational symmetry: The complex dance of various roles and states of consciousness in a fluid system. (16)

Second training: The development of mastery in following something mysterious and intimate, even when it can't be described by signals and structural patterns. It is ineffable but leads to the core of a group's self-organizing tendency. (16)

Self-awareness: The conscious awareness and understanding of the assumptions, emotions, values, motives, and goals one holds and where they originate. (17, 20)

Self-efficacy: The confidence to take on challenging tasks and put in the necessary effort to succeed in them. (17)

Self-regulation: The ability to set internal standards and to evaluate discrepancies between such standards and potential or actual outcomes. In other words, self-regulation is behaving in accordance with inner thoughts and feelings by regulating the differences between internal standards and actual outcomes. (17)

Sequence analysis: A statistical procedure to calculate transition probabilities, that is, the probability of a specific event occurring after another specific event between different events. In group interaction, sequence analysis can be used to determine whether certain communication patterns such as *complaining cycles* occur significantly more often than chance would indicate. (3)

Social capital: The collective value of networks and the inclination to help one another that arises from those networks. (4)

Social constructivism: The movement in the social sciences that stresses the role played by language in the production of meaning. A central tenet is that people produce through *discourse* the social conditions by which their thoughts, feelings, and actions are determined. In this way, meaning is made in social contexts rather than given. (15)

Social forces: Variables from the organization, business, and larger environment of a group that influence the group's ability to produce desired results. (10)

Spiritual rank: The ability to ground oneself in something that comes from beyond space and time, giving one access to an inner sense of meaning. (16)

Split: An action that causes people to lose sight of the task by connecting with each other on the basis of mutual stereotypes. (1)

Stereotype: Images, beliefs, or assumptions about a group of people that do not take into consideration a person's individual differences. (7)

Stereotypical subgroup: An informal identity projected on others to reinforce an unfounded bias or assumption. (1)

Street power: An ability to be comfortable in a group that gives you intense negative feedback. (16)

Study Circle: A small, diverse group of people who meet several times to find common ground on a key public issue. Neutral facilitators and discussion materials help the participants examine issues from all sides and move from dialogue to action. (7)

Surface-level diversity: Diversity largely defined on the basis of observable differences, including, for example, gender, skin color, and age. Also referred to as demographic diversity and biodemographic diversity (cf. *deep-level diversity*). (6)

Sustained dialogue: A dialogue process that convenes the same group of participants over a long period of time (months or years) and seeks to move through understanding toward collective action. (15)

Sympathy: An understanding of somebody's feelings; a feeling of closeness and concern for the other person. Not to be confused with empathy, which entails also sharing those feelings and viewing the situation from the other person's position. (15)

Team coaching: Coaching that involves the whole team as a system. Team coaching is a process rather than a single intervention. The focus lies on the daily work of the team, integrating both supervisor coaching and various team intervention elements to improve team interaction and performance in the long term. (3)

Team functioning: Important organizational outcomes such as team performance, information exchange and processing, commitment, organizational citizenship behavior, conflict, and worker morale. (18)

Team leader communication about diversity: All the references made by the leader to the composition of the team when addressing the team. (18)

Team leader diversity beliefs: The leader's beliefs about the value of diversity for work group functioning. (18)

Technical eclecticism: The use of practices without a clear understanding of the reasons for using them. (20)

Theory-in-use: The subconscious thoughts, ideas, or principles that actually guide our actions—often outside our level of awareness. (20)

Timespirit: Roles that change with time, sometimes quite rapidly, and often move from one individual or group to another. (16)

Traditional diversity: Diversity defined principally on legal or ethical grounds. When approached from a legal perspective, diversity might be assessed as compliance with legislation. From an ethical perspective, emphasis is on maintaining an environment that is fair and that affords all opportunities for development and advancement. Diversity is likely operationalized as observable differences (cf. *nontraditional diversity*). (6)

Transference: Behavior similar to projection, but the feelings, emotions, and mental attributes projected are repressed and unresolved and normally stem from childhood or earlier experience. This makes it more difficult for individuals and groups to identify transference than projection. (19)

Voice: The capacity to speak on one's own behalf, in terms that are not given by others. (15)

REFERENCES

INTRODUCTION

Belasen, A. T. (2008). *The theory and practice of corporate communication: A competing values perspective*. Thousand Oaks, CA: Sage.

Campbell, J. P. (1977). On the nature of organizational effectiveness. In P. S. Goodman & J. M. Pennings (Eds.), *New perspectives on organizational effectiveness*. San Francisco: Jossey-Bass.

Cook, J. (1999). *The book of positive quotations*. New York: Gramercy/Random House.

Gladstein, D. (1984). Groups in context: A model of task group effectiveness. *Administrative Science Quarterly*, 29, 499–517.

Hare, A. P. (1976). *Handbook of small group research*. New York: Free Press.

Lipscomb, A. E., & Bergh, A. A. (Eds.). (1903–04). *The writings of Thomas Jefferson, memorial edition*. Washington, DC: Thomas Jefferson Memorial Association.

McGrath, J. E. (1964). *Social psychology: A brief introduction*. New York: Holt, Rinehart and Winston.

Parsons, T. (1959). General theory of sociology. In R. Merton, L. Broom, & L. S. Cottrell (Eds.), *Sociology today: Problems and prospects*. New York: Basic Books.

Quinn, R. E., & Rohrbaugh, J. (1983). A spatial model of effectiveness criteria: Towards a competing values approach to organizational analysis. *Management Science*, 29, 363–377.

Rohrbaugh, J. (1983). The competing values approach: Innovation and effectiveness in the Job Service. In R. H. Hall & R. E. Quinn (Eds.), *Organizational theory and public policy*. Thousand Oaks, CA: Sage.

Rohrbaugh, J. (1989). A competing values approach to the study of group decision support systems. In R. H. Sprague (Ed.), *Proceedings of the twenty-second annual Hawaii International Conference on System Sciences* (Vol. 4, pp. 158–166). Kailua-Kona, Hawaii, January 3–6.

Rohrbaugh, J. (2005). Assessing the effectiveness of group decision processes. In S. Schuman (Ed.), *The IAF handbook of group facilitation: Best practices from the leading organization in facilitation.* San Francisco: Jossey-Bass.

Rousseau, V., Aube, C., & Savoic, A. (2006). Teamwork behaviors: A review and an integration of frameworks. *Small Group Research, 37,* 540–570.

Schwarz, R. (2002). *The skilled facilitator: A comprehensive resource for consultants, facilitators, managers, trainers, and coaches.* San Francisco: Jossey-Bass.

Shaw, G. B. (2008). *Pygmalion.* Charleston, SC: Forgotten Books. (Original work published 1913.)

CHAPTER 1

Asch, S. (1952). *Social psychology.* Upper Saddle River, NJ: Prentice Hall.

Agazarian, Y. (1997). *Systems-centered theory for groups.* New York: Guilford Press.

Faucheux, C. (1984, October 10–13). Leadership, power and influence within social systems. In Suresh Srivastva, *The Functioning of the Executive.* Symposium. Case Western Reserve University, Cleveland.

CHAPTER 2

Ancona, D., & Bresman, H. (2007). *X-Teams: How to build teams that lead, innovate and succeed.* Boston: Harvard Business School Press.

Ancona, D., & Caldwell, D. (1992). Bridging the boundary: External activity and performance in organizational teams. *Administrative Science Quarterly, 37,* 634–655.

Bunderson, J., & Sutcliffe, K. (2002). Why some teams emphasize learning more than others: Evidence from business unit management teams. In E. Mannix & H. Sondak (Eds.), *Research on Managing Groups and Teams,* 4, 49–84. New York: Elsevier Science.

Cummings, J. (2004). Work groups, structural diversity, and knowledge sharing in a global organization. *Management Science, 50,* 352–364.

Gladstein, D. (1984). Groups in context: A model of task group effectiveness. *Administrative Science Quarterly,* 29, 433–442.

Reagans, R., & Zuckerman, E. (2001). Networks, diversity, and productivity: The social capital of corporate R&D teams. *Organization Science,* 12, 502–517.

Williams, K., & O'Reilly, C. (1998). Demography and diversity in organizations: A review of 40 years of research. In B. Staw & R. Sutton (Eds.), *Research in Organizational Behavior,* 20, 77–140. Greenwich, CT: JAI Press.

CHAPTER 3

Alberts, J. K., & Driscoll, G. (1992). Containment versus escalation: The trajectory of couples' conversational complaints. *Western Journal of Communication, 56,* 394–412.

Bales, R. F. (1950). *Interaction process analysis: A method for the study of small groups.* Chicago: University of Chicago Press.
Barsade, S. G. (2002). The ripple effect: Emotional contagion and its influence on group behavior. *Administrative Science Quarterly, 47,* 644–675.
Bartel, C. A., & Saavedra, R. (2000). The collective construction of work group moods. *Administrative Science Quarterly, 45,* 197–231.
Bavelas, J. B., Black, A., Lemery, C. R., & Mullett, J. (1987). Motor mimicry as primitive empathy. In N. Eisenberg & J. Strayer (Eds.), *Empathy and its development: Cambridge studies in social and emotional development* (pp. 317–338). New York: Cambridge University Press.
Bernieri, F. J., Reznick, J. S., & Rosenthal, R. (1988). Synchrony, pseudosynchrony, and dissynchrony: Measuring the entrainment process in mother-infant dyads. *Journal of Personality and Social Psychology, 54,* 243–253.
Brashers, D. E. (1991). Argument and organizational complaints: Application of the structuration coding scheme. In D. W. Parsons (Ed.), *Argument in controversy: Proceedings of the seventh SCA/AFA conference on argumentation* (pp. 147–153). Annandale, VA: The Speech Communication Association.
Brodbeck, F., Anderson, N., & West, M. (2000). *TKI Teamklima-Inventar* [Team climate inventory]. Göttingen: Hogrefe.
Forgas, J. P. (1992). On mood and peculiar people: Affect and person typicality in impression formation. *Journal of Personality and Social Psychology, 62,* 863–875.
Fornell, C., & Wernerfelt, B. (1988). A model for customer complaint management. *Marketing Science, 7,* 287–298.
Garrett, D. E., Meyers, R. A., & West, L. (1996). Comparing the communication characteristics of high competence and low competence customer service representatives. *Journal of Consumer Satisfaction/Dissatisfaction and Complaining Behavior, 9,* 64–74.
Garrett, D. E., Meyers, R. A., & West, L. (1997). Sex differences and consumer complaints: Do men and women communicate differently when they complain to customer service representatives? *Journal of Consumer Satisfaction/Dissatisfaction and Complaining Behavior, 10,* 116–130.
Gersick, C.J.G. (1991). Revolutionary change theories: A multilevel exploration of the punctuated equilibrium paradigm. *Academy of Management Review, 16,* 10–36.
Hackman, J. R. (1992). Group influences on individuals in organizations. In M. D. Dunnette & L. M. Hough (Eds.), *Handbook of industrial and organizational psychology* (pp. 199–267). Palo Alto, CA: Consulting Psychologists Press.
Hall, B. J. (1991). An elaboration of the structural possibilities for engaging in alignment episodes. *Communication Monographs, 58,* 79–100.
Hatfield, E., Cacioppo, J. T., & Rapson, R. L. (1994). *Emotional contagion.* New York: Cambridge University Press.

Hsee, C. K., Hatfield, E., & Chemtomb, C. (1992). Assessments of the emotional states of others: Conscious judgments versus emotional contagion. *Journal of Social and Clinical Psychology, 11*, 119–128.

Jordan, P. J., Lawrence, S. A., & Troth, A. C. (2006). The impact of negative mood on team performance. *Journal of Management & Organization, 12*, 131–145.

Kauffeld, S. (2006a). Self-directed work groups and their impact on team competence. *Journal of Occupational and Organizational Psychology, 79*, 1–21.

Kauffeld, S. (2006b). *Kompetenzen messen, bewerten, entwickeln* [Measuring, evaluating, and developing competencies]. Stuttgart: Schäffer-Poeschel.

Kauffeld, S. (2007). Jammern oder Lösungsexploration—Eine sequenzanalytische Betrachtung des Interaktionsprozesses in betrieblichen Gruppen bei der Bewältigung von Optimierungsaufgaben [Complaining or solution seeking—a sequence analysis of problem-solving interaction in industrial groups]. *Zeitschrift für Arbeits- und Organisationspsychologie, 51*, 55–67.

Kauffeld, S., Lorenzo, G., Montasem, K., & Lehmann-Willenbrock, N. (2009). act4-teams®: Die nächste Generation der Teamentwicklung [act4teams®: The next generation of team development]. In S. Kauffeld, S. Grote, & E. Frieling (Eds.), *Handbuch Kompetenzentwicklung* (pp. 191–215). Stuttgart: Schäffer-Poeschel.

Kauffeld, S., & Meyers, R. A. (2009). Complaint and solution-oriented circles: Interaction patterns in work group discussions. *European Journal of Work and Organizational Psychology, 18*, 267–294.

Kelly, J. R., & Spoor, J. R. (2006). Affective influences in groups. In J. Forgas (Ed.), *Affect in social thinking and behavior* (pp. 311–325). New York: Psychology Press.

Laird, J. D. (1984). The real role of facial response in the experience of emotion: A reply to Tourangeau and Ellsworth, and others. *Journal of Personality and Social Psychology, 47*, 909–917.

Larsen, R. J., & Diener, E. (1992). Problems and promises with the circumplex model of emotion. *Review of Personality and Social Psychology, 13*, 25–59.

Liker, J. (2006). *The Toyota way fieldbook*. New York: McGraw-Hill.

Mangold, P. (2005). *Interact handbook*. Arnstorf: Mangold Software & Consulting.

McIntosh, D. N., Druckman, D., & Zajonc, R. B. (1994). Socially-induced affect. In D. Druckman & R. A. Bjork (Eds.), *Learning, remembering, believing: Enhancing human performance* (pp. 251–276, 364–371). Washington, DC: National Academy Press.

Neininger, A., & Kauffeld, S. (2009). Kompetenzen durch Reflexionen im Team? Ein Beispiel aus der Produktion [Competencies through reflection in the team? An industry example]. In S. Kauffeld (Ed.), *Handbuch Kompetenzentwicklung* (pp. 233–255). Stuttgart: Schäffer-Poeschel.

Newell, S. E., & Stutman, R. K. (1988). The social confrontation episode. *Communication Monographs, 55*, 266–285.

Nielsen, T. M., Sundstrom, E. D., & Halfhill, T. R. (2005). Group dynamics and effectiveness: Five years of applied research. In S. Wheelan (Ed.), *The handbook of group research and practice* (pp. 285–311). Thousand Oaks, CA: Sage.

Sellers, P. (1988). Tapping into gripes and profits. *Management Review, 77,* 51–53.

Sims, D. E., Salas, E., & Burke, C. S. (2005). Promoting effective team performance through training. In S. Wheelan (Ed.), *The handbook of group research and practice* (pp. 407–425). Thousand Oaks, CA: Sage.

Sundstrom, E., McIntyre, M., Halfhill, T., & Richards, H. (2000). Work groups: From the Hawthorne studies to work teams of the 1990s and beyond. *Group Dynamics: Theory, Research, and Practice, 4,* 44–67.

Tannenbaum, S. I., Beard, R. L., & Salas, E. (1992). Team building and its influence on team effectiveness: An examination of conceptual and empirical developments. In K. Kelley (Ed.), *Issues, theory, and research in industrial/organizational psychology,* 82, 117–153. Amsterdam: Elsevier Science.

Watson, D., & Tellegen, A. (1985). Toward a consensual structure of mood. *Psychological Bulletin, 98,* 219–235.

Wheelan, S. A. (1999). *Creating effective teams.* Thousand Oaks, CA: Sage.

CHAPTER 4

Beegle, D. (2006). *See poverty . . . be the difference!* Portland, OR: Communication Across Barriers.

Bennett, M., Hammer, M., & Wiseman, R. (2003). Measuring intercultural sensitivity: The intercultural development inventory. *International Journal of Cultural Relations, 27,* 421–443.

Distefano, J. J., & Maznevski, M. L. (2000). Creating value with diverse teams in global management. *Organizational Dynamics, 29*(1), 45–63.

Hammer, M. R. (2002). *Intercultural conflicts style inventory (ICS) interpretive guide.* Portland, OR: Intercultural Communication Institute.

Hofstede, G. (1983). The cultural relativity of organizational practices and theories. *Journal of International Business Studies, 14*(2), 75–89.

Hofstede, G. (2003). *Culture's consequences: Comparing values, behaviors, institutions and organizations across nations* (2nd ed.). Thousand Oaks, CA: Sage.

Hofstede, G. (2005). *Cultures and organizations: Software of the mind* (2nd ed.). New York: McGraw-Hill. Retrieved December 14, 2008, from http://www.geert-hofstede.com/hofstede_dimensions.php.

Hogan, C. (2005). Successfully facilitating multicultural groups. In S. Schuman (Ed.), *The IAF handbook of group facilitation: Best practices from the leading organization in facilitation* (pp. 255–280). San Francisco: Jossey-Bass.

Northouse, P. (2001). *Leadership: Theory and practice.* Thousand Oaks, CA: Sage.

Pedersen, P. (2000). *A handbook for developing multicultural awareness.* Alexandria, VA: American Counseling Association.

Putnam, R. (2000). *Bowling alone: Collapse and revival of American community.* New York: Simon & Schuster.

Schauber, A. C. (2002). *Working with differences in communities.* Corvallis: Oregon State University Extension Service.

Scheffert, D., Horntvedt, J., & Chazdon, S. (2007). *Social capital and our community.* St. Paul: University of Minnesota. Retrieved December 14, 2008, from http://www.extension.umn.edu/community/00007.pdf.

Schlossberg, N. K. (1989). Marginality and mattering: Key issues in building community. In D. C. Roberts (Ed.), *Designing campus activities to foster a sense of community.* New Directions for Student Services, no. 48. San Francisco: Jossey-Bass.

Taylor, S. (2007). *Diversity and intercultural communication.* Paper presented at a conference at Medica. Woodbury, MN: Sentient Consultants.

Ting-Toomey, S. (1999). *Communication across cultures.* New York: Guilford Press.

CHAPTER 5

Andersson, L. M., & Pearson, C. M. (1999). Tit for tat? The spiraling effect of incivility in the workplace. *Academy of Management Review, 24,* 452–471.

Aquino, K. (2000). Structural and individual determinants of workplace victimization: The effects of hierarchical status and conflict management style. *Journal of Management, 26,* 171–193.

Bandura, A. (1977). *Social learning theory.* Upper Saddle River, NJ: Prentice Hall.

Bell, M. P., Quick, J. C., & Cycyota, C. S. (2002). Assessment and prevention of sexual harassment of employees: An applied guide to creating healthy organizations. *International Journal of Selection and Assessment, 10,* 160–167.

Berdahl, J. L. (2007). Harassment based on sex: Protecting social status in the context of gender hierarchy. *Academy of Management Review, 32,* 641–658.

Bies, R. J., & Tripp, T. M. (2001). A passion for justice: The rationality and morality of revenge. In R. Cropanzano (Ed.), *Justice in the workplace: From theory to practice* (Vol. 2, pp. 197–208). Mahwah, NJ: Erlbaum.

Björkqvist, K., Østerman, K., & Lagerspetz, K.M.J. (1994). Sex differences in covert aggression among adults. *Aggressive Behavior, 20,* 27–33.

Bowling, N. A., & Beehr, T. A. (2006). Workplace harassment from the victim's perspective: A theoretical model and meta-analysis. *Journal of Applied Psychology, 91,* 998–1012.

Brown, M. E., & Trevino, L. K. (2006). Socialized charismatic leadership, values congruence, and deviance in work groups. *Journal of Applied Psychology, 91,* 954–962.

Cortina, L. M. (2007). Unseen injustice: Incivility as modern discrimination in organizations. *Academy of Management Review, 33,* 55–75.

Davenport, N., Schwartz, R. D., & Elliott, G. P. (2002). *Mobbing: Emotional abuse in the American workplace* (2nd ed.). Ames, IA: Civil Society Publishing.

Duffy, M. K., Ganster, D. C., Shaw, J. D., Johnson, J. L., & Pagon, M. (2006). The social context of undermining behavior at work. *Organizational Behavior and Human Decision Processes, 101*, 105–126.

Dunlop, P. D., & Lee, K. (2004). Workplace deviance, organizational citizenship behavior, and business unit performance: The bad apples do spoil the whole barrel. *Journal of Organizational Behavior, 25*, 67–80.

Einarsen, S. (1999). The nature and causes of bullying at work. *International Journal of Manpower, 20*, 16–27.

Einarsen, S., & Hoel, H. (2001, May). *The Negative Acts Questionnaire: Development, validation and revision of a measure of bullying at work.* Paper presented at the 10th European Congress on Work and Organizational Psychology: Globalization—Opportunities and Threats, Prague.

Felps, W., Mitchell, T. R., & Byington, E. (2006). How, when, and why bad apples spoil the barrel: Negative group members and dysfunctional groups. *Research in Organizational Behavior, 27*, 175–222.

Field, T. (2008). *Case histories at Bully OnLine.* Retrieved July 23, 2008, from http://www.bullyoffline.org/cases/index.htm.

Fox, S., & Spector, P. E. (1999). A model of work frustration-aggression. *Journal of Organizational Behavior, 20*, 915–931.

French, J., & Raven, B. H. (1959). The bases of social power. In D. Cartwright (Ed.), *Studies in social power* (pp. 150–167). Ann Arbor, MI: Institute for Social Research.

Gibbs, J. R. (1961). Defensive communication. *Journal of Communication, 11*, 141–148.

Hancocks, D. (2006a). *Sample code of conduct policy.* Retrieved July 16, 2008, from http://www.hrinfodesk.com/Articles/codeofconductpolicysample.htm.

Hancocks, D. (2006b). *Sample workplace harassment prevention policy.* Retrieved July 16, 2008, from http://www.hrinfodesk.com/Articles/workplaceharassment policy.htm.

Hébert, S. P., & Ravary, R. (2008). *Employers' lessons from Québec's experience with psychological harassment.* Retrieved July 16, 2008, from http://employmentlaw post.com/northernexposure/2008/06/24/lessons-from-quebecs-experience-with-psychological-harassment/.

Hepworth, W., & Towler, A. (2004). The effects of individual differences and charismatic leadership on workplace aggression. *Journal of Occupational Health Psychology, 9*, 176–185.

Hershcovis, S., & Barling, J. (2008). *Comparing the outcomes of sexual harassment and workplace aggression: A meta-analysis to guide future research.* Working paper.

Hershcovis, S., Barling, J., Turner, N., Arnold, K. A., Dupre, K., Inness, M., Leblanc, M., & Sivanathan, N. (2007). Predicting workplace aggression: A meta-analytic approach. *Journal of Applied Psychology, 92*, 228–238.

Hoel, H., & Cooper, C. (2001). Origins of bullying: Theoretical frameworks for explaining workplace bullying. In N. Tehrani (Eds.), *Building a culture of respect: Managing bullying at work* (pp. 3–20). New York: Taylor & Francis.

Hoel, H., & Giga, S. B. (2006). *Destructive interpersonal conflict in the workplace: The effectiveness of management interventions*. Retrieved July 16, 2008, from http://www.bohrf.org.uk/downloads/bullyrpt.pdf.

Jehn, K. A. (1997). A qualitative analysis of conflict types and dimensions in organizational groups. *Administrative Science Quarterly*, *42*, 530–557.

Jehn, K. A., & Bendersky, C. (2003). Intragroup conflict in organizations: A contingency perspective on the conflict-outcome relationship. *Research in Organizational Behavior*, *25*, 187–242.

Judge, T. A., Woolf, E. F., Hurst, C., & Livingston, B. (2009). Leadership. In J. Barling & C. L. Cooper (Eds.), *Handbook of organizational behavior* (pp. 334–352). London: Sage.

Keashly, L., & Jagatic, K. (2003). By any other name: American perspectives on workplace bullying. In S. Einarsen, H. Doel, D. Zapf, & C. Cooper (Eds.), *Bullying and emotional abuse in the workplace: International perspectives in research and practice* (pp. 31–61). London: Taylor & Francis.

Keashly, L., & Nowell, B. L. (2003). Conflict, conflict resolution, and bullying. In S. Einarsen, H. Hoel, D. Zapf, & C. L. Cooper (Eds.), *Bullying and emotional abuse in the workplace: International perspectives in research and practice*. London: Taylor & Francis.

Leymann, H. (1993). *Mobbing: Psychoterror am arbeitsplatz und wie man sich dagegen wehren kann*. Hamburg: Powohlt Taschenbuch Verlag GmbH.

Leymann, H. (1996). The content and development of mobbing at work. *European Journal of Work and Organizational Psychology*, *5*, 165–184.

Mathisen, G. E., Einarsen, S., & Mykletun, R. (2008). The occurrences and correlates of bullying and harassment in the restaurant sector. *Scandinavian Journal of Psychology*, *49*, 59–68.

McLaughlin, J. (2000). The anger within. *OH & S Canada*, *16*, 30–36.

Namie, G., & Namie, R. (2000). *The bully at work: What you can do to stop the hurt and reclaim your dignity on the job*. Naperville, IL: Sourcebooks.

Namie, G., & Namie, R. (2008). *Workplace bullying institute legislative campaign*. Retrieved July 23, 2008, from http://workplacebullyinglaw.org/.

Neuman, J. H., & Baron, R. A. (1996). Aggression in the workplace. In R. A. Giacalone & J. Greenberg (Eds.), *Antisocial behavior in organizations* (pp. 37–67). Thousand Oaks, CA: Sage.

Neuman, J. H., & Baron, R. A. (1998). Workplace violence and workplace aggression: Evidence concerning specific forms, potential causes, and preferred targets. *Journal of Management*, *24*, 391–429.

O'Reilly, J., & Raver, J. L. (2008, August). *Rewards, surveillance, and leadership: Cross-level effects on employee deviance and citizenship.* Paper presented at the annual conference of the Academy of Management, Anaheim, CA.

Randall, P. (1997). *Adult bullying: Perpetrators and victims.* London: Routledge.

Raver, J. L. (2007, May). *Sexual harassment vs. generalized workplace aggression: Construct differentiation and contextual antecedents.* Paper presented at the annual conference of the European Association of Work and Organizational Psychology, Stockholm, Sweden.

Raver, J. L. (2008, March). *Workplace aggression from supervisors and coworkers.* Paper presented at the Seventh International Conference on Occupational Stress and Health, Washington, DC.

Raver, J. L., & Barling, J. (2008). Workplace aggression and conflict: Constructs, commonalities, and challenges for future inquiry. In C.K.W. De Dreu & M. J. Gelfand (Eds.), *The psychology of conflict and conflict management in organizations* (pp. 211–244). Mahwah, NJ: Erlbaum.

Raver, J. L., Dawson, J., Grojean, M., & Smith, D. B. (2008, April). Contextual predictors of organizational-level aggression from staff and patients. In M. S. Hershcovis & T. C. Reich (chairs), *Bringing the relationship into the experience of workplace aggression.* Symposium conducted at the annual conference of the Society for Industrial and Organizational Psychology, San Francisco.

Raver, J. L., & Gelfand, M. J. (2005). Beyond the individual victim: Linking sexual harassment, team processes, and team performance. *Academy of Management Journal, 48,* 387–400.

Robinson, S. L., & O'Leary-Kelly, A. M. (1998). Monkey see, monkey do: The influence of work groups on the antisocial behavior of employees. *Academy of Management Journal, 41,* 658–672.

Ryan, L. (2007, February 12). Why "forced" job rankings don't work. *BusinessWeek.* Retrieved June 24, 2007, from http://www.businessweek.com/careers/content/feb2007/ca20070212_272450.htm.

Saint-Cyr, Y. (2004). *Are your harassment policies and procedures sufficient?* Retrieved July 16, 2008, from http://www.hrinfodesk.com/Articles/workplaceharassment hrpao.htm.

Salin, D. (2003). Ways of explaining workplace bullying: A review of enabling, motivating and precipitating structures and processes in the work environment. *Human Relations, 56,* 1213–1232.

Schein, E. H. (1985). *Organizational culture and leadership.* San Francisco: Jossey-Bass.

Smith, A., & Williams, K. D. (2004). R U there? Ostracism by cell phone messages. *Group Dynamics: Theory, Research, and Practice, 8,* 291–301.

Sutton, R.I. (2007a). Building the civilized workplace. *McKinsey Quarterly, 2,* 47–55.

Sutton, R. I. (2007b). *The no asshole rule: Building a civilized workplace and surviving one that isn't.* New York: Warner Books.

Tajfel, H., & Turner, J.C. (1985). The social identity theory of intergroup behavior. In S. Worchel & W. G. Austin (Eds.), *Psychology of intergroup relations* (2nd ed., pp. 7–24). Chicago: Nelson-Hall.

Townsend, J., Phillips, J. S., & Elkins, T. J. (2000). Employee retaliation: The neglected consequences of poor leader-member exchange relations. *Journal of Occupational Health Psychology, 5*, 457–463.

Vartia, M. (1996). The sources of bullying: Psychological work environment and organizational climate. *European Journal of Work and Organizational Psychology, 5*, 203–214.

Wageman, R., & Donnenfeld, A. (2007). Intervening in intra-team conflict. In K. M. Behfar & L. L. Thompson (Eds.), *Conflict in organizational groups: New directions in theory and practice* (pp. 261–280). Greenwich, CT: JAI Press.

Williams, K. D. (2007). *Ostracism. Annual Review of Psychology, 58*, 425–452.

Zapf, D. (1999). Organisational, work group related and personal causes of mobbing/bullying at work. *International Journal of Manpower, 20*, 70–85.

Zapf, D., & Gross, C. (2001). Conflict escalation and coping with workplace bullying: A replication and extension. *European Journal of Work and Organizational Psychology, 10*, 497–522.

Zapf, D., Knorz, C., & Kulla, M. (1996). On the relationship between mobbing factors and job content, social work environment, and health outcomes. *European Journal of Work and Organizational Psychology, 5*, 215–237.

CHAPTER 6

Amason, A. C. (1996). Distinguishing the effects of functional and dysfunctional conflict on strategic decision making: Resolving a paradox for top management teams. *Academy of Management Journal, 39*, 123–148.

Chenhall, R. H. (2004). The role of cognitive and affective conflict in early implementation of activity-based cost management. *Behavioral Research in Accounting, 16*, 19–44.

Cunningham, G. B. (2006). The influence of group diversity on intergroup bias following recategorization. *Journal of Social Psychology, 146*, 533.

Cunningham, G. B., & Sagas, M. (2004). Group diversity, occupational commitment, and occupational turnover intentions among NCAA Division IA football coaching staffs. *Journal of Sports Management, 18*, 236–254.

Harrison, D. A., & Klein, K. J. (2007). What's the difference? Diversity constructs as separation, variety, or disparity in organizations. *Academy of Management Review, 32*, 1199–1228.

Harrison, D. A., Price, K. H., & Bell, M. P. (1998). Beyond relational demography: Time and the effects of surface- and deep-level diversity on work. *Academy of Management Journal, 41*, 96–107.

Horwitz, S. K., & Horwitz, I. B. (2007). The effects of team diversity on team outcomes: A meta-analytic review of team demography. *Journal of Management, 33*, 987–1015.
Ilgen, D. R., Hollenbeck, J. R., Johnson, M., & Jundt, D. (2005). Teams in organizations: From input-process-output models to IMOI models. *Annual Review of Psychology, 56*, 517–543.
Jehn, K. A. (1995). A multimethod examination of the benefits and detriments of intragroup conflict. *Administrative Science Quarterly, 40*, 256–282.
Jehn, K. A. (1997). A qualitative analysis of conflict types and dimensions in organizational groups. *Administrative Science Quarterly, 42*, 530–558.
Jehn, K. A., Northcraft, G. B., & Neale, M. A. (1999). Why differences make a difference: A field study of diversity, conflict, and performance in workgroups. *Administrative Science Quarterly, 44*, 741–763.
Kerr, N. L., & Tindale, R. S. (2004). Group performance and decision making. *Annual Review of Psychology, 55*, 623–655.
Lawrence, B. S. (1997). The black box of organizational demography. *Organizational Science, 8*(1), 1–23.
Liang, T. P., Liu, C. C., Lin, T. M., & Lin, B. (2007). Effect of team diversity on software project performance. *Industrial Management & Data Systems, 107*, 636–653.
McGrath, J. E., Berdahl, J. L., & Arrow, H. (1995). Traits, expectations, culture and clout: The dynamics of diversity in work groups. In S. E. Jackson & M. M. Ruderman (Eds.), *Diversity in work teams: Research paradigms for a changing workplace.* Washington DC: American Psychological Association.
Mooney, A. C., Holahan, P. J., & Amason, A. C. (2007). Don't take it personally: Exploring cognitive conflict as a mediator of affective conflict. *Journal of Management Studies, 44*, 733–758.
Morris, W. (Ed.). (1982). *American heritage dictionary of the English language.* Boston: Houghton Mifflin.
Phillips, K. W., & Loyd, D. L. (2006). When surface and deep-level diversity collide: The effects on dissenting group members. *Organizational Behavior and Human Decision Processes, 99*, 143–160.
Parayitam, S., & Dooley, R. S. (2007). The relationship between conflict and decision outcomes: Moderating effects of cognitive- and affect-based trust in strategic decision-making teams. *International Journal of Conflict Management, 18*(1), 42–73.
Priem, R. L., Lyon, D. W., & Dess, G. G. (1999). Inherent limitations of demographic proxies in top management team heterogeneity research. *Journal of Management, 25*, 935–953.
van Knippenberg, D., De Dreu, C.K.W., & Homan, A. C. (2004). Work group diversity and group performance: An integrative model and research agenda. *Journal of Applied Psychology, 89*, 1008–1022.
van Knippenberg, D., & Schippers, M. C. (2007). Work group diversity. *Annual Review of Psychology, 58*, 515.

CHAPTER 7

Asante, M., & Davis, A. (1985). Black and white communication: Analyzing workplace encounters. *Journal of Black Studies, 16*(1), 77–93.

Brown, C. R., & Mazza, G. J. (2005). *Leading diverse communities: A how-to guide for moving from healing into action*. San Francisco: Jossey-Bass.

Campbell, S. L. (1998). *A guide for training facilitators*. Pomfret, CT: Topsfield Foundation.

Clark, M. A., Anand, V., & Roberson, L. (2000). Resolving meaning: Interpretation in diverse decision-making groups. *Group Dynamics: Theory, Research, & Practice, 4*, 211–221.

Collier, V. A. (1992). Synthesis of studies examining long-term language minority student data on academic achievement. *Bilingual Research Journal, 16*, 187–212.

Darling-Hammond, L. (2000). Teacher quality and student achievement: A review of state policy evidence. *Education Policy Analysis Archives, 8*(1). Retrieved Nov. 15, 2009, from http://epaa.asu.edu/epaa/v8n1/.

Faircloth, B. S., & Hamm, J. V. (2005). Sense of belonging among high school students representing four ethnic groups. *Journal of Youth and Adolescence, 34*, 293–309.

Gouran, D. S., & Hirokawa, R. Y. (1996). Functional theory and communication in decision-making and problem-solving groups: An expanded view. In R. Y. Hirokawa & M. S. Poole (Eds.), *Communication and group decision-making* (2nd ed.). Thousand Oaks, CA: Sage.

Gouran, D. S., & Hirokawa, R. Y. (2005). Facilitating communication in group decision-making discussions. In S. Schuman (Ed.), *The IAF handbook of group facilitation: Best practices from the leading organization in facilitation* (pp. 351–360). San Francisco: Jossey-Bass.

Guzmán, M. R., Santiago-Rivera, A. L., & Hasse, R. F. (2005). Understanding academic attitudes and achievement in Mexican-origin youths: Ethnic identity, other-group orientation, and fatalism. *Cultural Diversity and Ethnic Minority Psychology, 11*(1), 3–15.

Jehn, K. (1994). Enhancing effectiveness: An investigation of advantages and disadvantages of value-based intragroup conflict. *International Journal of Conflict Management, 5*, 223–238.

Landesman, J. (2008). Using study circles to engage racially diverse parents, staff, and students in dialogue and problem solving. *NCPIE Update*. Washington, DC: National Coalition for Parent Involvement in Education.

Larkey, L. K. (1996). Toward a theory of communicative interactions in culturally diverse workgroups. *Academy of Management Review, 21*, 463–491.

Lasley, M. (2006). Difficult conversations: Authentic communication leads to greater understanding and teamwork. *Group Facilitation: A Research and Applications Journal, 7*, 13–20.

Lau, D. C., & Murnighan, J. K. (1998). Demographic diversity and faultlines: The compositional dynamics of organizational groups. *Academy of Management Review, 23*, 325–340.
Milliken, F. J., & Martins, L. L. (1996). Searching for common threads: Understanding the multiple effects of diversity in organizational groups. *Academy of Management Review, 21*, 402–433.
Montgomery County Public Schools. (2003). *Our call to action: Pursuit of excellence. The strategic plan for MCPS 2003–2008*. Rockville, MD: Author.
Ogbu, J. U. (1992). Adaptation to minority status and impact on school success. *Theory into Practice: Literacy and the African-American Learner, 31*, 287–295.
Schwarz, R. (2002). *The skilled facilitator: A comprehensive resource for consultants, facilitators, managers, trainers, and coaches*. San Francisco: Jossey-Bass.
Sibbet, D. (2005). Graphic facilitation: The art of drawing out the best in people. In S. Schuman (Ed.), *The IAF handbook of group facilitation: Best practices from the leading organization in facilitation*. San Francisco: Jossey-Bass.
Slaughter-Defoe, D. T., Nakagawa, K., Takanishi, R., & Johnson, D. J. (1990). Toward cultural/ecological perspectives on schooling and achievement in African- and Asian-American children. *Child Development, 61*, 363–383.
Spencer, M. B., & Markstrom-Adams, C. (1990). Identity processes among racial and ethnic minority children in America. *Child Development, 61*, 290–310.
Study Circles Resource Center. (2006). *A guide to training study circle facilitators* (2nd ed.). Pomfret, CT: Author.
Wigfield, A., & Wentzel, K. (2007). Introduction to motivation at school: Interventions that work. In K. R. Wentzel & A. Wigfield (Eds.), Motivational interventions that work. Special Issue, *Educational Psychologist*42, 191–196.
Wade, J. (2007). *Evaluation of the Montgomery County Public Schools Study Circles Program*. Rockville, MD: Montgomery County Public Schools.

CHAPTER 8

Asch, S. E. (1951). Effects of group pressure upon the modification and distortion of judgments. In H. Guetzkow (Ed.), *Groups, leadership, and men* (pp. 177–190). Pittsburgh: Carnegie Press.
Bass, B. M. (1990). *Bass and Stogdill's handbook of leadership: A survey of theory and research* (3rd ed.). New York: Free Press.
Bazerman, M. H., & Moore, D. (2009). *Judgment in managerial decision making* (7th ed.). Hoboken, NJ: Wiley.
Beach, L. R., & Connolly, T. (2005). *The psychology of decision making: People in organizations* (2nd ed.). Thousand Oaks, CA: Sage.
Benne, K. D., & Sheats, P. (1948). Functional roles of group members. *Journal of Social Issues, 4*, 41–49.

Bennis, W. (2007). The challenges of leadership in the modern world. *American Psychologist, 62*, 2–5.

Festinger, L. (1957). *A theory of cognitive dissonance.* Evanston, IL: Row Peterson.

Festinger, L. (Ed.). (1964). *Conflict, decision and dissonance.* Stanford, CA: Stanford University Press.

Folger, J. P., Poole, M. S., & Stutman, R. K. (2009). *Working through conflict: Strategies for relationships, groups, and organizations* (6th ed.). Boston: Pearson Allyn & Bacon.

Gouran, D. S. (1982). *Making decisions in groups: Choices and consequences.* Glenview, IL: Scott, Foresman.

Gouran, D. S. (2003a). Communication skills for group decision making. In J. O. Greene & B. R. Burleson (Eds.), *Handbook of communication and social interaction skills* (pp. 835–870). Mahwah, NJ: Erlbaum.

Gouran, D. S. (2003b). Leadership as the art of counteractive influence in decision-making and problem-solving groups. In R. Y. Hirokawa, R. S. Cathcart, L. A. Samovar, & L. D. Henman (Eds.), *Small group communication theory and practice: An anthology* (8th ed., pp. 172–183). Los Angeles: Roxbury.

Gouran, D. S., & Hirokawa, R. Y. (1996). Functional theory and communication in decision-making and problem-solving groups. In R. Y. Hirokawa & M. S. Poole (Eds.), *Communication and group decision making* (2nd ed., pp. 55–80). Thousand Oaks, CA: Sage.

Gouran, D. S., & Hirokawa, R. Y. (2005). Facilitating communication in group decision-making discussions. In S. Schuman (Ed.), *The IAF handbook of group facilitation: Best practices from the leading organization in facilitation* (pp. 351–360). San Francisco: Jossey-Bass.

Harvey, J. B. (1974). The Abilene paradox: The management of agreement. *Organizational Dynamics, 3*, 63–80.

Herek, G., Janis, I. L., & Huth, P. (1987). Decision making during international crises: Is quality of process related to outcome? *Journal of Conflict Resolution, 31*, 203–226.

Hersey, P., & Blanchard, K. H. (1993). *Management of organizational behavior: Using human resources* (6th ed.). Upper Saddle River, NJ: Prentice Hall.

Hirokawa, R. Y., & Rost, K. M. (1992). Effective group decision making in organizations: Field test of the vigilant interaction theory. *Management Communication Quarterly, 5*, 267–288.

Janis, I. L. (1972). *Victims of groupthink: A psychological study of foreign policy decisions and fiascoes.* Boston: Houghton Mifflin.

Janis, I. L. (1982). *Groupthink: Psychological studies of policy decisions and fiascoes* (2nd ed.). Boston: Houghton Mifflin.

Janis, I. L. (1989). *Crucial decisions: Leadership in policymaking and crisis management.* New York: Free Press.

Janis, I. L., & Mann, L. (1977). *Decision making: A psychological analysis of conflict, choice, and commitment.* New York: Free Press.

Jehn, K. A., & Mannix, E. A. (2001). The dynamic nature of conflict: A longitudinal study of intragroup conflict and group performance. *Academy of Management Journal, 44*, 238–251.

Keyton, J., & Frey, L. R. (2002). The state of traits: Predispositions and group communication. In L. R. Frey (Ed.), *New directions in group communication* (pp. 99–120). Thousand Oaks, CA: Sage.

Northouse, P. G. (2007). Introduction. In P. G. Northouse (Ed.), *Leadership: Theory and practice* (4th ed., pp. 1–14). Thousand Oaks, CA: Sage.

Poole, M. S. (1991). Procedures for managing meetings: Social and technological innovations. In R. A. Swenson & B. O. Knapp (Eds.), *Innovative meeting management* (pp. 53–109). Austin, TX: 3M Meeting Management Institute.

Schanck, R. L. (1932). A study of a community and its groups and institutions conceived of as behaviors of individuals. *Psychological Monographs, 43*(2). Whole No. 195.

Schultz, B., Ketrow, S. M., & Urban, D. M. (1995). Improving decision quality in the small group: The role of the reminder. *Small Group Research, 26*, 521–541.

Senge, P. M. (1990). *The fifth discipline: The art and practice of the learning organization.* New York: Currency Doubleday.

Seibold, D. R., & Krikorian, D. H. (1997). Planning and facilitating group meetings. In L. R. Frey & J. K. Barge (Eds.), *Managing group life: Communicating in decision-making groups* (pp. 270–305). Boston: Houghton Mifflin.

Shaw, M. E. (1981). *Group dynamics: The psychology of small group behavior* (3rd ed.). New York: McGraw-Hill.

Socha, T. J. (1997). Group communication across the life span. In L. R. Frey & J. K. Barge (Eds.), *Managing group life: Communicating in decision-making groups* (pp. 3–28). Boston: Houghton Mifflin.

Surowiecki, J. (2004). *The wisdom of crowds.* New York: Doubleday.

Torrance, E. P. (1954). Some consequences of power differences on decision making in permanent and temporary three-man groups. *Research Studies, Washington State College, 22*, 251–278.

Wahrman, R. (1972). Status, deviance, and sanctions: A critical review. *Comparative Group Studies, 3*, 203–224.

Zaccaro, S. J. (2007). Trait-based perspectives of leadership. *American Psychologist, 62*, 7–16.

CHAPTER 9

Armstrong D. (2004). Emotions in organizations: Disturbance or intelligence. In C. Huffington, D. Armstrong, W. Halton, L. Hoyle, & J. Pooley (Eds.), *Working below the surface.* London: Karnac.

Barge, J. K. (2001). Creating healthy communities through affirmative conflict communication. *Conflict Resolution Quarterly, 19*(1), 89–100.

Bowling, D., & Hoffman, D. (2003). *Bringing peace into the room: The personal qualities of the mediator and their impact on the mediation.* San Francisco: Jossey-Bass.
Bunker, B. (2000). Managing conflict through large group methods. In M. Deutsch & P. T. Coleman (Eds.), *The handbook of conflict resolution: Theory and practice.* San Francisco: Jossey-Bass.
Chasin, L., & Herzog, M. (2006). *Fostering dialogue across divides.* Watertown, MA: Public Conversations Project.
Cloke, K. (2001). *Mediating dangerously: The frontiers of conflict resolution.* San Francisco: Jossey-Bass.
Fisher, R. J. (2000). Inter-group conflict. In M. Deutsch & P. T. Coleman (Eds.), *The handbook of conflict resolution: Theory and practice.* San Francisco: Jossey-Bass.
Folger, J. P., Poole, M. S., & Stutman, R. K. (1993). *Working through conflict: Strategies for relationships, groups, and organizations.* New York: HarperCollins.
Goleman, D. (2004). *Primal leadership: Learning to lead with emotional intelligence.* Boston: Harvard Business School Press.
Kouzes, J., & Posner, B. (2002). *The leadership challenge.* San Francisco: Jossey-Bass.
Lang, M., & Taylor, A. (2000). *The making of a mediator: Developing artistry in practice.* San Francisco: Jossey-Bass.
LeBaron, M. (2002). *Bridging troubled waters: Conflict resolution from the heart.* San Francisco: Jossey-Bass.
Mayer, B. (2000). *The dynamics of conflict resolution.* San Francisco: Jossey-Bass.
Mayer, B. (2004). *Beyond neutrality: Confronting the crisis in conflict resolution.* San Francisco: Jossey-Bass.
Mohr, B. J., & Watkins, J. M. (2001). *Appreciative inquiry.* San Francisco: Jossey-Bass.
Schwarz, R. (1994). *The skilled facilitator: Practical wisdom for developing effective groups.* San Francisco: Jossey-Bass.
Stanfield, R. B. (Ed.). (1998). *Winning through participation.* Gabriola Island, BC, Canada: New Society Publishers.
Weeks, D. (1992). *The eight essential steps to conflict resolution: Preserving relationships at work, at home, and in the community.* New York: Tarcher Penguin.
West, M. A. (2004). *Effective teamwork: Practical lessons from organizational research.* Leicester, UK: British Psychological Society and Blackwell.
Wilson, G. (2002). *Groups in context: Leadership and participation in small groups.* New York: McGraw-Hill.

CHAPTER 10

Janis, I. L. (1972). *Victims of groupthink: A psychological study of foreign policy decisions and fiascoes.* Boston: Houghton Mifflin.
Kantor, D., & Lehr, W. (1975). *Inside the family.* San Francisco: Jossey-Bass.
Ober, S. (2000). *Cracking the culture nut: Human systems consulting—an implementation package.* Cambridge, MA: Innovation Associates/Arthur D. Little.

Ober, S., & Kantor, D. (1996). Achieving breakthroughs in executive team performance. *Prism, Q3*, 83–95.
Ober, S., Kantor, D., & Yanowitz, J. (1995). Creating business results through team learning. *Systems Thinker, 6*(5), 1–5.

CHAPTER 11

Aiello, J. R., & Kolb, K. J. (1995). Electronic performance monitoring and social context: Impact on productivity and stress. *Journal of Applied Psychology, 80*, 339–353.
Alge, B. J., Ballinger, G. A., & Green, S. G. (2004). Remote control: Predictors of electronic monitoring intensity and secrecy. *Personnel Psychology, 57*, 377–410.
Avolio, B. J., & Kahai, S. S. (2002). Adding the "e" to e-leadership: How it may impact your leadership. *Organizational Dynamics, 31*, 325–338.
Bradley, L. (2008). The technology that supports virtual team collaboration. In J. Nemiro, M. Beyerlein, S. Beyerlein, & L. Bradley (Eds.), *Handbook of high performance virtual teams: A toolkit for collaborating across boundaries* (pp. 331–365). San Francisco: Jossey Bass.
Bradley, L., & Beyerlein, M. (2005). Facilitation of the future: How virtual meetings are changing the work of the facilitator. In S. Schuman (Ed.), *The IAF handbook of group facilitation: Best practices from the leading organization in facilitation*. San Francisco: Jossey-Bass.
Cascio, W. F., & Shurygailo, S. (2002). E-leadership and virtual teams. *Organizational Dynamics, 4*, 362–376.
De Dreu, C.K.W. (2008). The virtue and vice of workplace conflict: Food for (pessimistic) thought. *Journal of Organizational Behavior, 29*, 5–18.
DeSanctis, G., & Jackson, B. M. (1994). Special issue: Information technology and organizational design. *Journal of Management Information Systems, 10*, 85–110.
DeSanctis, G., & Poole, M. S. (1997). Transitions in teamwork in new organizational forms. *Advances in Group Processes, 14*, 157–176.
Dorfman, P. W., & House, R. J. (2004). Cultural influences on organizational leadership. In R. J. House, P. J. Hanges, M. Javidan, P. W. Dorfman, & V. Gupta (Eds.), *Culture, leadership, and organizations* (pp. 51–73). Thousand Oaks, CA: Sage.
Edmondson, A. (1999). Psychological safety and learning behavior in work teams. *Administrative Science Quarterly, 44*, 350–383.
Ellemers, N., De Gilder, D., Haslam, S. A. (2004). Motivating individuals and groups at work: A social identity perspective on leadership and group performance. *Academy of Management Review, 29*, 459–478.
English, A., Griffith, R. L., & Steelman, L. A. (2004). Team performance: The effect of team conscientiousness and task type. *Small Group Research, 35*, 643–665.
Fiore, S. M., Salas, E., & Cannon-Bowers, J. A. (2001). Group dynamics and shared mental models. In M. London (Ed.), *How people evaluate others in organizations* (pp. 309–335). Mahwah, NJ: Erlbaum.

Gibson, C. B., & Gibbs, J. L. (2006). Unpacking the concept of virtuality: The effects of geographic dispersion, electronic dependence, dynamic structure, and national diversity on team innovation. *Administrative Sciences Quarterly, 51*, 451–495.

Hackman, J. R. (1990). *Groups that work (and those that don't).* San Francisco: Jossey-Bass.

Hackman, J. R. (2002). *Leading teams: Setting the stage for great performances.* Boston: Harvard Business School Press.

Hambley, L. A., O'Neill, T. A., & Kline, T.J.B. (2007a). The effects of leadership and communication medium on team interaction styles and outcomes. *Organizational Behavior and Human Decision Processes, 103*, 1–20.

Hambley, L. A., O'Neill, T. A, & Kline, T.J.B. (2007b). Virtual team leadership: Perspectives from the field. *International Journal of e-Collaboration, 3*, 40–64.

Harrison, R. (1972). Role negotiation: A tough-minded approach to team development. In W. W. Burke & H. A. Hornstein (Eds.), *The social technology of organization development.* La Jolla, CA: University Associates.

Hertel, G., Konradt, U., & Voss, K. (2006). Competencies for virtual teamwork: Development and validation of a web-based selection tool for members of distributed teams. *European Journal of Work and Organizational Psychology, 15*, 477–504.

Hofstede, G. (1980). *Culture's consequences: International differences in work-related values.* Thousand Oaks, CA: Sage.

Ilgen, D. R., Hollenbeck, J. R., Johnson, M., & Jundt, J. (2005). Teams in organizations: From Input-process-output models to IMOI models. *Annual Review of Psychology, 56*, 517–543.

Jarvenpaa, S. L., Knoll, K., & Leidner, D. E. (1998). Is anybody out there? Antecedents of trust in global virtual teams. *Journal of Management Information Systems, 14*(4), 29–64.

Jarvenpaa, S. L., & Leidner, D. E. (1999). Communication and trust in global virtual teams. *Organization Science, 10*, 791–815.

Javidan, M., Dorfman, P. W., de Luque, M. S., & House, R. J. (2006). In the eye of the beholder: Cross cultural lessons in leadership from project GLOBE. *Academy of Management Perspectives, 20*, 67–90.

Jonassen, D. H., & Kwon, H. (2001). Communication patterns in computer mediated versus face-to-face group problem solving. *Education Technology Research and Development, 49*, 35–51.

Kirkman, B. L., & Mathieu, J. E. (2005). The dimensions and antecedents of team virtuality. *Journal of Management, 31*, 700–718.

Kirkman, B. L., Rosen, B., Gibson, C. B., Tesluk, P., & McPherson, S. (2002). Five challenges to virtual team success: Lessons from Sabre, Inc. *Academy of Management Executive, 16*, 67–79.

Kline, T.J.B. (1999a). *Remaking teams: A revolutionary research-based guide that puts theory into practice.* San Francisco: Jossey-Bass.

Kline, T.J.B. (1999b). The Team Player Inventory: Reliability and validity of a measure of predisposition toward organizational team-working environments. *Journal for Specialists in Group Work, 24*, 102–112.

Kline, T.J.B., & McGrath, J. (1998). Development and validation of five criteria for evaluation team performance. *Organization Development Journal, 16*, 19–27.

Kline, T.J.B. & McGrath, J. (1999). A review of the groupware literature: Theories, methodologies, and a research agenda. *Canadian Psychology, 40*, 265–271.

Kline, T.J.B., & Sell, Y. P. (1996). Cooperativeness vs. competitiveness: Initial findings regarding effects on the performance of individual and group problem solving. *Psychological Reports, 79*, 355–365.

Kock, N. (2004). The Psychobiological Model: Towards a new theory of computer-mediated communication based on Darwinian evolution. *Organizational Science, 15*, 327–348.

Latham, G. P., & Marshall, H. A. (1982). The effects of self-set, participatively set and assigned goals on the performance of government employees. *Personnel Psychology, 35*, 399–404.

MacDonnell, R., O'Neill, T. A., Kline, T.J.B., & Hambley, L. H. (2009). Bringing group-level personality to the electronic realm: A comparison of face-to-face and virtual contexts. *The Psychologist-Manager Journal, 12*, 1–24.

Markus, M. L. (1983). *Systems in organization: Bugs and features*. San Jose, CA: Pitman.

Montoya-Weiss, M. M., Massey, A. P., & Song, M. (2001). Getting it together: Temporal coordination and conflict management in global virtual teams. *Academy of Management Journal, 44*, 1251–1262.

O'Neill, T. A., Hambley, L. A., Greidanus, N., MacDonnell, R., & Kline, T.J.B. (2009). Predicting teleworker success: An exploration of personality, motivational, situational, and job characteristics. *New Technology, Work, and Employment, 24*, 144–162.

O'Neill, T. A., Lewis, R. J., & Hambley, L. A. (2008). Leading virtual teams: Potential problems and simple solutions. In J. Nemiro, M. Beyerlein, S. Beyerlein, & L. Bradley (Eds.), *Handbook of high performance virtual teams: A toolkit for collaborating across boundaries* (pp. 213–238). San Francisco: Jossey-Bass.

Pinder, C. C. (1998). *Work motivation in organizational behavior*. Upper Saddle River, NJ: Prentice Hall.

Wageman, R. (2003). Virtual processes: Implications for coaching the virtual team. In R. S. Peterson, & E. A. Mannix (Eds.), *Leading and managing people in the dynamic organization* (pp. 65–86). Mahwah, NJ: Erlbaum.

Walther, J. B. (1992). Interpersonal effects in computer-mediated interaction: A relational perspective. *Communication Research, 19*, 52–90.

Walther, J. B., & Bunz, U. (2005). The rules of virtual groups: Trust, liking, and performance in computer-mediated communication. *Journal of Communication, 55*, 828–846.

Walton, R. E. (1969). *Interpersonal peacemaking: Confrontations and third party consultation.* Reading, MA: Addison-Wesley

Witte, E. H. (2007). Toward a group facilitation technique for project teams. *Group Processes and Intergroup Relations, 10,* 299–309.

CHAPTER 12

Angelica, M. P. (1999). *Resolving conflict in nonprofit organizations.* St. Paul, MN: Amherst H. Wilder Foundation.

Beckhard, R. (1967, March-April). The confrontation meeting. *Harvard Business Review, 45,* 149–155.

Bell, N., & Nurre, S. (2005). The big picture: Creating an ongoing client relationship. In S. Schuman (Ed.), *The IAF handbook of group facilitation: Best practices from the leading organization in facilitation.* San Francisco: Jossey-Bass.

Block, P. (1981). *Flawless consulting: A guide to getting your expertise used* (2nd ed.). San Francisco: Pfeiffer.

Boulton, A. C. (2005). *The art of board development* (3rd ed.). Salt Lake City: Utah Arts Council. Available at http://arts.utah.gov/services/publications/handbooks/board.html.

Carver, J. (1990). *Boards that make a difference: A new design for leadership in nonprofit and public organizations.* San Francisco: Jossey-Bass.

Dannemiller, K. (1988). Team building at a macro level, or "Ben Gay" for arthritic organizations. In W. B. Reddy (Ed.), *Team building: Blueprints for productivity and satisfaction.* Alexandria, VA: NTL Institute.

DeWine, S. (2001). *The consultant's craft: Improving organizational communication* (2nd ed.). New York: Bedford/St. Martin.

French, W. L., & Bell, C. H. (1984). *Organizational development: Behavioral science interventions for organization improvement* (3rd ed.). Upper Saddle River, NJ: Prentice Hall.

Gibb, J. R. (1961). Defensive communication. *Journal of Communication, 11,* 141–148.

Howe, F. (1995). *Welcome to the board: Your guide for effective participation.* San Francisco: Jossey-Bass.

Hunter, D., & Thorpe, S. (2005). Facilitator values and ethics. In S. Schuman (Ed.), *The IAF handbook of group facilitation: Best practices from the leading organization in facilitation.* San Francisco: Jossey-Bass.

Kimberly, J., & Miles, R. (1980). *The organizational life cycle.* San Francisco: Jossey-Bass.

Larson, S. (2008). Unique nature and struggles of traditional small nonprofits. In C. McNamara (Ed.), *Basic overview of nonprofit organizations.* Retrieved July 17, 2008, from http://www.managementhelp.org/org_thry/np_intro.htm.

McNamara, C. (2008). Founders syndrome: How corporations suffer—and can recover. Retrieved July 17, 2008, from http://www.managementhelp.org/org_thry/np_intro.htm.

Robinson, M. K. (2001). *Nonprofit boards that work: The end of one-size-fits-all governance.* Hoboken, NJ: Wiley.

Rodas-Meeker, M. B., & Meeker, L. (2005). Building trust: The great enabler. In S. Schuman (Ed.). *The IAF handbook of group facilitation: Best practices from the leading organization in facilitation.* San Francisco: Jossey-Bass.

Rohrbaugh, J. (2005). Assessing the effectiveness of group decision processes. In S. Schuman (Ed.). *The IAF handbook of group facilitation: Best practices from the leading organization in facilitation.* San Francisco: Jossey-Bass.

Schwarz, R. M. (2002). *The skilled facilitator: A comprehensive resource for consultants, facilitators, managers, trainers, and coaches* (2nd ed.). San Francisco: Jossey-Bass.

Simon, J. S., & Donovan, J. T. (2001). The five life stages of nonprofit organizations. St. Paul, MN: Amherst H. Wilder Foundation.

Sline, R. W. (2006). Who owns the jazz festival . . . ? A case of facilitated intergroup conflict management. In L. Frey (Ed.), *Facilitating group communication in context: Innovations and applications with natural groups.* Cresskill, NJ: Hampton Press.

Van Maanen, J. (1988). *Tales of the field: On writing ethnography.* Chicago: University of Chicago Press.

Wolf, T. (1999). *Managing a nonprofit organization in the twenty-first century.* New York: Simon & Schuster.

Wood, J. (2007). *Interpersonal communication: Everyday encounters* (7th ed.). Belmont: CA: Wadsworth.

CHAPTER 13

Axelrod, R. (1984). *The evolution of cooperation.* New York: Basic Books.

Carter, B., & Cieply, M. (2007, December 29). Letterman and writers guild reach agreement. *New York Times.* Retrieved June, 26, 2008, from http://www.nytimes.com/2007/12/29/business/media/29strike.html?_r=1&sq=d&oref=slogin.

Cieply, M. (2008, February 12). Writers vote to end strike. *New York Times.* Retrieved June 26, 2008, from http://www.nytimes.com/2008/02/12/business/media/12cnd-strike.html?_r=1&oref=slogin.

Cohen, T. R. (2008). The effects of empathy on intergroup conflict and aggression: Examining the dual roles of empathy in fostering positive and negative intergroup relations (Doctoral dissertation, University of North Carolina at Chapel Hill, 2008). *Dissertations & Theses Database.* (Publication No. AAT 3304253)

Cohen, T. R., & Insko, C. A. (2008). War and peace: Possible approaches to reducing intergroup conflict. *Perspectives on Psychological Science,* 3, 87–93.

Cohen, T. R., Montoya, R. M., & Insko, C. A. (2006). Group morality and intergroup relations: Cross-cultural and experimental evidence. *Personality and Social Psychology Bulletin, 32*, 1559–1572.

Colman, A. M. (1995). *Game theory and its applications in the social and behavioral sciences* (2nd ed.). Oxford: Butterworth-Heinemann.

CNN. (2008, February 13). Strike over, Hollywood writers head back to work. Retrieved June 26, 2008, from http://www.cnn.com/2008/SHOWBIZ/TV/02/13/writers.strike/index.html.

Eisenberg, N., Guthrie, I. K., Cumberland, A., Murphy, B. C., Shepard, S. A., Zhou, Q., & Gustavo, C. (2002). Prosocial development in early adulthood: A longitudinal study. *Journal of Personality and Social Psychology, 82*, 992–1006.

Ellison, H. (2008). Harlan Ellison reacts to the proposed WGA contract. *United Hollywood.* Retrieved July 19, 2008, from http://unitedhollywood.blogspot.com/2008/02/harlan-ellison-reacts-to-proposed-wga.html.

Fisher, R., Ury, W., & Patton, B. (1991). *Getting to yes.* New York: Penguin.

Gaertner, S. L., & Dovidio, J. F. (2000). *Reducing intergroup bias: The common ingroup identity model.* Philadelphia: Psychology Press.

Graziano, W. G., Habashi, M. M., Sheese, B. E., & Tobin R. M. (2007). Agreeableness, empathy, and helping: A person x situation perspective. *Journal of Personality and Social Psychology, 93*, 583–599.

Hoyle, R. H., Pinkley, R. L., & Insko, C. A. (1989). Perceptions of social behavior. Evidence of differing expectations for interpersonal and intergroup interactions. *Personality and Social Psychology Bulletin, 15*, 365–376.

Insko, C. A., Schopler, J., Gaertner, L., Wildschut, T., Kozar, R., Pinter, B., Finkel, E. J., Brazil, D. M., Cecil, C. L., & Montoya, R. M. (2001). Interindividual-intergroup discontinuity reduction through anticipation of future interaction. *Journal of Personality and Social Psychology, 80*, 95–111.

Insko, C. A., Schopler, J., Hoyle, R. H., Dardis, G. J. & Graetz, K. A. (1990). Individual-group discontinuity as a function of fear and greed. *Journal of Personality and Social Psychology, 58*, 68–79.

Insko, C. A., Schopler, J., Pemberton, M. B., Wieselquist, J., McIlraith, S., Currey, D. P., & Gaertner, L. (1998). Long-term outcome maximization and the reduction of interindividual-intergroup discontinuity. *Journal of Personality and Social Psychology, 75*, 695–710.

Kelley, H. H., Holmes, J. G., Kerr, N. L., Reis, H. T., Rusbult, C. E., & Van Lange, P.A.M. (2003). *An atlas of interpersonal situations.* New York: Cambridge University Press.

Kelley, H. H., & Thibaut, J. W. (1978). *Interpersonal relations.* Hoboken, NJ: Wiley.

Littleton, C. (2007, December 19). WGA strike taking toll on L.A. *Variety.* Retrieved October 28, 2008, from http://www.variety.com/article/VR1117977983.html?categoryid=1066&cs=1.

Malhotra, D., & Liyanage, S. (2005). Long-term effects of peace workshops in protracted conflicts. *Journal of Conflict Resolution, 49*, 908–924.

McCallum, D. M., Harring, K., Gilmore, R., Drenan, S., Chase, J., Insko, C. A., & Thibaut, J. (1985). Competition and cooperation between groups and between individuals. *Journal of Experimental Social Psychology, 21*, 301–320.

Meier, B. P., & Hinsz, V. B. (2004). A comparison of human aggression committed by groups and individuals: An interindividual-intergroup discontinuity. *Journal of Experimental Social Psychology, 40*, 551–559.

Morgan, P. M., & Tindale, R. S. (2002). Group vs. individual performance in mixed motive situations: Exploring an inconsistency. *Organizational Behavior and Human Decision Processes, 87*, 44–65.

Pemberton, M. B., Insko, C. A., & Schopler, J. (1996). Memory for and experience of differential competitive behavior of individuals and groups. *Journal of Personality and Social Psychology, 71*, 953–966.

Pinter, B., Insko, C. A., Wildschut, T., Montoya, R. M., Kirchner, J. L., & Wolf, S. T. (2007). Reduction of interindividual-intergroup discontinuity: The role of leader accountability and proneness to guilt. *Journal of Personality and Social Psychology, 93*, 250–265.

Poundstone, W. (1992). *Prisoner's dilemma*. New York: Doubleday.

Rea, A., Insko, C. A., Wildschut, T., & Cohen, T. R. (2009). *Intergroup competition as a function of Campbell's indices of entitativity: The primacy of common fate*. Manuscript in preparation.

Ridley, M. (1996). *The origins of virtue*. London: Penguin.

Schopler, J., Insko, C. A., Drigotas, S. M., Wieselquist, J., Pemberton, M., & Cox, C. (1995). The role of identifiability in the reduction of interindividual-intergroup discontinuity. *Journal of Experimental Social Psychology, 31*, 553–574.

Schopler, J., Insko, C. A., Graetz, K. A., Drigotas, S. M., & Smith, V. A. (1991). The generality of the individual-group discontinuity effect: Variations in positivity-negativity of outcomes, players' relative power, and magnitude of outcomes. *Personality and Social Psychology Bulletin, 17*, 612–624.

Schopler, J., Insko, C. A., Graetz, K. A., Drigotas, S. M., Smith, V. A., & Dahl, K. (1993). Individual-group discontinuity: Further evidence for mediation by fear and greed. *Personality and Social Psychology Bulletin, 19*, 419–431.

Schopler, J., Insko, C. A., Wieselquist, J., Pemberton, M. B., Witcher, B., Kozar, R., Roddenberry, C., & Wildschut, T. (2001). When groups are more competitive than individuals: The domain of the discontinuity effect. *Journal of Personality and Social Psychology, 80*, 632–644.

Stephan, W. C., & Finlay, K. (1999). The role of empathy in improving intergroup relations. *Journal of Social Issues, 55*, 729–743.

Takemura, K., & Yuki, M. (2007). Are Japanese groups more competitive than Japanese individuals? A cross-cultural validation of the interindividual-intergroup discontinuity effect. *International Journal of Psychology, 42*, 27–35.

Ury, W. (1993). *Getting past no: Negotiating your way from confrontation to cooperation.* New York: Bantam Books.

Whedon, J. (2008, February 6). Do not adjust your mindset. *United Hollywood.* Retrieved June 26, 2008, from http://unitedhollywood.blogspot.com/2008/02/from-joss-whedon-do-not-adjust-your.html.

White, M., & Fixmer, A. (2008, February 13). Hollywood writers return to work after ending strike. *Bloomberg.* Retrieved June 26, 2008, from http://www.bloomberg.com/apps/news?pid=20601103&sid=aKdwR90C54WM.

Wildschut, T., & Insko, C. A. (2007). Explanations of interindividual-intergroup discontinuity: A review of the evidence. *European Review of Social Psychology, 18*, 175–211.

Wildschut, T., Insko, C. A., & Gaertner, L. (2002). Intragroup social influence and intergroup competition. *Journal of Personality and Social Psychology, 82*, 975–992.

Wildschut, T., Insko, C. A., & Pinter, B. (2007). Interindividual-intergroup discontinuity as a joint function of acting as a group and interacting with a group. *European Journal of Social Psychology, 37*, 390–399.

Wildschut, T., Lodewijkx, H.F.M., & Insko, C. A. (2001). Toward a reconciliation of diverging perspectives on interindividual-intergroup discontinuity: The role of procedural interdependence. *Journal of Experimental Social Psychology, 37*, 273–285.

Wildschut, T., Pinter, B., Vevea, J. L., Insko, C. A., & Schopler, J. (2003). Beyond the group mind: A quantitative review of the interindividual-intergroup discontinuity effect. *Psychological Bulletin, 129*, 698–722.

Winquist, J. R., & Larson, J. R., Jr. (2004). Sources of the discontinuity effect: Playing against a group versus being in a group. *Journal of Experimental Social Psychology, 5*, 675–682.

Wolf, S. T., Cohen, T. R., Kirchner, J. L., Rea, A., Montoya, R. M., & Insko, C. A. (2009). Reducing intergroup conflict through the consideration of future consequences. *European Journal of Social Psychology, 39*, 831 841.

Wolf, S. T., Insko, C. A., Kirchner, J. L., & Wildschut, T. (2008). Interindividual-intergroup discontinuity in the domain of correspondent outcomes: The roles of relativistic concern, perceived categorization, and the Doctrine of Mutual Assured Destruction. *Journal of Personality and Social Psychology, 94*, 479–494.

CHAPTER 14

Fisher, R. (2008). Fractionating conflict. In J. V. Bondurant, & M. W. Fisher (Eds.), *Conflict: Violence and nonviolence.* Piscataway, NJ: Aldine Transaction. (Original work published 1964).

Hackman, J. R. (2002). *Leading teams.* Boston: Harvard Business School Press.
Martinez-Moyano, I. (2006). Exploring the dynamics of collaboration in interorganizational settings. In S. Schuman (Ed.), *Creating a culture of collaboration: The International Association of Facilitators handbook.* San Francisco: Jossey-Bass.
Schaffer, R. (1991, March-April). Demand better results—and get them. *Harvard Business Review,* pp. 142–149.
Schwarz, R. (2002). *The skilled facilitator: A comprehensive resource for consultants, facilitators, managers, trainers, and coaches* (2nd ed.). San Francisco: Jossey-Bass.
Sole, K. (2006). Eight suggestions from the small-group conflict trenches. In M. Deutsch & P. T. Coleman (Eds.), *The handbook of conflict resolution: Theory and practice.* San Francisco: Jossey-Bass.
Ulrich, D., Kerr, S., & Ashkenas, R. (2002). *The GE Work-Out. How to implement GE's revolutionary method for busting bureaucracy and attacking organizational problems—fast!* New York: McGraw-Hill.

CHAPTER 15

Chambers, R. (1994). The origins and practice of participatory rural appraisal. *World Development, 22,* 953–969.
Cornwall A., & Jewkes J. (1995). What is participatory action research? *Social Science and Medicine, 41,* 1667–1676.
Fals-Borda, O. (1991). Some basic ingredients. In O. Fals-Borda & M. A. Rahman (Eds.), *Action and knowledge: Breaking the monopoly with participatory action-research* (pp. 3–12). New York: Apex.
Halpern, J., & Weinstein, M. (2004). Rehumanizing the other: Empathy and reconciliation. *Human Rights Quarterly, 26,* 561–583.
Hartling, L. M. (2005, December 15–16). *Humiliation: Real pain, a pathway to violence.* Preliminary draft of a paper prepared for Round Table 2 of the 2005 Workshop on Humiliation and Violent Conflict, Columbia University, New York. Available at http://www.humiliationstudies.org/documents/HartlingNY05meetingRT2.pdf.
Hicks, D. (2002). Dignity matters. *Centerpiece, 16*(1), 8–9.
LeCompte, M. D. (1995). Some notes on power, agenda, and voice: A researcher's personal evolution toward critical collaborative research. In. P. L. McLaren & J. M. Giarelli (Eds.), *Critical theory and educational research* (pp. 93–112). New York: State University of New York Press.
Petersen, R. (2002). *Understanding ethnic violence: Fear, hatred, and resentment in twentieth-century eastern Europe.* Cambridge, England: Cambridge University Press.
Reid, C., & Frisby, W. (2008). Continuing the journey: Articulating dimensions of feminist participatory action research (FPAR). In P. Reason & H. Bradbury (Eds.), *Handbook of action research* (pp. 93–105). Thousand Oaks, CA: Sage.

Ross, M. H. (2007). *Cultural contestation in ethnic conflict.* Cambridge, England: Cambridge University Press.

Rothman, J. (1997). *Resolving identity-based conflict in nations, organizations, and communities.* San Francisco: Jossey-Bass.

Rothschild, J. (1981). *Ethnopolitics: A conceptual framework.* New York: Columbia University Press.

Saunders, H. (2001). *A public peace process: Sustained dialogue to transform racial and ethnic conflict.* New York: Palgrave Macmillan.

Winslade, J., & Monk, G. (2001). *Narrative mediation: A new approach to conflict resolution.* San Francisco: Jossey-Bass.

CHAPTER 16

Einstein, A. (1931). Living philosophies. Retrieved December 6, 2004, from http://www.bartleby.com/63/17/3117.html.

Einstein, A. (2004). *Collected quotes from Albert Einstein.* Retrieved December 6, 2004, from http://rescomp.stanford.edu/~cheshire/EinsteinQuotes.html.

Harper, D. (2001). Learn. Retrieved June 3, 2008, from the *Online Etymology Dictionary,* http://www.etymonline.com/index.php?term=learn.

Mindell, A. P. (1989). *The year 1: Global process work.* New York: Arkana.

Mindell, A. P. (1992). *The leader as martial artist: An introduction to Deep Democracy.* San Francisco: HarperSanFrancisco.

Mindell, A. P. (1995). *Sitting in the fire: Large group transformation using conflict and diversity.* Portland, OR: Lao Tse Press.

Mindell, A. P. (2000). *Quantum mind: The edge between physics and psychology.* Portland, OR: Lao Tse Press.

Mindell, A. P. (2010). *Processmind: The mind of God in personal life and the world's future.* Wheaton, IL: Quest Books.

Mindell, A. S. (1995). *Metaskills: The spiritual art of therapy.* Tempe, AZ: New Falcon.

Morin, P. (2002). *Rank and salutogenesis: A quantitative and empirical study of self-rated health and perceived social status.* Unpublished doctoral dissertation, Union Institute & University, Cincinnati.

Schupbach, E. (2004). *The gold at the end of the rainbow: A hermeneutic study of a therapist's spiritual experience.* Unpublished doctoral dissertation, Union Institute & University, Cincinnati.

Schupbach, M. (2007). Worldwork: Ein Multidimensionales Change Management Modell. *Organisations Entwicklung, 4* (Erfahrung), 56–64. Available at http://www.maxfxx.net/my_publications.asp.

Schupbach, M., & Schupbach, E. (2008). Organizational Change Seminar. Manly, Australia: www.maxfxx.net.

CHAPTER 17

Avolio, B. J., Gardner, W. L., Walumbwa, F. O., Luthans, F., & May, D. R. (2004). Unlocking the mask: A look at the process by which authentic leaders impact follower attitudes and behavior. *Leadership Quarterly*, *15*, 801–823.

Avolio, B. J., & Gardner, W. L. (2005). Authentic leadership development: Getting to the root of positive forms of leadership. *Leadership Quarterly*, *16*, 315–338.

Avolio, B. J., & Luthans, F. (2006). *The high impact leader: Moments matter for accelerating authentic leadership development*. New York: McGraw-Hill.

Avolio, B. J., Luthans, F., & Walumbwa, F. O. (2004). *Authentic leadership: Theory-building for veritable sustained performance*. Working paper, Gallup Leadership Institute, University of Nebraska, Lincoln.

Bandura, A. (1982). Self-efficacy mechanism in human agency. *American Psychologist*, *37*, 122–147.

Batt, R. (2004). Who benefits from teams? Comparing workers, supervisors, and managers. *Industrial Relations*, *43*(1), 183–212.

Bierhoff, H., & Müller, G. F. (2005). Leadership, mood, atmosphere, and cooperative support in project groups. *Journal of Managerial Psychology*, *20*, 483–497.

Cooper, C. D., Scandura, T. A., & Schriesheim, C. A. (2005). Looking forward but learning from our past: Potential challenges to developing authentic leadership theory and authentic leaders. *Leadership Quarterly*, *16*, 475–493.

Cranton, P. (2006). Fostering authentic relationships in the transformative classroom. In E. W. Taylor (Ed.), *Teaching for Change: Fostering Transformative Learning in the Classroom*. New Directions for Adult and Continuing Education, no. 109, 5–13. Hoboken, NJ: Wiley.

Eagly, A. H. (2005). Achieving relational authenticity in leadership: Does gender matter? *Leadership Quarterly*, *16*, 459–474.

Endrissat, N., Müller, W. R., & Kaudela-Baum, S. (2007). En route to an empirically-based understanding of authentic leadership. *European Management Journal*, *25*, 207–220.

Frankforter, S. A., & Christensen, S. L. (2005). Finding competitive advantage in self-managed work teams. *Business Forum*, *27*(1), 20–25.

Gardner, W. L., Avolio, B. J., Luthans, F., May, D. R., & Walumbwa, F. (2005). Can you see the real me? A self-based model of authentic leader and follower development. *Leadership Quarterly*, *16*, 343–372.

Gardner, W. L., & Schermerhorn, J. R. (2004). Unleashing individual potential: Performance gains through positive organizational behavior and authentic leadership. *Organizational Dynamics*, *33*, 270–281.

Glassop, L. I. (2002). The organizational benefit of teams. *Human Relations*, *55*, 225–249.

Greer, L. L., Jehn, K. A., & Mannix, E. A. (2008). Conflict transformation: A longitudinal investigation of the relationships between different types of intragroup conflict and the moderating role of conflict resolution. *Small Group Research*, *39*, 278–302.

Guzzo, R. A., Yost, P. R., Campbell, R. J., & Shea, G. P. (1993). Potency in groups: Articulating a construct. *British Journal of Social Psychology, 32*, 87–106.
Harter, S. (2002). Authenticity. In C. R. Snyder, & S. Lopez (Eds.), *Handbook of positive psychology* (pp. 382–394). Oxford: Oxford University Press.
Homan, A. C., van Knippenberg, D., Van Kleef, G. A., & De Dreu, C.K.W. (2007). Bridging faultlines by valuing diversity: Diversity beliefs, information elaboration, and performance in diverse work groups. *Journal of Applied Psychology, 92*, 1189–1199.
Ilgen, D. R. (1999). Teams embedded in organizations: Some implications. *American Psychologist, 54*, 129–139.
Jansen, S. M., & Luthans, F. (2006). Relationship between entrepreneurs' psychological capital and their authentic leadership. *Journal of Managerial Issues, 18*, 254–273.
Luthans, F., & Avolio, B. J. (2003). Authentic leadership: A positive developmental approach. In K. S. Cameron, J. E. Dutton, & R. E. Quinn (Eds.), *Positive organizational scholarship* (pp. 241–261). San Francisco: Barrett-Koehler.
Luthans, F., & Youssef, C. M. (2004). Human, social, and now positive psychological capital management: Investing in people for competitive advantage. *Organizational Dynamics, 33*(2), 143–160.
Luthans, F., Youssef, C. M., & Avolio, B. (2007). *Psychological capital.* New York: Oxford University Press.
Raven, B. H. (1959). The dynamics of groups. *Review of Educational Research, 29*, 332–343.
Sargent, L. D., & Sue-Chan, C. (2001). Does diversity affect group efficacy? The intervening role of cohesion and task interdependence. *Small Group Research, 32*, 426–450.
Schminke, M., Wells, D., Peyrefitte, J., & Sebora, T. C. (2002). Leadership and ethics in work groups: A longitudinal assessment. *Group and Organization Management, 27*, 272–293.
Shamir, B., Dayan-Horesh, H., & Adler, D. (2005). Leading by biography: Toward a life-story approach to the study of leadership. *Leadership, 1*, 13–29.
Shamir, B., & Eilam, G. (2005). What's your story? A life-stories approach to authentic leadership development. *Leadership Quarterly, 16*, 395–417.
Shea, G. P., & Guzzo, R. A. (1987). Groups and human resources. In K. M. Rowland & G. R. Ferris (Eds.), *Research in personnel and human resources management* (pp. 323–356). Greenwich, CT: JAI Press.
Sosik, J. J., Avolio, B., & Kahai, S. S. (1997). Effects of leadership style and anonymity on group potency and effectiveness in a group decision support system environment. *Journal of Applied Psychology, 82*(1), 89–103.
Webber, S. S., & Donahue, L. M. (2001). Impact of highly and less job related diversity on work group cohesion and performance: A meta-analysis. *Journal of Management, 27*, 141–162.

Weiss, H. M., & Cropanzano, R. (1996). Affective events theory: A theoretical discussion of the structure, causes, and consequences of affective experiences at work. *Research in Organizational Behavior, 18*, 1–74.

Wright, B. M., Barker, J. R., Cordery, J. L., & Maue, B. E. (2003). The ideal participative state: A prelude to work group effectiveness. *Journal of Business and Management, 9*, 171–188.

CHAPTER 18

Ashfort, B. E., & Mael, F. (1989). Social identity theory and the organization. *Academy of Management Review, 14*, 20–39.

Bass, B. M. (1990). *Bass & Stogdill's handbook of leadership: Theory, research, and managerial applications* (3rd ed.). New York: Free Press.

Bass, B. M., Avolio, B. J., Jung, D. I., & Berson, Y. (2003). Predicting unit performance by assessing transformational and transactional leadership. *Journal of Applied Psychology, 88*, 207–218.

Blau, P. M. (1977). *Inequality and heterogeneity*. New York: Free Press.

Brewer, M. B. (1979). In-group bias in the minimal intergroup situation: A cognitive-motivational analysis. *Psychological Bulletin, 86*, 307–324.

Chemers, M. M. (2000). Leadership research and theory: A functional integration. *Group Dynamics: Theory, Research, and Practice, 4*, 27–43.

Chin, J. L. (2007). Diversity and leadership. *American Psychologist, 62*, 608–609.

Dovidio, J. F., Gaertner, S. L., Isen, A. M., & Lowrance, R. (1995). Group representations and intergroup bias: Positive affect, similarity, and group size. *Personality and Social Psychology Bulletin, 21*, 856–865.

Earley, P. C., & Mosakowski, E. (2000). Creating hybrid team cultures: An empirical test of transnational team functioning. *Academy of Management Journal, 43*, 26–49.

Ely, R. J., & Thomas, D. A. (2001). Cultural diversity at work: The effects of diversity perspectives on work group processes and outcomes. *Administrative Science Quarterly, 46*, 229–273.

Gaertner, S. L., Dovidio, J. F., Banker, B. S., Houlette, M., Johnson, K. M., & McGlynn, E. A. (2000). Reducing intergroup conflict: From superordinate goals to decategorization, recategorization, and mutual differentiation. *Group Dynamics: Theory, Research, and Practice, 4*, 98–114.

Harrison, D. A., & Klein, K. J. (2007). What's the difference? Diversity constructs as separation, variety, or disparity in organizations. *Academy of Management Review, 32*, 1199–1228.

Harrison, D. A., Price, K. H., Gavin, J. H., & Florey, A. T. (2002). Time, teams, and task performance: Changing effects of surface- and deep-level diversity on group functioning. *Academy of Management Journal, 45*, 1029–1045.

Hobman, E. V., Bordia, P., & Gallois, C. (2003). Consequences of feeling dissimilar from others in a work team. *Journal of Business and Psychology, 17*, 301–325.

Homan, A. C., Greer, L. L., Jehn, K. A., & Koning, L. (in press). Believing shapes seeing: The impact of diversity beliefs on the construal of group composition. *Group Processes and Intergroup Relations.*

Homan, A. C., Hollenbeck, J. R., Humphrey, S. E., van Knippenberg, D., Ilgen, D. R., & Van Kleef, G. A. (2008). Facing differences with an open mind: Openness to experience, salience of intra-group differences, and performance of diverse groups. *Academy of Management Journal, 58*, 1204–1222.

Homan, A. C., van Knippenberg, D., Van Kleef, G. A., & De Dreu, C.K.W. (2007a). Bridging faultlines by valuing diversity: The effects of diversity beliefs on information elaboration and performance in diverse work groups. *Journal of Applied Psychology, 92*, 1189–1199.

Homan, A. C., van Knippenberg, D., Van Kleef, G. A., & De Dreu, C.K.W. (2007b). Interacting dimensions of diversity: Cross-categorization and the functioning of diverse work groups. *Group Dynamics: Theory, Research, and Practice, 11*, 79–94.

Horwitz, S. K., & Horwitz, I. B. (2007). The effects of team diversity on team outcomes: A meta-analytic review of team demography. *Journal of Management, 33*, 987–1015.

Hostager, T. J., & De Meuse, K. P. (2002). Assessing the complexity of diversity perceptions: Breadth, depth, and balance. *Journal of Business and Psychology, 17*, 189–206.

Jackson, S. E. (1991). Team composition in organizational settings: Issues in managing an increasingly diverse work force. In S. Worchel & W. Wood (Eds.), *Group process and productivity* (pp. 138–173). Thousand Oaks, CA: Sage.

Jehn, K. A., Northcraft, G., & Neale, M. (1999). Why differences make a difference: Field study of diversity, conflict, and performance in workgroups. *Administrative Science Quarterly, 44*, 741–763.

Kearney, E., & Gebert, D. (2009). Managing diversity and enhancing team outcomes: The promise of transformational leadership. *Journal of Applied Psychology, 94*, 77–89.

Kossek, E. E., & Zonia, S. C. (1993). Assessing diversity climate: A field study of reactions to employer efforts to promote diversity. *Journal of Organizational Behavior, 14*, 61–81.

Kozlowski, S.W.J., & Bell, B. S. (2006). Work groups and teams in organizations. In R. J. Klimoski, W. C. Borman, & D. R. Ilgen (Eds.), *Handbook of psychology: Industrial and organizational psychology* (Vol. 12, pp. 333–375). Hoboken, NJ: Wiley.

Lau, D., & Murnighan, J. K. (1998). Demographic diversity and faultlines: The compositional dynamics of organizational groups. *Academy of Management Review, 23*, 325–340.

Levine, M., Prosser, A., Evans, D., & Reicher, S. (2005). Identity and emergency intervention: How social group membership and inclusiveness of group boundaries shape helping behavior. *Personality and Social Psychology Bulletin, 31*, 443–453.

Milliken, F. J., & Martins, L. L. (1996). Searching for common threads: Understanding the multiple effects of diversity in organizational groups. *Academy of Management Review, 21*, 402–433.

Mor Barak, M. E., Cherin, D. A., & Berkman, S. (1998). Organizational and personal dimensions of diversity climate: Ethnic and gender differences in employee perceptions. *Journal of Applied Behavioral Sciences, 31*, 82–104.

Pelled, L. H., Eisenhardt, K. M., & Xin, K. R. (1999). Exploring the black box: An analysis of work group diversity, conflict and performance. *Administrative Science Quarterly, 44*, 1–28.

Randel, A. E. (2002). Identity salience: A moderator of the relationship between group gender composition and work group conflict. *Journal of Organizational Behavior, 23*, 749–766.

Schaubroeck, J., Lam, S.S.K., & Cha, S. E. (2007). Embracing transformational leadership: Team values and the impact of leader behavior on team performance. *Journal of Applied Psychology, 92*, 1020–1030.

Shin, S. J., & Zhou, J. (2007). When is educational specialization heterogeneity related to creativity in research and development teams? Transformational leadership as a moderator. *Journal of Applied Psychology, 92*, 1709–1721.

Somech, A. (2006). The effects of leadership style and team process on performance and innovation in functionally heterogeneous teams. *Journal of Management, 32*, 132–157.

Stogdill, R. M. (1974). *Handbook of leadership: A survey of theory and research.* New York: Free Press.

Strauss, J. P., Connerley, M. L., & Ammermann, P. A. (2003). The "threat hypothesis," personality, and attitudes toward diversity. *Journal of Applied Behavioral Science, 39*, 32–52.

Tajfel, H., & Turner, J. (1986). The social identity of intergroup behavior. In W.A.S. Worchel & W. G. Austin (Eds.), *Psychology and intergroup relations* (pp. 7–24). Chicago: Nelson-Hall.

Thatcher, S.M.B., Jehn, K. A., & Zanutto, E. (2003). Cracks in diversity research: A contingency perspective on the conflict-outcome relationship. *Group Decision and Negotiation, 12*, 217–241.

Turner, J. C., Hogg, M. A., Oakes, P. J., Reicher, S. D., & Wetherell, M. S. (1987). *Rediscovering the social group: A self-categorization theory.* Oxford: Blackwell.

Van der Vegt, G. S., & Van de Vliert, E. (2005). Effects of perceived skill dissimilarity and task interdependence on helping in work teams. *Journal of Management, 31*, 73–89.

Van Ginkel, W., & van Knippenberg, D. (2008, April). *Leadership, diversity mindsets, and group performance.* Paper presented at the 23th annual conference of the Society for Industrial and Organizational Psychology, San Francisco.

van Knippenberg, D., De Dreu, C.K.W., & Homan, A. C. (2004). Work group diversity and group performance: An integrative model and research agenda. *Journal of Applied Psychology*, *89*, 1008–1022.
van Knippenberg, D., Haslam, S. A., & Platow, M. J. (2007). Unity through diversity: Value-in-diversity beliefs as moderator of the relationship between work group diversity and group identification. *Group Dynamics: Theory, Research, and Practice*, *11*, 207–222.
van Knippenberg, D., & Schippers, M. C. (2007). Work group diversity. *Annual Review of Psychology*, *58*, 515–541.
Webber, S. S., & Donahue, L. M. (2001). Impact of highly and less job-related diversity on work group cohesion and performance: A meta-analysis. *Journal of Management*, *27*, 141–162.
Williams, K. Y., & O'Reilly, C. A. (1998). Demography and diversity in organizations. *Research in Organizational Behavior*, *20*, 77–140.
Yorges, S. L., Weiss, H. M., & Strickland, O. J. (1999). The effect of leader outcomes on influence, attributes, and perceptions of charisma. *Journal of Applied Psychology*, *84*, 428–436.
Zellmer-Bruhn, M. E., Maloney, M. M., Bhappu, A. D., & Salvador, R. B. (2008). When and how do differences matter? An exploration of perceived similarity in teams. *Organizational Behavior and Human Decision Processes*, *107*, 41–59.

CHAPTER 19

Bion, W. R. (1961). *Experiences in groups*. London: Tavistock.
Campbell, J. (1993). *The hero with a thousand faces*. London: Fontana Press. (Original work published 1949)
Heron, J. (1999). *The complete facilitator's handbook*. London: Kogan Page.
Hopper, E. (2007). Theoretical and conceptual notes concerning transference and countertransference processes in groups and by groups, and the social unconscious: Part II, *Group Analysis*, *40*, 29. Thousand Oaks, CA: Sage.
Maynard, B., & Champoux, T. (1996). *Heart, soul and spirit: Bold strategies for transforming your organization*. Redmond, WA: Effectiveness Institute.
Pearson, C. S. (1991). *Awakening the heroes within*. San Francisco: HarperSanFrancisco.
Snowden, D. (2005). Simple but not simplistic: The art and science of story. Retrieved November 18, 2009, from http://www.cognitive-edge.com/ceresources/articles/43_simple_not_simplistic_final.pdf.

CHAPTER 20

Anderson, R. D., & Price, G. E. (2001). Experiential groups in counselor education: Student attitudes and instructor participation. *Counselor Education and Supervision*, *41*, 111–119.

Argyris, C., & Schön, D. A. (1996). *Organizational learning II: Theory, method and practice*. Reading, MA: Addison-Wesley

Bendaly, L. (2000). *The facilitation skills training kit*. New York: McGraw-Hill.

Bens, I. (2005). *Advanced facilitation strategies: Tools and techniques to master difficult situations*. San Francisco: Jossey-Bass.

Biggs, J., & Tang, C. (2007). *Teaching for quality learning at university: What the student does* (3rd ed.). Maidenhead, England: Open University Press.

Brockbank, A., & McGill, I. (1998). *Facilitating reflective learning in higher education*. Buckingham, England: SHRE and Open University Press.

Claxton, G. (2000). The anatomy of intuition. In T. Atkinson & G. Claxton (Eds.), *The intuitive practitioner: On the value of not always knowing what one is doing* (pp. 32–52). Buckingham: Open University Press.

Ghais, S. (2005). *Extreme facilitation: Guiding groups through controversy and complexity*. San Francisco: Jossey-Bass.

Havergal, M., & Edmonstone, J. (1999). *The facilitator's toolkit*. Aldershot, England: Gower.

Hogan, C. F. (2002). *Understanding facilitation: Theory and principles*. London: Kogan Page.

Hunter, D. (2007). *The art of facilitation: The essentials for leading great meetings and creating group synergy*. Auckland, New Zealand: Random House.

Hunter, D., Bailey, A., & Taylor, B. (1999). *The essence of facilitation: Being in action in groups*. Auckland, New Zealand: Tandem Press.

Jenkins, J. C., & Jenkins, M. R. (2006). *The nine disciplines of a facilitator: Leading groups by transforming yourself*. San Francisco: Jossey-Bass.

Killion, J. P., & Simmons, L. A. (1992). The Zen of facilitation. *Journal of Staff Development*, *13*(3), 2–5.

Kirk, P., & Broussine, M. (2000). The politics of facilitation. *Journal of Workplace Learning: Employee Counselling Today*, *12*(1), 13–22.

Kottler, J. A. (2004). Realities of teaching group counseling. *Journal for Specialists in Group Work*, *29*(1), 51–53.

Mindell, A. (1995). *Sitting in the fire: Large group transformation using conflict and diversity*. Portland, OR: Lao Tse Press.

Ringer, M. (2002). *Group action: The dynamics of groups in therapeutic, educational and corporate settings*. London: Kingsley.

Robson, M., & Beary, C. (1995). *Facilitating*. Aldershot, England: Gower.

Schneider-Corey, M., & Corey, G. (2006). *Groups: Process and practice* (7th ed.). Belmont, CA: Thomson Brooks/Cole.

Schwarz, R. (2002). *The skilled facilitator: A comprehensive resource for consultants, facilitators, managers, trainers, and coaches* (2nd ed.). San Francisco: Jossey-Bass.

Schwarz, R. (2005). The skilled facilitator approach. In R. Schwarz & A. Davidson (Eds.), *The skilled facilitator fieldbook: Tips, tools, and tested methods for consultants, facilitators, managers, trainers, and coaches* (pp. 3–13). San Francisco: Jossey-Bass.

Thomas, G. J. (2007). *A study of the theories and practices of facilitator educators.* Unpublished doctoral thesis, La Trobe University, Melbourne.

Thomas, G. J. (2008a). Facilitate first thyself: The person-centered dimension of facilitator education. *Journal of Experiential Education, 31,* 168–188.

Thomas, G. J. (2008b). Preparing facilitators for experiential education: The role of intentionality and intuition. *Journal of Adventure Education and Outdoor Learning, 8*(1), 3–20.

Thomas, G. J. (in press). The theories and practices of facilitator educators: Conclusions from a naturalistic inquiry. *Group Facilitation: A Research and Applications Journal.*

Warren, K. (1998). A call for race, gender, and class sensitive facilitation in outdoor experiential education. *Journal of Experiential Education, 21*(1), 21–25.

Weaver, R. G., & Farrell, J. D. (1997). *Managers as facilitators.* San Francisco: Berrett-Koehler.

White, S. A. (1999). Participation: Walk the talk! In S. A. White (Ed.), *The art of facilitating participation: Releasing the power of grassroots communication* (pp. 15–32). London: Sage.

Yalom, I. D., & Leszcz, M. (2005). *The theory and practice of group psychotherapy* (5th ed.). New York: Basic Books.

NAME INDEX

SUBJECT INDEX

Page references followed by *fig* indicate an illustrated figure; followed by *t* indicate a table; followed by *e* indicate an exhibit.

D

Printed and bound by CPI Group (UK) Ltd, Croydon, CR0 4YY

23/04/2025

14660928-0001